Devastation on the Delaware
Stories and Images of the Deadly Flood of 1955

by

Mary A. Shafer

The first printing of this book was sponsored by
H.J. Opdyke Lumber

A PROFESSIONAL CHOICE

FRENCHTOWN • BELLE MEAD
BOONVILLE, NY

in commemoration of its fiftieth anniversary
as a Delaware Valley merchant.

Opdyke Lumber was born amid the devastation of the 1955 flood
on the Delaware River and is proud to have helped other valley residents
and businesses similarly recover from that flood
and from those that have happened since.

Word Forge Books • Ferndale, Penns

Devastation on the Delaware: Stories and Images of the Deadly Flood of 1955
ISBN 0-9771329-0-0

Library of Congress Control Number: 2005907230

Published by Word Forge Books
PO Box 97
Ferndale, PA 18921
Phone   610-847-2456
Fax   610-847-8220
Email   floodbook@thewordforge.com
Web   www.55flood.com

Written by ·
Mary A. Shafer
floodbook@thewordforge.com
www.thewordforge.com

Edited and indexed by
Rebecca A. Valentine
The Write Stuff
Windsor, CO 80550
mzwrite@frii.com
www.thewritestuffonline.com

Cover design and illustration by
Laura Pritchard
Pritchard Design
Doylestown, PA 18901
laura@pritcharddesign.com
www.pritcharddesign.com

Devastation on the Delaware

Dedication

This work is dedicated to the memory of those who did not survive the flood of 1955, the strength of those they left behind, and the spirit of those who forged ahead into better times.

This watermark, meant for southbound readers, is one of two located on Route 32 near Lumberville, Pennsylvania. Such reminders of the flood of 1955 aren't uncommon in communities along the river. — Collection the author

Foreword

For this meteorologist (dare I say, most meteorologists), the fascination with weather goes back to childhood. The weather bug bit early in life and never let go. Since a young age, this passion for all things atmospheric has helped frame the passage of time: the traditional calendar marked with holidays and birthdays has always been supplemented by personal points of reference linked to significant weather events.

Of course, my definition of "significant" has changed considerably over the years. As an elementary school student, I considered any spring rain a disaster. That's because my father was the baseball coach at the local high school, and I was his official scorekeeper. Rain meant a possible cancellation of what was certainly the most fun part of a ten-year-old's day. So each evening, I sat next to the television, twirling the dial from channel to channel (no remotes!) to catch each weathercast, praying for a dry forecast for the next day.

A few years later, a tropical system named Agnes redefined my perspective. It was mid-June 1972, coincidentally the week that I spent with my grandparents in Pittsburgh that summer. That time was always a highlight of the year, except that year. It rained. And rained. And rained. I never played so many card games in my life. The Ohio River ran so high that the bridges were closed, extending my "vacation" a few days. And the damage in western Pennsylvania paled in comparison to that in central and eastern parts of the state. To this day, Agnes remains the worst natural disaster in Pennsylvania history.

Decades later, as Storm Analyst at The Weather Channel, I report on significant weather events every day, including winter nor'easters, spring tornado outbreaks, and autumn hurricane landfalls. Though few affect me directly, I nonetheless feel an uneasy connection as I track these storms: I know what makes them tick

3

and the widespread disruption they potentially bring.

Flooding from Hurricane Floyd in September, 1999 and Tropical Storm Allison in 2001 did affect me personally, and they remain the most vivid recent memories on my own weather calendar. Though I did not experience Connie and Diane, I have lived in Conyngham and Warrington, two of the Pennsylvania towns affected by the 1955 floods. I have spoken with individuals in those communities who vividly remember, decades later, those awful August days. And that's why I'm pleased that Mary Shafer has chosen to tell the story of the Delaware Flood of 1955. It's these individual stories of heroism and, sadly, tragedy, that remind us of the awesome power of the atmosphere.

That power remains untamed, though it is now much better understood, better observed, and better anticipated. In 1955, weather radar was in its infancy, the launch of the first weather satellite was still five years away, and the first generation of primitive computer weather models was still in development. Television weather was more of a novelty than a serious and instantaneous means to convey critical and potentially live-saving information.

The year before Connie and Diane, in October 1954, a fast-moving hurricane named Hazel had demonstrated the inland wind power of tropical systems, cutting a path of destruction through the Mid-Atlantic and producing the highest wind gust ever officially recorded in Philadelphia, 94 mph.

Fifty years later, awareness of the impacts of tropical systems has never been greater following the 2004 hurricane season, the costliest in U.S. history. Though Florida was by far hardest hit, flooding from Ivan extended all the way to Pennsylvania and New England. In fact, over the last thirty years, inland flooding has been the most deadly component of tropical systems.

When a tropical system is so costly or deadly that the future use of its name for a different storm would be inappropriate or confusing, the National Hurricane Center may "retire" that name. "Connie" and "Diane" have been retired, as have "Andrew," Floyd," and more than fifty others, including four from the 2004 season. And undoubtedly, the list of retired names will continue to grow in future years.

That's because society's vulnerability to tropical systems is greater now than ever, despite the fact that our ability to forecast them and foresee their impacts is also unprecedented. More than half of the U.S. population lives within fifty miles of a coast, most along Atlantic or Gulf shores. More people and property are potentially in harm's way than ever before, and investment in these high-risk areas shows no sign of slowing. Meanwhile, each summer and fall, new tropical storms will be born in the Atlantic. Though not yet even a twinkle in the atmosphere's eye, some will inevitably make landfall, occasionally with the wind power of a Charley or the flooding rains of a Diane.

Dr. Jon M. Nese
Storm Analyst, The Weather Channel
Former Franklin Institute Chief Meteorologist
Author, *The Philadelphia Area Weather Book*
Atlanta, Georgia
April, 2005

Author's Note

Telling the story of a natural disaster poses many challenges to an author, not the least of which is deciding what the scope of coverage should be. The Delaware River flood of 1955 was just part of the far-reaching effects of Hurricanes Connie and Diane. Communities from South Carolina to Maine were ravaged by the wind and rain of these sister storms.

As bad as it was, the devastation in the Delaware Valley region wasn't the worst of it. New England, especially Connecticut, suffered greater property damage than did Pennsylvania, New Jersey or New York. But the loss of life in Monroe County, Pennsylvania alone was greater than that of all New England put together. This disaster did more to change life in the Delaware Valley than almost any other single event in its history.

Once I began the research, my decision to write the story was rewarded with the kind of gratifying response one can only hope for, but never expect. People were most generous in taking the time to share their stories with me. It was clear they felt both validated and somehow relieved to finally be able to relate their memories to someone who would put it all together, in a form that made sense of all the fragmented accounts they'd heard over the years.

This is the best thing about writing history: the author is given a public trust to record a shared experience. In a sense, the result is an acknowledgment of something life-changing. Something about committing a story to paper makes it more real. It creates a touchstone for those whose powers of recall have dimmed with the passage of time.

So here is where I must apologize to those whose stories I didn't gather, whose personal memories and photos won't appear in these pages. More than halfway through the research for this book, I realized that no matter how long I worked on it, or how many people I interviewed, I would never be able to tell everyone's story. I couldn't possibly talk to or see or even hear about all the people whose lives were altered by this event. Instead, I had to do that most difficult of all things a writer must do: Weed out everything but the essence of the story, eliminating sometimes fascinating detail because it doesn't serve its efficient telling. I have tried to find the right balance.

Part of achieving that balance was determining the geographical area to be covered. Because what happened there had a direct bearing on what happened on the Delaware River proper, I have included the Pocono Mountain region, of which Scranton is the far western edge. The Lehigh River Valley suffered its own extensive trauma, worthy of a separate book, and is covered here only insofar as it affected the Delaware region.

Other nearby areas—such as Montgomery and Chester Counties and metro Philadelphia—were affected, but not to the same drastic extent, so what's described previously is the region on which this book concentrates. I decided this not to minimize anyone else's experience or suffering, but to keep the scope of the project manageable.

One important geography note will affect the reader's understanding of the Pocono region account: Official highway numbers have changed since 1955. Where the story refers to Route 90, the current designation is Route 191. What is now Route 447 at the time of the flood was called Route 290.

A note about the photographs: I made every effort to locate and be able to use the best photos possible to illustrate my manuscript. In some cases, I was able to find and use images that are now only available as second-generation scans of already-printed materials. In this case, they appear with an unavoidable screen pattern in the book. I felt they were important enough to include despite this annoyance.

I was extraordinarily fortunate to gain access to some truly unique shots. Some of these are from personal collections, and I'm grateful to their owners for their permission.

On the other hand, some shots I believe would have enhanced the book were not available for one reason or another. Unfortunately for this history-rich area, some of its news organizations have strict policies limiting the use of their photo archives. If you notice a lack of what might seem obvious images to include, it's likely these policies are the reason the images don't appear. It certainly wasn't for lack of trying to secure their use.

My goal in writing this book was to create a very readable account of a tragic natural disaster, as opposed to a dry historical treatise. For this reason I chose to present the story as narrative nonfiction. I have attempted to stay as close to actual fact as I was able to discern it through several years of archival research and first-person interviews.

Quite a few of the "characters" in this story are no longer living or were unavailable for interview, and many who are still with us had difficulty remembering exact times, dates, thoughts and conversations that occurred fifty years ago in the midst of sometimes urgent and chaotic situations.

In most cases, especially in references to dates, times, locations, relationships and meteorological data, I have stuck absolutely to verifiable facts. However, the sources normally used to verify such things— news agency or government account and reports—sometimes conflict with individual interviewees' memories, and even with each other. Such is the nature of reportage, especially around such confusing and chaotic events as disasters. In other instances, where there is no available historical reference material, I have based the writing on my own personal observations of what it's like to live along the Delaware River.

Where I was unable to know for certain what a person was thinking or doing, or what they said or felt at any given point, I chose to conjecture. I based my choices on what I felt a reasonable person or persons would likely have been thinking, feeling, saying or doing in such situations. I took into consideration what knowledge I could glean about each individual's personality from newspaper interviews and accounts, or from my own personal interviews with these people or those who knew them.

All dialogue appearing in quotation marks are actual statements recorded from these sources. Dialogue appearing in italics, without such punctuation, is my idea of what might likely have been said, but it is unverifiable.

All Weather Bureau bulletins and advisories are verbatim as they came off the teletype machines at weather and news stations. Though some have been edited for length, no words have been added or altered, and no meanings have been changed.

When I found discrepancies between two or more archival sources (and there were many, even from official sources), I used the information contained in that which seemed most reliable. Always, my intent has been to present the most historically accurate account possible.

I live just a few miles from several of the hardest-hit 1955 flood areas along the Delaware River. In an almost unbelievable twist, another flood of similar but less significant proportions occurred when the remnants of Hurricane Ivan passed through in September, 2004, just as I was completing my research for this book. As I was finishing the manuscript, an even greater flood occurred on April 3-4, 2005.

Respectively, these crests were the fourth and third highest recorded on the Delaware River to date. My heart goes out to those for whom these more recent deluges caused much loss, trouble and expense. Having talked with some of these people, I found their sense of violation and helplessness enormous. Yet most are choosing to remain "river people," a testament to the loyalty the river inspires.

My own losses were small, and I must admit—with a certain amount of guilt—that for me as a writer, these experiences provided the kind of timely insight one can't possibly even hope for. I was able to live for myself many of the emotions and activities previously only described to me secondhand. Especially in dealing with an historical subject, this was tremendously valuable. There is a level of detail and understanding one finds in experiencing such an event that would elude one after the fact, regardless how skilled a researcher or how compassionate a listener one may be.

In an ironic way, the situation has a certain poetic justice. I believe this experience helped me do a better job of relating what happened to the '55 flood's survivors, and to those who didn't survive; an effort to which I feel a strong obligation.

I hope you will feel I have honored their stories.

Mary A. Shafer
Ferndale, PA
July, 2005

Prologue

1955 was an unusually active hurricane year. It began with a completely atypical storm—Alice—that reached hurricane strength on New Year's Day. In all, there were thirteen tropical storms, ten of which reached hurricane force. Five years earlier, there had been eleven hurricanes in the season, setting the record. Typical hurricane seasons carry the expectation of ten tropical storms, with six reaching hurricane strength.

Hurricane seasons that produce large numbers of storms, especially ones that threaten the eastern coast of the United States, are usually referred to as "Bermuda High" years. That's when a huge, clockwise-rotating weather system sets up long-term residence in the high altitudes in the vicinity of the island of Bermuda and the surrounding middle Atlantic Ocean. This strong weather "bubble" acts much like a bumper in a pinball machine, helping to steer tropical storms first west, then north as they head toward the North American coast.

In mid-August of 1955, two training hurricanes—Connie and Diane—inundated the eastern seaboard of the United States within five days of each other. They both came ashore in the Carolinas and ravaged their ways north through Virginia, Maryland, Delaware, New Jersey, and Pennsylvania. Though Connie had once been a Category 4 (Extreme damage) storm and Diane a Category 3 (Extensive damage), when they made landfall, they both weakened considerably after leaving warm ocean waters.

When they reached the Delaware Valley, they had weakened further, to tropical storm status. Neither was all that dangerous as a wind threat. But together, they dumped close to two feet of rain in some areas of the Mid-Atlantic region and parts of New England.

This book deals primarily with the effects of this massive rainfall on the Delaware River and its tributaries in Pennsylvania and New Jersey.

The Delaware River is fed by countless tributaries and surface runoff, beginning at the river's headwaters in the Catskill Mountains of upstate New York. In the space of thirty-six hours on August 18 and 19, its normally docile, shallow channel turned into a raging torrent.

As the river rose, cities and towns on both sides in Pennsylvania, New Jersey, and New York became surrounded by the swirling, muddy waters. Some were swallowed almost entirely. Several islands, many camps and quite a number of summer getaways along the channel suffered immensely, some wiped completely out of existence. It eventually crested between seven a.m. on Friday, August 19 and nine a.m. the next day, at the highest level ever recorded at most gauging stations along its length.

The most horrific destruction happened along creeks and tributaries, whose narrow channels couldn't accommodate the sudden, exponential increase in their usual volume. Raging water bulldozed entire buildings, bridges, trees, train cars, and anything else in its path. It widened existing channels by gouging out saturated stream banks. In some places, the violence of the charging water could no longer be contained. There, it leapt its banks completely, carving new channels where previously had been roads, rail beds, tunnels, streets…even homes and businesses.

Many Delaware Valley communities, some of the oldest in the country, were changed drastically and forever in less than forty-eight hours. For these communities the flood of 1955 was, in every sense, a watershed event.

Along with washing away tangible parts of these communities' lives, the flood also sliced through their collective psyche. It cut the decade almost in half, creating a point of reference for everything that would follow. In a way, the flood finished the job that the Second World War had begun. It erased the last vestiges of a slower, quieter way of life that had held on even after America had lost its isolationist naiveté in that global struggle.

Quaint, covered wooden bridges and family-owned country stores were swept away, as if to make room for the modern world of

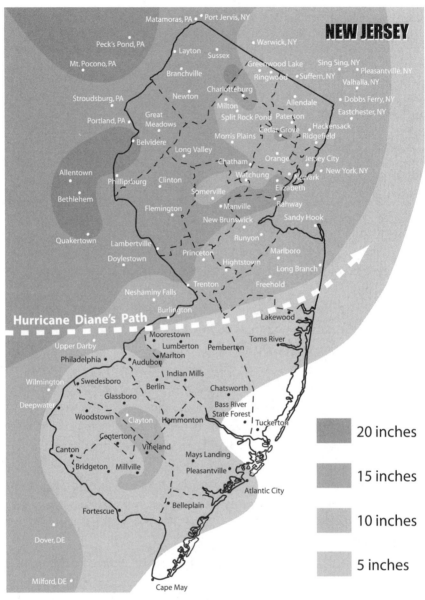

Hurricanes Connie and Diane swept up the Eastern Seaboard and through the Mid-Atlantic within five days of each other in mid-August, 1955. After ravaging the Carolinas with mighty winds and lots of water, they continued into the Delaware Valley. By then, neither was of much danger as a wind threat, but that didn't stop them from wreaking havoc. Together, the sister storms dumped up to two feet of rain in some upper reaches of the Delaware Watershed. By the time all that precipitation collected in the river, the stage was set for the most devastating flood in the region's recorded history.

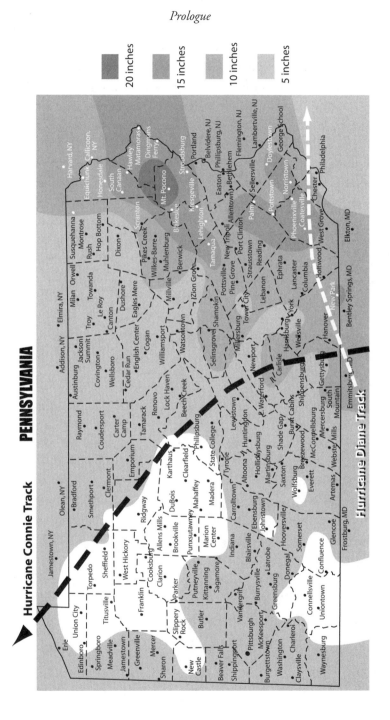

– Maps based on those from U.S. Weather Bureau Technical Paper No. 26.

clean-lined steel spans and bustling supermarkets. Some "mom-and-pop" diners along river roads, while digging out of the muck, lost their regular crowds to the novelty of chain establishments. Downtown shopping districts in some larger towns never quite recovered from losing everything.

This is the story of some of these communities. It's an exploration of the uniquely symbiotic relationship between rivers and river towns, and what happens when the fragile balance of that association is disturbed.

The story offers both an assurance and a warning: that nothing—not winning a war against another human foe, no matter how intimidating; not creating the most destructive weapon on the planet; not even building cities that reach into the heavens—makes any society invulnerable to the caprices of Mother Nature.

Though usually quiet, she has been known occasionally to rage. During such times, she trumpets her disapproval at the hubris of puny mankind. Despite all our technology and study, she can—and, it seems, more frequently does—still surprise.

Section I
The Calm

DELAWARE RIVER BASIN

The Delaware is one of the country's longest free-flowing rivers. It drains the Catskill and Pocono ranges of the Appalachian Mountain chain, and is the source of water for drinking and commercial uses in some of the most populous areas of America.

— Based on a map from the Delaware River Basin Commission

Between a War and a Hard Place

Friday, August 12, 1955

Friday dawns red, if you can see the sun at all. At most places along the Delaware River, it has begun to cloud over. Most people in the valley are aware that what's left of Hurricane Connie is making its way up the coast. They expect rain, maybe a few wind gusts. Nothing much to worry about, the weatherman had said.

Bill Coleman hasn't heard the news about the coming rain, but he isn't thinking about the weather, anyway. Bill is thinking about getting out of his bunk at Camp Pahaquarra, a Boy Scout camp located on the side of Kittatinny Mountain, about ten miles north of Delaware Water Gap on the Jersey side of the river. It's his second year at Pahaquarra, or, as the guys all call it, "Paquarry."

Like last year, Bill is the camp's official bugler, but this year there's a bonus. He just turned fourteen at the end of July, and is old enough to be a clerk at the camp store. He likes the job. It's a position of trust, and he feels grown up to be earning his own pay. That pay is a generous five dollars per week plus free room and board, along with the fun of all the regular camp activities.

He swats at a fly buzzing around his tousled head and punches off the alarm clock. He has half an hour to get himself presentable before it's time to bring the camp to life with seven o'clock *Reveille*. Pulling off the sheet and light blanket, he scans the room for his bugle. It's his school instrument, tarnished and dented from being dropped too many times. It's where he left it. He picks it up, shakes it and blows through it to make sure no one has pulled any funny business overnight.

He's never forgotten the morning he put his lips to the mouthpiece and blew, only to be surprised when no sound came out. He'd tried another time or two before figuring out that something was blocking the air. Upon inspection, he'd discovered the marble some wise guy had dropped into the tubing, trying to buy himself and his friends a few extra winks. Now Bill keeps the horn close to his bunk, where he's able to hear and wake up if someone messes with it.

The concrete floor of the three-sided Adirondack shack he shares with three other campers is pleasantly cool to his feet. Cool is something there hasn't been much of this summer. He's heard some of the counselors talking about this year's heat setting a record, and he isn't surprised. It has been relentless, and he's glad he decided to take the job at Paquarry.

The camp is up in the Pocono Mountains, farther north than his hometown of Titusville, which also sits along the banks of the Delaware. Paquarry is close enough to allow Bill to visit his parents on his day off, but still far enough into the country to be pleasantly rustic. The camp is a thousand acres of heaven, with all kinds of wildlife, and trees that shade the camping platforms and most activity areas. There are bubbling streams and even a waterfall. And, of course, there is the river.

A view from the overlook at Camp Pahaquarra, the venerable Boy Scout camp in the Delaware Water Gap. Located on the side of Mt. Kittatinny between the Delaware River and the Appalachian Trail, the sprawling camp played host to thousands of young men over the years of its existence.   – *Collection Lawrence Gering*

Chapter 1

Bill knows he's lucky to be able to plunge into the Delaware's cooling waters almost any time he wants to. A river kid all his life, he'd easily passed his swimming test last year, allowing him into the deeper water toward mid-channel. As in most spots on the lazy Delaware, there is a sluggish current there, but nothing even worth thinking about. This river is made for fun, not worry. He loves diving off the floating platform into it, clowning around and yelling with a bunch of his buddies, showing off with the big splash of a cannonball.

He also loves the serenity of the river when he takes a sunset canoe ride. The sky turns yellow, then orange, pink and finally, purple. The humidity concentrates into a haze that creeps over the water's surface. That's the magic time, when the camp settles down for stories and toasted marshmallows around campfires. The smell of wood smoke mingles with the scent of pine and that certain, pleasantly earthy aroma every river person knows as "the river smell."

As the first evening stars appear in the sky, it turns quiet out on the water. Now, you might be able to hear a whippoorwill beginning its nightly serenade or, if you're lucky, the slap of a bass on the surface after it rises for the evening's first flies. All the boys, even those who aren't the best swimmers, enjoy their proximity to the gentle Delaware. The river is their friend, and they love it.

Bill feels that affection even more keenly, because his shack is one of those on the flats leading down to the riverbank. He is assigned there so he can be near the parade ground for his bugle call duties, but the location has a benefit much coveted this year: Occasionally, a rare, merciful breeze skims over the water, picking up some of its coolness and swirling it right into the open side of the shack. After a long, active day in the heat, it's the perfect incentive to relax into deep, refreshing sleep.

Bill shakes off that sleep now, gets dressed and makes his bed. Stowing his nightclothes in the footlocker, he gives his hair a quick once-over with the comb. He plucks the bugle off the bed and sets off across the parade ground to wake 350 sleeping Scouts.

Up the river at Matamoras, the summer tourist season is winding down. This town sits across the Delaware from its sister city, Port Jervis, New York. Here, the river forms a border between Pennsylvania, New

Jersey and New York. The Tri-State region is dotted with lakes and webbed with streams, creeks and rivers, all tributaries to the Delaware. These natural amenities give the region its character and form the basis of its evolving economy.

After white settlers had displaced the Native Lenni Lenape residents, the area had developed into a prime railroad junction between the busy stations of New York City and the anthracite coalfields of northeastern Pennsylvania. As shipping and air flight gradually replaced canal and train travel, industrial commerce slowed. The region's business shifted to a service-oriented economy, catering to city dwellers who sought relief from crowded urban conditions in its bucolic forests and streams.

By August, 1955, the tourism trade is firmly entrenched, and supports the lives of many families spread throughout area valleys and along the waterways. The whole northeast corner of Pennsylvania, including such towns as Honesdale, Newfoundland, Milford and Dingman's Ferry now depend on the draw of the Pocono landscape for their sustenance. Tiny Hawley straddles the service and industrial worlds, sitting as it does on the banks of beautiful man-made Lake Wallenpaupack. The lake is a mecca for watersports enthusiasts, while its hydroelectric dam on the Lackawaxen River provides power to the entire region.

The tourism economy is fortuitous for these small towns, since America has, in the last decade, become an unprecedentedly mobile society.

Exactly ten years have passed since the terror and uncertainty of World War II abruptly ended with the introduction of an even more dreadful certainty: We could, at any moment, blow ourselves and every other living thing off the face of the planet. The sheer, unimaginable horror of this concept has somehow managed to keep world events at a manageable level since then.

The home front sports a shiny, new face of optimism. Gone are the decades of privation that had beaten us down during the Great Depression. Gone are wartime rationing and other austerity measures. Giddy with the new abundance surrounding us, we need only look about to witness the wonders we have already wrought since returning from the battlefield.

The newly robust automobile industry is churning out big cars that will come to define the word "classic." The '55 Chevy Bel Air, with its eyebrowed headlights and pillared wraparound windshield, embodies the new "Motoramic" styling. Oldsmobile's popular and commodious Super 88 muscles along on its trend-setting Rocket 88 engine and gangster whitewalls. Ford rocks the blacktop with its new two-door Thunderbird, "the boulevard sports car" with a unique peek-a-boo opera window. The roomy Mercury station wagon is the mini-van of its day, accommodating growing families.

It is the prime of the summer camp, and a good number of them exist in the Poconos; family and church camps, sports and scout camps like Pahaquarra, hunting and fishing camps. From limited-service day camps to full-season resorts with all the amenities, hundreds of such getaways line the banks and islands of the Delaware and its tributaries.

Those who can afford it go away to the mountains, lakes, and rivers to commune with nature and each other. Mom and the kids stay all week, Dad drives up from the city to join them for the weekend. Hiking, canoeing, and crafts split the schedule with singing, campfires, and an endless slumber party until campers fall exhausted into their bunks each night.

Residential air conditioning is still fairly rare, so these camps are particularly attractive to the region's families during the oppressively hot, dry summer of 1955. Like young Bill Coleman, they are looking for a break from the relentless heat and drought that has plagued the eastern seaboard all season. In the relative cool of forested Pocono hills and along the Delaware Water Gap, many city dwellers find the refuge people have been seeking there for centuries.

Pocono place names themselves often reflect the high esteem in which new settlers held their beautiful surroundings. Promised Land and Lords Valley share space in the mountains with Lake in the Clouds and Paradise Falls. The Falls is located on Paradise Creek next to Lake Crawford, another manmade dam reservoir.

One of several resorts in the area, Paradise Falls is owned and run by a Lutheran association and caters to families in its congregation. Seventeen-year-old Ruth Stielau is staying in one of its cottages with her mother, Lydia and younger sister, Edna. They are waiting for her father, Edward and older sister, Carolyn to arrive that evening. Edward and Carolyn will come up from the family home in Malvern, Long Island, where they stay while working in the city during the week.

Ruth enjoys the weekends most, when everyone is together for a few days. During the week, she keeps busy playing with her sister and their friends. She also enjoys Harold Bates, their neighbor in a cottage up the hill. Mr. Bates lives in Crawford, New Jersey, and is an inventor. He came up with the idea to use metal "dog tags" worn around the neck to identify military personnel in the field. He is very smart, and the girls and their mother think highly of him. He is also friendly, and keeps an eye out for the Stielau girls while their dad is away.

Ruth loves to roam outside, exploring the "wilds" of the area. She is disappointed to see that today will be a rainy one, though her mother is happy that the lawn and garden will finally get a decent drink. The few spotty showers they've had in the past few weeks haven't been nearly enough, and everything is beginning to turn brown and shrivel. She would welcome a return to the lush greenness that usually characterizes their vacation getaway.

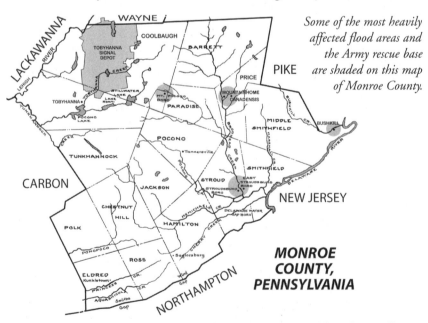

Some of the most heavily affected flood areas and the Army rescue base are shaded on this map of Monroe County.

MONROE COUNTY, PENNSYLVANIA

– Based on an historic map from the Monroe County Public Library collection.

22

The gateway to the Pocono leisure area in Pennsylvania is across the river from Pahaquarra, at the twin cities of Stroudsburg and East Stroudsburg. These cities, like Hawley, ride a comfortable line between industrial and service economies. Some of the residents work at the silk and paper mills along the Brodhead Creek and the Delaware. Others run stores that supply the needs of folks headed for vacationland.

Still others work as faculty or support staff at East Stroudsburg State Teachers College, which will later become East Stroudsburg University. One of those people is lifelong East Stroudsburg resident Helen Brown.

At 32, Helen has been a teacher at the college since 1947, following a stint in the Army during World War II. She has lived in the Stroud Hall dormitory since returning to civilian life. It's invigorating and keeps her attuned to campus goings-on, but by 1952, she feels it's time for a more private lifestyle. She moves to an apartment on Main Street in East Stroudsburg, which she rents from her niece, Katheryn Eyre, and Katheryn's husband Ed. The Eyres live downstairs with their two children.

Family is important to Helen. Her roots reach deep into the Pocono region's history. Her Uncle Peter owns the Peters House Hotel, and will eventually buy the resort known as Bushkill Falls. Her parents own a boarding house in Stroudsburg, about a mile west of town on old Route 209. It was hit by lightning in 1926 and burned down. They replaced it with ten guest cabins, from which they now derive their income.

During the Great Depression of the 1930s, Helen had learned compassion from her parents, who often took in homeless strangers and fed them. Watching them, she developed an attitude of service to her fellow beings. A widower once told her "Service is the rent we pay for the space we occupy." It's a lesson she takes to heart, and to which countless people will soon owe their comfort and well-being, if not their lives.

Helen is an adventurous sort, what some might in the future call a feminist, long before it is any kind of fashionable social movement. She has always done for herself just what she wanted to do, regardless of whether others approve or not. Hers are a sharp mind

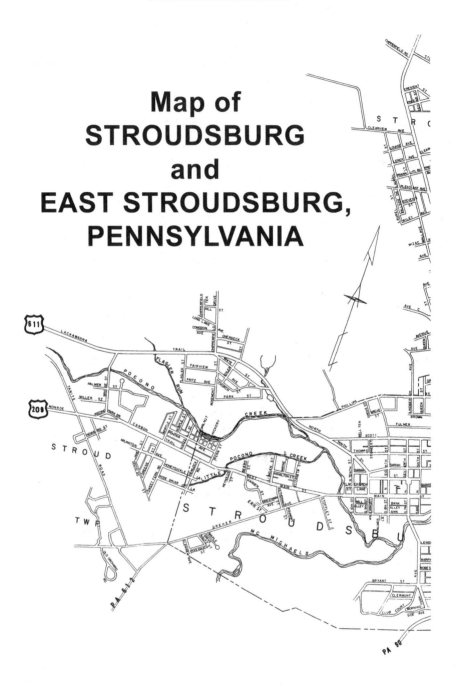

Map of
STROUDSBURG
and
EAST STROUDSBURG,
PENNSYLVANIA

This 1955 map of Stroudsburg and East Stroudsburg shows how the twin boroughs evolved around a network of creeks and streams that would come to define some of their

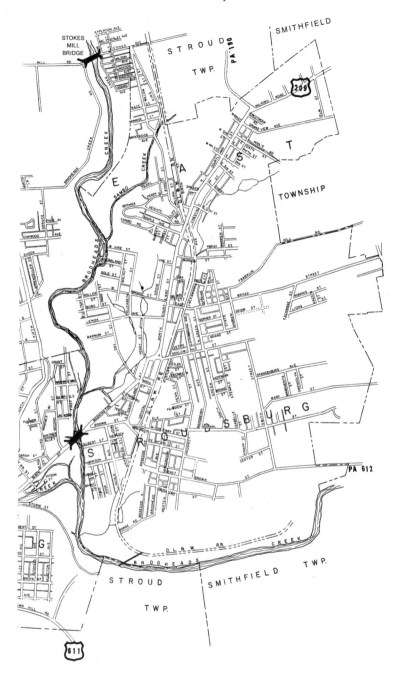

boundaries and, in August of that year, destroy significant parts of both towns.
— Based on an advertising map by Photolith Advertising Co., Forked River, N.J.

and a quick wit, and she uses both without hesitation. As a teenager, she had gotten herself a motorcycle on which she buzzed about all over the area's back roads and byways. The experience will serve her well in the days to come.

True to form, at the end of the previous school year, Helen had pulled her tiny camping trailer out west to Wyoming for the summer. She looked forward to returning to where she had served as a captain in the Women's Army Corps during the war. This summer, she has taken classes and again explored the wild, open country. Now she is on her way home, about a week away from her destination and eager to settle back in for another school year.

She is also anticipating a visit from her sister when she gets back. Always thinking ahead, before taking off for Wyoming, Helen had moved all her own clothes out of her first-floor closet and into the basement, so her sister will have room to hang her outfits. When she gets home, she won't have to worry about such chores. She can concentrate on getting herself back into the rhythm of her regular life, and she is looking forward to it.

Fifteen-year-old Bob Herman is also getting ready to go back to school in East Stroudsburg. He will be a sophomore at the high school. Bob lives near the school's stadium, on Walnut Street. Brodhead Creek, the boundary between the Stroudsburgs, is his neighbor. It runs less than two football fields away from the house he shares with his parents, older brother Donald, nineteen, and their older sister, Charlotte, twenty-one.

Though he's lived there all his life, Bob has never seen the Brodhead do any major flooding. Sure, there has been some high water during spring snowmelt from the mountains, but nothing threatening. And today's rain, though it is getting heavy, doesn't seem dangerous. After all, the summer has been so dry that the creek is now barely more than a trickle.

Bob is enjoying the last days of his summer freedom before having to go back to the confines of the classroom. They will be the last truly carefree days of his youth. The events of the next week will shove Bob through the door to manhood and slam it shut behind him.

Chapter 1

In Forks Township, Pennsylvania, just north of Easton, twenty-year-old Peggy Beling is looking forward to the Labor Day holiday. It will be the last big fling of the summer before she and her fiancé, Mike Fackenthal, head back to Penn State. Peggy is studying to be an elementary school teacher, and Mike, one year her senior, is a sociology major. He is the son of a family friend, and for years, Peggy has been visiting the Fackenthals at their place along the river on North Delaware Drive, also known as Route 611.

She loves how their low-slung, Craftsman style bungalow nestles into the gentle slope, dominating the broad expanse of manicured lawn and looking out over the river. She enjoys the long evenings with Mike's family, talking, laughing, and playing games. Mike's father, J. Douglas Fackenthal, is a prominent attorney and a thoughtful man. He remains on the perimeter of the activity, drawing deeply on a corncob pipe and exhaling slowly, enjoying his own thoughts but rarely missing a bit of the spirited conversation.

Peggy looks up to Mr. Fackenthal, a man with a reputation for honesty and integrity. He's the kind of guy who makes everyone feel safe, that any situation is under control if he's around. And she loves his son.

Mike is an energetic young man with many interests, and he likes his fun. At the beginning of the summer, he and his brother John had bounded down the concrete steps and taken sickles to the tall weeds growing at the river's edge. They made a path down to Sopal Beach, a small, private sand spit that serves as playground and picnic area all season for a sizable group of boys and girls they hang around with.

Mike and Peggy often cross the river with their friends to explore the wonderful beaches on the Jersey side, which is dotted with summer cottages. Just a ways downriver, there's a spring where they can always get fresh, teeth-freezing water. They watch the carp and "sunnies" that dart about in the clear river there.

Mike builds wooden boats, and there are always one or two of these sturdy craft moored at the beach. This summer, his favorite is a larger one he has outfitted with a 22-horsepower outboard engine. He has plans for that boat.

Mike and a few of his buddies are fashioning homemade water skis from boards, and fitting them with bindings cut from old inner tubes. They test out different designs until they find one that holds the foot fast to the ski, then it's time to create a ski jump. The girls watch as some of the boys bring the skis down and try them on, while the others wade out to the swim dock anchored in the river.

After a few exploratory dives to the anchor, the boys decide on a plan. They use some cables, bolts and boards to angle up one end of the dock, while sinking the other and securing it to the bottom. Once they are satisfied that their "ski ramp" will hold, they rub it down with soap and splash it with water to prepare the surface for a smooth jump. When all is ready, the boys draw straws to see who will be the first to try out their latest engineering feat.

Mike gets the honors, and the girls wait onshore while the guys shuttle Mike out to drop in and put his skis on. They throw him the tow rope. He checks the knot, and gives the skis a last quick check. Taking a deep breath, he positions his legs and signals to the driver. It's now or never.

"Go!"

He hears the engine throttle up and feels the rope go taut as he tightens his grip. There is a tug on his shoulder sockets and he lunges forward. The warm water rushes over him as he straightens his legs and rises out of the water. The skis are staying on. It's working!

His friends take him for a few turns around the wide part of the channel to get a feel for the skis. He enjoys the rush of air, cooling the already hot day. He chances letting go of the bar with one hand to wave at Peggy, who is watching intently from the beach. She waves back, and he can see her shouting encouragement, but can't hear it over the drone of the outboard. He's ready.

Smiling, he gives the "thumbs up" to his friend in the boat, and immediately it turns for the final, long run at the ramp. He hears the voice of all twenty-two horses tighten into a high whine as the boat speeds up. Approaching the ramp, he instinctively pulls on the bar, shifting his center of gravity over his knees. The guys who have been watering the jump move away as he comes closer. He feels the boat swing away, launching him into the final trajectory. His ski tips make a smooth transition to the solid ramp, and he straightens up.

At the top, he feels the exhilaration of soaring into space. As he hangs suspended in mid-air for a brief moment, he becomes vaguely aware of cheers erupting from the beach. He drops the bar, savoring the free-floating sensation before his skis head back toward the surface. He bends his knees to absorb the impact, and momentum carries him several more yards after he hits the water. The boat is already circling back to pick him up, and all the guys are yelling and clapping as they hoist him aboard.

"You did it! Yeah!"

He can see the adoration in Peggy's eyes when they drop him back at the beach, and for the rest of the day they all take turns skiing and jumping. They'll sure have a blast on Labor Day weekend. Three whole days of this fun…they can't wait.

Since she was three years old, Sally Packard has loved old Joe Muller. That was when he had first taken her with him on his mail route through her hometown of Kintnersville, Pennsylvania. Joe breathes a little funny. He'd lost a lung after being gassed on the battlefields of France during The Great War. He wheezes once in a while, but it doesn't scare Sally, because she knows he's nice. He even gives her an orange with peppermint sticks stuck in it for her to suck on while they drive.

Joe hasn't let his awful experience embitter him. He remains the same kind person he's always been, especially to the many uneducated farmers on his long rural route. Sally watches him write down orders from the Burpee Seed Catalog or the Sears and Roebuck *Christmas Wish Book* for his customers who can't read or write. He never makes them feel funny or treats them differently than anyone else. They hand him an envelope and he addresses it for them, and they buy a stamp for it.

She always loves the look of anticipation on their faces as Joe slips their order into his mailbag and heads back to the truck. When they finish the last leg of the long, double-loop route, Joe drops Sally off back at her home on Lehnenburg Road, near its intersection with Route 611.

The building has been converted to a house from the old Monroe Hotel and Wagon Spoke Factory. Joe is Sally's step-grandfather, and he owns the building. His parents had run it until about 1950; then Sally's parents, Arlene and James Tingle, took it over. Now the business is the Monroe Tearoom, Gas Station and Restaurant.

Joe and his wife Imogene live across Lehnenburg Road from them. Arlene's great aunts, Maude Hollingshead and Kate Stiles, live up the hill. Their house has a pipe running beneath it from which artesian spring water bubbles all year.

Sally is sixteen now, almost seventeen. She hasn't gone out on the mail route with Joe for several years, but the closeness remains, as it does between all her family members. Even her Uncle Don, who lives over in Runnemede, New Jersey, stays in close contact with everyone. It's a happy life.

She sometimes goes swimming up at the Cascade Lodge with the owners' son, Howard Knuth. They hang around and watch all the New York tourists who spend their summers there. Walking home, she listens to the birdsong from robins, wrens and the especially beautiful tune of the brilliant red cardinals. She watches ruby-throated hummingbirds flit about among the azaleas or the late season trumpet vines.

She walks by stands of colorful jewel weed and goldenrod that have recently appeared along the road. She passes by Al and Ed Pagliaro's Chevy dealership, which has been there since the '30s. If the guys are out, they wave, and she waves back, then continues over the hot macadam road to home. The heat shimmers over the surface in the high sun, and the smell of road oil rises to her nostrils.

In the evenings, she sits outside and breathes in the fresh smell of the woods. Every night, like clockwork, she hears the long, mournful wail of the "Pennsy" diesel engine whistle as it hurtles down the tracks across the river. And she watches the moon rise huge and white, its reflection sparkling on the water. This easy, natural rhythm of life along the river in Kintnersville feels safe to Sally, and never fails to lull her into a deep, peaceful sleep.

Farther down the river, in Upper Black Eddy, May Snyder knows it's going to rain, and maybe a lot. The bridge cops from Milford had come over at lunch and told her so. But she's too busy to worry about rain. A couple of the guys from across the river hung around longer than usual today, reliving Ted Williams' two-thousandth hit against the Yankees. Now it's getting late, and she still has to clean up from the lunch crowd before the afternoon rush on ice cream starts. Even though the sun isn't shining, it's still hot, and before too long, the late day crowd will be coming through the door.

At 37, May runs the Riverview Lunch, while her husband Donald works his shift across the river at the Riegel Paper mill. She operates the stand on the bottom floor of their two-story frame house near the Milford bridge. While an obscure entrepreneur named Ray Kroc is gambling on the launch of a small hamburger stand far away in Chicago, the concept of "fast food" is just gaining acceptance in America. Riverview Lunch is the closest thing to it along the river in upper Bucks County. It caters mostly to the lunch crowd from the mill and other businesses nearby, serving one-dish meals that can be enjoyed on the run or back at the office; mostly soups, sandwiches, mac and cheese, chicken, spaghetti.

The luncheonette also stocks a few convenience items—gum, candy, cigarettes. But there is a secondary clientele that becomes important in the summertime: tourists and kids who stop by for some cool refreshments before heading back to the river for more swimming or boating.

This summer, it's hard keeping up because nobody can get cool enough. May is constantly re-ordering Breyer's ice cream and bottles of soda pop. It's great for sales, but between ordering and serving and cleaning, she is going full bore all day long. Her three boys, fourteen-year-old Jim, eleven-year-old Barry, and seven-year-old Leonard, aren't yet old enough to be much help. Besides, kids need time to just be kids. So most of the time, May is on her own until Don gets home.

Still, she likes the stand. She likes knowing their food is keeping the mill workers fed while they toil, and she enjoys their compliments when the chicken fries up extra good or she's serving someone's favorite soup. She really likes being able to stay in touch with all the local news, and sometimes even being first to hear it. She gets to see many of her friends while she works, even visits a little when it's slow. And there is something to be said for being your own boss. Makes you feel like you're really part of building your community.

Community matters to May. She has lived in Upper Black Eddy all her life, and her parents still do, right up Bridgeton Hill from her. This is home, and she likes being an integral part of the fabric of its everyday life.

The river is an integral part of that life, too. May likes the river as much as anyone, but she has another feeling for it that a lot of them don't share: respect. May's mother has lived through the flood of 1903, and she's told May about the river's awesome power. As a member of the fire company's Ladies Auxiliary, May has heard enough about river rescues to know that the river, though a constant presence, shouldn't be taken for granted. She knows what it can do.

Lots of times, she hears the tourists bragging about some trick they've performed on the water, or about how fast their fancy motor-boats can go. She sometimes thinks they're foolhardy, but keeps that sentiment to herself while she smiles and serves their double-dip cones. Still, she thinks, one of these days there's going to be an accident or something. People will learn what that river's really all about.

Connie

The night of September 8, 1900, was a turning point in the way Americans thought about weather. The lesson had become a distant memory by 1955, and the cost of forgetting would be high.

A long, intense heat wave had oppressed the island of Galveston, Texas, with stifling humidity and sweltering temperatures throughout that first summer of the century. The mercury stayed well into the eighties, even after the sun disappeared below the ocean waves on the horizon. This misery culminated in the terrible night of September 8, with the arrival of a ferocious hurricane that bore down directly on the city from off the Gulf of Mexico.

Before the sun rose the next morning, between six and ten thousand people—no one has ever been able to ascertain the actual figure—were dead, victims of a record high storm surge. The waves rolled over the low island, breaking up houses and commercial buildings, smashing everything and everyone in their way. When they retreated back into Galveston Bay, they pulled with them the corpses of humans and animals and the debris of what had been one of America's most prosperous cities.

Among the bodies were those of Cora Cline and her daughters, Allie May and Rosemary. These were the pregnant wife and two young children of Isaac Cline, chief meteorologist at the island's U.S. Weather Bureau office. Isaac himself survived, along with his youngest daughter, Esther, and his brother, Joseph. But his was to be a life of regret, for he had been one of many whose disregard for the power of nature had led to such tragedy.

Isaac had known the storm was coming far enough in advance to have warned his friends and neighbors to evacuate the island. His own recollections notwithstanding, historic records show he did little, if any, of that. Instead, he put his faith in the ability of man's engineering and

33

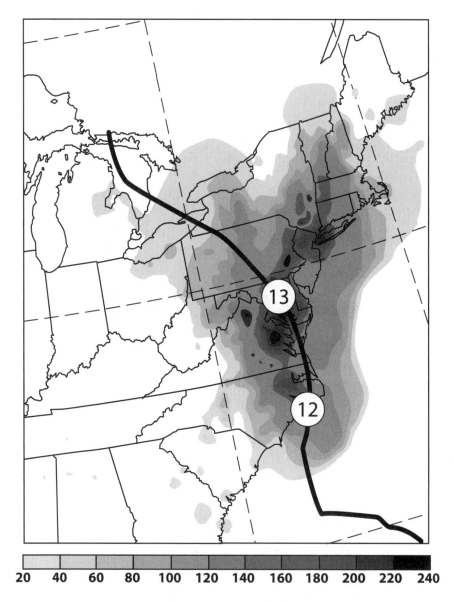

20 ml = .79"   100 ml = 3.94"   160 ml = 6.3"   240 ml = 9.46"
Conversion: 1 ml = .0394 inch

This map shows the storm track and rainfall distribution (in milliliters) of Hurricane Connie along the entire eastern seaboard of the United States, including indicators of the position of the storm's "eye" on August 12 and 13, 1955.
—Based on a map from the National Climatic Data Center

technology to protect him, his family, and neighbors. He was a man of his time, sublimely confident in human supremacy. He simply refused to believe, despite his own experience to the contrary, that nature could throw anything destructive enough at his hometown that its sturdy buildings couldn't shelter them from.

By the time he finally realized the danger of the powerful storm, it had been too late. He would pay a chilling price for his hubris, and spend the rest of his career in the Weather Bureau studying the causes and effects of tidal storm surge. Isaac was a man possessed, doggedly blaming surge as the primary source of danger in a hurricane, though many argued that it was the extreme winds that did the most damage. He published two books on the subject and became one of the most sought-after experts in his field. Eventually, long after his death, his theory would be proven scientifically correct.

Though Isaac courted the recognition and financial reward accruing to his expertise, no amount of acclaim could erase the fact that he'd lost nearly everything of personal value in that awful storm. It couldn't fill the void in his life, or assuage the guilt he carried with him for the remainder of it. Isaac never remarried and retired from the Weather Bureau in 1935. He sought relief in beauty, dabbling in art over the next twenty years.

At eight thirty on the evening of August 3, 1955, ninety-three-year-old Isaac Cline's memory ceased to be tortured. At the very moment of his death in New Orleans, an ironic emergence of another kind was taking place far to the southeast.

A wave of low pressure had rolled off the west coast of Africa, churning the sea below and creating its own heat-and-moisture engine. A cluster of thunderstorms was forming around its center on the surface of the Caribbean Sea. Just after midnight, the San Juan Weather Bureau issued this advisory:

```
ADVISORY NO. ONE CONNIE 1 A.M. 0500Z
AUGUST 4 1955.
TROPICAL STORM OF SLIGHT TO MODERATE
INTENSITY IS CENTERED AT 1 A.M.0500Z…AT
ABOUT LATITUDE 16.6N LONGITUDE 48 W OR
ABOUT 850 MILES EAST OF GUADALOUPE FRENCH
WEST INDIES. IT APPEARS TO BE MOVING
SLOWLY WESTWARD TO 8 MPH AND IS ATTENDED
```

BY WINDS OF 50 TO 55 MPH IN SQUALLS OVER
A SMALL AREA NEAR THE CENTER. PRESENT
INDICATIONS ARE FOR INCREASING INTENSITY
AND CONTINUED WEST TO WESTNORTHWEST MOVE-
MENT DURING NEXT 6 TO 12 HOURS AT ABOUT
SAME RATE. VESSELS IN PATH SHOULD EXER-
CISE CAUTION. THE NEXT ADVISORY WILL BE
ISSUED AT 6 A.M. EST 1000Z.

HIGGS WEATHER BUREAU

Hurricane Connie had been born.

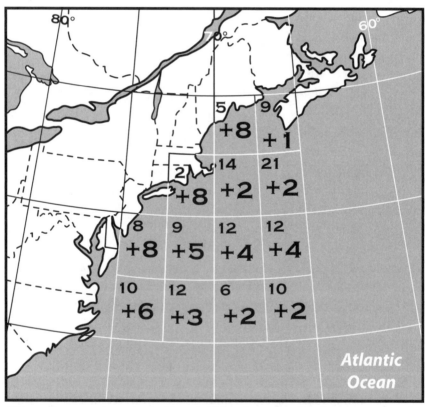

*This gradient map shows the significantly higher-than-normal surface temperatures that
fueled the active and destructive 1955 Atlantic hurricane season. The small figures in
upper left indicate how many measurements were made inside each 2.5° square.*
– Based on map from U.S. Weather Bureau Technical Paper No. 26, 1956

Before Connie arrived in the Mid-Atlantic region, it had been a dry, hot year. In the northeastern United States and adjacent waters of the Atlantic Ocean, a general lack of storminess and clouds allowed a constant stream of sunshine. Surface waters were measuring an average of five to six degrees higher than normal. Without storms to disturb the surface, Atlantic waters were heating to a depth much greater than usual.

Records were being set for high temperature and lack of rainfall. Farmers were getting nervous. Most of them were old enough to remember the Dust Bowl days of the Great Depression, when much of the country had suffered from severe and prolonged drought. Crops had withered in fields, animals had starved or died of dehydration, and whole farms had literally blown away in the unceasing winds that moaned across America's Great Plains. Though it hadn't been quite as bad in the northeast, the drought's effects had been felt here, nonetheless.

In the Delaware Valley, February and March, 1955 had seen a surplus of precipitation, mostly in the form of snow, but that would be followed by two months of deficits. April was off the average by 48 percent, May by 73 percent. June experienced a slight bump, then July was down by 77 percent.

A Doylestown *Intelligencer* editorial at the beginning of August gives an idea of the general weariness felt about the weather. Headlined "Hot and Dry, July—Goodbye," it offered a summary that, by the end of August, would appear to fairly glow with irony:

> July, 1955, is now history, and history is welcome to it. True, the month broke records, but they were of a kind much better left intact. …Rather than anticipate August, 1955, however, we prefer to be thankful to be rid of July. Rid of a month which set an all-time record for heat in the 90s. Even worse, a month which was one of the driest on record.
>
> One need only drive through the countryside to see July's handiwork. Parched crops; burned fields;

wilting trees; stagnant streams. Dr. Thurlow C.
Nelson, chairman of the New Jersey Water Policy
and Supply Council, notes that July was far more
serious than the "usual summer dry spell." And he
warns that if August follows suit "we may be heading
into the worst drought" in local experience.

As the excerpt tells, the lack of rainfall was exacerbated by continuous, sweltering heat. Even in February, there had been a dozen days
above 50°, the highest being the 28th, when the temperature hit 66°.
March was warmer yet, with a 73° day in mid-month. The last day of
April it was 80°, and from there, the scorching began. From mid-May
on, high temperatures would not fall below 70° again until September
22, with the exception of three days in early June. More often, highs
were in the mid-to-high 80s, and there was at least one day each in July
and August when the mercury hit 100° in Philadelphia. Plenty of days
in the high nineties surrounded those.

So it was that with no small amount of fervor, farmers in the
Mid-Atlantic and New England were praying for rain by August.
Nonfarmers, sick of watching their gardens shrivel and their lawns
turn brown, also thought a bit of precipitation would be a good idea.

With all the interest in the weather at the time, it may surprise
modern readers to learn how primitive forecasting methods still were
in the mid-1950s. Though far advanced from Isaac Cline's America at
the turn of the last century, techniques in 1955 were far less sophisti-
cated—and much less accurate—than those we take for granted today.

Back then, there was no Weather Channel broadcasting television forecasts and storm tracking around the clock. Most people didn't
yet even own a TV set. They still got the majority of their news from
the daily papers and, in some areas, AM radio stations.

There was no Doppler radar, nor earth-orbiting weather satellites
to detect storms. Even if there had been, no efficient, affordable computers existed to parse all the data they would have relayed to tracking
stations. Forecasters could not easily have created timely, usable reports.

Marine readings were received on a catch-as-catch-can basis, from
cooperative ship captains and fishing vessels who understood the value

of accurate weather forecasts to their own safety and productivity. Inter-governmental cooperation between countries in sharing weather data was a victim of the distrust fostered by the Cold War, and there would be no system of dedicated weather buoys until 1967.

Atmospheric readings were still taken manually using simple tools that remain the best for capturing specific types of data even today. The problem is that such readings are strictly local, and aren't of much value in creating accurate, longterm forecasts over large geographic areas. Weather doesn't occur in a vacuum, and it was the critical relativity data that was missing.

Following the massive destruction and loss of life caused by killer hurricanes Carol, Edna and Hazel in 1954, Congress had appropriated a record budget of $571,000 to the Weather Bureau. The funding was used to beef up their hurricane forecasting abilities with what the Stroudsburg *Daily Record* called "a whole new arsenal of ultra-modern devices and methods."

The bureau began launching stratosphere-probing meteorological rockets more than a hundred miles into space to provide upper level wind data not previously available. They also created a network of reporting stations throughout the Caribbean, a common birthplace for tropical storms, and began building twenty-five stations along the East Coast of the United States.

These stations were equipped with various types of cameras, newly developed gust recorders, and radar units whose technology had been developed during World War II. Connie had been the first hurricane ever to be located and reported by one of the Caribbean stations.

Their first-generation radar units could, indeed, image a storm on a screen that located it relative to a surrounding area. They even had the capability to render the spiral pattern of hurricane rain bands, providing meteorologists their first real evidence of the circulatory nature of tropical cyclones. However, the images they generated weren't anywhere near the resolution quality and versatility of those even civilians now know and use daily.

These radar units were also saddled with serious limitations. They were useful only within a fairly short distance range, and were too bulky and heavy to be sent airborne on most planes to follow active systems.

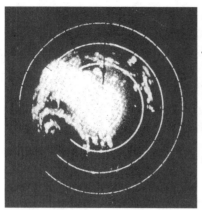

Radar in 1955 was still very primitive and limited, compared to modern technology. It generated crude light images of precipitation, but did not indicate windspeed or direction of travel. This is the image of Hurricane Diane's rain pattern as seen by U.S. Weather Bureau operators on the radarscope at Cape Hatteras, North Carolina at 7:50 a.m. EST on August 17, 1955. Distance between the range circles is 50 nautical miles.

– From Technical Paper No. 26, April 1956

Still more frustrating, weather forecasters couldn't pinpoint with an acceptable degree of accuracy where any given storm was headed and how soon it would get there. There were several theories about what atmospheric mechanism steers hurricanes, but not enough empirical information to prove or disprove most of them. This particular question remains something of a mystery even in the beginning of the twenty-first century.

There was also the issue of data richness. Aside from speed and direction, forecasters need to know about storm intensity. Without Doppler technology, there was no knowledge of how much precipitation was occurring inside a storm or whether its clouds obscured a dangerously spinning vortex.

A *Philadelphia Inquirer* article in the August 11, 1955 edition sums it up nicely:

> Experts…tackle that task, basing their forecasts largely on wind directions aloft and air pressure (or weight) surrounding the storm. The interplay of winds and pressure, themselves subject to scores of variables, decide the future path of the hurricane.

> Scientists make the best predictions they can, recognizing they still are far from the precision they would like.

This problem persists today, evidenced by the notorious "cone of uncertainty" shown on every modern hurricane forecast map.

The discovery and movement of storms over large bodies of open water in 1955 were reported to local weather bureau stations by ships at sea, commercial airline pilots, fishing vessels, Coast Guard stations and lighthouse keepers, oil rigs and military bases. In the case of hurricanes, it had been discovered that their massive waves produce vibrations on the ocean floor of significant enough intensity to be picked up by seismographs, the instruments used to measure earthquake strength. Therefore, alerts were sometimes issued from seismograph observers stationed in tropical zones, as well.

Once weather stations had been alerted to the existence of any kind of tropical disturbance, they turned to America's national Hurricane Forecast Center to track it as it developed. Then, as now, the Hurricane Center depended on a unique arm of military pilots to provide the ongoing data they needed to track over the life of any tropical storm.

The Weather Bureau had been working in conjunction with the Navy and Air Force since 1947 to provide round-the-clock hurricane warnings. Pilots from the Naval Air Station in Jacksonville, Florida covered aerial reconnaissance missions over the eastern Atlantic and Caribbean Sea, while the Air Force's 53rd Squadron tracked hurricanes in the western Atlantic Ocean and the Pacific. Informally, these squadrons were—and still are—referred to as "Hurricane Hunters."

The first intentional flight into a hurricane had been made about five years before the official effort took shape. It had happened during the war, quite on a lark. Col. Joseph Duckworth, a pilot training instructor at Bryan Field in—ironically—Galveston, was trying to impress upon his nervous British flight students the sturdiness of their AT-6 "Texan" training aircraft.

It had not been an officially sanctioned flight, and only when the daredevil colonel and his navigator, Lt. Col. Ralph O'Hair, returned safely did it became an event to be celebrated. After the war, Duckworth served as the first instructor of those who would become Hurricane Hunters.

Since then, hundreds of successful flights had been made into and through the monstrous storms. They had developed workable methods for gathering the data they needed while maintaining their own safety, and over the years, hurricane reconnaissance flight techniques had been refined. It was one of the few meteorological tools that really worked well in 1955.

MIAMI WEATHER BUREAU BULLETIN 8 PM EST
AUGUST 11 1955

FOR THE LAST THREE HOURS HURRICANE CONNIE
HAS MADE NO NEW FORWARD PROGRESS AS SHE
HAS PROCEEDED ON HER ERRATIC COURSE AND
WAS STILL CENTERED ABOUT 75 MILES SOUTH-
EAST OF WILMINGTON NC. HIGHEST WINDS ARE
ESTIMATED AT ABOUT 100 MPH AND GALES
EXTEND OUT 150 TO 300 MILES FROM THE
CENTER. WINDS AT WILMINGTON HAVE BEEN UP
TO 50 MPH WITH GUSTS TO 80 MPH. A LIGHT
SHIP STATIONED IN THE ATLANTIC NEAR WILM-
INGTON HAS HAD GUSTS UP TO 100 MPH IN
SQUALLS. TIDES AT SOME PLACES ARE RUNNING
4 TO 6 FEET ABOVE NORMAL. HURRICANE CON-
NIE IS EXPECTED TO CONTINUE MOVING SLOWLY
ON AN ERRATIC COURSE FOR THE NEXT FEW
HOURS BUT SHOULD MOVE MOSTLY TOWARD THE
NORTH NORTHWEST OR NORTH AT ABOUT 5 MPH.
WINDS WILL CONTINUE TO INCREASE ALONG THE
NORTH CAROLINA AND VIRGINIA CAPES AS THE
STORM APPROACHED. HURRICANE WARNINGS ARE
DISPLAYED FROM CAPE ROMAIN SC TO THE
VIRGINIA CAPES AND NORTHEAST STORM WARN-
INGS ELSEWHERE FROM SOUTH OF MANASQUAN NJ
TO CAVANNASH GA. ALL PRECAUTIONS SHOULD
BE CONTINUED IN THE AREA OF DISPLAY.
NEXT ADVISORY AT 11 PM EST.

GENTRY WEATHER BUREAU

Connie was actually the second hurricane of the '55 season, but she was the first to threaten any serious destruction. Alice had been a freak occurrence, essentially a "New Year's storm," occurring completely outside the regular tropical storm season of June 1 through November 30. In fact, she had been such a surprise to those U.S. Weather Bureau meteorologists responsible for naming the storms that she caught them unprepared. They didn't have a new list of hurricane names chosen for the New Year yet, so they simply recycled the name of the first 1954 hurricane, which poses something of a problem for researchers delving through that year's records.

Alice developed on December 30, 1954, and was upgraded to full hurricane status on New Year's Eve. On January 2, 1955, already on the wane, she battered the Leeward Islands with 85-mile-per-hour winds before dying out in the Caribbean. There was something ominous about her anomalous life. In retrospect, she was a portent of an Atlantic hurricane season that would become one of the most active and destructive on record.

Tropical storm Brenda came next, emerging more expectedly from the Gulf of Mexico in July. She dissipated near Louisiana almost immediately, without reaching hurricane strength. Looking back, it's almost as if these first two storms were rehearsals for the real thing, which was about to upstage nearly every other weather event of the year.

Connie first appeared about 600 miles west of the Cape Verde islands in the middle of the Atlantic before moving to her first reported position. She played a dangerous game of "Will I? Won't I?" with the islands of the Caribbean. It was this kind of behavior that had the press classifying her as a "coquette." She ended up snaking north between Bermuda and the Bahamas, skirting and sparing Puerto Rico, the Virgin Islands and the Leewards, and heading for the U.S. mainland.

Hurricane flags were hoisted all along the east coast, with many jittery people still recalling the onslaught of Hurricane Hazel and her sisters Carol and Edna the year before. Just 200 miles off the coast of North Carolina, Connie halted, moving about in indecisive circles. This was perceived alternately as a cruel taunt and an annoying prolonging of the inevitable. Again, the press had a field day. The *Philadelphia Inquirer* reported on August 12 that "Irritated male observers saw in her conduct vindication of the Weather Bureau's decision—which had been criticized last year—to continue to identify hurricanes by feminine names.

" 'She can't make up her mind,' they said. 'Just like a woman.' "

In Washington, New Jersey, *Newark Evening News* reporter Richard Harpster is also observing Connie's progress, monitoring what he thinks might become a serious local story. He's watching the front pages of other papers like the *Philadelphia Inquirer,* following the progress of Hurricane Connie toward the Mid-Atlantic. An August 11 headline tells of gales whipping the Carolina coast, bringing tornadoes along with them. Beneath two forbidding photos on page one was another headline, this one carrying the voice of warning for Dick and his neighbors: "Storm Threat Hovers Over Area With Force of Blow Unpredictable."

No one could forget the hundred-mile-an-hour winds that had ripped trees from the White House lawn the year before, when Hazel had torn through in October. A rare hurricane that had kept her tropical characteristics long after moving inland, she had done similar damage in the Delaware Valley. Philly had reported 94 m.p.h. peak gusts, and air traffic controllers had been forced to abandon their towers for fear they would be blown down. That storm had dropped a lot of rain, but it was the wind that was most frightful. To those in her path, it seemed she would never die out. Even after Hazel had moved up into Ontario, Canada, she had killed eighty people and left thousands more homeless.

Yet already, people are talking about other reports that say the wind threat from Connie is dying, and that she's losing power. Even the top headline on August 12 says the Philadelphia area will escape the storm's fury, and that the Weather Bureau has lifted its hurricane alert north of the Delaware breakwater.

Still, having witnessed some impressive storms in the South Pacific, Dick knows weather is unpredictable, especially tropical cyclones. They had been called typhoons over there, but it was the same kind of storm. He isn't taking any chances on missing a story. Besides, in a smaller article, he notices that another tropical tempest has shown up near San Juan. And already, there have been a number of lightning strike incidents during a significant electrical storm, just last night. He is going to be ready, no matter what.

At 31, Dick has established himself as a crack news pro. He had been a staff sergeant in World War II, serving on Guam under General Curtis LeMay, who had masterminded the bombing of Tokyo. Dick had been the radio teletype operator who'd sent all the messages issuing orders for the dropping of the first atomic bomb on Hiroshima.

Surrounded by such drama, he had developed a knack for story-telling. He'd written many letters home, entertaining friends and family so much that they told him he should use that talent to make a living. When Dick had returned to the States, he'd taken advantage of the G.I. Bill and begun taking night courses in journalism. As soon as he'd graduated, he'd walked into the offices of the *Washington Star* and asked for a reporting job. They'd hired him on the spot for $35 a week, a position that would allow him to marry and start a family.

Dick had soon proven himself adept at the professional journalism trade. Before too long, he'd established the chops to move up to the *Newark Evening News,* the state's largest newspaper. They publish five editions, with reporters stationed all along the Delaware Valley.

Dick's beat is Warren County, and he writes for the State edition. Always "Johnny-on-the-spot," he keeps his car's gas tank full, with a few high quality cameras in the trunk. The industry darling—a 4x5 Speed Graphic—is his favorite, and he makes sure it's always stocked with film. A true pro, he's always ready for a breaking story.

Knowing his success depends on being able to gain access to breaking news, Dick stays on the good side of emergency response personnel. He's careful never to photograph a state trooper with his hat off or his sleeves rolled up: it would be considered unprofessional of them and reflect poorly on their careers. He shares information with rescue squads and fire companies if they need it. He develops a rapport with these public servants built on trust, and he will soon parlay that into some of the best reporting of his career.

Downriver a few miles, some four hundred people are enjoying life on the river in the summer colony of Carpentersville. The small Pohatcong Township vacation settlement has grown over the years to eighty-nine cottages and bungalows. Residents consist primarily of seasonal dwellers, though a few have begun living year-round in some of the mostly unheated, non-insulated buildings.

One of the buildings in this enclave is a typical river cottage owned by Virginia Sutton's family. Virginia is the eldest of nine children. She had been twenty-four when her parents found the place. It had been just a shell, but it was 1938, during the Great Depression, and they had been able to buy it for a song. Virginia's dad was a handy guy, and between him and the rest of the family and friends, they'd managed to renovate it into a comfortable summer getaway. They'd christened it the "All Inn," and proceeded to make it the site of a cherished ritual; the annual trek from their Easton, Pennsylvania, home to stay for the summer.

Virginia's aunt already owned the place next door, which they called "LaFayette." It had been nice to know you'd like your neighbors before you even moved in, and Virginia and her family quickly established themselves in Carpentersville.

When they'd first bought the All Inn, Virginia's family would get on the trolley that ran to Doylestown from Easton, and pay their dime for a ride to the Raubsville stop. From there, they would telephone her aunt, asking her to row across the river to pick them up. If nobody was home at LaFayette, they would walk across the canal bridge in Raubsville and walk down to the water's edge. Inevitably, there would be someone out on the water in a boat, and the newcomers would hitch a ride.

One of the attractions of the location is the group of several large shade trees that surround their cottage on two sides. Along with the welcome shade, they provide shelter for the many songbirds native to the region. The birds' spirited chirping and trilling is a natural soundtrack for summer life at All Inn.

Virginia's dad has built a card table and painted a layout for a game called "Michigan" on its top. On Saturday nights, six or eight of the gang get together around it to play cards all evening. Other times, they host parties for the whole crew and their friends. All of Virginia's brothers and sisters—and as they get older, their spouses and in-laws—come to share food and drinks and long summer nights at All Inn.

Of course, one of the mainstays of cottage activity is swimming in the river. Without air conditioning or insulation, the small building quickly turns stuffy during the hot, humid Delaware Valley summers. Rowboats are another way to relax and have fun. At night, many river people row up and down their stretch of the Delaware or paddle merrily along in canoes, camp lanterns lighting their way. There aren't too many people with motorboats yet, so the water is still fairly quiet other than the sounds of splashing and laughing.

Virginia has recently married Cliff Sutton, a Phillipsburg man in his early forties, close to her own age. Cliff is also a river person, having spent much time at his parents' summer place at Harvey Station, north of Phillipsburg. He slides easily into the rhythm of All Inn.

Every summer, the Carpentersville community holds their Water Carnival. They decorate watercraft of all types and parade up and down the riverfront. Sometimes they showcase new residents in a baby parade. Nearby, Hap's Pavilion sells ice cream, soda and candy for the kids, and beer for adults. Saturday nights hop with the sounds of dance music, and the ice cream and cool drinks help ease the strain of the constant heat.

As Connie ambles up the coast, she drops a good bit of rain on Carpentersville and the whole Delaware Valley. The river rises and even floods a little, but not too much more than anyone has seen before, during regular spring freshets caused by snowmelt.

No one gets too excited. Besides, it really does help the growing things. Though it's more indoor-oriented, life goes on as usual at the All Inn.

Philadelphia Inquirer, August 13, 1955 – Front Page:

Area On Guard For Connie Fury

Philadelphia, made wary by the erratic behavior of Hurricane Connie and with an eye on another tropical storm following in her wake, remained on the alert throughout last night as the outer fringes of the disturbance buffeted the city.

For the second successive day, pelting rains drenched the five-county area, flooding highways and cellars here at the same time that they brought welcome relief to farmlands parched by a summer-long drought. Steadily increasing winds, expected to reach 40 miles an hour this morning, began blowing in midafternoon.

Late last night, the wind at Wildwood had mounted to a velocity of 50 miles an hour, the Coast Guard reported. Heavy gusts blew down several signs in front of businesses…

As Connie approaches, other headlines trumpet disturbing news. Ten people are dead and four more missing from a vacation schooner that has been capsized by high winds and wild waves, 3,000 yards offshore near North Beach, Maryland. Two Rehoboth Beach children's camps are evacuated. Residents hunker down, wondering what Connie might dish up for them.

She arrives August 12 in the Delaware Valley at tropical storm force, just below that of a hurricane. Gale winds and torrential rains lash coastal and inland sections of northern New Jersey. Bergen County is particularly hard hit, with power outages caused by trees taking wires down with them as they fall. In the Raritan Bay area, nearly three hundred summer residents are evacuated to higher ground from colonies in the Clifford Beach area by Red Cross disaster units. The Plainfields and Watchung are flooded and parts are without power when a substation is knocked out.

Downed lines interrupt telephone service in a wide area that includes South River, Jersey City, Hoboken, Bayonne, Elizabeth, and Chatham. The police in Perth Amboy log almost nine thousand distress calls, with flooded conditions reported throughout the city. The beachfront at Asbury Park is under several inches of water from rainfall, though there is no damage to the park itself. Route 17, the main travel artery to New York's upstate resorts, is flooded in multiple locations.

Flooded roadways and downed trees cause miles of traffic snarls for motorists, and five people are killed in car accidents. One man is electrocuted when he comes into contact with a dangling power line. Two people are missing. Newark Airport Weather Station reports $3\frac{1}{4}$ inches of rain in the previous 24 hours, an August record…for the time being.

Meanwhile, another tropical storm, Diane, makes her debut and reaches hurricane status, as well. Only 400 miles across, Diane is being dragged into her older sister's 500-mile diameter path by a process known as the Fujiwara effect.

Decades earlier, a Japanese scientist of that name had noted that two vortices—or whirling storms—in close proximity will tend to curl around each other, pulled toward the other's center by a complex interplay of their swirling winds. Meteorologists will later figure that it was Diane's influence that, in this way, caused Connie to suddenly stop moving forward and instead to sashay around in circles off the Carolina coast.

When a low pressure trough opens the way landward, Connie finally escapes her little sister's hold and she strikes out over Morehead City, North Carolina. Her absence leaves a vacuum of sorts, which clears the way for Diane to continue her own advance toward the coast.

Meanwhile in Pennsylvania, Phoenixville's Camp Council sends its 160 campers and 30 counselors home a day early, fearing a repeat of Hazel's performance. Several units of Philadelphia's National Guard leave for weekend drill at Fort Indiantown Gap, but Connie is on everyone's minds. One of those people is the state's Adjutant General, Maj. Gen. A. J. Drexel Biddle, who is running their training maneuvers. He tells the papers that the troops are ready to move out "at a moment's notice in the event of an emergency." They will soon be called to do exactly that.

Philadelphia and vicinity is reporting the heaviest rainfall in 57 years, with a 24-hour total of 4.83 inches. The Delaware and Schuylkill Rivers are both topping their banks, as are many smaller streams. Fourteen-year-old John Judge is rescued from a small island in Darby Creek. His friends Larry Greb and Charles Carter swim to safety through the raging waters after their canoe overturns, then go to get help for John. Residents along several waterways are evacuated.

Many boats are ripped from their moorings along the Neshaminy Creek in Bucks County. Members of Croydon, Seaford, and Wright boatyards and the Bucks County Yacht Club retrieve them before they can be completely washed away. Several families in the Riverside section of Bristol Township and the Echo Beach section of Bensalem are flooded out of their homes.

Doylestown reports steady winds of 45 m.p.h. with gusts up to 60 m.p.h., downed power lines, and telephone outages. The Neshaminy Creek is overflowing at several points, including the intersection of Old York Road and Route 611. In Warrington, the entire fire company is on standby in case they're needed for rescues. The northeast branch of the Perkiomen Creek overflows in Perkasie, prompting the borough's fire company to turn out for cellar pumping duty at three o'clock in the morning. Sellersville also catches overflow from the creek.

Water pouring over the banks of Licking Run Creek filters down between the stones and dirt of two Quakertown home foundations and buckles their cellar walls. The Tohickon Creek also leaves its banks in the village.

During her tenure over the Delaware Valley, Connie drops a wide range of rain totals, all of them high. The majority of it falls in the northern reaches of New Jersey and Pennsylvania. Between August 11 and 14, the Philadelphia Airport logs 60 m.p.h. winds and 5.48 inches of rain; Doylestown 7.87 inches; Phoenixville 7.55; Scranton 3.73; Tamaqua, in the Lehigh Valley, 4.88; Lehighton 6.17; Stroudsburg 6.9; Hawley 6.47; Mt. Pocono 9.45; and Matamoras 5.72.

In New Jersey, during the same time period, Trenton receives 6.29 inches of rain; New Brunswick 8.9; Lambertville 7.8; Belvidere 6.17; Phillipsburg 7.28; and Sussex 6.28. The Delaware River at Trenton reaches 5.61 feet over flood stage at 10:00 on the morning of the thirteenth, but any other flooding is moderate. The Assunpink Creek—one of its tributaries running through Trenton—reaches its highest stage of the month, surging 2.02 feet over the highest stage it will reach even during Diane the following week.

Connie does cause extensive flooding on the Passaic and Raritan Rivers in New Jersey, though damage is spotty and not excessive. There are patchy power outages up and down the valley, mostly due not to wind, but to trees losing their grasp in the spongy soil and toppling over onto wires. Most outages are repaired within a very short time, and utility companies express their relief and happy surprise at how unexpectedly "gentle" Connie has been.

She causes one drowning death in Monroe County, when an elderly Presbyterian minister from Princeton drives his car through a bridge guardrail over the Tobyhanna Creek and plunges into its swollen waters. He had been vacationing in nearby Pocono Lake Preserve with his family. At least seven other deaths are attributed to Connie in Pennsylvania. Still, given her destruction in the South, Connie goes easy on the Delaware Valley.

Civil Defense workers and emergency personnel are alerted throughout Philadelphia and its suburbs, but the downpours finally dwindle out around 10:30 on the morning of the fourteenth. Utility repair crews and those from street and highway departments take advantage of the break in the weather to fix or replace damaged roadways, flooded substations and downed power lines. By storm's end, Pennsylvania damages are estimated in the $350 million range.

Port Jervis gets 7.5 inches of rain, as do many of its surrounding neighbors in upstate New York. LaGuardia airfield reports a total of 12.2 inches, falling in a 38-hour period on the twelfth and thirteenth. Southern New England also receives a great deal of rain from Connie. Nearly 6 inches are recorded at Stamford, Connecticut, on August 13, along with power outages and tides one to two feet above normal.

Other areas are suffering as well. Many residents of the Delmarva Peninsula are isolated by power outages and downed lines, and a 250-ton cargo vessel sinks in the Choptank River near Chesapeake Bay. Four Maryland deaths are blamed on the storm, and more than a hundred traffic accidents result. New York reports several cruise ships pulling in to port up to thirty-three hours late. The Big Apple itself is flooded by more than nine inches of rain and buffeted to a standstill by 70 m.p.h. winds before power is restored to affected areas. Eleven of the state's residents are dead in storm-related incidents. But it is to the south that Delaware Valley residents look and count their blessings.

Though South Carolina reports relatively mild damage, mostly limited to fishing piers and oceanfront homes on Myrtle Beach, North Carolina is battered and reeling. Unofficial estimates put total damage between seven and ten million dollars. Governor Luther Hodges requests President Eisenhower's declaration of a major disaster area to release funds for cleanup and rebuilding. Amazingly, no deaths are reported, but there is one notable birth. A High Point couple, Mr. and Mrs. Clarence Hill, welcome a new baby, born August 13. They name her Connie Diane.

With the storm past, seventeen workmen return to the still-intact Texas Tower, so called because it's being built with the help of oil riggers used to working with such structures. It will house an Air Force radar station being installed 100 miles off of Cape Cod, to monitor just such storms. The workers had been evacuated with twenty-three others the previous Wednesday, due to fears that the half-built structure might not withstand the storm.

WASHINGTON WEATHER BUREAU BULLETIN 2 PM
EST AUG 13 1955

STORM CONNIE HAS CONTINUED MOVING TOWARD
THE NORTH NORTHWEST ABOUT 22 MPH DURING
THE PAST 3 HOURS AND IS NOW CENTERED IN
NORTH CENTRAL PENNSYLVANIA 95 MILES
NORTHEAST OF PITTSBURGH. WINDS OF 30 TO
40 MPH WITH GUSTS TO ABOUT 50 MPH EXTEND
AS FAR AS 200 MILES NORTH AND NORTHWEST
OF THE CENTER AND GUSTS UP TO 45 MPH ARE
STILL BEING REPORTED ALONG THE COAST FROM
NEW JERSEY THROUGH SOUTHERN NEW ENGLAND.
MOVEMENT TOWARDS THE NORTH NORTHWEST 20
TO 25 MPH IS INDICATED FOR THE NEXT 12
TO 24 HOURS AND THE STORM CENTER WILL
CONTINUE TO FILL. HEAVY RAINS WILL OCCUR
IN WESTERN AND CENTRAL NEW YORK THIS
AFTERNOON AND TONIGHT AND WINDS TO THE
NORTH AND NORTHWEST OF THE STORM WILL
CONTINUE 30 TO 40 MPH WITH GUSTS TO 50
MPH. WINDS WILL GRADUALLY DIMINISH ALONG
THE COAST THIS AFTERNOON AND TONIGHT BUT
TIDES ARE EXPECTED TO BE 2 TO 4 FEET
ABOVE NORMAL THIS AFTERNOON AND TONIGHT
ALONG THE EXPOSED COASTS OF CONNECTICUT
RHODE ISLAND AND MASSACHUSETTS. STORM
WARNINGS REMAIN DISPLAYED FROM DELAWARE
BREAKWATER NORTHWARD TO EASTPORT MAINE
BUT WILL BE LOWERED LATER THIS AFTERNOON
FROM LONG ISLAND SOUTHWARD AS WINDS
DIMINISH. FURTHER ADVICES ON THIS STORM
WILL BE CARRIED IN ROUTINE STATE AND
LOCAL FORECASTS. THIS IS THE FINAL NEWS
BULLETIN TO BE CARRIED BY WASHINGTON ON
CONNIE.

SCHMIDT WEATHER BUREAU WASHINGTON

Ironically, after an entire summer of total sunshine, Connie threatens to rain out the annual employee picnic of the Line Material Company in Stroudsburg, Pennsylvania, scheduled for August 13. However, several of L-M's employees are members of the East Stroudsburg Fire Department, and they arrange for the event to be held in the newly renovated Firemen's Hall. The hall is located in the municipal park on Day Street, on the eastern bank of the Brodhead Creek in an area known as The Flats.

The building has been modernized to serve as a meeting and recreational hall, as well as to function as the local Civil Defense headquarters in an emergency. Most often, it is used by the fire department for fundraising events. But on this Saturday, it serves as a shelter from the downpour for hundreds of Stroudsburg area residents as they eat, drink, and enjoy each other's company outside of work.

There's more than a little pride on the part of those fire company volunteers present. Lots of time, energy, and sweat from scores of people had gone into raising the funds to perform the renovations, plus the work itself. Now they look around and see the direct benefit of their labors among their friends, neighbors, and coworkers. It's a satisfying feeling. It's all been worth it.

What remains of Connie continues on a northwesterly path across the Great Lakes region before petering out in Canada on Monday, August 15. At her peak, she had been a Category 4 hurricane with sustained winds of 145 m.p.h. and a core low pressure of 936 millibars or 27.64 inches. Her official lifespan has been twelve days. All told, Connie is responsible for twenty-five deaths and $40 million in damages.

The weather forecast for that Monday morning predicts a cloudy, humid day, 85° with showers and scattered thunderstorms for southeast Pennsylvania. Delaware Valley farmers are rejoicing. The significant rainfall has revived their hopes to produce a crop to rival the record one of 1948. Perhaps the weather will be their friend, after all.

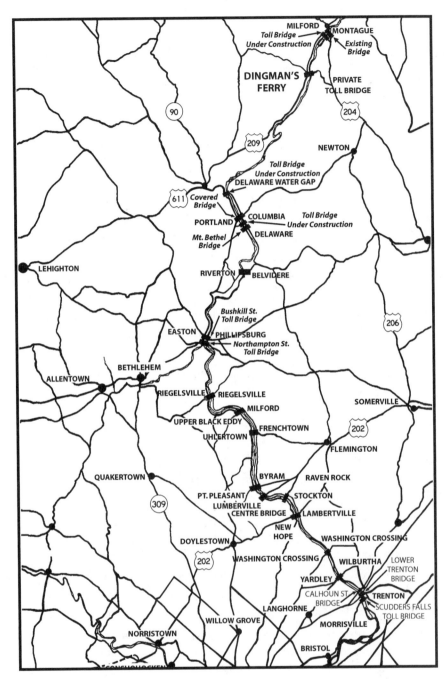

The Middle Delaware and the locations of its major crossings in 1955, just before the flood. Based on a map contained in the 1955 Delaware River Joint Toll Bridge Commission (DRJTBC) Report.   — *Map from 1956 report by DRJTBC*

The Delaware:
Cutting a Swath Through History

Monday, August 15, 1955

The town of Lumberville draws its name from the timber operation that has existed on its riverbank for centuries. That business has been in the Tinsman family since its inception, and has fallen victim to more than one of the Delaware's rampages. The battered photo albums in Tinsman Lumber's company archives are filled with images of flooded buildings and stacks of lumber wallowing in swirling water.

A crackled tintype from 1890 and browning silver prints from 1901 and 1903 are evidence of an unusually active period of flooding on the river. Bill Tinsman Sr. grew up looking at those pictures, and listening to the stories of The Great Flood of "Ot-Three," shared between his father and their customers. That one flooded all the surrounding farmers' fields, snatching thousands of pumpkins and floating them down the river in a darkly comical Halloween parade.

Now 29, Bill is watching the same river rush past at an impressive clip, close to the bank tops but not over them. Connie has been a close call, but coming as she did on the heels of the long dry spell, was more welcome than feared. Bill knows there are a few places where the Delaware is actually flooding, but Lumberville isn't one of them, this time. You take your breaks where you get them, and he is thankful.

He turns the key in the office door, and figures some of his customers' construction crews, who've been working solid all summer in the brutal heat, are probably pretty thankful, too. Everyone needs a break from it. Besides, the hard rain had only lasted through Friday and then was quite a bit lighter on Saturday. The down time had been just like a weekend off, no harm done.

It's only drizzling a little now, and the cloud cover will keep the heat down. Maybe everybody will come back refreshed today, and not so irritable. Tempers have been getting kind of frayed lately, and he, for one, will welcome a return to the easy smiles and friendly joshing at the counter.

Almost everyone has heard of the historic Delaware River crossing of George Washington and his bedraggled troops on Christmas Night in 1776, allowing the Continental Army a critical, morale-boosting victory in the Battle of Trenton. The event has been commemorated by artists over the years, from the famous 1851 image by Emmanuel Leutze to the lesser known but more historically accurate "Second Crossing," by contemporary Lambertville painter Robert Beck.

What may not be so well known or celebrated is the biography of the river itself. Its background gave the river its geological and topographical characteristics, which bore significantly on how the 1955 flood would play out, and on related events in its aftermath.

For a river whose primary commercial characteristic is a lack of consistent navigability, the Delaware has managed to cut an impressive swath through our nation's history. In latter years, this very quality is what inspires for the river a large and devoted following among paddlers, hikers, bikers, and environmental enthusiasts. Over the years, though, it has—time and again—been the impetus for efforts to dam the river, deepen its channel, and perform other engineering that would force the Delaware to do man's bidding. But this is one river that has never shown an inclination to be forced into anything…occasionally, not even back into its own banks.

Perhaps this kind of orneriness becomes more understandable when one considers that the Delaware is one of the older rivers on our continent, and perhaps just a little cranky. It has been—literally—through a lot.

There were the eons of the building up and wearing away of various rocks and soils that would ultimately become the landscape we see today, if we traverse the boundary between New Jersey and Pennsylvania. Then ancient continents slid together, heaving tectonic plates up against each other. The resulting violent thrust of sedimentary ocean floor up through the earth's crust formed the basis of the Appalachian Mountains.

Later, on its upper reaches, the area was compressed under the incomprehensible weight of at least three glacial ice sheets, each miles thick. And all this was going on before the river was even born.

Before that, the area we know as current-day Pennsylvania and New Jersey was located south of the Earth's equator, torqued nearly 45° clockwise from its present orientation. Before the supercontinent Pangea began breaking up about 200 million years ago, North America slowly revolved counter-clockwise, as convection currents in the planet's mantle "floated" the landmass into the Northern Hemisphere.

Magma—molten rock that boils around the earth's core—plays a large part in the movement of its tectonic plates. By forcing the continents apart, it also created a new sea, which we now call the Atlantic Ocean. Massive erosion about 42 million years ago carved out the lower elevations along what is now the Atlantic coast, establishing the early stage of today's watershed drainages. Still, the Delaware River wasn't yet even a twinkle in its channel's eye.

That birth came approximately 18 million years later. With the change to a cooler, drier climate as the continent drifted northward, the physical weathering and erosion of the landscape increased. Geologists believe the entire surface of eastern Pennsylvania and New Jersey may have been lowered by several hundred feet in this process. It also increased the difference in elevation between the highest and lowest points, beginning the formation of some of the Delaware Valley's majestic bluffs and breathtaking gorges.

This activity gave the area the physical characteristics we recognize today, and marked the actual birth of the river. In fact, the whole system of rivers, creeks, and streams that now drain the Appalachian Basin was established then. As water will do, it sought the lowest places via routes offering the least resistance, and eventually worked its way out to the johnny-come-lately Atlantic.

On the way, when it ran into the ultra hard igneous rock of the various geologic eras, the Delaware simply went around them through the softer sedimentary layers. While it was finding those easier paths, its waters carried along boulders and gravel. Together, water and stone scoured and drilled pockets along the banks, which formed deep whirlpools and eddies that still arrest errant craft.

Fast-forward to just over 20,000 years ago. Those who study such things believe that the vast amount of water needed to produce the glaciers was drawn out of the regular hydrology cycle, causing ocean levels to recede. This exposed huge areas of land, which are now submerged under higher water levels.

One of these expanses was the shallow shelf between present-day Alaska and Siberia, called Beringia. Geologists believe this broad, continent-sized expanse was not ice-covered. Rather, studies suggest it was covered in cool, wet grasslands, capable of supporting large herds of grazing animals. They believe numerous species of animals migrated across Beringia between the present-day Asian and North American continents. It's likely that the first human migrants also walked across this shelf in pursuit of migrating herds of woolly mammoth, mastodons, or perhaps the more manageable deer or bison.

It's from this hardy stock that the Delaware Valley's first recorded residents, the Lenni Lenape Indians, descended. They inhabited the valley from its northernmost reaches in present-day New York state's Catskill Mountains north to New England and south and east to the sea. Their low impact lifestyle found the river more than adequate in meeting most of their needs.

Its waters were clean and thirst-quenching for them and the prey they sought along its edges; deer, bear, raccoon, and the occasional possum. It gave up a bounty of nutritious fish—trout, bass, shad—and culinary variety with its offerings of eel and turtle.

The Lenape learned that corralling their catch in a water-filled basin until it was needed kept the fish fresh and safe from other predators, yet still convenient to recapture. One of these original live wells was eventually laid across with timbers to serve as the foundation for a hotel and tavern during the lively heyday of the Delaware and Lehigh Canal. Today, that venerable building serves much the same function it did in the early 1800s, operating as the Indian Rock Inn on Highway 32 in Pennsylvania's Upper Black Eddy.

The lazy current of the Delaware allowed relatively safe and easy access to its life-sustaining treasures as well as to an ongoing source of hygiene and recreation. Its often rocky and shallow channel was rarely a challenge to dugouts and canoes, the light and supremely maneuverable craft favored by the Indians. The ribbon of water also

The Indian Rock Inn, a popular Bucks County dining and entertainment establishment, has been part of life in Upper Black Eddy since the canal was built in the early 1800s. It was constructed over a natural stone pool that served as a live well for the Lenni Lenape native people who first inhabited the area. — Collection Ted Schweder

served as a reliable mode of transportation between their villages and, eventually, trading posts.

By the time Europeans arrived in earnest in the early 1600s to establish those posts, the Lenape had already for thousands of years been familiar with—and respectful of—the river's rhythmic cycles of low water and bank-topping freshets. They took this changeability into account when establishing semi-permanent village sites. Though home was located within walking distance of the waterway, the villagers carefully avoided putting themselves inside the danger zone of the flood plain during the fairly regular spring snowmelt and fall tropical storm high water seasons.

Since these villages were portable, there was never an issue with any permanent building within the flood plain. That particular problem began with the entrenchment of white settlers looking for convenient sources of drinking, cooking and cleaning water, and cheap power for their many grist- and sawmills. They also saw the river as a potential transportation route to get the products of these mills—as well as those from farms and coal and iron mines—to market.

Many of these establishments were erected hard on the banks of the river, and the settlers, too, soon realized the dichotomy of the Delaware: Its frequent floods could and did sometimes wash away the fruits of all their labors, but without those floods the channel was often too shallow to float their products downstream. Philadelphia and ships in its port waited to convert these cargoes into much-needed cash.

And so began the "push me-pull you" relationship between modern civilization and the Delaware River.

Just as towns along a river's edge take much of their character from the waterway, so the river is partly defined by what occurs along its banks. The greatest of these influences are the character and location of its tributaries.

Shallow, fast running creeks and brooks push their contents rapidly into the main channel, frequently causing whirlpools in the current. Over time, their swirling backflows dig permanent shoreline eddies and riverbed rifts. Some of these hold hazards for watercraft. The river's flow can stagnate there and trap slow moving boats; or treacherous, uneven bottoms may catch unsuspecting navigators and hold them fast.

On the Delaware, many of these spots sometimes stranded nineteenth-century timber raftsmen for extended periods. Over the years, some of these areas grew into purposeful rest stops and, eventually, settlements. Town names like Sandts Eddy, Upper Black Eddy and Foul Rift attest to some of their more prominent members.

The deeper, slower running streams, runs, or "kills"—a hangover term from the times of the first Dutch settlers—usually have longer histories as the genesis of intentional settlements. Because of their more navigable channels—some are small rivers in themselves—and dependable good fishing, they attracted more activity and settlers than smaller waterways. This longer history has often given them more time to grow into larger towns. Each waterway has lent something of its personality to that particular stretch of the Delaware it occupies, and vice-versa.

Like the towns they serve, the fortunes of many modes of transportation—timber rafting, pig iron shipping in Durham boats, early experiments in steamboats, ferries and canals on both banks, and eventually railroading—have risen and fallen with the levels of the Delaware River. Nowhere has this liquid roller coaster been so clearly delineated as in the river's flood history.

The Lenape people advised the colonists that the Delaware and its tributaries flooded roughly every fourteen years. It's not known exactly how they defined "flood." White settlers called high water that stayed within the waterways' banks "freshets." Anything that swelled over the top was a flood. Whatever these deluges were called, the Indians had the good sense to stay out of their way.

Tuesday, August 16, 1955

Eleanor Sciss looks across Route 32 from her Upper Black Eddy home, just south of May Snyder's Riverview Lunch. The rain from Connie has come and gone, and the river is high. Real high. She's heard it had topped its banks in some places up and down the valley, but her husband Lester assures her it will start going down now. He must be sure, she thinks. He's going off to work.

Les is a supervisor across the river at Milford's biggest employer, the Riegel Paper Company. He's working the night shift now, and she knows he wouldn't go across the bridge if he thought he couldn't get back. He kisses her and grabs his lunch pail as he heads out the door.

Eleanor is glad they had chosen this spot to build their house back in the '40s. It's on a slight rise along River Road, and affords a beautiful view. Better still, their neighbors had lived through the big flood of 1903, and had told her and Les that their property had remained untouched by even those high waters. In February of 1941 they had moved in, not quite a year before the Japanese attacked Pearl Harbor. She had been comforted then, when the war started, that she and Les had had time together with baby Barbara in their new house before all the killing started and the world got so crazy.

That's all behind them, thank God, and now they have a son, too. Nine-year-old Don likes to help his dad out in the shop when Les isn't too busy to keep an eye on him. And what a shop it is: thirty foot square, with modern electric and lots of room to grow. They had just built it in the spring to house Lester's burgeoning lawn-mower repair business. Les is hoping to get enough work to be his own full time boss before too long. The new shop is a big step, and they're proud of it. They both worked hard and saved a long time to be able to build it.

Eleanor decides it's silly to worry. The new building sits as high as the house, and further back off the river. And the river has never gotten that high that anyone can remember. Besides, the rain has stopped, and Les says the river will be going down now. But there is just that little tug at the back of her brain, the one that reminds her about what she'd read in the paper on Saturday. It had said there was another big storm on its way. She thinks they're calling this one Diane.

Official records dating back over two centuries indicate that, up until recently, six events with an average interval of twenty-five years had held the top five positions for most severe flooding on the Delaware. Measurements for these records were taken at the Riegelsville Bridge, where flood stage is twenty-two feet.

The flood of January 8, 1841, called the "Bridges Freshet" because it wiped out so many Delaware spans, and that of January 5, 1862 were tied for fifth worst flood at 28.5 feet. Those records were dislodged by the flood caused by the remnants of Hurricane Ivan on September 19, 2004, with a river gauge reading of 31 feet. March 19, 1936's St. Patrick's Day flood registered 32.45 feet to claim third place. That record was also dislodged by the rain and snowmelt-induced event of April 3-4, 2005. The second highest flood ever measured on the Delaware remains the great "Pumpkin Freshet" of October 10, 1903, so called because of the many pumpkins washed downriver from farm fields, then seen bobbing along in the current.

The worst flood since records have been kept happened August 19, 1955, with a crest of 38.85 feet, nearly 14 feet above flood stage. This flood cut a swath through more than just history. It went through the lives of individuals, families and whole communities, at an intensity never before seen in the Delaware Valley. It sliced through the nation's belief in the invincibility of our knowledge and technology.

In terms of every measurement—lives lost, property damaged and destroyed, bridges washed out—August 1955's flood was a recordbreaker. That some of this loss, particularly among human lives, could have been avoided makes it a tragedy, as well.

So...why?

Why, if it was possible, wasn't some of the loss avoided? What happened?

The answer is actually more about what didn't happen. The disaster of the Delaware River flood of 1955 was a function of the unique set of circumstances that defined the time. There are reasons why it shouldn't happen again.

There are more to explain why it could, and likely will.

August 16, 1955

Fred Johnson and his son Johnny had been working slavishly on a construction project before Connie's rains hit. The Johnsons had been a little south of Lumberville and across the river in New Jersey every weekend, building their new house on Stockton-Sergeantsville Road. They'd been finishing the foundation when Connie's rain had begun.

Now they're headed back to install a temporary roof because they've heard there might be another storm on the way. The floor has been poured, the well drilled, and they've even hooked up a sink, so they want to keep any more rain out of what will be the cellar. The tarpaper they had tacked to a simple frame has done a pretty good job keeping out most of what Connie dropped, but it won't hold up under another big drenching.

Sixteen-year-old Johnny helps his dad pick up sheets of plywood and more tarpaper from Niece Lumber's Lambertville location, and they drive out to the site of their future home.

Meanwhile, Johnny's sister, Greta, is working the day shift as a switchboard operator at the Bell Telephone Company in Stockton. Greta enjoys the convenience. She only has to walk the few blocks to Union Street from the house they rent on Bridge Street, the first one on the canal. She loves everything about living in Stockton, but she understands why her parents want the house on Stockton-Sergeantsville Road.

They want to own, and it will be much more affordable than anything in town. She'll be moving out soon, anyway. 21 years old, she is engaged to Nick Fresco, and they'll be married by this time next year. With just her parents and Johnny, who will be only a year away from leaving for college, they won't need all the room of the Stockton house. The single-story Cape Cod they're building will be plenty.

Still, she'll miss the Stockton house. Errico's Market, friendly and full of everything they might need, is an easy walk away. She enjoys how the town comes alive on weekends, when they watch all the tourists who drive down from New York in their grand cars to eat at Colligan's. She loves their fancy clothes, and listening to them talk about their exciting careers. She can hear the soft but upbeat strains of Big Band music escaping from the open doors. And walking along the canal with Nick on moonlit nights…it's all so romantic.

As she heads off to work, Greta's thoughts turn to the plans her mom, Paula, is helping her make for the wedding. Right now, Mom is finishing canning this year's garden produce. Then she's going to work some more on the crocheted circles that she'll eventually stitch together into a bed coverlet for Greta's wedding present.

Greta climbs the stairs to the second-story switchboard office and wishes a good morning to her supervisor, Chief Operator Helen Malloy. Helen nods acknowledgement as she connects a call. Greta takes a seat at her station and hears one of her coworkers talking with someone about how high the river is. Greta hasn't really noticed, but she's glad it has almost stopped raining.

Much of the Delaware Valley hasn't shared as deeply in the spoils of war as the rest of America has. In the 1940s and '50s, a great deal of the valley is still primarily agricultural land.

Like many other rural communities, those along the Delaware have lost many members of their upcoming generation on the beaches and battlefields of Europe and the Pacific. Many farm families have lost more than one son. This is double the tragedy it is for urban families, because these young farming men weren't just family. They had been members of the clan's primary work force, and often inheritors of the family farm itself.

While recovering from personal tragedy, these farming families have also to deal with replacing critical workers in their production processes. Sometimes this is not an easy task, and extended periods will pass before a particular operation regains full production capacity. As with any business, lack of production is reflected in lack of profit.

So at a time when many Americans are experiencing unprecedented prosperity, some farm families continue to struggle.

Such struggles reach beyond individual farms to the surrounding communities in a ripple effect. If the community is comprised mostly of farmers, and those farmers don't have as much money to spend at the grocery store, restaurant, or gas station, the local economy suffers. Everyone feels it: the barbershop, beauty salon, movie theater, even the doctor.

This ripple effect is still being felt in many parts of the Delaware valley in the mid-fifties. Consequently, there are many families who need two incomes just to stay solvent. It must be a strong incentive for women to take outside jobs during a time when stay-at-home moms aren't just the rule, but practically a social moré.

Local governments of such places, where every inch of arable land must be pressed into service, don't have the support they need to pass strict floodplain zoning laws. This issue is also a problem in more urban areas. Though a fairly serious flood had occurred on the river in 1942, there had been a war on, and the human mind has a funny way of forgetting rather quickly when it comes to disasters.

Perhaps it's a desire to put pain and suffering in the past as soon as possible, or maybe just that the problems of everyday life are sometimes so overwhelming that nobody wants to go looking for more trouble. Whatever the reason, no one wants to be the one to tell developers—who are also potential employers and taxpayers— that they can't build on otherwise attractive riverfront property because it's in a floodplain.

The extreme optimism of the fifties also plays a part. Nobody wants to question the virulent can-do attitude of most post-war individuals. So the valley remains a place where many assets are located in areas vulnerable to serious flood damage.

People thus preoccupied with their financial wellbeing don't have time to think about, or money to invest in, such desirable but unnecessary things as emergency communication systems. It's enough of a burden that they have to install air raid sirens and put shelter signage in place to be ready for a nuclear attack by the Reds.

In the minds of many, the whole Civil Defense program is simply confounding. Inside it, optimism and cynicism often walk hand-in-hand. The war is over, and people believe the Korean problem has been taken care of, yet municipalities are still required to continue spending precious tax dollars on a silly program that no one's sure will do any good if "The Big One"—a dreaded atomic bomb—is actually dropped.

In stark contrast to the united front the United States presented during the war, more than a few people now consider the whole Civil Defense organization a downright joke. When people had feared air raids, they'd been willing to put up with the self-importance of some overzealous blackout wardens, but all the annoying drills and inconvenient precautions ended up being pointless. No bombing raids had ever materialized, and now citizens aren't about to put up with any more government-sponsored nonsense. By and large, they are simply tired of the war mentality in any form, and don't want to hear about any more supposed threats.

With such lack of public support, few municipal governments prioritize budgets—or even staffs—for their Civil Defense programs. Those that do so accomplish it at the cost of credibility with some of their constituents. In the end, they generally work up lists of volunteers, duty descriptions, and a hierarchy of authority. But that's often where the effort stops. Regardless how impressive some of the more serious Civil Defense efforts may look on paper, almost none are supported by appropriate infrastructure.

Those forward thinkers who are successful in convincing taxpayers of the need for such equipment and communication systems sometimes have a hard time attracting anyone to drill regularly in using it. Aside from a few volunteer ham radio operators and some gung-ho guys with two-way radios, dedicated emergency communications are catch-as-catch-can. Delaware Valley communities will come to owe a great deal to such committed volunteers.

Meanwhile, areas further inland are being developed at an equally rapid pace as their riverfront peers. The biggest boom that will ever be recorded in new housing construction is underway all over America. The novel concept of the "planned community" has given Bucks County Levittown: 5,500 acres filled with 17,000 single-family homes. It is hailed as an engineering marvel, a sociological breakthrough, and a boon to the tax base.

Nobody talks about the amazing amount of permeable soil that

According to Peter Bacon Hales of the University of Illinois, Levittown "capitalized on the housing crunch of the immediate postwar years, offering affordable housing to returning GIs and their families, in the form of small, detached, single-family houses equidistant from New York City and the burgeoning defense industrial plants on Long Island."
– Reprinted with permission of LevittownPA.org

has been paved over with concrete and asphalt to accommodate the driveways, sidewalks, and streets that make up such developments. Yet rain will continue to fall at the levels it always has, and the water that results will have to go somewhere.

If it doesn't soak in where it falls, it will run off to someplace else. The first places it will go will be along roadway drains and into sewer grates, and from there into streams and creeks. Some of it will simply collect in low areas until it runs over into someone's swimming pool, garden, or house. And all of it will eventually end up in the main waterway after which the watershed is named: the Delaware River.

This explosion of development is happening more in some places than others, but it isn't isolated, and it's not just an urban problem. Though many farmers are practicing enlightened agriculture, such as terracing their fields on slopes to help conserve topsoil, not everyone is. These practices take more time and effort, and so eat into profitability. Some farmers feel they can't afford it, and continue to plow indiscriminately.

The result of these development and farming practices is thousands of paved-over acres and poorly maintained fields running off into hundreds of tributaries that pour their contents directly into a single river.

The last serious factor in the Delaware Valley "ripe for disaster" scenario is a matter of insufficient technology. Aside from the telephone and radio, there is no early warning system for serious flood threats. Even those methods are relatively impotent without timely, accurate information to pass along.

Without satellite images of the larger weather picture, people have limited warning time of excessive precipitation headed their way. Then, once it arrives, their means to measure rising water and to pass the word along on a mass basis aren't much better.

The free bridges on the Delaware each have a box suspended on a chain from the middle of the span. The chain is marked with a depth gauge, and the weighted box is cranked up and down, into and out of the water, to take river level measurements. Readings are taken at varying intervals, depending on navigational traffic and expectation of flooding along the waterway at that point.

However, once the water rises to four feet above normal at any gauging point, Delaware River Joint Toll Bridge Commission operators begin taking readings every hour, on the hour. Readings are given in terms of "feet above normal low," which differs at each location.

The Bridge Commission provides estimates of cresting times at each bridge, a function that will later be performed by local offices of the National Weather Service, which is yet called the Weather Bureau. During a flood, operators (whom most people call bridge guards or bridge cops) relay by telephone their readings and crest forecasts to anyone they think will need them. News reporters call in from their respective broadcast stations or newspapers to get the latest, and guard-house numbers are listed in the telephone book for local residents to call, as well. The problem with this system is its lack of timeliness and limited reach.

Telephone alerts work well for local reports, and the bridge-to-bridge telephone relay is fairly effective in reaching those immediately along the river. However, unsophisticated technology once again slows things down. There is no Call Waiting feature to let someone tying up a line know there's an important call trying to get through. In fact, residents often share party lines, which can keep a single line busy interminably. A resident on the Middle River might not get an alert from the upper reaches for hours, losing precious preparation and evacuation time, unless someone is successful in convincing an operator to break into a conversation.

Radio listening is not as prevalent as it will be in the future, and with television in its infancy, few people get their news that way, either. The main news media, the daily paper, can have content that's already half a day old by the time it reaches readers. In a situation requiring quick decisions, it simply isn't enough.

Marie Petranto is sick of the rain. It seems like that's all it has done for two weeks straight, and she's bored. Worse yet, all her campers are bored, and that's getting to be a problem.

At fifteen, Marie has a good deal of responsibility on her shoulders as a junior counselor for the Campfire Girls on Pennington Island. She has been there since the end of June, when she stepped off the barge that brought everyone over from Erwinna, on the Pennsylvania side. It's her first summer as a counselor, having come up through the rank of Bluebird to earn enough achievement beads and merit badges as a Campfire Girl.

Now she's sitting in the crafts and folklore hut, leading rounds of "Row, Row, Row Your Boat" for the sixth time this week. She senses the girls' restlessness, even catches a few rolling their eyes when she suggests they sing again.

"We want to go outside!" they say. Marie wants to go, too. After all, it is still very warm out, and the rain isn't cold. But there has been so much of it that the ground is saturated and will turn to mud immediately under any kind of traffic. She can just imagine shoes and boots getting sucked off of feet, and the angry parents when little girls come home with permanently soiled clothes. She can't be irresponsible enough to allow any of them to catch cold because their heads got wet, either.

"I know, I know. But we just can't, so we'll have to keep ourselves busy in here, okay?" Groans and heavy sighs. "Come on, we're Campfire Girls! We have good imaginations…let's think of something fun to do in here!" Marie sounds perkier than she feels, but she knows it's important to show leadership. The girls will take their cue from her.

She slaps at a mosquito on her leg. With all the standing water, they've gotten worse than they usually are. Between them and the ticks that seem to be everywhere, all the campers and counselors are afflicted to one degree or another. The worst is trying to sleep at night. It's too hot and sticky to stay inside your sleeping bag, but if you leave anything exposed, the biting will wake you up. And then you'll be scratching all night.

She hears on her transistor radio that this rain is all part of a big storm that used to be a hurricane named Connie. Connie's winds have done some serious damage, even killed people in the south, so Marie guesses they are lucky the camp isn't getting hit with that. Well, Connie can just keep right on moving, she thinks.

Marie is getting stiff from too much sitting around. She wants to get out and ride a bike, or go hiking. Anything but this! Very soon, she will get her wish.

Diane: The Jealous Sister

Wednesday, August 17, 1955

MIAMI WEATHER BUREAU BULLETIN 7 AM EST
AUGUST 17 1955

HURRICANE DIANE FINALLY MOVED INLAND THIS
MORNING ABOUT 520 AM EST ON THE NORTH
CAROLINA COAST ABOUT OVER WILMINGTON…MOVING
TOWARDS THE NORTH NORTHWEST AT ABOUT 14
MPH. HIGHEST WIND REPORTED AT WILMINGTON
WAS 74 MPH AND LOWEST PRESSURE 29.27
INCHES. GUSTS…TO 95 MPH…REPORTED. THE
HURRICANE WILL SLOWLY LOSE FORCE…EXPECT
STRONG TO GALE FORCE WINDS AND HEAVY RAINS
AS THE HURRICANE MOVES NORTHWARD…

                    DAVIS MIAMI WEATHER BUREAU

Forty-eight-year-old Jennie Johnson is enjoying what's left of a five-week vacation at Davis Cabins with her family, before the kids go back to school. She is especially glad that her daughter, Nancy, has been able to make it. At nineteen, Nancy is taking a break from her nursing studies at Christ Hospital in their hometown of Jersey City, New Jersey. Her schedule is starting to get busy. Her oldest son, Joe Jr., is away in the Air Force, and another older daughter, Lorraine, couldn't get away from work.

The boys, fourteen-year-old Roy and David, ten, are getting to the point where they'll expect more from summer break than a few quiet weeks at Bible camp. Jennie knows this may be the last time they'll be able to have most of the family together for a vacation.

Davis Cabins—called Camp Davis by outsiders—isn't anything fancy. It's a cozy place with some cabins and bungalows—thirteen in all—and enough land to provide a sense of freedom while vacationers share some family time. Nestled along a placid little stream called the Brodhead Creek just south of Analomink in the Poconos, it appeals to families like the Johnsons. It's rustic enough to feel like a vacation but close enough to home that you don't have to spend half your time off driving here.

It's not really an official camp, but any place with rustic accommodations in the Poconos is referred to that way. It takes its name from founder Reverend Leon Davis, a retired Baptist minister from Nanuet, New York. Sometimes he comes to stay with his wife and his daughter's family, the Liebfreds. His grandson, Billy, is twelve now, and doesn't need as much supervision as he did when he was small. This year, Billy's parents have allowed him to visit the camp with his grandparents and great-grandmother, eighty-year-old Bertha Polly, while they stay home in the city.

The Davis family began the camp with the main building, a sturdy one-story farmhouse with an attic. Some people call it "the Big House," because most of the other dwellings are small in comparison. Others call it "the Winter House" because it's heated and sometimes houses hunters or other guests in the off-season. The rest of the buildings are either glorified one-room cottages or military surplus wooden Quonset huts. They might have a bed or two, perhaps a sitting room, and a galley kitchen if there's one at all.

Most Davis residents spend much of their time outdoors all summer, with food preparation for communal gatherings taking place in a mess hall that provides use of appliances. Some cabins have the luxury of spare indoor plumbing such as a commode and crude shower, but most Davis people take their baths in the Brodhead. Parents find that even children normally predisposed against bathing don't seem to mind when it's combined with a swim in the refreshing creek water.

Mrs. Polly lives with Billy in another, more permanent building closest to the water. The Winter House is the only one large enough

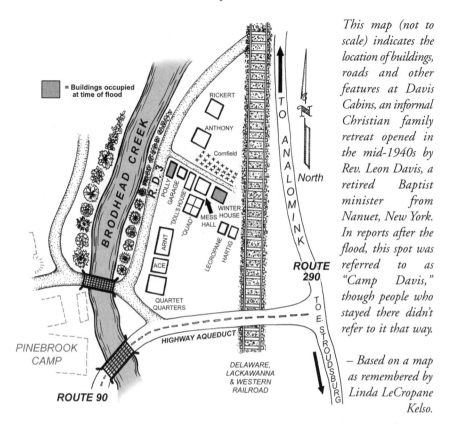

This map (not to scale) indicates the location of buildings, roads and other features at Davis Cabins, an informal Christian family retreat opened in the mid-1940s by Rev. Leon Davis, a retired Baptist minister from Nanuet, New York. In reports after the flood, this spot was referred to as "Camp Davis," though people who stayed there didn't refer to it that way.

— Based on a map as remembered by Linda LeCropane Kelso.

to accommodate the extended Weber clan. There are nine of them staying this trip.

Edna Winfield, her seven-year-old son, Rowan, and eight-year-old daughter, Karen, are occupying one of the small bungalows near the mess hall. Mrs. Winfield is the camp manager, taking care of check-ins, housekeeping, supply ordering, and guest requests. Karen and Rowan are getting old enough to help her. They're also good company, and are usually with Edna while her husband, Raymond, works back home in Rutherford, New Jersey.

Jennie likes that the Davises spend a good deal of time at the camp, mingling with the guests and making them feel at home. They are kindly, decent people, and she likes the family atmosphere they encourage. She never worries that the kids will get into trouble like they might in the city. Here, she can relax and know that everyone is safe, even when her husband, Joe, is gone.

These two images, taken around 1950, show where the buildings were located at Davis Cabins, just south of Analomink. The one above was taken from R. D. 3, the camp's access road. Bertha Polly's house is at far right, then the garage, which was turned into living quarters. Next left is the "Doll's House," where the Hartigs had previously lived, with a car parked between it and the garage; then the Mess Hall, with a tree at its right corner. The outhouse is next left, then the Winter (Big) House. The duplex, referred to as "the quad," where the Johnsons and Thompsons lived in 1955, is behind and between the Mess Hall and the Doll's House, not yet built when this photo was taken.

The one below was taken from the tracks of the DL&W Railroad, looking northwest. The the Winter (Big) House is at far right, across the field from Davis Cabins. The back of the Arnts' property, possibly a barn, is to the far left.

– Collection Linda LeCropane Kelso

Above: Henry Hartig took this photo of his wife, Lillian (left) chatting over the clothes-line with longtime Davis Cabins neighbor, Gladys Thompson, circa 1950-51. The wooden military surplus quonset hut in the background is where the LeCropane family—whose daughters, Sara and Linda, were the Hartigs' grand-nieces—lived. The Hartigs' original small, wooden cottage their nieces liked to call "the Doll's House" is just out of the frame at right, on the other side of the path Gladys stands next to. The day of the flood, the Hartigs took their niece Linda into town to celebrate Henry's completion of a new, larger house for him and Lillian. Below: Four-year-old Linda poses in the doorway of "The Doll's House" in 1946.   – *Collection Linda LeCropane Kelso*

Joe works a checking job at Brooklyn's Isthmian Steamship Company during the week, then drives down with Lorraine on Friday for the weekend. The cares of his week melt away with each increasingly beautiful mile. By the time he arrives, he's happy and ready to spend a pleasant weekend with her and the kids. It really is the perfect summer arrangement.

Irene Weber has her two younger children, nine-year-old Betty Jane and five-year-old Bobby, with her in the Winter House. Her mother, sister-, and brother-in-law are also there with their son. Irene's husband, Ed, has been with them, but must get back to work. He will leave the next day for home in West Paterson, New Jersey, with Ed Jr. At twelve, Eddie is their oldest son, and has some things he wants to get done at home before school starts up again.

Irene has been hoping to pack a lot of fun into the next three days, since their vacation will end Saturday. She's dismayed at the way the weather has turned out. For the last week, it's rained at least a little nearly every day. A big reason they stay at Camp Davis is to enjoy the sunshine and fresh air they can't get in the city. Having to spend so much time indoors has been disappointing, but she decides to make the best of it.

Perhaps they'll take a trip into town to see a movie tomorrow evening. What is it the kids want to see? She thinks it's that new one with Fess Parker...Davy Crockett, is that the title? Well, it's a Disney film, so it'll be good and she knows the kids will enjoy it. She'll have to think about it.

Mom might not enjoy it so much, but then she might. You just never know with Josephine. At sixty-two, she isn't slowing down as much as one might expect, and Irene is thankful. She has bounced back from Dad's death, and it's clear she enjoys time with the kids. But a theater full of them? Well, they'll figure it out.

Helen and Chris Lawyer, Ed's sister and brother-in-law, could take the kids. Their Allen, just a year younger than Eddie, is still at the age where such adventure films are much-anticipated treats. Anyway, she doesn't have to decide this minute. Right now, she's enjoying a bit of rare sunshine and watching the kids play down at the water's edge. The weather says it will probably rain again later, so she doesn't want to waste her chance.

She sees Donnie Christensen, one of the boys Eddie pals around with when he's here. At fifteen, Donnie is a handsome young man. Lean and tanned, he's all muscle and sharp blond crew cut. Standing there in his plaid swim trunks, a flashy watch on his wrist, he could be a model. She suspects he knows it, as he is attentive to his looks, but he isn't conceited.

On the contrary, he's very kind and polite, even to the smaller kids, including his sister, Linda. She's four years younger, with adorable blond curls. She's small for her age. Irene notices that Donnie keeps an eye out for her. You have to love a kid like that. At an age where most boys pick on their sisters, Donnie is protective of his.

Louise, Donnie's mom, is watching the kids. The water is down from its high level after the rain earlier in the week, but it's still higher than usual and pretty muddy. The smaller kids could get lost if they slipped beneath the surface. She knows Louise won't let any of them get into the deeper, faster current. No one needs to end the summer with an accident.

Storms can be so relentless and frightening that it can seem they have minds of their own and are "out to get us." This has always made it easy to attribute human emotions to severe weather. While the Weather Bureau has always gone out of its way to maintain scientific objectivity, the news media of 1955 feels no such obligation.

Reporters can't pass up the temptation to compare the "sister storms" of Connie and Diane in the somewhat hyperbolic and markedly sexist language typical of the times. The fact that forecasters employ solely female names to differentiate hurricanes gives reporters license to liberally sprinkle their stories with references to tantrums, female indecision, and sisterly spats.

Quite in contrast to this picture of sibling rivalry, the actual relationship of the two hurricanes is closer to one of mutual support.

From the beginning, Diane has been a weaker storm than Connie, a common scenario when a second hurricane follows a recent precursor. Because these storms thrive on heat, the first one to develop over calm seas will always benefit from surface water that's been heated to a greater depth than those roiled by recent disturbance.

However, at the point between August 9 and 11, when Diane had been pulled inside the fringe of Connie's circulation, the second storm had been able to gain strength to the detriment of the first. Though Connie hadn't lost much in power, her forward progress was temporarily stalled. This was when she'd seemed to wander aimlessly about, just off the Carolina coast.

It was only when an irresistibly attractive low pressure system had pulled her inland that she'd left her little sister on the open water to fend for herself. Though the trough had eased her way forward, Connie might still have wobbled back over water, but Diane had blocked that backslide. She had pushed her big sister on toward her destiny.

Being left on her own strengthens Diane. While both hurricanes make landfall at a Category 3 level, Diane is initially the more powerful. With a central low pressure of 28.02 inches, she will later earn the rank of 31 on the National Oceanic and Atmospheric Administration's list of the sixty-five most intense hurricanes to strike the United States from 1900 to 2004. Connie's pressure at landfall had been 28.41 inches, putting her at number 60 on NOAA's list.

Newspapers and radio stations, though, are still relatively unsophisticated in this understanding of tropical storms. They really only look at wind speed and circulation area to gauge strength. From the beginning, they have portrayed Connie as the more dangerous storm because her winds had been higher when she had reached populated areas, and her circulation more massive than Diane's. She had also carried some not-insignificant amounts of rain.

Peter and Alice Barry have their hands full. They're in the middle of moving from their home in Stockton, New Jersey. They've found one across the Delaware on Street Road in Buckmanville. It's south of New Hope and just the other side of Bowman's Hill from the river. Frank, the eldest of their five kids, is away visiting friends in Vermont. Kathy, David, Roxana, and Bethany are doing their best to help with the move. Pluto, their German Shepherd mix, is not adapting well, and they're concerned because he won't eat.

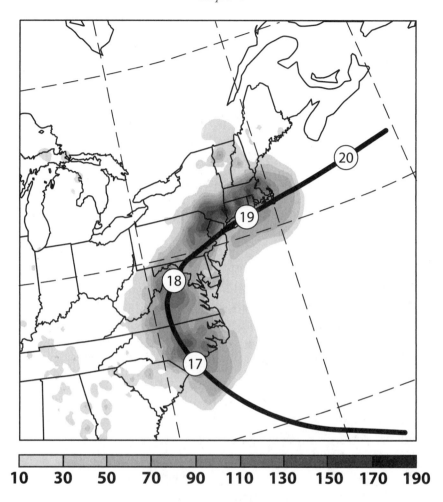

10 ml = .39"   70 ml = 2.76"   130 ml = 5.07"   190 ml = 7.49"
Conversion: 1 ml = .0394 inch

This map shows the storm track and rainfall distribution of Hurricane Diane along the entire eastern seaboard of the United States, including indicators for the position of the storm's "eye" on August 17-20, 1955. This map does not indicate some of the storm's highest recorded values, because they occurred in such small areas. However, several official and unofficial sources recorded localized rainfall in excess of 12 inches in such areas as Mt. Pocono, Pennsylvania.

– Based on a map from the National Climatic Data Center

Peter is preparing to spend the next morning painting window shutters on the new house and doing some other detailing. Alice is finishing the last of the packing in Stockton so they'll be ready when the moving van comes.

Peter teaches religion and art history at the Buckingham Friends School, where he is also the principal. Alice is a regular columnist for the *New Hope Gazette*. She keeps a journal so she can remember items of interest for her weekly, "Alice's Column." Between unpacking boxes and arranging furniture, she pens a few lines about the move, thinking it will be the most exciting entry she'll make this year.

Another couple is on the move as well. Twenty-year-old Marion Edwards and her husband, Don, twenty-six, have just gotten married on July thirtieth. Mikey and Choc, as they're known to friends, have found a third-floor apartment on Church Street in Lambertville, New Jersey, and are getting settled in. Both Lambertville natives, they're happy to have found a place in town they can afford.

Mikey works as a checker at the Acme Market on South Union Street, and Choc is a bridge guard for the Delaware River Joint Toll Bridge Commission. He is stationed on the bridge at Morrisville, but occasionally rotates to others when the need arises.

Around home, they both enjoy the tempting smell that wafts from the Korn Kurlz snack factory just along the river, over near Lewis Island. Mikey had grown up spending lots of time on the river, as most Lambertville kids do. As a young girl, she had made friends with old Mr. Lewis, "Poppy," as all the kids called him.

Poppy lives with his family out on the island, just north of the New Hope-Lambertville Bridge. He makes his living fishing for shad with big nets they spread between the piers in the river, and is proud that his family business is one of the last private fisheries on the Delaware.

Growing up, Mikey had heard from her parents about the big flood of 1903, and knew there had been others over the years. It seemed to her that Poppy had probably been around for most of them, and so she'd asked him how it was that his house never got wrecked in any of the floods. After all, the island is actually out in the channel, way below the level of the bridge deck. It had to have been underwater at times.

"I'll tell you," he'd said, squinting one eye and nodding in the direction of his home. "My house will never go down the river. I built it to stay." She'd had no reason to doubt him. When the river had come up back in '42 when she was seven, she'd watched and worried that his house would let loose and tumble downstream, but it never had.

Today Choc has gone off to Morrisville, and now it's time for her to set out for the Acme. She leaves time for a leisurely stroll and maybe a hello or two. After all, that's part of the fun of living in a small town and being able to walk to work. And even her job is nice. She gets to see people she knows all day long and helps them get the things they need. Mikey is a "people person," and likes helping them. She'll get plenty of opportunity in the next few weeks.

The media's overlooking Diane is understandable. As she makes landfall just before 5:30 a.m. on the seventeenth over the vicinity of Wilmington, North Carolina, her winds almost immediately die down to Category 1—or minimal hurricane—status. But if there is anything for certain, it's that Diane doesn't need to be a jealous sister, as she's being portrayed.

What she has going for her is some serious moisture, even greater than that Connie had unleashed on the Delaware Valley. She has been absorbing it in abundance over the abnormally steamy ocean for a week. Her track takes her inland over the central Appalachians, of which the Poconos are a northern part. This causes a rain-increasing phenomenon meteorologists call "orographic enhancement."

This process occurs when storm winds encounter the upward slopes of mountain ranges or other elevated topographic features. The slopes act like giant chutes, guiding the winds upward and providing lift to the moist air within the storm. As this moist air moves higher into the atmosphere, it cools rapidly, eventually condensing into raindrops. The longer a storm lingers over such an upslope, the more rain will be generated.

The bumpy terrain does more than create greater precipitation, however. Diane's travel over it also causes frictional drag against her forward motion, slowing her down. This gives her lots of time to drop her load of rain, which is increasing by the minute.

Forecasters, lacking satellite imagery, do not see a strong, cool low pressure system rapidly building in from the northwest at the same time Diane's loaded rain bands reach the Delaware Valley. This low will completely stall the storm's movement, and its cooler air will further enhance the amount of rainfall.

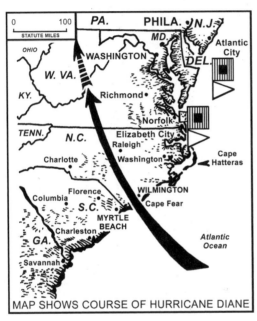

MAP SHOWS COURSE OF HURRICANE DIANE

Next to the headline "Diane Puffs Way Into Virginia," this map appears in the Philadelphia Inquirer *on Thursday morning, August 18, 1955, with this caption: "Map shows how weakening Diane hit mainland and is expected to continue on a north-northwest course. Storm warnings are up from Cape Hatteras to Atlantic City."*

In fact, as the paper is being printed, Diane has already begun a sharp swing to the northeast that will take her almost directly over Philadelphia and then parallel to the Delaware River Valley the whole way to the Water Gap, before heading out to sea over New Jersey and New England.

All these factors combine to most devastating effect. Essentially, the greatest possible moisture available is collecting within the storm, being multiplied by an amazing factor, and will be dumped within a relatively small area. That this area centers roughly on Mt. Pocono and is surrounded by other peaks and valleys means there is precious little level surface to absorb the deluge. Nearly all of it will run off the slopes.

The flats below aren't going to absorb it, either. The substantial rains from Connie haven't soaked in far enough to replenish depleted reservoirs and underground aquifers, so officials in Pennsylvania's Monroe County keep restrictions on lawn sprinkling and car washing in place. The ground's surface, however, is saturated.

The straw that breaks the proverbial camel's back is that Diane's movement isn't following Connie further west over the Alleghenies, as the Weather Bureau had predicted. Instead, it's under the influence of the unforeseen low pressure now sitting there. The low pushes Diane's track directly over and parallel to the Delaware Valley itself, assuring that most of her precipitation will be concentrated on the river and its tributaries.

Meteorologists have not yet amassed a long enough track record of hurricane damage data to establish what Isaac Cline had posited and what will later become common knowledge: The majority of hurricane-related deaths are caused by drowning, either in coastal storm surge or during inland flooding due to excessive rainfall. Meteorologists still believe violent winds pose the most danger, and so don't over-emphasize flooding in their forecasts. This lack of knowledge, added to their unawareness of the approaching low, are two of the final elements setting up the scenario that will lead to Diane's high toll in death and destruction.

Forecasters can't react to threats they don't know about. Without this knowledge, they can't warn Pocono residents that most of them are sitting at the bottom of natural drainage routes, beneath what is rapidly developing into a kind of inland "perfect storm."

The last factor ensuring devastation nearly the entire length of the Delaware Valley will be the nature of the flooding itself. Unlike floods that occur over a longer period of time from a gradual buildup of water, those triggered by Diane will be of the flash flood variety: too much rain, all at once, in a concentrated area.

No one is ready.

Carolinas Expect Diane This Morning

Charlestown, S.C. Aug. 16 (AP) – Hurricane Diane, still roaring with 100-mile-an-hour winds in her center, veered slightly northward late today, headed for the Carolina coast. …At 9 p.m., it was 140 miles from Myrtle Beach. The bureau said that continued movement at about the same rate toward the west northwest with a gradual trend more toward the northwest would give Diane a landfall early tomorrow forenoon along the upper South Carolina or the North Carolina coast.

Diane lost some of her fury during the day-long churn up the Atlantic. Early today her winds had been clocked at 115 miles an hour, but by mid-afternoon 85 miles an hour with gusts up to 100.

...A Weather Bureau spokesman said: "I hope nobody will relax their vigilance, because the storm still packs a punch. She's still just a little less dangerous...She may weaken still further, and if she does we'll hurry the word along."

– *Daily Record*, Stroudsburg, PA

People read or hear this advisory, but seem only to register the part about weakening winds, and either don't notice or ignore the part about heavy rain. With the exception of those old enough to remember the 1903 flood, few valley residents can recall any seriously rising waters in their lifetime. They believe it will be business as usual, just as it has been with Connie. A few spill-overs here and there, no big deal. They are perhaps preoccupied with the possibility of an upcoming "Subway Series" between the Dodgers and the Yanks, or with thoughts of going back to school. The weather hasn't been great, but it's more a minor annoyance than anything else.

What eleven-year-old Sandy Smith is looking forward to is returning from her stint at Tohicony Girl Scout Camp in Quakertown, Pennsylvania. She has enjoyed camp, but now her parents are about to leave on a trip to Canada, and she wants to see them off. She knows her mom will have picked up some new clothes for the trip, and she is excited to get a look at them before they get packed away in the suit-case. It won't be long now, though. Sandy's going home tomorrow.

Home. For her that's New Hope, Pennsylvania. Already famous as a haven for artists and creative types, it's a small, friendly town that swells its summer ranks with hordes of tourists from all along the eastern seaboard. They come to haunt the antique shops and art galleries, hoping a little of the wild bohemian mystique might rub off on them before they have to return to their nine-to-fives in the cities.

Sandy lives with her parents on Parry Street, along River Road between the river and the Delaware and Lehigh Canal. Her Uncle Hug lives next door, right beside the canal. It has long since stopped being used for its original purpose of transporting coal from the anthracite region to Philadelphia, and is now a popular tourist attraction.

People come from out of town and pay to ride up and down the canal in a replica of one of the old flatboat barges. They love the novelty of being pulled along its mirror-like waters by a mule at the end of a long rope. The mule is coaxed along the raised towpaths on either side of the waterway with a mixture of reward and threat; a feedbag and a switch. At least that's the line. Sandy has never once seen an operator switch a mule.

She loves hearing the oddly flat, merry clank of the bells worn around the mules' necks. When she first hears that sound after a long winter, she knows that tourist season has arrived. On a still day, she can hear it grow louder as the mule approaches, and diminish after it passes by, along with the soft clop of hooves on the packed dirt of the towpath.

At night, "music circuses" hold big parties aboard the barge, culminating around midnight, and she can hear raucous laughter between the lilting refrains of some happy air. On the last Saturday night of a run, she sometimes hears the unmistakable voice of some big star like Robert Goulet or Louis Armstrong, as they perform their "theater in the round." After the sounds of celebration die down, she will be lulled to sleep by the deep *Barrrr-UMP! Bwomp!* of huge bullfrogs seeking companionship on a warm summer night.

Tourists bring their vacation attitudes to New Hope, and with their arrival, the town comes alive with a Mardi Gras atmosphere. The hum and whine of speedboat races on the river are punctuated by the explosion of fireworks. The colorful bursts blossom into gigantic, phosphorescent flowers overhead, reflected in dancing fragments on the surface of the Delaware.

Sandy's parents make a little extra money by renting out a downstairs room to bit players from the Bucks County Playhouse. The bed and breakfast concept hasn't yet caught on in America, and rare, affordable lodging is much appreciated by struggling actors. Sandy is equally appreciative of the company, getting to know a new lodger every season, or enjoying an old acquaintance who has returned.

It's a great life for a gregarious kid. Sandy knows everyone on both sides of Main Street and often sends or returns greetings while flying up the sidewalk on her steel-wheeled roller skates. Her hair blows out behind her as she spins along. She inhales the earthy scent of the river mingling with the enticing potpourri of different foods, which drifts into the street from open restaurant doors.

Other kids play in the streets, riding bikes with trading cards clipped in the spokes to simulate engine noise. Cars roll by, usually slowly because there are so many people walking everywhere, so it's hardly dangerous. Screen doors slam, somewhere a radio blares Bill Haley's "Rock Around the Clock," and the pulse of energetic life throbs through the ever-present humidity of the Delaware Valley in August.

Sometimes Sandy goes into the New Hope Pharmacy at the corner of Main and Bridge Streets for some candy or gum. Benny Sidon, the owner, looks up with a smile from whatever concoction he is formulating and says, "Hi!" Benny is a friendly guy, unassuming, just the kind of person you'd want for a neighbor.

Sandy likes the way the orange neon of his Rexall Drugs sign reflects off the cobalt blue oval behind it. The moon-like Breyer's Ice Cream sign that hangs over the sidewalk from the corner of Benny's big brick store has enticed her inside more than once on a hot day like today.

Yes, Sandy is ready to go home. She just hopes the rest of the summer break won't be too boring.

Laura Slack works at the Solebury National Bank in New Hope, located kitty-corner from Benny's. She lives with her husband, Cliff, on Sugan Road near where Route 179 meets 202 just outside the downtown area. It's still pastoral there. The road is unpaved, and occasionally the farmer's cow across the road lets out a lonesome low. The most excitement they get around their place is one of the cows getting out of the fence and wandering into some unsuspecting neighbor's yard.

Laura and Cliff are friends with the Fennimore family, who own Hendricks Appliances across the bridge in Stockton. The Fennimores have a little shore house down in Gilford Park and have invited the Slacks to stay for a few days. Cliff isn't able to get off work on short notice, so they agree Laura will ride down with the Fennimores and he'll meet her down there on Friday after work. So she leaves, looking forward to some relaxing beach time.

Laura doesn't find much of that "down the shore." As if that darned Connie hadn't been enough, now they find out another hurricane is on the way. And you don't have to be a genius to see it for yourself: The ocean is riled, wind whipping up the waves and driving sand so that time on the beach wouldn't even be pleasant. Still, it's hot, and the thought of being housebound doesn't appeal to Laura. But Cliff has the car and she doesn't want to burden her hosts, so she just has to find a way to keep herself entertained.

She reads a little, but something in the air makes her tense, unable to concentrate. She talks with the Fennimores, reads some more, and finally settles in to watch their television set. It's still a fairly new experience, and she enjoys it. She watches some game shows, a little Arthur Godfrey, and in the evening, "I Love Lucy" makes her laugh. Still, she can't shake the feeling of disquiet. Laura decides to go to bed.

WEATHER BUREAU WASHINGTON NATIONAL AIRPORT
WEDNESDAY AUGUST 17 1955 BULLETIN DIANE
11 PM EST

THE STORM DIANE WAS CENTERED OVER SOUTH
CENTRAL VIRGINIA IN THE VICINITY OF
LYNCHBURG AT 11PM EST. IT IS MOVING IN A
GENERAL NORTHERLY DIRECTION ABOUT 13 MPH
AND HAS CONTINUED TO FAIL AND WEAKEN. THE
CENTRAL PRESSURE IS NOW ABOUT 29.40 INCHES
WINDS HAVE CONTINUED TO DIMINISH GRADUALLY
AND NOW AVERAGE BETWEEN 20 OR 30 TO 35
MPH WITH A FEW GUSTS UP TO 40 MPH. …MOD-
ERATE TO HEAVY RAINS…WILL LIKELY SPREAD
NORTHWARD INTO CENTRAL PENNSYLVANIA DURING
THURSDAY.…INDICATIONS ARE THAT THIS STORM

WILL CONTINUE TO FILL AND WEAKEN AS IT
MOVES NORTHWARD AT ABOUT THE SAME SPEED
DURING THE NEXT 12 TO 18 HOURS PM. THE
ONLY SERIOUS DANGER NOW IS FROM HEAVY
RAINS AND FLOODING. ...THIS WILL BE THE
FINAL BULLETIN ON THIS STORM.

NORQUEST WEATHER BUREAU WASHINGTON

The next day, New Hope and Stockton will receive just under two inches of rain from Diane. The deceptive storm is saving its command performance for the vulnerable hill country to the north. The weather station at Mount Pocono, near the Brodhead Creek watershed, will record 10.75 inches from Wednesday night to Friday. Most of it will fall in the twelve-hour period between two o'clock in the afternoon on Thursday and two in the morning on Friday.

An inch of rain over an acre of ground adds up to 27,150 gallons or 113 tons of water. Multiply that by 10 inches, and you're looking at 1,130 tons of water distributed on each acre. This water volume and its weight are pulled by gravity to seek the lowest elevations.

The Brodhead Creek watershed encompasses thousands of acres, most of them mountainous. All of it drains down through valleys, many of them quite steep and narrow. For instance, Bushnell Hill has an elevation of 2,112 feet above sea level. Located 17 miles from the Stroudsburgs, which stand at a 550-foot elevation, its runoff gains momentum from the drop of nearly a hundred feet per mile.

When all this runoff finally collects in the Brodhead, it will swell the creek's normally 3-to-5-foot depth by up to ten times. At first contained in the relatively narrow channel, this burgeoning volume will accelerate to speeds estimated at up to 25 miles per hour through the Minisink Hills, and eventually gush into the Delaware River at the Water Gap, just east of the Stroudsburgs.

Hydrologists have proven that just two feet of water moving at eight miles per hour exerts the same force as do the winds of an F5 tornado, the strongest twister with winds greater than 260 miles per hour. At the height of its rampage, the Brodhead will be packing water levels up to fifteen times that high and moving at perhaps more than three times the speed.

But on Wednesday the seventeenth, even after the up-to-twelve inches of rain left in the area by Connie, the Brodhead is already dwindling back toward the trickle it has been most of the long, parched summer. Nobody sees anything to be even remotely concerned about.

Then Diane approaches on a track far to the east of that predicted by the Weather Bureau. A dark cloud bank preceding her fills the evening sky around Scranton, Pennsylvania with enough humidity to produce a rainbow over West Mountain. Even as the final hurricane advisory bulletin is hitting the wires, intermittent showers are beginning in the Poconos. Before midnight, almost imperceptibly, the Brodhead again begins to swell.

Section II
The Storm

It Wasn't Supposed To Be This Way

Thursday, August 18, 1955
Morning until 8:00 p.m.

The river is a big part of life in Titusville, New Jersey. Most residents of this tiny village tucked between the river and the Delaware & Raritan Canal belong to the local boat club. On the Fourth of July, club members put on their annual Water Show, to the delight of participants and spectators alike. Most homes along River Drive sport summer porches. Many have sunbathing decks perched atop the steep bank, and there are more than a few permanent stairways to that particular heaven known as the Delaware.

For kids growing up in Titusville, learning to swim is like learning to walk, and getting your boat pilot's license is almost a rite of passage into adulthood. The river is so tightly woven into the fabric of community life that all who own motorboats understand the cardinal agreement with the minister of the church on River Drive: No motors on the river before noon on Sunday. After all, you don't want to risk the wrath of God by winding out your engine just as the pastor is delivering the homily. Besides, it just wouldn't be the neighborly thing to do.

Charles "Dusty" Scudder is one of those with a boat, and he happily observes the Sunday morning ban by sleeping in late. Or, more accurately in summer, by sleeping out late on his parents' summer porch. He's back from Rutgers for the summer, where he has just graduated with a degree in Dairy Husbandry. It will likely be his last free summer, and he intends to enjoy it.

Dusty likes lying in screened-in comfort, feeling the cool

breezes waft in off the water, bringing with them the slightly musty scent of the river. It's hard to describe: a heady cocktail of damp leaf litter and rich, dark humus; of green, growing things and just a touch of aquatic life.

Dusty listens happily to the night sounds: hooty owls, bullfrogs, and the occasional burst of laughter from a neighbor's late-night backyard barbecue. Sometimes, after he has turned off the transistor radio on which he's been listening to a Phillies game, he lies back with one hand tucked behind his head and breathes deeply. He watches moths fluttering around the yellow squares of light escaping from his mom's kitchen window, and hears their soft bodies bouncing off as they fling themselves at the screen.

There's little traffic up on Highway 29, especially late at night, and he imagines he can hear forever up and down the river. Once in a while, if he closes his eyes and really concentrates, he thinks he can detect the splash of a startled turtle hurling itself off a log and into the safety of the water. It always makes him smile.

Diane Wearing Herself Out As She Blows
Northwest; Only Minor Damage Caused

RICHMOND, Va., Aug. 17 (AP) – Weary
Hurricane Diane, fast wearing herself out in her
overland journey after eight fierce days at sea, swept
into south central Virginia tonight from North
Carolina.

…It was too early to assess the extent of the
damage to corn and tobacco crops, hurt in some
cases seriously last week by Connie, a much wetter
and more worrisome hurricane than Diane.
– *Daily Record,* Front Page, Stroudsburg, PA

This same issue of the newspaper carries a smaller article near the bottom of the page, headlined "Area Awaits Heavy Rains," but no one in the Poconos is really paying attention. It's still tourist season, and they're busy.

In the valley south of Easton, most people are reading—and relying on the accuracy of—local forecasts, like that printed in the morning edition of the *Philadelphia Inquirer.* "Southeastern Pennsylvania and Southern New Jersey: Cloudy with occasional rain today. Windy this morning, diminishing in afternoon. High 80 to 85 degrees. Tomorrow, partly cloudy and warmer."

Rarely has a forecast been so off the mark, more for what it leaves out than for what it says. Regardless, the result will be the same: thousands of people surprised by significant developments whose effects they might have been able to change, had they known what to expect. But with other headlines such as "Tired Diane Puffs Way Into Virginia," carrying subheads like "No Hurricane Now," "Diane Is Weaker," and "Miraculously Light" damage reports, who would be expecting anything worse than Connie?

Certainly not Dorothy Grider. She's using the dreary day to take a break from her busy illustration career, traveling to visit a friend in Selinsgrove. She had caught the morning train leaving the station in New Hope. She lives there along Main Street with her friend Lydia Gudemann and Lydia's father, "Pops." Their backyard sits atop the western bank of the Delaware, just north of the downtown area.

She's looking forward to seeing her friend, but throughout the trip Dorothy experiences a sense of foreboding. There's nothing she can actually see to make her feel this way—perhaps some standing water here and there, nothing serious—but she finds the rain has also dampened her spirits, which is unusual. Something's wrong, but she can't place it.

For the past few hours at Camp Davis, it has been raining so hard you can't see more than two or three feet in front of you. Already this morning, residents resign themselves to yet another day of keeping busy indoors.

David Johnson walks across the porch to the Thompsons' adjoining cabin to play with Bruce. Bruce is closer to his brother Roy's age, but Roy seems more interested in playing their older brother Joe's trumpet than doing anything with him.

Henry and Lillian Hartig, who have lived through several hurricanes and their attendant high waters, take a cab into town. They're up for a little shopping and lunch at Wyckoff's department store with their teenaged grandniece, Linda LeCropane. Henry buys a fancy new flashlight with an SOS beacon on the back end. A lover of gadgetry, he thinks someday it might come in handy.

The Hartigs are sending a postcard to the Liebfreds — the Rev. Davis' daughter and her husband. Mrs. Liebfred now handles most of the camp's correspondence for her aging father. Henry, the camp's unofficial maintenance man, feels duty-bound to let her know what's going on.

"Creek rising rapidly," his wife Lillian has written, "and we are beginning to become concerned." He drops the postcard into the mailbox in Stroudsburg and looks up at the sky. The overcast goes on as far as he can see, no sign of the rain letting up. This has gone on for the better part of a week now, and it's dropped no small amount of rain.

The Hartigs' concern isn't for the campers' safety, as the Brodhead has never, as far as Henry knows, risen dangerously. He's more concerned about what the high water might do to the creek banks and the make-shift stone "dam" that corrals creek water for swimming. Everyone in camp swims there, and most find it suitable for bathing. More high water threatens to make a mess out of them. He's also concerned about what all the water might do to the camp's crude septic system.

Henry doesn't realize that technically, the camp is built directly on the Brodhead's ancient floodplain, but it wouldn't matter anyway: there hasn't been a really serious flood there in his lifetime. The water had gotten high around the turn of the century and again during the war, but it had never threatened the camp. Still, he thinks it's prudent to keep the Liebfreds informed. He and Lillian will just keep their eyes on things a little more closely than usual once they get back to camp.

In mid-afternoon, the rain lets up a little. Irene Weber, having exhausted her patience for indoor activities, decides to go shopping in Stroudsburg. Upon leaving a store, she notices it has stopped raining entirely, and decides to head back up Route 90 to enjoy some time outdoors at the camp before evening falls. When she arrives, she smiles at the kids running around in their swimsuits, some taking a cautious dip in the high creek water. Everyone's glad to get outside for a while.

About five p.m., twenty-five-year-old Will Dobron, a volunteer with his hometown fire company, stands out in his yard on Ferry Road in Point Pleasant, Pennsylvania. He's watching a heavy sky, lowering to the point of looking as if he could reach out and touch the clouds. He thinks it can't be good, after the gully-washers that had come with the remnants of Connie.

But it's clear there's something coming, and he decides to stick close to home. If there's any more heavy rain, it's sure to cause some rockslides on River Road or other hilly areas, and the fire department will be called out. Casting a last, long glance at the threatening sky, Will decides he'll stay near the phone and make sure nobody else stays on it too long, in case he's needed.

Retired Army Col. A. M. Heritage is the Bucks County Director of Civil Defense. Maybe because it's based in the county seat, or perhaps due to the serious and intelligent nature of Col. Heritage, Bucks is one CD chapter that is properly structured, reasonably well funded, and attentively maintained.

After the minor to moderate flooding from Hurricane Connie's remnants, Col. Heritage had put the Bucks County CD headquarters on routine alert level. Once he'd read the newspaper accounts of the day's storm, however, he'd returned the office to a normal state of operations earlier in the evening. Satisfied that all is well, Col. Heritage returns to his Newtown home, a picturesque farm along the Neshaminy Creek.

The Neshaminy, though beautiful in spots, has a history of being flood-prone. Its West Branch rises in the Hatfield-Lansdale area, the North Branch in Doylestown. The creek runs fifty miles through twenty-five suburban Philadelphia municipalities, most of which are still fairly rural in character. Fed by nineteen tributary streams and creeks, it also receives storm water runoff from some of the most densely populous, heavily paved areas of southeast Pennsylvania. That's a lot for one little, steep-sided creek to handle. And so, as the rain continues to fall on Thursday, the Neshaminy rises more quickly than most other waterways in the region.

Just outside of Newtown, the Neshaminy winds through hundreds of acres of beautiful, rolling farmland that comprise the private Tyler Estate, still a working farm. Young Bob Maxwell's father rents a place on the farm, where they live and work. When Bob has the chance, he loves to ride his bicycle around the area, exploring the many woods, fields, and country roads. Today there is little farm work to be done in the sodden, mucky yard, so he takes off on his bike. His dad has said the creek is up, so he turns down Newtown-Richboro Road to get a look.

The Spring Garden Mill, which has for over a century used the creek's power to grind meal between its massive stones, sits along the Neshaminy's banks, just off the road. Its waterwheel has long since fallen into disrepair, though, and the miller now uses horsepower to turn the millstones for small, private orders. Bob knows the miller and his wife, friends of his dad.

The mill and its old covered wooden bridge have seen better days. Highway traffic now crosses over a massive concrete affair with many times its utility and not an ounce of its charm. The miller uses the neglected wooden bridge as a storehouse. Bags of feed, bales of hay and old, broken tack now cover its planks, and shelter beneath its shake roof.

Bob thinks it's a shame. At thirteen, he's old enough to appreciate the care with which the covered bridge had been designed and built, and feels bad that people can no longer enjoy it. From the outside, the bridge isn't all that impressive, but if you go inside, you can see the huge, laminated wood arches that support the span and its lavish construction methods. He thinks it will make the perfect vantage point from which to watch the rising waters of the Neshaminy.

When he arrives, it begins to rain again. He walks out on the bridge's deck, and sees that the water is nearly up to its beams. He thinks about the miller and his wife, who rent the mill and the stone house just uphill from it. Bob wonders how they will fare if the water gets really high.

The rain is quickly becoming heavier. Bob thinks he'd better get home.

Further upstream, the Neshaminy flows through New Britain, a little town sandwiched between Doylestown and Chalfont in central Bucks County. As evening falls, Marian Detwiler and her husband Jerry are there, nervously watching the creek's waters creeping slowly up the yard toward their house on Upper State Road.

Jerry and Marian have felt some apprehension before, but never really worry about it. The water has come up during hard rains, but it's never done any damage until Connie had come through last week. Then, the creek had risen to the point where it had filled their basement. Jerry has just finished a whole week of cleaning up, drying it out and whitewashing the walls...and now Diane shows up.

The timing couldn't be worse. Jerry, a teacher at Central Bucks West High School, is trying to get ready for the upcoming school year. Marian, thirty-four, is eight-and-a-half months pregnant.

Their son, Dick, is five years old and his little sister, Susan, is two. They are both quietly occupied in the playroom as their parents try to distract themselves with magazines.

It doesn't work. After the recent inundation, Jerry and Marian are concerned. Trying to be nonchalant so as not to worry the children, they now find themselves quietly making the circuit back and forth between the window and their seats. Finally, it gets too dark to see much outside, and they resign themselves to just waiting it out.

Things are beginning to happen on the other side of the Delaware, as well.

Just north of Phillipsburg, Warren County Fair goers are eyeing the sky, which has been leaden all day. When a light drizzle begins to fall just after lunch, most of them smile. They're farmers concerned about their crops, which are near ruin after the exceedingly dry summer. Even Connie's rains only gave a brief respite to their hard, cracked fields. Many of them will listen to State Governor Robert Meyner's speech tonight, telling them what New Jersey's drought committee is doing in response to their increasing clamor for federal aid. Meanwhile, they'll enjoy the Holstein judging, a sheep exhibit, and a tractor pull.

Farther north, Branchville sits astride the confluence of Dry Brook and Culvers Creek, just a few miles southeast of Culvers Lake on Highway 206. The lake spreads out at the base of the Kittatinny

Mountain range, with the river running parallel a few miles on the other side.

Culvers Creek flows southeast from the lake's narrow south end through Branchville. In 1868 a small dam had been built on the creek in town, to power a gristmill. Another larger and more substantial dam had been built by the mill owner's son in 1907 at the outlet of Culvers Lake, to power a turbine generator he had installed to light his mill.

Branchville had prospered because of this newer dam. The generator was large enough to supply power within a three-mile radius, and had been the genesis of the Branchville Electric Power, Light and Water Company. New Jersey Power and Light had bought out the pioneering little company in 1923 and moved all its generating facilities to Newton. The earth-and-log dam was then abandoned.

After years of neglect, the dam had threatened to fail under the onslaught of heavy rains in 1937. The emergency had been met by reinforcement with sandbags, narrowly avoiding a dam break, but something permanent needed to be done. The original builder's daughter, Irene McNellie, had inherited the dam with the rest of her father's property, and had been approached about her responsibility to maintain it.

That had been the middle of the Great Depression, and even the McNellies couldn't afford to perform a major dam overhaul. Still, Irene had realized her duty to the safety of her neighbors and her own home. She had allowed the village fathers to keep the dam's sluice gates open, avoiding further pressure that might weaken the structure.

Since then, the dam has only filled when feed water volume has exceeded drain capacity. For the last eighteen years, this has meant an irregular cycle of filling and draining, which works fine to keep undue pressure off the dam. The only problem is that the dam's log superstructure remains exposed to repeated wetting, swelling, drying, and shrinking cycles, as well. Not only does this exposure encourage the development of dry rot, the resulting movement allows the fill material between and around the logs to slowly shift, settle and degrade.

The torrential rains from Hurricane Connie have brought flow back to the previously parched waterways of Sussex County, as they have to surrounding areas. They've also ruined the much-anticipated

County Farm and Horse Show in mid-run, but left crops revived in what seems like a consolation offering.

Now, after Diane's rains have begun in earnest, a few folks not pre-occupied with agricultural pursuits look out at the drops coming down with the force of a fire hose, and immediately think of the dam. By evening there is enough concern to send a group to check it out. What they see is not good.

The structure is beginning to bulge in an alarming manner, but no one thinks the rain can possibly keep up this unbelievable pace. They don't want to panic anyone—what a mess that would be. The group decides not to issue any warnings just yet, not even to those whose homes and businesses lie in what would be the direct path of destruction. They will simply take turns keeping vigil throughout the night. If things take a turn for the worse, they'll sound the fire siren.

Up the Delaware in Port Jervis, New York, residents are used to hearing from tourists how lovely their area is. Situated at the spot where their state meets New Jersey and Pennsylvania, Port Jervis is surrounded by the beauty of mountains, rivers, and lakes. All that beauty comes with a price, however.

The Delaware River, where it hooks decidedly to the southwest, forms the city's southern boundary. Almost immediately, it enters a series of deep gorges left over from its glacial period. There's little floodplain to speak of here. Overabundant water simply piles up the sides of the gorge, waiting to spread out where the terrain flattens…near Port Jervis.

The Neversink River comes in from the north, running along the city's eastern frontier and separating a small section of it from the rest. A brook runs through the northern part of town, and there are several reservoirs nearby.

What ups the ante is that the Delaware gets a major volume boost not far from here. About thirty miles upstream, it is joined by the Lackawaxen River, which drains huge, man-made Lake Wallenpaupack after meeting the long Lackawanna River in Carbondale. In short, Port Jervis is not a place you want to be when the water's getting high.

Naturally, there is always some anxiety there during potential flood times, and it's not without justification. Serious flooding had affected the city three times between 1901 and 1904. In 1922, a reservoir dam above it had its splashboards pulled to keep it from bursting, and parts of the city had been washed out. Eleven years later, another section was engulfed and in 1942, floods washed the bodies of drowning victims all the way down from Hawley on Lake Wallenpaupack.

It's no surprise, then, that everyone's nerves are on edge as Diane's rains swell surrounding waterways.

About twenty miles down the Lackawanna from Carbondale sits Scranton, the largest city in northeastern Pennsylvania. Built with profits from the iron and coal industries and the railroads that serve them, Scranton's location at the base of two significant mountain ridgelines has always made it particularly vulnerable to flash floods. Unfortunately, time between major flooding episodes plays on the human tendency to forget or to think it can't happen again.

Residents in 1955 can't see that, from a mile up, their area looks like nothing so much as a giant drainage ditch. If they could, they wouldn't hesitate to believe a disaster of epic proportions is on its way. One look at the image of their fair city lying at the bottom of this elongated trough laced with rivers, creeks, and streams, and they'd understand the inescapable nature of their predicament.

But 1955 Scrantonites don't have satellite images or aerial topography schematics. All they have to go by are the best guesses of the Weather Bureau and some tales of long-ago floods that hardly seem relevant to their busy, urban lives. Even if they did realize what's coming, there would be little they could do about it other than an earlier, more planned version of what some of them will end up having to do anyway: grab what they can carry, and get out of the way.

On the east side of town, a feeder stream called Roaring Brook enters town from the east. Its name emphasizes its reputation as, according to one historian, "the noisiest tributary of the Lackawanna." It also reveals the brook's rambunctious character even in times of normal flow.

The Delaware, Lackawanna & Western Railroad's main line to Hoboken roughly parallels the brook along its north bank, supported at turns by box culverts. The Erie Railroad line and its maintenance shops sit about twenty yards above the DL&W line.

This afternoon, mechanics in the Erie yard have just finished several months of repairs to the railroad's largest maintenance-of-way crane. Flatbed and gondola cars are being coupled on, in anticipation of returning the huge beast to service tomorrow.

Just past this area, Roaring Brook swings a little more than ninety degrees south of its northwest bearing, on its way to join forces with the Lackawanna. It continues between the Erie line and Union Avenue, over Ash Street into the Little England section of Scranton.

Elliott and Ella Highfield, a retired couple, live in a modest frame house at the corner. They've been watching the brook rise all afternoon, and it's beginning to alarm them. As daylight fades, they can see the white foam shooting up where the brook is starting to splash over its embankments at the turn. Full of itself and the runoff from the length of the ridgeline, it doesn't want to stay in its channel anymore, but to continue straight ahead. The only problem is that, in less than a block, it will run directly into the Highfields' front door.

One more block to the southwest, thirty-eight-year-old Charlie Schane is busy with other things. If he hears the increasing volume of the brook living up to its name, he's apparently not concerned about it.

About ten meandering blocks downstream, Roaring Brook turns northwest again, traveling along Front Street toward Washington Avenue, where it will swing back southwest on the last leg of its journey to meet the Lackawanna. The same thing is happening there, with the brook leaving its banks to pioneer a new channel.

By the time it gets dark, it's obvious to everyone in the vicinity that the water is going to continue building in height and power. The Southside Flats along Washington Avenue are largely surrounded by the errant water. Their inhabitants are stranded on a virtual island of houses and apartment buildings, wondering whether their foundations will hold out. They frantically phone contacts outside the area, hoping the lines won't go dead before they can get out their calls for help.

Friends, neighbors, and family members arrive in motorboats, trying to save those they can. It's getting more difficult by the minute to negotiate what are quickly becoming Class A rapids. Soon, they can't wait for people to gather their belongings or even pets. The moment a person appears at a window—the doors are already underwater—they're grabbed and pulled into the boats.

As soon as all are safe within the craft, throttles are thrown open. The boats disappear into the dark, navigating four, five, six feet above what had been streets. They dodge street signs, telephone poles, and power lines as they make their escape. The shaken rescuees, most carrying nothing at all, look back to watch their homes being battered by walls of water and the debris now being washed along with it. The frightening images recede into the darkness, and for many, it's the last glimpse they will ever have of their homes.

Uptown, farther from the brook, Kay Cody has been happily shopping with her maid of honor, Joanne Martinelli. They are oblivious of the destruction happening just a few dozen blocks away.

Kay is engaged to be married on Saturday to John "Jake" Sengel at the Mountainhome Methodist Church. She and Joanne had braved the rain and left their pre-ceremony accommodations at Skytop Lodge in Mountainhome this morning to fill the car with the necessities to furnish her and Jake's new apartment.

When they come out of the last store, they're astonished to see the streets awash in several inches of water, and to hear rumors of serious flooding in several parts of town. Not knowing how bad it might be on the roads back to Mountainhome, Joanne suggests they spend the night at her place, just a short distance away in Dunmore, a Scranton suburb.

The wedding's not till Saturday, so Kay agrees. They'll have plenty of time to get back tomorrow.

Southeast of Scranton and almost directly south of Honesdale, the Wallenpaupack Creek emerges from the dam on Lake Wallenpaupack. After a half-moon curve to the northwest and back down, it heads generally south until jogging around East Sterling. Then it heads south again, roughly paralleling Route 507. For its entire length before crossing into Monroe County, the creek forms the border between Wayne and Pike Counties, and eventually empties into the Lehigh River.

Greentown sits just east of that line, where the Wallenpaupack is joined by Greentown Creek. A little farther south and just west of the Wayne County line lies the small village of Newfoundland. Its eight hundred or so residents live mostly in the downtown area.

There, Route 507 comprises a short main street lined with houses, shops and a few offices. Several mountains rise on all sides of the town, creating something of a bowl shape at the bottom.

June Schafer loves the lay of the land at her Newfoundland home. A young wife and mother, she enjoys looking up into the mountains while she washes dishes or hangs laundry to dry in the fresh air. This summer, though, has been one of extremes. Up until last week, it had been brutally hot and as dry as anyone had ever seen it. Then, since last week, there haven't been any days dry enough to hang out the wash. Today, it's been raining nonstop since she woke up.

Her husband, Robert, is a major in the U.S. Army. Stationed at the Tobyhanna Signal Depot, about eight miles to the southwest, he serves as Assistant Chief of its Storage Division. They have a good-sized yard for their two daughters to play in as they grow, and June and Robert get along well with the Robackers, their downstairs neighbors in the old farmhouse they rent.

Though they receive rural route mail delivery, they're still considered to live in "downtown" Newfoundland. They're located on one of two main roads that form the downtown intersection. The house sits not far from the lumberyard where Bob Robacker works, and about 150 yards across the road is an offshoot stream of the Wallenpaupack Creek. The main channel runs behind the lumber-yard, roughly parallel to highway 507.

A little after five o'clock in the afternoon, June sees Bob walking up the steps from work, and goes out on the porch to greet her neighbor. He tells her the creek is rising, and they talk a while. She says she's expecting Robert home for dinner any time now, and excuses herself to finish getting ready.

Within half an hour, Bob can see from the porch that the stream is up over the road in quite a few places. He takes his wife, Edith, and their young son, Bobby, further toward the creek to look at the high water. When they come back, June again meets them on the porch. She has seen the headlights of cars driving up the ridge roads, and asks Bob if he thinks perhaps they, too, should move their cars to higher ground.

"It never gets any higher," Bob says, "and I've lived here all my life." He doesn't think they need to take any action.

Robert swings in the driveway, and pulls his car into the barn, next to Bob's. They all remark on the weather, then retire to their apartments for supper.

A little after six o'clock, the wind kicks up and the Schafers' daughter, four-year-old Marie, points out the window at their swing set. The swings are being tossed about by wind gusts, and the rain begins to come down much harder. Within a few minutes, the sound on the roof is tremendous, actually making it difficult to hear their conversation.

The Schafers go to the window to watch the rain, but it no longer looks like individual raindrops. Instead, the water is cascading from the sky in solid sheets like those that pour forth from a bucket. They've never seen anything like it.

After the dishes are done, Robert and June join the Robackers on the porch. Robert says he's beginning to get concerned.

Bob still maintains that the water's never been this high before, but this time he allows, "When it reaches the porch, we'll start to worry." His voice maintains a joking tone, but June notices that the mirth is gone from his eyes. She glances at Robert to gauge his reaction, but he's focused on the water, saying nothing. She goes inside to put Marie and ten-month-old Patricia to bed.

Just up the way in Greentown, the Greentown Creek is also swelling, and now there's a bigger problem. The Wallenpaupack has become so engorged that its stronger current is blocking normal entry of waters from the Greentown, just past Route 507/90. With nowhere else for its waters to go, the tributary begins backing up. The unique combination of currents forms a powerful backwash whirlpool. It starts eating away at all surrounding banks, rocks, trees, signs, and anything else in its way.

Soon, the volume of water has pushed the violent eddy back to the highway bridge. The angry swirl of water and rocks scours out the banks from beneath it. Within hours, its concrete abutments crumble. The heavy concrete roadway and guardrails drop into the creek, to be smashed into pieces and carried downstream like a fleet of naval battering rams.

Just to the south, the rain has been swelling the Brodhead Creek all day, as well.

The Brodhead is normally a gentle-running, coldwater creek, with an average depth of five or six feet. Along with its many tributaries, it has a reputation among avid flycasters for its abundant native brook trout populations. Such distinguished personages as United States president Grover Cleveland and Wild West stars Buffalo Bill Cody and Annie Oakley had often visited its waters, staying in the Henryville House Hotel between fly fishing jaunts.

Over the years, many small, earthen dams have been erected on the creek and its feeder streams to encourage the deep, still pools that attract trout. The long, dry summer of 1955 has blown deposits of broken branches, tumbleweeds of dried grass, nesting material from various rodents, and balled-up, discarded fishing line into the channel. The rains from Connie had already gathered such clumps of debris into coagulated masses that had lodged against many of these dams. They lay where they had dropped when the water receded.

Energized by the fresh influx of Diane's water, the current again picks them up and carries them along. Here and there, a mass snags on a stick or rock in front of one of the dams. This obstruction collects enough other debris, until finally the mass has grown to significant size.

With the current picking up volume and speed, larger logs and even a few stones are pushed up against it. Soon, the ends of these logs catch more flotsam, which in turn catches loose material of its own. Within an hour, the dam has enlarged enough to trap a considerable volume of water behind it.

This obstruction holds and builds until finally, the strengthening current hurls a massive boulder at it. In an instant, the accumulation explodes with a loud crash and the unique grinding sound of wood being splintered and chewed by boulders tumbling in the current like stones in a cement mixer.

The wall of water it's been holding back rushes over and through the few remaining sticks, crushing what's left of the dam. Confined within narrow creek walls, the towering swell rides downstream at a quickening pace. When it enters the Brodhead's main channel, it spreads out and flattens just a bit, but remains several feet above the water level directly ahead of it.

One of these pile-ups alone would be enough to raise the Brodhead's level, with steep sides maintaining its fairly narrow channel. But this process has been happening over and over again on many tributaries for miles upstream, the dams sometimes forming and self-destructing within minutes of each other. Each surge of volume adds to the height of the current.

Now a veritable wall of water, ten or even fifteen feet high, is rolling downstream in the dark. It passes through many Pocono villages, picking up speed and power—and sizable streambed boulders—with every mile. No longer just a passive, mild creek, the Brodhead has become a surging, shape-shifting bulldozer.

Around five p.m., it begins raining hard again at Camp Davis, sending everyone back indoors. Jennie Johnson is using the time inside to get some ironing done. Nancy has invited the Thompsons, neighbors in the "quad" cabins, over for a game of Flinch.

Irene Weber and Edna Winfield are in the Winter House with their children, discussing whether or not to drive over to Pinebrook, the nearby Bible retreat, for the evening service. Everyone is getting tired of being inside the house, but the rain is really coming down now. It's cascading down in almost impenetrable sheets, and Irene doesn't want to have to walk through that. She looks at the clock. It's already seven, and it's getting dark. She decides not to chance it.

The kids let out a collective groan, disappointed they won't at least get outside for a bit and break the monotony of their enforced indoor stay.

Irene looks at Edna, understanding their letdown. *How about we have a party?* she suggests, trying to raise everyone's dampened spirits.

Really? asks Bobby, warming to the idea.

Yeah! enthuses Rowan, looking up at his mother for confirmation.

Edna doesn't hesitate. *Sure! I'll make a cake, and we can have an end-of-the-summer party later this evening. How does that sound?*

Rowan, Bobby, and Betty Jane all cheer, smiles returning to their faces.

Well then, we'll need some decorations, so you children had better get busy, says Irene. *Go get your crayons and paper, and I'll find a pair of scissors.*

The kids scramble to collect their materials and gather around the kitchen table. Irene helps them draw suns and rainbows and make paper chains, while Edna whips up a chocolate cake.

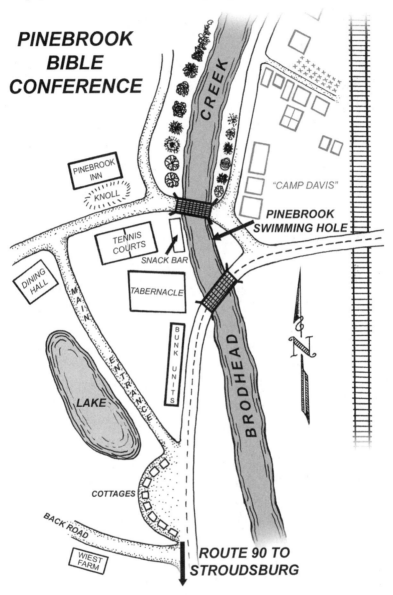

Pinebrook Bible Conference retreat layout (not to scale) as it was in 1955. This map shows the various buildings and their general locations on the grounds and in relation to roads, bridges, the Brodhead Creek and Davis Cabins (Camp Davis).

— Based on a sketch by Linda LeCropane Kelso.

The Hartigs' grandnieces, seventeen-year-old Sara and thirteen-year-old Linda, have been making plans with their visiting friend, Marion Baker, fifteen. The girls want to attend the evening service over at Percy Crawford's Pinebrook Camp, just across a small bridge at the top of the Brodhead's western bank. Most of the Camp Davis visitors attend Sunday and evening services there.

The LeCropane girls are regular visitors, and want to keep up on the teen "soap opera;" who's sweet on who, who's no longer together. Part of this constantly changing social scene at Pinebrook is the Youth on the March male quartet. They're also eager to sing the latest "hits" from the popular Pinebrook songbook.

Uncle Henry and Aunt Lily aren't too keen on the idea of the girls walking over to Pinebrook tonight, though. They're concerned about them going across the metal bridge during all the lightning, and in the strong, gusty winds. But the girls are staying in their family's cabin, which Henry had built for them right next door. They realize they can get away with slipping out if they're careful not to be seen by their relatives.

Linda isn't burning to go as strongly as her sister and Marion are. She misses their mother, who is back home in New York with their dad for a blood transfusion to treat her worsening leukemia. The girls, testy from all the bad weather, have had a spat, and Linda is also in a funk from that. Finally, Sara stands and announces that she and Marion are going to Pinebrook, whether Linda comes along or not. She watches the door close behind them as they sneak away.

Like many hormonal teenage girls, Linda finds herself just sitting on the edge of her cot, wondering what to do. She wants to go to the service, but she's still angry with her sister. She just sits, until her sister and Marion return to get their galoshes about ten minutes later. Linda is surprised to see them.

The older girls are all excited, telling her, "You ought to see what's going on down at the creek! The kids are playing in deep puddles, like wading pools!" They pull on their boots and are once again out the door.

Linda is interested and wants to see the rising water, but her ennui gets the better of her, and she continues pouting for several more minutes. She thinks about her aunt and uncle next door in their newly completed cabin. She'd like to go over there, but they'd ask about Sara and she'd get the girls in trouble, so she just stays put.

Suddenly, for a reason she can't put her finger on, she gets the feeling that she needs to get out of the cabin. Instinctively obeying this strong feeling, she gets up, ducks below the window so her aunt and uncle won't see her, and grabs an umbrella from their deck. She walks down the lane between the creek and the cabins. By now, everyone else has returned to their cabins, and it's strangely quiet.

The water is now up to the road, and when she reaches the creek bridge, nobody else is there. She stands on the bridge, looking down through the steel grid and watching the water rush underneath. She turns to face north, arms on the railing, and sees eddies swirling along the banks.

As she was growing up, Linda had always feared falling off the bridge and being washed down the creek into the Delaware. Now she watches logs and barrels shooting down the channel, frightening herself by imagining them as people. As one swirls toward the bank, she imagines that this object will be "saved," while others will continue downstream and be "lost."

She remains in this reverie for five or ten minutes. A car approaches from the Pinebrook side, and crosses over to R. D. 3, which runs north along the creek. It is the Arnts, neighbors and close friends of her family. They wave and head home to their farmhouse up the road.

Linda glances over at a tree with a waterline marked on it, and realizes how high the water is. Where the bridge ends on the Pinebrook side, people are noticing the same thing, exclaiming that it's higher than they've ever seen it. The comment jolts her from her reverie. Again, the sense that she needs to keep moving kicks in. and she finally walks the rest of the way across.

She approaches the large, timber-framed tabernacle, entering through the back door because she's late. Sara looks back and sees her come in and sit down. Their eyes meet and Linda knows their spat is over. Sara turns back toward the front.

The meeting soon becomes strange. Staffers, wearing bathing trunks, are going up and down the aisles. They're requesting that some people from the congregation leave to help secure rowboats on the pond, and other camp property in danger of being blown away by the storm.

A little boy who has been living with his grandparents in an Airstream trailer near the creek is called out. One of the ushers whispers something to him, and he begins to cry. Odd.

Meanwhile, across the creek in the Johnson bungalow, Jennie looks away from Nancy's and Beverly Thompson's card game and notices her boys getting restless.

David had come back from the Thompsons' when Bruce and his sister Beverly came to play cards, and Roy has been hanging around playing his older brother's trumpet much of the day. After several hours of squeaky, off-key notes from a beginner in the small, closed area, Jennie's ready for a break.

She looks out the window at the waning light and sees the rain has slacked off again. She also notices quite a few of the other summer residents down near the water. Apparently, no one wants to negotiate the rain to attend Pinebrook services this evening. She suggests a walk down to see what's going on, and the card players agree that a stretch of the legs would be welcome.

She and Nancy stay under their umbrellas, while Roy, David, Bruce, and Beverly run ahead, not caring about getting wet. The Brodhead's waters are running fast, so Jennie reminds them not to get too close. The boys throw sticks into the water and watch them get taken by the rushing current, then find a few rocks to toss in.

Jennie is surprised to find even old Mrs. Polly at the water's edge, along with the Kochs, the Russos, Beth Deubel and her mother Martha, and the Weber's in-laws, the Lawyers. The little McCaffery boys join hers in tossing rocks into the current.

The water is up to the edge of the road that runs parallel to the creek. Jennie watches white bubbles elongating and glittering in the half-light of an overcast dusk, just beneath the surface of the swift current.

It's almost pretty, don't you think? she asks Nancy.

Nancy smiles and nods, a faraway expression on her face. She never looks away from the water. Its constant motion is soothing, almost hypnotic.

Roy remarks that the flight of steps he helped his dad build two years before, from the top of the bank to the water's edge, is now underwater. Fourteen steps, with an average nine-inch rise; the water has risen nearly ten feet throughout the day.

Henry Hartig has already been down to see it, though, and has satisfied himself that nothing is amiss. He's gone back to his cabin.

Still, water running off the bank above is collecting in the road that Linda LeCropane has recently left. Instead of running down to meet the creek water, it's now coursing along in its own stream. The kids take off their shoes to splash around in it. Jennie thinks the two streams look like they will soon merge, and sends the boys to go get Mr. Hartig again.

He comes from his cabin to take another look. No, he reassures them, the creek has never risen any higher than the road. They have nothing to fear, and should really just go back to their cabins and relax. The crowd has no reason to think otherwise, and starts moving away from the creek.

Then a murmur rises from those near the water's edge, and Jennie Johnson turns to see the cause. A virtual wall of water is heading toward them, only about two feet high, but disquieting in its unexpectedness. It looks for all the world like a breaker rolling up on a beach. It reaches them, but unlike a breaker, the water does not recede again once it has passed. One moment the campers are standing on dry ground, the next they are up to their knees in water. They can feel small stones and sticks hitting their legs.

Jennie supposes a dam has broken somewhere. She can't know that it's actually the result of numerous small, old earthen structures built over the years as "improvements" to countless fishing streams and brooks to the north. She doesn't realize that, at this very moment, more of them are giving way one after another, like a set of dominoes stood on end and tapped. All she does know is that her legs and feet are getting wetter by the moment, and the umbrellas suddenly seem ridiculous.

The water now covers a significant portion of the wide spit on which Camp Davis stands. The creek has overrun R.D. 3 and has left its banks to sluice along the railroad. Davis' now seems like an island. Everyone agrees that it's probably best to seek the safety of the buildings.

Little David Johnson is spooked by the odd phenomenon and scoots ahead of his mother into their bungalow.

"Don't be scared," Jennie encourages, while realizing that indeed there might be some danger to all this. She follows David into the cabin and takes his hand. Roy and Nancy are right behind, and Bruce and Beverly cross the porch to their cabin.

Children, Jennie says, I think it might be a good idea for us to go up to the Winter House. The water could come up higher. She notices David's furrowed brow and widening eyes. Not wanting to frighten him further, she gives him a reassuring smile and tousles his hair. Not much higher, I think, but the Big House is sturdier. Why don't you bring a book or something to do, and I'll go see if the Thompsons might want to come, too.

She doesn't think they'll be gone long, and goes out to talk with Gladys. To her surprise, Gladys and the children are already on the stoop. Jennie notices just a hint of concern in her neighbor's eyes.

Are we thinking the same thing? Jennie asks.

The Winter House? Gladys nods. *Yes. Just until the water goes down a bit.*

Jennie turns as her children come out on the porch. She reaches around the wall and flips off the light switch. The two families troop up to the Winter House, which sits slightly higher than the rest of the spit, and farther from the creek than the other buildings. They notice quite a few of their fellow campers also heading for the big house. Several others go instead to Mrs. Polly's, the most sturdily built of the cabins.

Surely, Jennie thinks, the water won't come up that far.

Hell in the Headwaters

Thursday, August 18, 1955
8:00 p.m. to 10:00 p.m.

A heavy rain is falling as New Jersey governor Robert Meyner arrives for his speech at the Warren County Fair. He steps through the mud to the main office, where the Stewartsville Grange is serving hamburgers and french fries. He shakes hands with old acquaintances and chats up the farmers regarding the topic of tonight's speech. Asked about the chances of Warren County receiving federal aid for losses they believe will be incurred from the season-long drought, the governor tells them such a decision will be up to the president.

The crowd is finishing their snack when fair officials tramp in, dripping. They tell the governor that, regretfully, they must cancel his speech. He has been upstaged by the weather. They bring him to look out at the sea of umbrellas and raincoats, explaining that people can't sit in such pouring rain to listen; in fact, might not even be able to hear for the loud drumming on surrounding tent tops, fuel drums, and trailers.

Good naturedly, the governor asks them to extend his regrets, likely relieved not to be under the microscope on this issue yet again, but sorry he won't have the chance to campaign on behalf of upcoming political candidates.

As he's leaving, he sees several cars bogged in the mud, and a bulldozer hauling out a mired ladder truck belonging to the New Jersey Hose Company.

Helen Brown is still on her way home to Stroudsburg. She has made it to Pottsville, where she stops in to see her sister, who will be coming for a visit of her own the following week. They spend the evening finalizing their plans, then Helen must leave. It's getting late, she still has a few hours' drive ahead, and it has begun to rain quite hard.

About an hour into the trip, Helen feels drowsy, so she pulls off at the Lehighton Diner to get a cup of coffee. As she waits for her drink, she hears people talking about high water in Stroudsburg. She's not surprised, given how hard it has been raining, but the creeks at home frequently rise during such downpours. It's never been anything to get excited about.

Still, she unhitches her trailer in case she has to drive through high water. She leaves it in the diner parking lot, where it will be safe until she comes back to get it in a few days.

She drives on toward her exit at Route 209 in Saylorsburg. When she pulls up to make her turn, a Civil Defense volunteer is guarding the road. He tells Helen that Route 209 is blocked off, and she can't go any further. Glad she has left the trailer behind, she turns around and takes a back route through Cherry Valley, remembering the way from her motorcycling days. As she gets closer to town, she begins to see signs of severe flooding; road washouts, deep crevasses on the hillsides that were never there before, every waterway full to its banks. It takes a while, but she finally makes it back home to Main Street in Stroudsburg.

The highway in front of the Schafers' and Robackers' Newfoundland house now lies under a foot of water, and cars are stalling in it. Within an hour, it has risen another foot. Bob Robacker takes a flashlight and wades back to the barn. It sits lower than the house, and the water there is over the tops of the tires. He realizes they couldn't leave now even if they wanted to. Still, he can't imagine the stream getting any higher. It's already swollen to the width of three football fields.

Bob returns to the house, and reports what he's found in the barn to Robert. Both men keep their concerns to themselves, but the tension has become palpable. By ten p.m., the water has not only reached the porch, it's up over the top and within six inches of the Robackers' front door. Edith asks if June would mind taking little

Bobby from his bed to their apartment upstairs, just in case. June agrees, and carries the small boy up to tuck him into hers and Robert's bed. She has the feeling they won't be using it tonight. She checks on the girls, then goes back downstairs.

When she gets there, Robert tells her they're going to start bringing the Robackers' furniture upstairs to their apartment. She's surprised, but nods, noting the look of stunned disbelief on the faces of her husband and their neighbors. Edith is moving almost as if in a trance, and Bob has stopped joking.

They silently go about moving the antiques upstairs first. As they've got a bed mattress halfway up, the power goes out. Maneuvering as best they can in the dark, June and Edith gather candles and place them around on tables and shelves. They're glad the kids are asleep, so they won't become frightened.

By eight thirty, Edna Winfield's chocolate cake is done baking, and Irene and the children finish hanging the decorations. In their busyness, they've been unaware of the developments outside. Answering a rap at the door, they're surprised to see the line of people waiting outside. Short explanations are made, and the visitors are welcomed in. After all, it's a party—the more, the merrier. They consider how to cut the cake to accommodate so many extra kids.

It also becomes quite warm in the Winter House, with thirty people crowded into the dining room. Though it's the camp's largest building, it is by no means commodious. Jennie discusses with Louise Christensen the possibility of leaving camp for the night.

They send Bruce Thompson and Donnie Christensen to check for possible exit routes. The boys, feeling grown-up to be trusted with such an important task, set off into the growing darkness with a flashlight.

Everyone tries to find a comfortable place to sit, but it's not easy. Finally, the young children clamber onto a large bed in the corner, while older children and adults seat themselves around it on the floor. Several adults serve slivers of cake to the children and talk quietly amongst themselves. The kids, having been bored most of the day, are happy for the diversion of each other's company, and there's a sense of adventure in the air.

Jennie begins to wonder where the boys are, and looks out the window, then at Irene, registering the first real concern she's seen on anyone's face. It's concern she shares.

Well, Irene says with a cheer she doesn't feel, *we'd better think about what we might have to do to stay the night in the attic.* She sees the other adults' faces change as the reality of their situation sets in. *Just in case, you know.*

I'll get some candles, Edna says, rummaging through drawers and cabinets where they're kept for candlelight services and emergencies.

Irene asks Jennie to help her carry some food upstairs. She pulls the rope on a hatch in the hallway ceiling, revealing a drop-down ladder stairway to the attic. Edna follows with bundles of candles and matches.

It's even warmer on the second floor, and the air is stagnant and stale. The women open windows, pleased to find that the rain has dwindled almost to nothing. But replacing the pounding of the rain now is the roar of water surrounding them, sluicing through the trees and probably, Jennie thinks, the cabins below. She wonders if she remembered to close their door.

She can still see the lights of Mrs. Polly's cabin, so she knows the people there are still all right. And with the rain stopping, the water will probably start dropping back. Everything should be fine by morning.

Today has been a long one for Dusty Scudder. It has rained incessantly, hard enough to keep him and his pal, "Mudguard," from taking the boats out. Tomorrow will be better, he thinks. The weatherman is calling for this wet stuff to come to an end in Titusville, and they'll finally get out on the water. He immediately falls into a deep sleep as only tired young men can.

In New Britain, the Detwilers are agitated about the water rising in the darkness outside, but they can't believe the Neshaminy Creek will get much higher. Jerry goes back to reading. Marian, unable to keep still, figures she might as well put the excess energy to use. She decides to make some soup for the weekend.

In the kitchen, she pulls some chicken out of the refrigerator and puts a pot on the stove. By the time she prepares the meat, the water has begun to boil. While the chicken cooks, she dices vegetables. When it's done cooking, she leaves the pot to cool before putting it back in the fridge. Then she checks on the kids in the playroom.

As she returns to the living room, she and Jerry both hear a trickling noise. They shoot each other a silent glance, then go to investigate. Jerry opens the basement door to find his recent handiwork completely covered again by the creek's waters. Only this time, they reach clear to the top, and are lapping at nosing on the first step. Frustrated and shaken, Jerry backs away and softly closes the door. As he turns, Marian appears from around the corner, ashen-faced.

It's coming in under the doors, she says quietly.

Jerry sees the fear in her eyes. He goes around with her to check all the doors. Sure enough, chocolate-colored water is seeping onto their floors. It seems absurd to them both, bizarre. Nobody has said a thing to either of them about it ever flooding here before. And now, two weeks in a row?

What shall we do? she asks.

He considers for a moment. Last time, it didn't get this high. How much farther can it go, really? *Let's wait a while,* he replies. *It can't get much higher than this.*

Marian agrees, but she doesn't want the children staying downstairs, just in case. The water isn't coming in the playroom yet, but it soon might. *Let's go upstairs, children,* she tells them. *Bring something to play with until bedtime. Mommy and Daddy need to move some things.*

So Dick and Susan select a plaything or two and head upstairs with their mother, while Jerry begins rolling up rugs. The water continues to rise as Jerry and Marian scurry to move what furniture will fit up the old, curved farmhouse staircase. Marian's pregnancy prevents her from helping to lift the heavy things, so most of it stays where it is.

Suddenly, the lights go out. They realize it could get dangerous downstairs, so after gathering flashlights and candles and putting the kids in bed, they stay upstairs. Every few minutes, they look down from the top of the stairs to see if the water has progressed any further. When it reaches four-and-a-half feet with no sign of leveling off, Jerry decides it's time to get out.

I'm going up to Wayne's to see if we can stay with them, he tells her.

The Lapps are good friends, and he's sure they'll be welcome there.

How will you get there?

Jerry hesitates a moment. *I guess I'll swim.*

Marian is now genuinely frightened. This whole situation is just surreal. It's dark, the water is getting very deep, and who knows what kind of current it has?

Jerry, please...be careful.

He hugs her and starts down the stairs. He bumps things floating in the rooms. As he pulls the back door open, he fights suction and feels the water swirl against his legs. It's shallowest there, and he swims through the yard until he reaches the slope to the Lapp's house. Marian tries to watch for him, but it's impossible to see much other than some shadowy movement.

Soon, Jerry is on his way back to the house. Marian's eyes have adjusted to the dark now, and she watches him try to enter the water from the other side of the yard. After moving a few feet into it, he stops. It's plainly deeper than when he went across the first time, and she realizes the current must have gotten too strong. Slowly, he turns around and trudges back up the hill, and Marian feels a chill move through her.

Jerry comes back with a rope, in which he makes a loop at one end, tying the other to a tree where he stands. He tosses the looped end toward a tree close to his house. It catches on a branch, and he pulls himself along the rope toward it. Holding on to the tree, he pulls in the rope's slack and yanks the loop off the branch. Then he winds the length once around the trunk and grabs the looped end again.

He kicks off the trunk, giving himself enough momentum to make it back to the door. Tying the end loop tightly around the doorknob, he wades back into the house. Marian is waiting for him at the top of the steps.

We need to get you and the kids out, fast, he says, out of breath.

Marian nods, and they climb the stairs to wake the children. She fights to control her rising fear as she explains to the kids that their house is flooding, and Daddy is going to take them all over to Mr. and Mrs. Lapp's house for the night. She tries to act calm, like it's no big deal. Susan is too young to comprehend, and looks as though she might fall back to sleep. Dickie seems more intrigued than anything. Marian is glad they aren't showing signs of panic.

Jerry carries Dick downstairs first. Dick looks around as they slosh through the playroom. In the beam of his father's flashlight, he dimly sees his toys covered with water, and some of their books beginning to float to the surface. The image will stay with him all his life.

Marian and Susan are close behind. The water has become rather chilly, and the shock of it through Marian's clothes is startling. She hopes it won't hurt the baby. Wading to the door, she tells Dick to be sure to hold on very, very tightly to Daddy as he swims.

She watches intently as they make their way through the water. Jerry holds Dick tightly to him with one hand, dragging himself along the rope with the other. When she sees they have made it safely, she sighs with relief, unaware she had been holding her breath. Susan goes next, and Marian can't remember ever being so acutely anxious as she is while watching her children go through that water.

At last, Jerry comes back for her. The water has risen past her chest. She's amazed at how powerful the flow is, and so thankful for the guide rope and Jerry's strength. She turns to face downstream as much as possible, trying to avoid being struck in the stomach by anything being flung along in the current.

As she leaves the water, Marian is exhausted from the effort and the chill of the water. She has to rest before making the slow climb up the hill in the rain. She's terrified she'll slip and somehow injure the baby, and Jerry understands. He holds her hand the whole way, staying with her until they reach the top.

When they make it to the Lapps' house, Mrs. Lapp has towels and dry clothes for them to put on after they get cleaned up. Marian is shivering, more from fear than cold, and Mrs. Lapp gives her an encouraging smile. She hands Marian a pair of underwear, and Marian looks at it quizzically.

For Susan, Mrs. Lapp says. *I haven't anything else she can wear!*

Marian laughs—what else can she do? As she towels off, she wonders if their house will withstand the raging water through the night.

Three branches of the Paunacussing Creek meet at the tiny hamlet of Carversville, Pennsylvania, before winding through some of the most scenic vistas in Bucks County. From there, the creek tracks alongside the dirt surface of Fleecydale Road, past the charming ruins of an old mill. Then it winds between steep, wooded ridges that provide picturesque cover for myriad wildlife before slipping past the homes of Bill Tinsman's family and those of his neighbors, then emptying into the Delaware River at Lumberville.

Usually, the creek serves along with the woodland canopy to maintain cooler summer temperatures in Carversville. Even when the rest of Bucks County is sweltering, Carversville residents enjoy a more comfortable existence, thanks to the Paunacussing. The creek is crossed by two bridges, one on each side of town at two of the three access points.

This unique lay of the land is funneling an amazing amount of the heavy rain runoff from the steep ravines into the creek's local branch. Its two other branches are bringing similar cargo from farther west and north in the county, where they rise. The water is rapidly deepening as the hours wear on, and the owner of Bartleman's General Store in the town square realizes his stock of farm machinery is in jeopardy. His son works in the waning light to move what he can to higher ground, and to chain down what he can't relocate.

Little Robbie Winans is driving up River Road with his mom and dad to pick up his younger brother in Lumberville. His grandmother has been watching the boy all day. The Winanses plan to turn up Cuttalossa Road to her house, but when they get close, they're stopped by a fireman in the murky dark, just south of where the road passes over Cutalossa Creek.

The Cutalossa empties into the Delaware on the south end of Lumberville much the way the Paunacussing does on the north end. The fireman tells Robbie's father it's up over the road, and they can go no further.

Undaunted, Robbie's mother, a fearless farm woman, insists she can wade across. She wants to assure her mother that they are all right. A long discussion with the fireman ensues, during which both men and Robbie several times believe she will actually try to make it across on foot. Much to their relief, the fireman finally persuades her that even if she's strong enough to negotiate the current, she could be struck by a log or other large piece of debris beneath the surface, and be carried off into the river.

She gets back in the car, and they drive the long way around to her mother's house. They fear the roads have become too dangerous to travel in the dark, so they stay overnight and decide to check things out in the light of day.

Sandy Smith has made it home to New Hope from camp and is sitting at her kitchen table with her friend Kathy. The girls are listening, spellbound, to Sandy's mother telling the story of her brother who had passed away and been buried in a glass coffin. Sandy has heard the story before, but never tires of its exoticism, and Kathy can't get enough.

Sandy's mom, Mary, is having a hard time concentrating on her story. For the umpteenth time, she stops mid-sentence because the pounding of the rain on the roof is nearly drowning out her words. She goes to the window again.

She has told Kathy several times that she should go home, because they don't know how bad it's going to get outside, but Kathy only prods her on with her eerie tale. This time, Mary won't be put off.

"Kathy, really. You need to get home. We can finish the story some other time. Who knows what you'll run into? Go on, now."

Kathy realizes she's not going to get another word out of Mrs. Smith, so she thanks her and says goodbye to Sandy. She hesitates for a moment at the door, then dashes out into the downpour and runs down the sidewalk, splashing up a bucketload of water with each slap of her sneakers. Sandy and her mom watch until Kathy disappears into the curtain of rain and darkness.

By nine p.m., the center of Carversville is awash in six to nine feet of swift-running water, as the creeks charge over their banks and into the heart of the town. The force of its movement picks up piece after piece of Bartleman's farm equipment and pushes it across town, lodging it beneath the bridge. The piece that had been chained down does its best to break free, but stays put, turning sideways in the current, parallel to the storefront.

The violent tide scours away at the side of the road until it manages to pry up the lip of the asphalt. It lifts the crumbling edge, then proceeds to roll it up like so much carpet across the square.

Soon, there's nothing left of the roadway but one long rut that's serving as a new creek channel.

In the dark, drivers who are unaware of the destruction drive onto roadways that are no longer there. Potholes swallow parts of cars and endanger their occupants. As people scream for help, neighbors hear their pleas and telephone the fire department to dispatch rescue crews. Will Dobron's hunch had been correct, and he will spend the night rescuing people from encroaching water.

Bill Tinsman is getting nervous. All evening, he and his wife, Sue, have been listening to the roar of the Paunacussing Creek grow louder by the hour. It runs right past their house across Fleecydale Road in Lumberville, and they always hear its noisy babbling when the windows are open in the summertime. But now that playful noise has built into a threatening roar. They begin to think it will leave its banks and start up toward their home, not knowing it's already done that and more, just upstream in Carversville.

Meanwhile, the Paunacussing is carrying all the Carversville debris downstream. The solid masses being thrown ahead of the crest are acting like crude snowplows, slamming into any obstacles and knocking them out. When this freewheeling blender reaches the area a hundred yards above the Tinsmans' house, it encounters the earth-and-stone dam built years before to provide water power for the old sawmill in the family's lumberyard.

Within seconds, the churning mass of debris chews a breach in the dam. Fortified with this new wreckage, it continues pushing ahead toward the Delaware. The Tinsmans have heard the commotion and are now out on their porch, waiting to see what's coming downstream. In the beams of their flashlights and porch light is an unlikely sight. Huge trees, boulders, logs, and other flotsam whoosh by, bucking on the crest of gigantic waves in the usually placid channel.

The Tinsmans watch in disbelief as the towering mass of debris knocks loudly against the bridge on River Road. Then the trees fall backward, dragged beneath the span and down to the broadened expanse of the river by the relentless, overpowering current. Before it's all over, the creek banks will be torn away and twelve families will have to evacuate their homes.

Concerned that their uphill neighbors might not know what's happening, the Tinsmans go next door to warn them. The neighbors say they're worried about their fuel oil tank in the basement. It's only half full, and they're concerned that if the basement fills with water, it will float the tank and spill the strong-smelling, flammable oil everywhere. Bill suggests they pump it full of water to keep it from floating, and that's what they do.

After returning home, Bill receives a phone call from a friend in the lumber business up in Belvidere. His friend tells him the river's getting very high there, that they've already had to rescue the island cottagers, and now they're expecting the Delaware to overflow its banks. He thinks Bill should call the Bridge commission to get the latest scoop, in case they're expecting flooding down his way. Maybe he can also find out what's going on further upstream. Then he has to go, because they may be evacuated.

Remembering his father's stories of the 1903 Pumpkin Freshet and his own memories of the 1936 and 1942 floods, Bill taps the cradle buttons and dials the operator.

Get me the Bridge Commission at Belvidere, please, he says, picturing in his mind the old flood waterlines marked on the lumberyard office.

One moment, please, replies the weary-sounding operator.

She must be busy, Bill thinks. That's probably not good.

After a moment, the Belvidere Bridge guard comes on the line, and Bill tells him what his friend has said, asking if there are any other details.

It's going to be bad, the guard says. We just don't know how bad. A few disturbing reports have been coming in from the north for a few hours now. From what we're hearing, it looks like it could be the worst flood ever on the river, at least in recorded history. Definitely higher water than oh-three.

Bill thinks of those water lines again. *How much higher?*

Can't tell yet. Sorry. But we do know the Poconos have gotten a tremendous amount of rain.

Thanks, anyway.

Bill settles the phone back in its cradle, and turns to Sue.

We need to start moving things, he says.

Is it going to be that bad, really?

He said they don't know exactly how bad, but definitely higher than ot-three. Bill thinks of his employee, who had bought his brother Dan's house the year before. *I'm gonna call next door to tell them they better get moving, too.*

Sue surveys the downstairs, collecting valuables to take to the second floor, while Bill calls the neighbor. His entreaties are met with a snort. His employee doesn't believe the river will come up that high, and says they won't be moving anything. Bill reminds him of the watermarks at the yard, but the neighbor says they're so old, plus they're down on River Road. The river won't come up Fleecydale, he believes.

Bill tells him what they've just seen of the creek and reminds him that it will likely back up into their homes if the river gets too high, and that's just as bad. Still, his neighbor remains unconvinced, and tells Bill he's going to bed.

Bill shakes his head slowly as he hangs up. Well, there are some sensible folks around here, he thinks. They'll listen. He calls as many neighbors down along the river in Lumberville as he can think of. They need to know it's going to flood.

When he's done, he rounds up the boys to help him move the heavy furniture. It's going to be a long night.

Lloyd Graff, committee member of the Quakertown Boy Scouts Troop, arrives in Camp Pahaquarra about nine thirty. It's his turn to serve as a counselor tonight. The trip up from Sidney, New Jersey, has taken nearly twice as long as usual. As he had started up through the Water Gap, streams of water had been gushing from the rocks over the road. George Ellis, a camp director from the Clinton area, greets him and asks about his trip.

"It was like going through the Cave of the Winds under Niagara Falls in an automobile!" Lloyd replies. He tells about the rising water he'd seen on the way up, and the two men decide to alert the rest of the camp to potential flooding danger. The main part of the camp is above the Old Mine Road and considered out of danger. The archery range, craft shop, counselor's bunkhouse, and parade ground—including Bill Coleman's Adirondack shack—lie between the road and the river, an area the men now recognize as a floodplain.

Before Bill plays Taps to signal lights out, all campers and
counselors are informed of the possibility that they may be mobilized
during the night to help secure the camp from flooding. If anyone's
frightened, there's no indication. Most of the campers just think of it
as a continuation of the outdoors adventure that Paquarry is known
for. The counselors, however, don't get much sleep. They know
they're responsible for the safety of hundreds of boys, as well as the
buildings and equipment belonging to the camp.

In Canadensis, Dale Price is upset. He wants to go to a dance in
town, but his father insists he stay home to help clear the gravity pipe
in their basement. It has backed up, and now water is collecting there.
By the time they finish, it's too late for the dance, so his dad suggests
they drive around to see what the heavy rain is doing elsewhere.

They set out down Dutch Hill Road in their truck but can't
get through the water blocking Highway 290 into Canadensis.
They turn around and try the back way, through The Pines and
north toward Coveville.

They're able to get on 290, but high water covers that route
farther toward Canadensis, too. With no other options at that late
hour, they go home to bed. Tomorrow, they'll take the big new
dump truck out. It's heavy and has lots of ground clearance. They're
sure to have more luck then.

Meanwhile, John "Jake" Sengel is enjoying his bachelor party in
Buck Hill Falls. He and four buddies are well into a hot hand of poker
when they hear the Buck Hill fire whistle. One of the young men,
Whit Schleiker, is a volunteer firefighter, so the game breaks up as he
leaves. As they shut the door, the guys hear cellar windows crashing
open and water pouring in. They had known it was raining all day but
hadn't realized it was becoming dangerous.

The phone rings. It's Whit, saying the highway bridge in
Canadensis has been washed out. They can't believe it. That bridge is
solid concrete, and well above the waterline. They decide to go see
for themselves.

Piling into Jake's 1932 Model A Ford, they drive down the Old
Canadensis Hill. As they near the bottom, they're surprised to find
water up to the steps at St. Ann's Catholic Church. What they'd be

even more surprised to see, if it weren't so dark, is the Brodhead Creek starting to rip out homes along its east bank.

Driving on a bit farther, they're stopped in front of Hugh Talmadge's log home by water coming through the floorboards. The guys get out of the car, but decide not to try pushing it backwards up the hill. One of them can't swim, and the water's coming up rapidly. Jake decides to abandon the car. His friends give Jake their good wishes for the wedding, and split up to walk home in the drenching downpour. Jake wonders how his bride-to-be is faring, but by the time he finally gets home, it will be too late to call.

As Jake trudges up the hill, all he can hear is the pounding of the rain on the road and swishing through the trees, and the roaring of the Brodhead Creek below. The rush of volume from the fishing dams crumbling upstream reaches Canadensis. It swells the already-high creek into a mass of roiling whitewater, but Jake is too far away to hear it begin tearing out the homes along Main Street.

Farther south, at Paradise Falls, the Stielau girls and their mother have received several visits from Harold Bates over the course of the day. The mountain runoff has become excessive, and he realizes there might be trouble with flooding and perhaps even mudslides. He checks in every so often to make sure they're okay, since Edward and Carolyn aren't expected to arrive until later.

Harold advises Lydia to run the bathtub full of water in case they lose power and can't pump any later. She does so, and not long afterward, the power does go out. Lydia's glad she followed Harold's advice, but what's that roaring she hears out back now? She finds a flashlight and goes to investigate.

To her astonishment, she sees a free-flowing cascade coursing down the slope behind the cottage. It's a regular waterfall emptying into the yard just past the building, and she immediately becomes concerned that it might undermine the foundation. Just five feet two, Lydia's no athlete, but her adrenaline begins to pump. She has two young girls to protect, and she's going to do what she can.

She begins searching around for large rocks, and Ruth and Edna watch from inside as her flashlight moves swiftly about the backyard. They are amazed to see her lifting huge rocks and carrying them to the middle of the yard, where she heaves them on top of one another. After a while, she has built up quite a barrier between the building and the water washing off the slope. She surveys her work, running the flashlight beam over the pile until she's satisfied it will serve its purpose.

Harold Bates has heard the roaring, too, and the girls see the beam from his flashlight come down the road just as Lydia is walking back to the cottage. He accompanies her inside, where he can see she's drenched and exhausted.

…must stay inside now, the girls hear him saying as he and Lydia come through the door, dripping. *It's dark and there are things being washed down the mountain. It's too dangerous!*

Ruth sees her mother's face, and knows the situation has become serious. Lydia promises Mr. Bates that they will stay put for the night, not to worry.

Aw, Mom! complains Edna, already dressed up for the "Halloween in Summer" party being held about a mile up the mountain tonight. *What about the party?*

Honey, I'm sorry, Lydia says, *but Mr. Bates is right. It's too dangerous to be out walking or even driving in this. You have no idea what might wash down on you. I'll be surprised if they're still even having the party, really.*

Lydia thanks Harold as he leaves and towels herself off. *Well girls,* she says, *I suppose we need to scout up some candles and make ourselves comfortable.*

At Camp Davis, the windows have all been opened now, in an attempt to get some fresh air circulating into the packed house. Irene Weber looks out the front window of the Winter House around nine thirty. Still no sign of the boys. In the house lights, she can see the water outside is up to the fenders of her 1948 Chrysler sedan, and mentions it to some of the others. But nobody is yet truly alarmed, because surely, if something were really wrong, they'd have heard from Mr. Hartig, whose cabin is situated at about the same elevation as the Winter House.

Just then, the door opens and the Hartigs come through, along with the Kochs. Julia Koch has brought her two boys, Mike and Frank McCaffery. Now it's clear to everyone that they are all in real danger.

Mr. Hartig says nothing, but strides to the rear of the house and presses his face to a window. He sees the lights on at the Polly cabin, but nowhere else. The storm must have knocked out a power line. But wait…

He puzzles for a moment, then asks if everyone in the room turned off their lights when they left their cabins. Jennie Johnson says she did, but everyone else looks kind of sheepish. Mr. Hartig looks back out the window, then back to the group.

We're all on the same electrical circuit here in camp, he says. *I see Mrs. Polly's lights, but no one else's.* He pauses. *It's a good thing you all came up here, because I think your places have washed away.*

There is a stunned silence, which Irene breaks with the news that her car is now covered up to the windshield, and that water is now washing over the front stoop. There are a few frightened noises from some children, while others are too young to comprehend their predicament.

Mr. Hartig takes his new flashlight out onto the stoop. He sees cars continuing to cross the highway bridge to Route 290, and he yells to them. He flips on the SOS beacon and waves his light to attract attention. Even if they can see it, they won't be able to hear him over the din created by the rushing water below. He realizes his efforts are likely in vain.

He can't see over to Pinebrook, less than a quarter-mile away. He supposes it has also been flooded, though it's on higher ground and on the mainland. He wonders if anyone there is aware of what's going on at Davis Cabins.

Pinebrook is indeed flooding, at the semi-circle of cottages near the creek. Their residents have abandoned them to the rising water. Most of them have moved to other accommodations and gone to bed. Even if it wasn't pitch dark outside, they wouldn't be able to see past the foliage screen over the road to Camp Davis, anyway. They don't have any idea what's going on across the creek.

However, three members of the Youth on the March Quartet have walked back to see how the farmhouse where they stay is faring. The young men are watching the normally twenty-foot-wide Brodhead Creek grow into a river three hundred yards across. It has already washed over the ends of the steel bridge, and they marvel at its power as it yanks trees from their roots and sends boulders hurtling past.

The crashing is tremendous, like that of a waterfall. Still, the lights glow in the buildings of Camp Davis, which they can see has now become an island. They don't see Henry Hartig's signal, since he's on a side of the house facing away from them. They think the inhabitants must be safe, since the lights are still on.

Those inhabitants listen anxiously as Irene Weber scans the radio dial seeking weather news. The announcer isn't reporting anything unusual, much to the group's relief. It seems the rain has stopped for good.

Julia Koch says she's grateful for this refuge in a house of the Lord, and perhaps a prayer of thanksgiving is in order. Everyone bows their heads, and Julia offers up a brief but heartfelt prayer. After "Amen," the group seems to come closer together.

Nancy Johnson suggests they sing to pass the time until the water goes down. She leads the children in "Let Your Light Shine," and afterward the adults join in. The familiar refrains of "My Lord Knows the Way Through the Wilderness" soon take the edge off the room.

Halfway through the hymn, Irene Weber looks over and sees water creeping across the floorboards from beneath the door. Hoping it'll stop. she says nothing to avoid alarming the children.

Only about a hundred yards upstream from Camp Davis, the Analomink classification yards of the Delaware, Lackawanna & Western Railroad are also being inundated. A freight locomotive crew has misjudged the Brodhead, too, and missed their chance to get to safety. Now, they just have to hope that the slightly higher rise of the railroad right-of-way will be enough to keep them above the surging current. Trapped inside their engine, they are subject to the terrifying clank of heavy objects smashing against its metal sides, and being rocked by the forceful current.

The nine cars of the DL&W's Train 5 are sitting with its load of passengers at the Cresco station by eight p.m. She had left Hoboken on her daily commuter run at a quarter to five and was past Cresco around a quarter past seven. The crew had been told to proceed with much caution, because of several potential washout areas. Sure enough, when they were about a quarter-mile past Devil's Hole, the engineer spotted a slide on the tracks ahead. He had backed the train up until it was sitting on the tracks just below the home of Forrest Evans, a fire inspector for the Pennsylvania Department of Forests and Waters.

In the flat, waning light, Evans had seen the train there. Just before, he had evacuated his sick wife and their dogs from their home, believing it might also be buried in a mudslide. He had seen that the earthen embankment beneath the Devil's Hole tracks looked like it might give way any moment.

Forrest had run down the hill, yelling at the engineer to back the train all the way to the station, because if they waited, they might not make it over Devil's Cut. The engineer had told him the conductor was walking back that way to check the situation, but Forrest knew there wasn't time. He had jumped into his Jeep and flown down the sodden road until he found the conductor, to whom he repeated the warning.

The conductor had run back to the train and ordered the engineer to back the train up to Cresco station immediately. He did so, and moments later, the expected washout occurred. Now the DL&W No. 5 is taking its chances sitting there, where at least they have access to a telegraph and automobile service if the situation becomes threatening.

Some of the two hundred-fifty riders, already restless and wanting to get home on a Thursday evening, question the necessity of such a drastic move. Conductors and stewards pass through the cars, explaining that it is being made for their safety. Most people don't quibble after being assured that the railroad is making arrangements to have the passengers bussed back to Scranton.

When the train arrives back at Cresco, railroad staff breathes a sigh of relief. Not long afterward, though, they must deliver yet more unwelcome news to their riders. The buses sent by management will not be arriving this evening. Too many roads and bridges have been washed out, and they can't reach the now-isolated Pocono outpost. However, they are assured, the train has plenty of fuel and food, enough to keep them comfortable for several days, if necessary.

Passengers are not told, however, what railroad officials already know about what's going on in Scranton: that they are actually safer sitting on the train track in Cresco than they might be in their own living rooms.

Number 44 had pulled out of Scranton with ninety people on board at seven o'clock, when the Roaring Brook's rampage was already in progress. The two coaches, three mail cars, and six milk cars had barely made it to Tobyhanna station when reports of washouts in both directions mandated an indefinite layover for her passengers and crew. It's a nervous time for railroad officials. They now have nearly four hundred people stranded along mountainous passes known for washouts and mudslides, in the dark of night during the worst flooding conditions anyone can recall.

Where the Brodhead empties into the Delaware River at the Water Gap lies Shawnee Island. Across the channel on the New Jersey side, the Binnekill River also empties into the river. All day long, cottagers on the island's south side have been watching the river rise, wondering if perhaps they should abandon their homes. By ten p.m., it's too late to go even if they want to: The water has become too turbulent to cross.

For an hour, the frightened cottage vacationers watch as the two creeks gush relentlessly into the Delaware. Though it's dark, surrounding house and yard lights reflect off the water's surface to reveal movement. Whitewater on the churning areas is also plainly visible in the night.

The rain has stopped, and the sky begins to clear. Without warning, the frothing current suddenly smoothes and the water becomes placid as a mountain lake. Huddled on the island's point, the campers can hardly believe what they see: The Delaware is flowing backwards!

The two tributaries have temporarily cancelled each other out. The force of their charging currents colliding has thrown up a liquid ridge across the river, interrupting its flows and forcing its water back upstream.

It's nothing short of a miracle, and the campers don't question it. They load their fishing boats with as many as can be safely carried and row across to the Pennsylvania mainland. It takes them eight trips, rowing madly, to offload everyone, but they manage to do it. They pull their boats up away from the water and lean exhausted on their oars, watching the unbelievable phenomenon as it continues.

Then, just as quickly as it had formed, the liquid ridge shrinks back into the river's channel, as critical mass shifts with the drop in new volume. The Delaware's current once again switches back to its usual direction. The volume that has collected behind the obstruction joins the already swollen river, and within minutes, Shawnee Island disappears completely beneath the black water.

Worlds Wash Away

Thursday, August 18, 1955
10:00 p.m. to 10:30 p.m.

In Newtown, Col. Heritage is awakened by a telephone call from State Civil Defense director Robert Gerstell. Camps on the islands near Erwinna are reporting an unusual rise on the Delaware River. Nobody really understands it, as the middle river area has only received an average of five or six inches of rain. It's a lot, but not enough to cause such a rise. Regardless, if it continues, several hundred children may be in grave danger.

Gerstell instructs the colonel to open up the Bucks County CD headquarters immediately and begin planning to evacuate the children. As he hangs up, Col. Heritage realizes the situation may have an added wrinkle. He's been keeping an eye on the Neshaminy all evening, and believes he may have trouble getting back to Doylestown. A quick trip down the road confirms this belief. As he turns to go back to the house, he's already formulating a plan to make the most of his single telephone line in coordinating the rescues.

His wife is waiting at the door, and she knows from the look on his face that they are trapped by the wild Neshaminy. She begins thinking of their friends and neighbors, but her husband tells her of the more pressing problem of the children on the islands of the Delaware. She realizes it will be a very long night.

I'll put on some coffee, she says.

Down the creek at the Spring Garden Mill, the miller and his wife are awakened by someone knocking. They sit up groggily, trying to orient themselves. The miller swings his legs over the side of the bed to put on his slippers, but instead of feeling soft, warm sheepskin, his feet hit a cool floor covered in several inches of water.

When his wife hears the splash, she looks at him, astounded. Both of them are now aware of the sound of rushing water outside, and they go to the window to look out. Even in the dark of night, they can see the whitewater rushing past, only a foot or so below the sill.

She screams in shock and fear, and in a shaky voice asks him what they'll do. He tries to calm her as she begins to cry. He tells her they'll have to go to the attic and just hope the Neshaminy doesn't get much higher. They both realize that it wasn't someone knocking at the door that woke them, but the sound of their furniture—now afloat—bumping against the kitchen ceiling below.

They have no flashlight, but the miller does manage to find a candle in a drawer in one of the other upstairs rooms. They take the quilt and pillows off the bed and trudge up the stairs to the attic. The smell of ancient dust and the scuttling of small creatures in dark corners frighten and unsettle his wife and she can't go to sleep, even in the comfortable chair they've brought up with them.

All night long, she is consumed with fear. She sits waiting for the foundation to cave in and the house to collapse. She vows to her husband over and over that, if they make it through this, she will never set foot in the house again, because she'll never feel safe from the water.

With water now washing over the bridge, the LeCropane girls are unable to get back across to Camp Davis after the service. Carl Van Buskirk, a Pinebrook staffer, offers them a ride, since he's on his way home to the old Gish farm on the East Stroudsburg side of the creek. They arrive in Stroudsburg only to find a long line of cars waiting to cross the State Bridge. It's pouring, thundering, and lightning. Electrical transformers pop, causing a bluish light show in the night sky. Soon, Carl has had enough. He turns around, pulling out of the line to try another crossing.

They start back north, pulling the vehicle up to and trying to cross a few smaller bridges, with no luck. They then make an attempt at the Stokes Mill Bridge, but still can't get across. There's no one blocking this span, but Mr. Van Buskirk can see in the light of his headlights that the water is too high. Perhaps if he didn't have three children in the back seat, he might try, but it's just too dangerous. Out of options, they return to Pinebrook.

Just to the northwest, the Lackawaxen River is already licking away at the tracks of the Erie Railroad's freight marshalling yard at Hawley. About a football field away, Middle Creek is scouring its banks, soon to eat into the foundation of the hardware store and chew the back corner off the white-tiled Texaco station.

One of the town's merchants is so awestruck by the sight that he runs for his camera. To get the best angle, he walks out onto the banks upstream of the hardware store. So intent is he on getting the shot, he doesn't notice the ground being washed away beneath his feet. Before he can do anything about it, he is sinking into the ground, which quickly liquifies and carries him tumbling sideways into the swift water. Too startled even to drop the camera, he's still clutching it as he disappears into the current.

A fellow storeowner has seen the whole thing, which happened so quickly he could do nothing about it. He's still standing in stunned

Middle Creek washes out its bridge in downtown Hawley as 55-year-old William Merz takes photos. The bank he stands on is washed out from beneath him, carrying him to his death. Two would-be rescuers are also washed away, but manage to save themselves by getting to shore. — *Courtesy Scranton Time-Tribune*

shock when, not too much later, the bridge also crumbles and follows his colleague downstream.

Over in the Eddy section of town, an unfortunate driver becomes trapped in his car when Main Street is overtaken by water. He struggles to open his door, but can't overcome the force of the tide surging against it. The water pours in from behind the dashboard, and he tries frantically to open one of the other doors, but the cab quickly fills. He tries kicking the glass out of the windshield, but can't get enough force going through the water. The last thing he's aware of as he's clawing at the door handle is a floating sensation. He ceases to struggle.

Across the Wayne County line, the Lackawaxen is fed by the Dyberry Creek at the county seat in Honesdale. The flood of 1942 had done a real number on this city, killing twenty-three people. It had been incentive enough for the area to invest a half-million dollars in flood control measures, which have just recently been completed. Today's rains will be the first real test of their effectiveness.

The precautions do manage to arrest the worst potential damage, but with that amount of rainfall, there is no way to prevent the two major waterways from rising where they meet. They hurl themselves against their banks like something alive. They become especially violent when they encounter the concrete-and-stone abutments that rise up along industrialized areas.

Carrying debris along with them, they begin battering these abutments beneath the Cloverleaf-Freeland Company plant. Though the supports hold out as long as possible, they eventually give way to the relentless pounding, scraping and gouging. With no solid foundation, it's only a matter of time before the soil beneath the building gives way in a whoosh of air. For a few moments, sill plates, beams, floorboards, and everything sitting on them hang out into empty space over the surging torrent.

Then, above the water's roar, a tremendous groaning and snapping of timbers is followed by multiple crashes and explosions, as the facility's boiler room collapses into the melee below. When the super-heated boilers hit the cool water, their huge cast iron shells crack and split. Plumbing pipes crumple and bend, forced by the water to wrap around poles in their way as they're pushed downstream. The boilers hiss and shriek, sighing a final, bubbling gasp as they disappear beneath the waves.

Some of the debris will get hung up on obstructions in the channel. Other fragments will move on downstream. One of the main bridges will come within inches of being breached. Parts of Main Street and the lower end of town will be covered with several inches of water and mud by morning. But this time Honesdale is lucky: no one will die.

Farther northwest, the Lackawaxen meets the Lackawanna River at Carbondale, in the heart of Pennsylvania's anthracite coal region. On this day, anywhere there is a confluence of waters in northeastern Pennsylvania is a flood waiting to happen, and it's no different in Carbondale. What is peculiar about this area is the color of the waters rushing by.

This city sits atop many abandoned mineshafts and drill holes. When they fill up with storm runoff, the water leaches off into nearby streams and rivers. It carries with it metals and minerals from leftover coal and slag heaps.

A chemical reaction to this iron-rich content causes oxidation, which appears as yellow or orangeish tinges on the surface, and rolls along in ribbons within the current. During still water, it can collect on rocks and other stationary surfaces, and form foamy slicks on top of the water, which old-timers refer to as "yellowboy."

When the sun comes up over Carbondale on Friday, it will reveal streets, houses and buildings wallowing in water the color, in places, of fermented orange juice.

Back on Ash Street in Scranton, the Highfields have been upstairs since water started seeping in under the door. Surely, they'd thought, it can't keep rising. But it has kept rising, and now the house is surrounded by raging water. They have waited too long to leave.

Terrified, they flinch every time something hits the house. They know when it's something large not just by the louder thud it makes, but also by the vibration they feel along the floorboards. Chunks of plaster have begun falling from the walls and ceilings. Things are

More than 50 people were trapped when even the amphibious Army "Duck" vehicle they were being evacuated in was overcome by the rising water in Scranton's South Side Flats area. Their National Guard escorts kept watch while they waited for the arrival of the fire department. When firefighters arrived with their aerial ladder truck, they quickly went into action to help the stranded passengers across it to safety. Though there were no human casualties, the ladder was severely damaged.

Many people stranded in their homes were rescued by a makeshift navy of rowboats and motorboats piloted by friends, family, and complete strangers. Below, a young man comforts an elderly woman whose home is being washed away as he watches.

– *Courtesy Scranton Times-Tribune*

being knocked from shelves and dishes rattle in the cupboards. Their home can no longer keep them safe.

There's only one thing to do, thinks Elliott. They need to get out to the roof, where someone will see them and they can signal for help. He grabs Ella's hand and leads her to the bedroom window overlooking the front porch roof. As he begins opening the window, she suddenly understands, and lets out a choked whimper of fear. Elliott throws up the sash and takes her hand.

Ella gives him a pained look as she sits on the sill. Trying to remain modest, she holds her dress tight against her trembling legs and swings them over the sill to the shingles. She runs her shoes across the granular surface before standing up. It's wet, and she's afraid she'll slip off.

Stay near the wall, he tells her, *and hold on. I'm right behind you.*

Meanwhile, down near Washington Avenue, more than fifty would-be evacuees are marooned. They had been escorted from their neighborhood in an amphibious DUKW—or "duck"—vehicle, driven by Marine Corps Reservists of the Sixth Truck Company. When it had turned left onto River Street in front of Bill's Lunch, even all their weight on the heavy truck hadn't provided enough friction to overcome the lift of several feet of swiftly moving water.

They feel themselves floating toward the brick building. Next thing they know, the duck wheels are pinned against the curb. The back of the vehicle jams against a mailbox. They won't be going anywhere else.

The driver radios his dispatcher, and tense moments click by until an aerial ladder truck arrives from the city fire department. The firemen extend the ladder across the roiling current, and one of them crosses to the duck. One at a time, he holds small children in one arm and the side rails with the other. He carefully negotiates each step. Trying not to become mesmerized by the water churning just feet below, he makes himself concentrate on making each step. He looks at the ladder rungs. Only the rungs.

He and his colleagues take turns bringing the children across, then escort the women. Finally, the men come across on their own. Crouched in a now-familiar waddle, they hope the ladder will hold out. Everyone can hear it creaking under the stress of a job it was not designed to do. As the last man steps off, there is a brief and subdued cheer before the fire truck takes off with its precious new cargo and a badly damaged ladder.

It will be none too soon—the area will quickly be completely awash.

East of town, past the Number Seven Reservoir of the Scranton-Springbrook Water Service Company, there are several streams, usually so nondescript they don't even have names. But tonight, one of them is emerging from obscurity as it tears down the embankment toward Roaring Brook. On its way, it gouges out an area fifty feet wide and twenty feet deep beneath the DL&W tracks.

Gravity drops the now unsupported steel rails of all three DL&W lines into the raging cataract, along with millions of tons of heavy square ties and ballast from the rail bed. This debris washes down into the main channel of the brook.

Farther upstream, past the curve beneath the Erie maintenance shops, the same runoff volume that gave the no-name stream its impetus now brings Roaring Brook fully to life. Its waters swell to the very tops of the bank; thirty and forty feet up, then over.

The force of it first kidnaps the train that was to deliver the maintenance-of-way crane, smashing its cars into kindling. Then the ravenous creek chews at the earth beneath the crane. There is a great clanking and moaning of failing steel as the behemoth machine succumbs to its own massive weight, collapsing into the water. Finally, the arm of water grabs the crane itself, pushing it a hundred yards while spinning it completely around in a tortured, ungainly pirouette. Finally, it dashes the crane against one of the shop buildings, where it crumples in defeat. The surge recedes.

The resulting debris now jams up along the embankments and under the DL&W box culvert at the curve. It swirls in a mad eddy for some moments, collecting more bulk until one log or rock or railroad tie too many tips the balance. Now, the entire mess heads downstream, riding high atop the forty-foot wall of water. It's headed straight for the lower Petersburg section and the turn into Little England.

In the dark, the Highfields can't see it coming, but they hear it; a terrifying cacophony of low rumble and constant grinding, punctuated by the pitched screech of metal scraping metal. Ella, clutching Elliott's arm, turns to face him. She's crying silently, and her legs begin to buckle. She stiffens them so she won't collapse.

140

Elliott doesn't know what's headed their way, but he knows it isn't good.

Hold on! he yells.

He pulls her toward the still-open window. Now frozen with fear, she won't move. He pulls again, this time as hard as he can. The menacing sound is dangerously close. Still, she doesn't budge. She turns her face away from the direction of the noise toward Elliott. She's so close that, even in the dark, he sees the abject terror in her wide eyes.

Suddenly, a whoosh and rapid gurgling draw his attention. He flicks his gaze to white foam breaking around the base of something on the crest. Two stories above and behind Ella's head, a jagged debris pile bigger than their house is bearing down right on them.

Reflexes kick in. With a last, desperate push, he flattens Ella against the front of the house with his body, shielding her beneath the eave as best he can. A horrible racket fills his ears as the black mass hits them like a gigantic, wet avalanche. In what feels like slow motion, it peels him away from her, pushing him like a rag doll across the roof ahead of it. Ella's being pushed directly behind him, and he reaches out to grab her with one hand as he catches the edge of the roof with the other.

He manages to jam his arm into the gutter and it somehow wedges him just tightly enough to let his body move aside, allowing the majority of the impact's force to pass him by. But Ella's not so lucky. The last Elliott sees of her are the whites of her eyes, and her mouth agape in a silent scream as she's torn from his grasp and becomes lost among the churning jumble of crushing debris.

The impact tears away the front of the house and wrenches it off its foundation. Elliott clings to the gutter, sputtering and hyperventilating. Now he spins slowly about in the darkness, a passenger on a drunken merry-go-round. Feeling the building bump up against something solid, he finally lets go, dropping onto a garage roof.

The tremendous whooshing and screeching continues on downstream, dulling with distance. He crouches, listening to what's left of his house creaking as it slips beneath the water's surface. He strains to see Charlie Schane's house on Richter Avenue, which had been square in the path of the churning bulldozer. Much of it is simply gone. He wonders about Charlie and his family.

Elliott can't see any farther in the dark. For the rest of the night, he calls Ella's name. There is no reply.

Like a mammoth, waterborne scouring pad, the mass of wreckage continues down the Roaring Brook into Scranton's south side flats, ripping away the walls of thirty-two homes and washing away their foundations. Outlying areas all around the city—Duryea, Moosic, Old Forge—are overrun by water, which washes out roads and tears out bridges. The waterways that had built the city and its industries are now tearing it down—brick by brick, board by board, rail by rail.

In the Winter House at Camp Davis, it has begun raining again. Henry Hartig backs slowly away from the window. His face is pale, and his wife, Lillian, thinks he might be shaking a little.

Henry, what...?

The lights in Mrs. Polly's cabin, he says quietly. *They're not there anymore.*

He doesn't look at her, or anyone else. The lights are still on in the Winter House, so it's not a power outage, and he can't believe the nine people inside the Polly cabin would willingly turn theirs out. That place is gone, he thinks, with all of them in it. He feels ill. All he can do is remember his earlier scoffing at the suggestion that the camp was in any kind of danger. And now, because he reassured them about staying, they really are.

Lillian frets out loud, wondering about the safety of their nieces and their friend, and about the Johnson and Christensen boys. She begins to pray.

Everyone becomes aware of things bumping about outside. Chris Lawyer, Irene's brother-in-law, looks down at the thin ribbon of water she's already seen snaking its way under the door and across the floor.

It's coming in, he reports. *We should go to the attic.*

It's the thing nobody wants to hear. It's dark up there, and the air is even more stifling than down here. Worst of all, it's their last resort. There is no higher place to climb than the attic. What has been a comforting option now looms as a chilling last resort.

The adults gather the children together, some of whom start crying. There are attempts to comfort them, but the little ones sense their elders' anxiety. One of the older boys ascends the drop-down ladder first with a flashlight, followed by the rest of the children. The adults come up last.

Edna Winfield is the last up the stairs, carrying the box of candles and matches. She hands them out. Some are small votives, and they're placed carefully around the stuffy attic. Some are the kind used for candlelight services, with cardboard drip catchers around the base so you can hold them. Their light, however small, is comforting, and Irene Weber thanks Edna as she takes one. Little Rowan and his sister Karen are helping their mother pass out candles, and Irene thinks their faces look angelic in the flickering light.

Henry pulls boards away from the small window and pokes his head out, pulling great lungfuls of fresh air. He grabs his flashlight and again flicks on the SOS flashing beacon, waving it in Pinebrook's direction.

Help! he yells. *Please help us!*

But there's no one outside now at Pinebrook, and nobody sees the signal light or hears Henry's pleas.

The attic group does the only thing they can think of to keep their hopes up and their minds off the frightening situation. They sing, "I've Got a Mansion Over the Hilltop," a Pinebrook favorite.

By the time the song ends, it's clear that no one has been able to respond to Mr. Hartig's SOS signals. The water's roar is simply too loud for anyone to hear above it. The boys haven't returned, and God knows what's happened to them. Likely, no one can get across the raging current. The trapped people send a prayer of intercession, asking God to keep them safe. A child starts to cry, but Mrs. Winfield comforts her.

That's okay, honey. Don't worry. It won't get higher than the attic. Besides, the Pinebrook people know we're here. They'll help us.

The child sniffs, and stops crying. Everyone hears Edna's words and wants to believe them, but in the short time they've been here, the water has already risen halfway up the ladder. Fifty-six-year-old Mae Koch decides she's not taking any chances. She puts on an inner tube she's brought with her.

Louise Christensen leans over to Nancy Johnson, saying, "Maybe it wasn't such a good idea to come up here." Nancy says nothing, just looks at her.

Mr. Hartig, always such a comforting and authoritative presence, now sags against a wall stud, looking shrunken and resigned.

With thirty people respiring and the open window allowing in more humidity than fresh air, the attic becomes increasingly warm and the musty smell intensifies. Everyone sweats, the beads of perspiration on their foreheads and upper lips glistening in the candlelight. The smell of warm, not-so-clean bodies mixes with that of dust and something else, something unfamiliar. It is the smell of fear.

Terror in the Night

Thursday, August 18
10:30 p.m. to Midnight

At ten thirty in Bucks County, Col. Heritage contacts the Naval installation in Warrington about dispatching helicopters to airlift threatened campers on Treasure, Pennington, and Marshall Islands in the Delaware. They don't have any craft they can release, but believe Lakehurst Naval Station in New Jersey does. Col. Heritage makes them aware of his single available telephone line, and they do what they can to relieve traffic for him by agreeing to relay the emergency request to Lakehurst. They will also be supplying other needed equipment, such as life rafts, life vests, rope, and as much manpower as necessary.

Though what's left of Hurricane Diane has lost most of its tropical characteristics and her eye has long since fallen in on itself, her rain clouds are still concentrated in typical hurricane bands, circulating slowly about Mt. Pocono. The rain has been on again-off again just four miles north in Analomink, but it has been pouring madly since ten p.m. in the Stroudsburgs. The rain no longer comes in drops but in huge, fat pellets that explode on every surface.

Eleven-year-old Joanne Shutt of Chatham, New York, is vacationing with her family in Henryville. She has talked her mother into driving her, her sisters Barbara and Linda, and their friend, Mary Lou Lilius, into East Stroudsburg for the theater's late show, Henry Fonda's *Mr. Roberts.* Her mother is afraid of storms and hadn't wanted to make the trip, but a house full of antsy girls all day has gotten to her.

The thunder and rain are so loud that they make some of the dialogue hard to hear in the cinema, but the girls enjoy the movie just the same. They're discussing how much they liked it as they leave the theater. The rain is now practically machine-gunning the rapidly thinning crowd, and the group makes a mad dash for the car.

Once inside, they find the pounding on the roof unbelievable, and Mrs. Shutt is clearly shaken by the storm's ferocity. She can't wait to get back to Henryville. The girls can barely see out the windows for the dense rain curtain, and the windshield wipers are so ineffective against the deluge, it's as though they aren't even working.

As the car starts up toward Route 90 North, its passengers become aware that the traffic is just creeping along. It doesn't look like there are that many cars on the road, and they didn't see that many people leaving the theater, so they have a hard time understanding the cause of the slowdown. Finally, they see a policeman standing in the street, waving people off over the Interborough Bridge.

Mrs. Shutt's knuckles are white as she takes the big sedan over the iron span. She can see the waters of the Brodhead splashing not far below its deck. It makes her especially nervous that the traffic going over is thick and moving very slowly. The situation is beginning to seem perilous, and she wants to get off the thing.

When they finally make it to the other side, they learn that the Route 209 bridge up ahead over the Pocono Creek has been washed out, and that the creek is also running deeply over Route 611 past North Ninth Street. Mrs. Shutt realizes they won't be getting back to Henryville this evening, and tells the girls they'll have to spend the night at the Penn-Stroud Hotel.

The girls, having always seen the hotel's valet sign saying, "We'll park your horse or car while dining," think it will be fun. But with many others in the same predicament, there are no rooms available at the Penn-Stroud. They finally find accommodations down the block at the Indian Queen.

Emergency vehicles are roaming everywhere, and the group begins to realize that something may be seriously amiss. As they park their car, the lights of Stroudsburg go out all around them. Checking in, they are each given a candle to be able to find their way upstairs to their room. They look at each other in wonderment, and the beginnings of worry.

Once in the room, Mrs. Shutt expresses her concern that without power or telephones, they won't be able to inform Mary Lou's parents that she's safe with them but won't be coming home tonight. Everyone makes themselves as comfortable as possible, but they get little sleep with loud noises just outside and spotlights coming in through the windows all night. They spend a lot of time watching all the activity out the front window, having no idea of the horrors taking place just blocks away.

Ed Burnett, a staff writer for the *Easton Express*, has been at the movies in East Stroudsburg, too. He has lingered a bit longer after the show, talking with friends. By the time he gets on the road to head back to Stroudsburg, the Interborough (State) Bridge is already closed. He and his companion turn about and hurry to the paper mill bridge in Minisink Hills. They cross just as waves are beginning to break over the sides of it.

Once home, he watches McMichaels Creek rapidly rising at a rate of nearly a foot every fifteen minutes. He's awestruck to see the gentle streams he played in as a boy turning to deadly, destructive rivers.

Police are running through the streets, blowing their whistles to alert residents to the danger. One of them tells Ed that he could hear cries from treetops near the State Bridge as the water swirled up around them. The cop had also seen a man straddling the street sign at Washington and Brown Streets. Others would later report seeing the man get washed away from his precarious perch.

Harry Leida, an employee of Stroudsburg's Line Material Company and an amateur photographer, has been staying at the home of his fiancée, Joyce Hewitt, and her parents. They live on Cedar Drive, just off Dreher Avenue on Stroudsburg's southwest side. This evening, he is across the Brodhead Creek visiting his parents and his nephew, Fred, who is staying with them on King Street, on the far north side of East Stroudsburg.

Their house backs up to the tracks of the DL&W Railroad and lies between the Brodhead and one of its tributaries, Sambo Creek. By the time Harry is ready to return to Joyce's house, the water is already too high, and nobody is being allowed across the bridges, so he returns to his parents' for the night.

Earlier, Eugene Heller and his wife Virginia had been eating supper at their home just up the street from Harry's parents, when the phone rang. Virginia's mother, Mrs. Dan Avery, was frantic on the other end. Their boarder, Bill Fleming, was in distress, and she thought he was having a heart attack. Virginia tells her to call the ambulance and then call back. When she and Eugene don't receive another call by the end of their meal, she rings her mother, but the line is dead. Very strange.

The Hellers feel they should drive the three miles to her parents' home in the Day Street Flats section of East Stroudsburg to make sure everything is okay. Eugene decides to drive their new Oldsmobile, rather than their unreliable old Dodge, in the worsening weather.

Now, nearing their destination, the Hellers are stopped by a Civil Defense volunteer blocking the road with his Jeep. He informs them that the road is covered by the flooding Brodhead Creek and they won't be able to get through. Undaunted, Eugene parks the Olds around the corner on Lenox Street, where no water has yet reached. He and Virginia cut through an alley to walk to her parents' home.

They come to a dip in the road, and suddenly the water is up to their knees. Approaching the house, they can see why the phone line is dead. The water is coming up to the outside steps, and has probably taken out many other services, as well.

Sure enough, when they get inside, Mrs. Avery tells Virginia and Eugene that the basement is flooded, and Mr. Fleming has died. The couple stays to pay their respects, but Eugene nervously looks out the window at the rising water. He has just bought the Olds, and doesn't want to take any chances on it getting ruined by the flood-waters. He tells Virginia that he's just going to go move it quickly, and will be right back.

She, too, has seen the water coming up, and tells Eugene she wishes he wouldn't take any chances. He insists on going, and she begs him, using her pet name for him, to reconsider.

Toy, please don't go. That water is getting dangerous now.

Oh, come on, he says. *It's a brand new car, and I'm not about to let anything happen to it.*

His wife is clearly upset at the prospect of something happening to him while he's gone, and he puts his hands on her shoulders in a comforting gesture.

"It's not going to amount to anything, Virginia. I'll be right back!" He bounds down the steps and splashes into the water.

She watches as he sloshes away toward Lenox, until he disappears around the corner.

Over the bridge in East Stroudsburg, Libby Ace is working the second shift at the Holland Thread Company, called simply "the silk mill" by the majority of Stroudsburg area residents. The plant is located south of Brown Street and east of Washington, where the Brodhead Creek takes a decided swing to the east along the foot of the Minisink Hills. The DL&W railroad follows along the creek's northern banks, over a small feeder creek at the turn.

The mill's second-floor workers had gone home at eight o'clock, and everyone remaining is too busy working to look out into the darkness to see anything unusual. They can't know that South Stroudsburg Falls, lying below the twin towns on the Brodhead Creek near where Interstate 80 will run in the future, has collected debris flowing down from disaster areas up north. A spontaneous dam has formed, and it's backing up the creek's monstrous volume of water. The low-lying industrial flats are the first to be swallowed by the backup.

Suddenly, Libby looks up to see her husband and uncle, soaking wet, rush into her workstation. They demand of her, "What are you doing here?"

Incredulous, she retorts, "We're working here, what do you think?"

"Get out!" her husband says, skipping all pretense of manners. "There's a flood coming!"

Libby knows he's serious and doesn't wait for any further explanation. She and her coworkers scurry after the men to the parking lot. As they rush out the front door, the waters of Brodhead Creek swirl in through the rear.

They jump in their vehicles and scramble out of the parking lot, which is rapidly being overrun by the spreading water. They make it out of the lowlands of the Silk Mill Flats, past Libby's flooding house and just ahead of water deep enough to swamp their cars and trucks. So intent are they on making it to safety, and so loud is the rain on their roofs and windows, they barely notice the flurry of activity off to their left at the corner of Washington and Brown Streets. Many people are standing there and yelling, looking and gesturing toward the creek.

Directly to the north, just blocks off "The Island" where Sambo Creek feeds into the Brodhead near the high school, young Bob Herman is trying to get to sleep in the warm, humid night. His window is open, and he can hear the rain pouring down. But there's something else, a sound he recognizes but can't place because it's out of context. He can hear distant sirens—quite a few of them, actually—but that's not it.

Bob closes his eyes and listens hard. Now he's got it. It's an outdoors sound; running water, like a stream. Okay…

His eyes fly open. If it's what he thinks he's hearing, it's definitely *not* okay. He springs up and puts his face close to the window screen. When the Brodhead has high water, he can usually see it from here, but not hear it. The channel is about two hundred yards away. But in the flashes of lightning, he can see it now, right down to the white froth of its current, and he can definitely hear it.

The Brodhead is not its usual, placid self, nor even its bolder, high-water incarnation. It is now a full-fledged river, and it's raging. Its near edge, already way over its bank, has swallowed the blocks of Vine, Oakland, and Gold Streets. Bob runs downstairs to get a better look. From his front porch, he sees it has begun flowing over Walnut Street in front of his house.

He ducks back inside to put on his fishing hip boots. When Bob comes back outside, the creek has passed over the road and is running between the houses on his block. He notices it also creeping up on a pile of lumber being used in the construction of a house across the street. He runs over and begins dragging it to higher ground.

In the middle of the task, the lights go out throughout the neighborhood, and he runs back home for a flashlight. He runs back over with the light, balancing it on the pile so he can see. A strong young man, Bob doesn't take too long to move the pile, maybe fifteen minutes. As he's finishing up, the water reaches over his knees. His family's car arrives, plowing through the water on Walnut. His parents drive up with his older sister, Charlotte, whom they had picked up from her job at the Bell Telephone Company over in Stroudsburg.

His father pulls the car up as far as he can near the house, which sits on higher ground than those surrounding it. He tells Bob that they had made it over the state bridge just before it washed away. They had then heard there was someone still on it when it went. It had been a close call, and everyone is shaken up by the night's events.

He tells Bob he'll stay with the house, but wants him to go with his mother and Charlotte up the hill to a friend's house, near the high school athletic field. Bob wants to stay with his dad, but his father is adamant about not taking any chances with his son's life. So Bob obeys and follows his mom and sister, helping them through waist-deep water and up the hill.

The whole time they're walking, he sees raindrops sparkling in the beams of spotlights over toward Washington Street. He hears the sirens, but can't imagine there could be a fire in this incredible downpour. After making sure the women are safe at the neighbor's, Bob does what any fifteen-year-old boy would do in such a situation: He worries his mother half to death by setting off to find out what's going on. He won't be held back, but promises to be careful.

Just south of where Jake Sengel had left his car along Route 290 in Canadensis, the Philadelphia vacationers at Price's Cottages are settling in for the night. The bedrooms are all located toward the rear of the tiny buildings, which sit atop the banks of the Brodhead Creek. Though it's been raining steadily for hours, no one has even thought about the possibility of a flood.

Retirees Edward and Mary Lang have already turned in for the night when the creek builds to a towering rage. Suddenly, it slams into their cabin with the force of a speeding freight train. The back wall is gone in an instant. They never know what hits them as the floor drops out from beneath their bed and the remaining walls and roof collapse on top of them. Jolted from the comfort of their covers and tumbling backwards into the frenzied waters, they are immediately overcome. It happens so fast that most of the other vacationers at the resort, even if they realize something is wrong, don't have time to react.

A few have managed to evade the water, however. Harry and Helen White and their eight-year-old son, Joseph, have climbed atop the roof of one of the cottages at the bidding of Joe Driscoll. Joe has been staying on the roof with his wife, Irene, and their young son, Jimmy. Irene's brother, David Harmer, is also there with his wife, Violet, and their eleven-year-old daughter, Barbara.

At eight p.m., they had heard the raging water. Finding themselves nearly surrounded by the spreading creek, they'd had the presence of mind to find a stepladder and scurry onto the roof. They'd tried to call out warnings to the other cabins, but their voices had been drowned out by the pounding rain and thundering creek.

For three hours now, they have been watching, terrified, as the water has picked up more and larger debris, and gained in height and speed. Joe estimates the current is now flying along at about 45 miles per hour. They have just watched it take out the Langs' cabin, and are certain the older couple was inside. There is nothing they can do.

Suddenly, the flash of a chrome auto bumper catches Joe's eye, just before the rest of the vehicle smashes into the cabin beneath them. The roof, left without support, crumbles into the torrent. The corner where the Whites are huddled goes first. They grab onto each other as they slide into the churning cauldron of raging water and pulverizing boulders.

The Harmers are next to fall in. The Driscolls watch them struggle not to go under as their own perch collapses into the water. Arm-in-arm, they try to stay together. They're successful until a jagged section of the roof slams into them. Joe is knocked unconscious, and his arms go limp.

He regains consciousness about a hundred yards away from the cabin, the roof section pressing him against the limbs of a tree, into which his arm and leg are jammed. He works himself loose, then interlocks his fingers around a branch to keep from being swept away. Even at the top of the tree, the water is up to his shoulders. He looks around and calls out, but nobody answers. The Whites are gone, along with the Harmers. Worse, Irene and Jimmy are gone.

Like so many others that night, the last sound they hear will be the muffled gurgle of liquid death surging over them, rolling and pushing them down toward the dark, cold bottom of the creek. Then, silence. By morning, Price's won't have any guests left.

Jake Sengel's Model A Ford lies on its side in front of Hugh Talmadge's Canadensis home. Rubble left by the marauding Brodhead Creek covers everything in sight.
—Courtesy Barrett Township Historical Society

Just up Route 90, the Greentown Creek has continued backing up from being unable to empty into the over-full main branch. The usually quiet little creek has swollen to six and seven times its normal width. Its backwash, having already undermined the Route 90/507 highway bridge and dropped it into the water, is now engulfing three residences and the American Legion Post 859 headquarters building in Greentown.

Sixty-three-year-old John Phillips, his wife, Myrtle, sister Kate, teenage son Raymond, and mother-in-law Annie Gilpin are asleep in their farmhouse when it is washed away. The large, two-story structure comes to rest two hundred yards downstream. Only the attic windows and part of the roof will be showing when the water recedes.

The bodies of the women will be found inside, and John's body will later be recovered near the wreckage, buried in four feet of rock and sand. Ray will be the sole survivor, spending the night and some of the following morning clinging to a tall tree until being rescued by a canoeist from an area hotel.

153

Fifty-two-year-old Helen Morieko is also asleep in her son's house along the creek banks. He and his wife are working in Connecticut, and Helen's watching their four children, who range in age from six months to six years. As they slumber, the house is wrenched from its foundation by a gigantic whirlpool, spun about, then smashed to bits against the trees downstream. The violence of the motion hurls them all from their beds. Some will drown, others will be crushed to death by pieces of their own home. Their bodies will be found a short distance downstream from the wreckage.

The Smith family—Robert, his wife, Pearl, and their daughter, Barbara— are awake when they hear the creek beginning to beat their frame house apart. With no other options, they head for the attic. Within a few terrifying minutes, the dwelling is pulverized by the pounding water and boulders tumbling in it. Robert and Barbara manage to grab some of the boards from the wreckage after they're tossed into the water. They are swept along together for about half a mile, until the churning water spits them out on a small knoll, where they will spend a fearful, shaky night. Pearl's body will be found the next day among the debris pile left near the former site of the house.

Volunteers join Pennsylvania State Troopers in bringing bodies out of the wreckage of several homes that were washed away along Greentown Creek. Several families were drowned along this particular stretch of the creek. – Courtesy Scranton Times-Tribune

Their neighbor, farmer Rowland Carlin, will spend the next two nights atop his silo, from where he will hear his house, barn, and outbuildings being demolished and washed away. The water will also undermine the silo, dropping half of it into the torrent. Fortunately for Rowland, the side he is on will keep him safe until he's rescued Saturday morning.

Fellow farmer Charles Drolsbaugh, seventy-four, is spirited out of his bed in South Sterling by the main branch of the Wallenpaupack as it pummels his home into matchsticks. His body will be found a half-mile away on a neighbor's property early the next morning.

Down the valley in Newfoundland, fifteen-year-old Geraldine Miller, an employee of the Vindabona Hotel, is getting more than she bargained for on the evening shift. She hears the cries for help from twenty-two-year-old Mildred McNiece, who has lost her footing and slid into the errant creek waters while trying to walk to the hotel owner's house from her stranded auto. Mildred had separated from her sister, Marie Fosgreen, who has managed to catch the branch of a bush near water's edge. But Mildred is clinging to some trees near the old Moravian cemetery. She can't hang on much longer under the constant barrage of water and rocks being hurled at her by the swollen creek.

Geraldine finds a rope and, tying it about her waist, begins swimming toward the trapped woman. But the rope is too short, and she must return to get a longer one. She finally reaches the New Jersey woman, honing in on her cries in the blackness. In a relay of catching bush branches jutting from the water and shinnying along the rope, they both finally reach the safety of the hotel three hours later.

In downtown Newfoundland, the Schafers and Robackers are ankle-deep in water. They continue carrying furniture and other valuables upstairs. By eleven p.m., they're wading in knee-deep water, and decide to give up the moving effort.

They all go up to the Schafers' apartment to rest and monitor the situation. Without electricity, they can't get any weather reports, but they can hear rain pounding on the roof with awful fury. The water downstairs has risen to the third step, and they begin hearing strange bumping and thumping noises both inside and outside the house.

They go to a window and shine a flashlight toward the ground. All they can see is an ocean of water. Large and small objects of every description are shooting by. They can distinguish some of these as trees and parts of buildings.

They wonder aloud about how the rest of the village is faring. It's clear that everyone is cut off from everyone else. June asks Bob about their home's foundation. His reply is not reassuring. He says it's just basically a pile of rocks, as the custom of the building period dictated. The house itself is sturdy and well-built, but Bob is privately concerned that the foundation could give way, and that the house might become waterborne itself if that happens.

Back in Port Jervis, the river rises to such a height that the fire siren is sounded at 10:30 to round up department volunteers. They need to stand by for emergency rescues. Already, the Neversink is smashing into houses in Ellenville, just twenty-five miles to the north in Ulster County. Roiling waters are forcing the evacuation of fifty homes and the closure of eight of the tiny town's streets.

Water is pouring down off the slopes of the Catskills and washing out the tracks of the Erie Railroad west of the city, forcing a shutdown of this major rail center. Route 6, the primary auto traffic artery through town, is taking a pounding from three different landslides.

Within hours, Mayor James Cole will declare a state of emergency and turn the city over to Civil Defense authorities.

Bob Herman walks the few blocks downhill to Washington Avenue in East Stroudsburg but finds the water so high he can't go much farther on his own. He sets out for the firehouse to see if he can be of any help there. In no position to turn down any aid, the firemen tell him to accompany a boatload of volunteers to help rescue people being washed down the creek. Bob can hardly believe this is really happening as he jumps in and they take off.

The water, though only a foot or two deep, is running far too swiftly for their small engine to negotiate. To their shock, the current overpowers the boat, turning it sideways and immediately swamping it. The volunteers all make it back to high ground, but with a bad

– Historic travel map

scare and a new respect for the incredible power of that water. It's a scene that would be repeated six more times in the immediate vicinity that night. With luck on their side, none of these rescuers will become victims themselves, but there will be many close calls.

The men make their way down to Lincoln Avenue, where they're horrified to see what was before just a theory: people actually caught in the rushing water and being carried away. They position themselves as far out in the current as they dare, forming human chains in some spots to anchor themselves to safety. It's become a particularly dangerous place to be, this current. Wreckage of all description is coursing down the channel between 35-45 miles per hour. Pieces of building walls, oil drums, mangled boats and garbage are mingling with rocks, boards, and boxes to make standing in the current a treacherous move.

People aren't the only creatures caught in the maelstrom. Every so often, a dog, sometimes still chained to its house, rides by on top of it as the little building is buffeted by turbulence. Raccoons, house cats, and other animals are seen clinging to logs and surfing along on piles of debris. The dogs' frantic barking can be heard over the water's crashing din, a pathetic plea from creatures who will likely not survive their journey downstream.

Bob, too young and inexperienced to be as cautious as some of the older fellows, volunteers to be on the business end of one of the rescue chains. In the darkness, he can hear a man yelling for help, and the cries are getting louder. He watches intently upstream in their direction.

Suddenly, a pale spot appears against the dark water. As it gets closer, Bob recognizes it as a human face. The man is completely drenched, hair plastered against his skull. His arms are flailing, and he's having difficulty keeping his eyes open against the pounding rain.

Bob's adrenaline pumps hard. He pushes his luck, fighting his way even deeper into the current. He extends his arms and legs farther than he ever thought possible, trying to reach the now hysterical man. Bob reaches out his hands, stretching his fingers to their limit, muscles burning with the effort.

The man struggles, madly slapping and scooping the water to pull himself nearer. He reaches out to Bob. Closer, closer, faster he comes toward the outstretched arm. Bob's heart is banging against his chest, and his throat closes up. Even in the rain, he knows he's sweating. He makes a final, desperate lunge for the extended hand.

The hapless soul remains too far into the channel. He rushes by, fingers clawing the air just inches from Bob's. In that instant, a lightning flash reveals the raw, naked terror in the man's eyes. It chills Bob to the bone and lodges in his gut. Then the man is gone, rushing toward the Delaware River.

Bob knows the man will die.

For a moment, Bob remains planted in the frothing water, feeling nothing. His mouth is dry and his stomach pulls tight. Then the current jars him back to reality, and he makes his way carefully back to the safer edge of the channel.

Again feeling the rocks and other flotsam smacking into his legs, he raises his eyes to those around him. Most look rapidly away, giving him what privacy they can. Those who hold his gaze do so with compassion, but it can't salve the wretchedness he feels.

Still, committed to doing what he can, Bob stays at his post until five the next morning. Every so often, the man's face reappears in his mind's eye, and his skin ripples with goose bumps. Finally, exhausted, cold, and emotionally numb, he trudges back to the neighbor's house, which has water halfway up its stairway leading to the second floor.

His mother is beyond relieved to see him come through the door. She's horrified by his story—which he carefully edits—and the danger that he has placed himself in, but she's also proud of his maturity and sense of responsibility. She will often worry for him, but they will never discuss the incident again.

His hosts hang Bob's clothes to dry while he gets a little sleep. When he closes his eyes, he again sees the image of the man's terrified face, and knows it will remain with him for the rest of his life.

Diane is causing mayhem further inland, as well.

For the first time in fifty-two years, the Little Schuylkill River is overflowing its banks in Tamaqua, northwest of Allentown and southwest of Stroudsburg. Having received the runoff from about three inches of rain over a six-hour period, the river, along with its tributary, the Wabash Creek, sloshes five feet of muddy water through the business district. At its height, the merged channel reaches one thousand feet wide, and many families in its path escape to the surrounding hills with their lives and little else.

The Atlas Powder Company, sitting astride the river, suffers water invasion into its blasting cap department. Water flowing back out of the plant takes ten thousand electric blasting caps with it on a wild ride down the Schuylkill. Below Tamaqua, the river runs through Reynolds, then the lower side of Pottstown and other, more rural areas before hitting Philadelphia. Half that part of Pottstown has already been evacuated to avoid flooding, so the danger in people returning to their residences is multiplied by the presence of the caps.

Every community for a hundred miles downstream is alerted by State Police bulletins of the danger of handling the deadly explosive devices, and newspapers will, for days, run illustrated articles describing what they look like and how to deal with them if found. Trying to put a better face on the public relations disaster, a company official calls to attention how fortunate it is that the dynamite section was not infiltrated. It's dubious comfort.

Forty-five-year-old Henry Allen of Tamaqua is on the porch of his West Broad Street home when he notices his neighbor's small daughter stepping off their porch into the current covering the street. He jumps off after her and manages to hand her to others watching from their porch. Just as he's about to climb out of the water himself, a powerful surge knocks him off his feet, and the other rescuers watch in horror as he disappears beneath the waves. Henry does not resurface. When he's finally pulled from beneath an abandoned car half a block away, he is dead.

Another small child, thirteen-month-old Virginia Farnsworth of Great Bend, isn't as lucky as her Tamaqua counterpart. She wanders to the edge of a swollen creek in her backyard and is carried to her death.

Two Conyngham men are swept away by the Conyngham Creek southwest of Hazleton while trying to rescue three women in a stranded automobile. Ironically, the women survive by just staying in their car until the water goes back down, while their would-be rescuers drown.

There are countless similar acts of selflessness that night and throughout the days to follow, many of which will never be known.

About a hundred women are gathered in the newly renovated fire hall on the Day Street Flats back in East Stroudsburg. Caught up in their weekly Thursday Night Bingo games, few are giving any thought to the weather. Nobody is aware of the turmoil broiling just outside the door.

Policeman Lou Carmella is plenty aware of it, though. On his nightly rounds, he drives by the hall as usual, to make sure no one is taking advantage of the ladies' concentration by doing any mischief to the cars parked in the lot. He sees the waters of the Brodhead creeping over nearby Barnum Street, and knows Day Street, on the other side of the fire hall, will be next. He stops to warn firemen on hall duty that the occupants are in danger. Realizing his mission is now critical, he begins to warn residents in the surrounding area.

The firemen at the hall interrupt the game in progress, telling the women they should clear out immediately, while they still can.

Most of them heed the warning and leave in time to save themselves. Bingo cards are left on the tables, corn kernel markers still in place.

Four of the women stay behind, however, insisting on waiting for their husbands to pick them up. Lena Cramer, Mamie Kautz, Martha Jane Sommers, and another friend feel they'll be all right if they stick together. Several others offer rides and urge the four to leave, but they stay put.

Patrolman Carmella is already across the street at the home of Ethel Nevil to warn her of the impending danger. Frightened and not knowing quite what to do, she asks if he will accompany her to safety. He says that he must continue warning others, but she is welcome to come along. They must leave right away.

They run into Caramella's colleague, Officer James Smith, who is rousing Mr. and Mrs. Dave Burd, an elderly couple. The Burds live in a mobile home, part of the trailer park located next to the bingo hall. Again, he shouts a warning to the women waiting in the doorway to leave now, but they won't budge. So the two officers, the Burds and Mrs. Nevil make their way in the rising water down Day Street, along the ball park fence line. High ground is just a few hundred feet away.

They pass the home of Mrs. Nevil's brother, Harry Hinton, and his wife, Sue. Harry's shouting for Sue to hurry up, and they pile into their car and also head down Day Street. Bubbles are rising from the tailpipe, but somehow the car doesn't stall. The Hintons escape the clutches of the water, which has risen from ankle deep to waist high in the time since Officer Carmella has brought Mrs. Nevil out of her house.

Now the force of the water is becoming too strong to get through, and the little party links arms until they can reach a tree. They move around to the lee side, hoping for some protection from the chunks of log and stone being driven beneath the surface, and hang on to the trunk to anchor them from being carried away themselves.

Suddenly, the Burds' trailer rises from its parking spot and is picked up by the rushing waters. It's now bearing down directly on the group. They huddle for protection behind the tree, but Mr. Burd's arthritis prevents him keeping a firm enough grasp, and he lets go his wife's hand. The desperate people watch him get sucked under by the current, and feel the increasing pressure of the still-rising water.

Within moments, Mrs. Burd, too, loses her grip and follows her husband downstream.

The two police officers and Mrs. Nevil are now hanging on to the tree for dear life, when they're startled by a tremendous crash at Fireman's Hall. Eugene Heller's new Olds, driverless, has struck the building, taking out the side wall.

The impact dislodges the women still waiting in the doorway. The friend manages to grab onto the chain link fence outside and pull herself to safety, but the remaining three are knocked backwards into the building, where they will drown. One of Lena's last thoughts is that she can't understand why her companion, Ira DeHaven, never showed up to get her. It's not like him to be unreliable… Ira's excuse is that, at that moment, he, too, is drowning in their home on Harrison Street.

Briefly, the entire site is lit up by the shorting out of the building's electrical service. The snapping and popping of wires, accompanied by the brilliant blue-white flashes of electricity unleashed, is terrifying. The wall clock is flung into the water, its hands stopped at ten forty-six p.m.

Officer Carmella realizes he and his two companions are directly in the line of danger and must move if they are to have any hope of surviving. He and Officer Smith see a nearby utility pole and hold on to Mrs. Nevil as they inch their way to it through the torrent. Yelling over the roar of the water, Officer Carmella tells her she must stay here, where she'll be relatively safe, until they can reach high ground and get help. As he says this, he unwraps the gun belt from his waist and straps her to the pole with it.

The two policemen assure Mrs. Nevil she'll be okay, but as they start away from her, she panics. Unbuckling the belt, she insists on accompanying them and starts toward them. The men see her lose her balance, and Officer Carmella grasps at her to keep her from being washed away. All he gets is a handful of her dress, and it's not enough to hold on to her. Without being anchored themselves, the policemen are also swept from their feet, and the three are carried away.

Mrs. Nevil has fallen backwards and so cannot orient herself to recover, but the two men are facing forward. It's enough to allow them both to grab onto trees at the end of the playground, but they lose Mrs. Nevil to the night and the inky black water.

They will manage to gain perches in the trees and stay there until being rescued hours later. Until then, they are tortured by the hopeless, hysterical cries of those they cannot help, many of them children still struggling since being thrust into the water at Camp Davis. Body after body floats past in the deadly current, and the public servants are overcome with frustration and sadness at their inability to save anyone.

It's after eleven p.m. when Mr. Van Buskirk arrives back at Pinebrook with the LeCropane girls and their friend. Mr. Van Buskirk drops the girls off, apologizing that he hasn't been able to help them. He tells them to stay here for now, until the storm is over and they can get back to Camp Davis. He leaves to continue trying to get back to his own home.

Things have gone crazy in the meantime. They're told the power has gone out and the pumps aren't working, so the camp now has no drinking water. Campers are going to bed anyway, at the separate Mountainbrook girls' camp and Shadowbrook boys' area. They've had all the excitement they can handle for one night. Young adults are heading for their outlying cabins around the main grounds. Those people still awake and active are camp staff.

Sara and Linda, longtime regular visitors to Pinebrook, are told they and Marion can stay at the Inn, because there will be no getting back over to Davis Cabins for the time being. They can sleep on the black leather-seated rockers on the screened porch. They've always liked these fancy chairs, and settle in to get as comfortable as possible.

A few miles south, in East Stroudsburg, the water is now invading the "Triangle" area bordered by Washington Street, Brown Street and South Courtland. Harry Heller and his wife, realizing what's happening, rush into the basement to turn off the refrigeration units of their store, Heller's Meat and Supply Company. If left running, their motors will surely be ruined by the gritty floodwater. By the time they've completed their precautionary measures, the water is already too high against the Hellers' ground-level door. They can't force it open.

They climb to the second floor to wait out the high water. Soon, though, they see it is still rising, not leveling off, and comprehend the danger they're in. It's a brick building, Harry reasons, and they won't be able to chop their way out if they get trapped inside. He and his wife crawl out a second-floor window and into an adjacent tree. They climb as high as they can into the top branches, and there they will spend the night.

Across Washington on Lincoln Avenue, the Van Gorder family is watching television when the pounding rain prompts Mrs. Van Gorder to take a look out the window.

"It's raining so hard," she remarks to her husband, George, "it's a wonder there isn't a flood!" Then some movement down the street catches her eye. "What are all those people going up Washington Avenue for?"

George now joins her at the window, and sees that there actually is a flood going on, and they're right in the middle of it.

"Let's get the kids together," he tells his wife. "I'll go down and get the car started." As he approaches the car, water is coming across the street up to his ankles. He is able to move the vehicle to higher ground, but by the time he returns to the house to collect his family, the water is waist high. Their four kids are too little to negotiate that kind of water, so George resigns himself to staying home and doing the best they can to ride out the flood.

On the other side of the Brodhead, the creek is ripping through and tearing up the lower part of Stroudsburg. First Street, near the Vassar Pocketbook factory, as well as Third and Fourth Streets, take the brunt of the punishment, but the damage is inconsistent. The Gulf service station near Third and Main Streets is left standing and still functional, but the houses and corner store just down the street are completely destroyed. Their shells will have to be bulldozed into a heap with the debris left on the streets.

On Second Street, Daniel Dingman and his girlfriend Jennie Berger are drowned while asleep in their home. McConnel Street is all but wiped out. A tavern located just before the State Bridge is washed away.

Just a few blocks away, the Shutt girls, along with their mother and friend, are at the window of their hotel room, wondering what's causing all the noise and commotion.

Back near the Day Street Flats in East Stroudsburg, retirees Mr. and Mrs. Herb Fenner are cowering on the roof of their small bungalow on Barnum Street. They had climbed up earlier when Herb had gone to let the dogs out because they were barking at the back door. He'd been greeted by water from the Brodhead, just outside the threshold. Herb had immediately taken his wife and the dogs up a ladder to the attic. Moments later, their young neighbors had run in with two small children and a baby, wondering what to do.

As the water had risen, they had all climbed out onto the roof, where they called for help. A short while later, a man in a motorboat had taken the young family off to safety. He had lingered as long as he could in the strengthening current, and then there had been no more room in the small boat. He'd looked apologetically at the Fenners as he told them he wouldn't be able to come back.

Since then, they've sat on the roof in the rain, Mrs. Fenner holding the smallest of their three dogs, The other two are floating on a mattress in the attic, and Mr. Fenner is watching for signs of other rescue boats. Now he hears screaming, and looks toward the center of the channel to see two young girls flying by in inner tubes, yelling for help. There is nothing he can do for them, and he and his wife just watch helplessly as they shoot past toward the Delaware River.

Then the Fenners both hear a sinister, hollow whooshing sound, interspersed with hissing and the "ploop-plooping" of bubbles. Just off the side of the house, they see what looks like a torpedo wake in the water, and lean over to get a better look. Just beneath the surface, a slender propane cylinder that has torn loose from its base is zooming by, propelled by the gas escaping from its broken valve.

The Fenners, at once surprised and horrified, watch it head out into the middle of the Brodhead's strong current and get turned downstream. They will cringe and brace themselves for an explosion each of the many times they hear the noise again during the night, imagining what will happen if one of the errant missiles happens to hit their house or a building nearby. Mr. Fenner wonders what kind of memories such sounds are dredging up for the many World War II vets who live in his community.

Around eleven thirty, the lights go out downstairs in Camp Davis' Winter House. Outside the circle of candlelight in the attic, something skitters across the bare floorboards. A little girl screams. A woman next to her picks her up and gathers her into her lap. Again, the group starts to sing, but they're interrupted by increasingly loud thumps as large items begin to jolt against the siding. They become aware of a dull, far-off roar. For a moment, everyone listens intently, until it's evident that the sound is growing louder.

Now children begin to cry, and nobody tries to stop them. Songs turn to fervent prayers. Irene Weber yanks an orange life vest she had grabbed on the way up onto Bobby and frantically secures its straps. She hopes she has enough time to put the other one on Betty.

Jennie Johnson hands her candle to Nancy and gathers her own sons closer, despite the stifling heat. Nancy looks around at the candle flames reflecting in the eyes of those whose aren't closed in prayer. Those eyes are wide, as she knows her own must be. She feels the pounding of her heart match that of the rain on the very near roof. Between it, the growing roar outside, and the thudding of objects against the house, even the children's crying is almost drowned out.

Shortly past midnight, a massive crash accompanies a sharp jolt. A sudden rush of air extinguishes the candles. Everyone gasps or screams, and Nancy realizes the house must have been knocked off its foundation. The floor is now sloping, like the deck of a keeling-over ship. A violent shudder precedes a tearing sound as the roof pulls apart. The noise is punctuated by nail pops in rapid succession, and the sound of breaking glass.

Bat droppings, clods of collected dirt, shingles and wood splinters fall in on the huddled group as the attic floor gives way beneath them. Parents yell their children's names, and clutch at them as they slide or are thrown into the water.

Beams split and fall on their heads; wiring drops around them like malevolent spaghetti. It winds around arms and legs, pulling them down, down into the black water. Children scream and claw at what's left of the floor breaking up beneath them. Hysterical wails rise from all corners. Frantic kicking and splashing is everywhere.

Irene grabs a strap on Bobby's life vest and tries to get hold of Betty Jane's hand, but misses. "Keep your head up out of the water,

Betty!" she yells, as all three are pulled underwater. Just before she submerges, she sees the Lawyers tumbling into the roiling water just yards away. It's the last she will ever see her in-laws alive.

Jennie Johnson plunges into the water as the floor drops out from under her. It doesn't feel cold, but it's moving swiftly and pushing her down. She fights her way back up, and after what seems forever, breaks the surface, gasping. She knows everyone has been dumped in along with her, and tries to get her bearings but can see nothing in the inky dark. She can hear them, though. They are splashing, trying to grab something—anything—as she is, to keep afloat. And they are screaming.

She pictures the dozens of little faces that had surrounded her just moments before, and wonders where her own children are. It has all happened so fast. She didn't see where the boys went, or Nancy. Jennie feels the rest of the house disintegrating around her. Things are hitting her body and legs below the surface. Then something large strikes her in the head, knocking her out.

Over at Pinebrook, the LeCropane girls begin hearing distant cries for help. They don't know where they're coming from. The Inn sits back off the road, and it's too dark to see anything. At first, the cries are close together. Some are barely audible over the roar of the water, the thunder, and the pounding rain. It doesn't occur to the girls that the cries might be coming from their family and friends in the Winter House. They seem too far away, and besides, Uncle Henry had said there'd never been a serious flood at Davis Cabins.

The Lackawanna Railroad crew can hear the screams, too. They stick their heads out the engine windows, straining to see what's causing the commotion. All they can make out is some white foam atop the area where the camp buildings had stood just moments before. The men hear the shrieks and cries of the women and small children. They make a concerted effort not to look at each other. One of them wipes his eye with a grease-embedded finger as they all stare off in the direction of the now-fading din.

Jennie Johnson, floating among pieces of wreckage, regains consciousness. She reaches out, feeling for something substantial. She finally locates a board, seizes it, then gives it up for a larger one. She floats downstream for what seems like hours, still hearing the agonizing cries of frightened children. A sob wracks her body.

What if those voices are David's and Roy's? How can she be so unable to help them? My God! And what about Nancy? Though she's older, she doesn't know how to swim. They must all be terribly frightened, and possibly in pain. Jennie cannot bear to think of it as she vaguely registers the sting of rocks and boards hitting her own legs.

She knows she is moving rapidly downstream, and that she's traveling a long way, because the cries and shouts are quickly growing distant. Suddenly, the board hits something and comes to an abrupt halt. The impact propels her from the water, but it's so dark she can't tell where she is, and she's afraid to move.

Irene Weber still has hold of Bobby in his life vest, and they bob to the surface together. She feels a wild surge of joy that she will at least be able to save one of her children. At that instant, something large hits her in the arm, knocking Bobby out of her grasp. Her blood runs cold. Clumsily, she scoops through the chunks of surface debris and windmills her legs until she again feels the vest strap and grabs it.

They ride along in the swift current for a few minutes. Irene hears Bobby's rapid breathing as she scans the water for any sign of Betty. She feels tears welling up, when suddenly they're both pushed into the branches of a tree that has been torn loose by the torrent. Bobby becomes hung up on the branches and is again pried from his mother's grasp as the tree rolls away from her. Other tree limbs grab Irene as she kicks toward Bobby. In her zeal to reach him, she forces their tensile limit. They spring back, flinging her onto the railroad embankment. She shrieks as Bobby is carried swiftly downstream, disappearing into the blackness.

Not feeling the many cuts and bruises she has received in the water, Irene scrambles on hands and knees to the top of the bank. Adrenaline pushes her to her feet, and she runs downstream, screaming hysterically after Bobby. If he answers, she cannot hear him over the roar of the water. Finally, she understands the futility and danger of continuing to run in the dark.

She sees a light shining feebly in the distance. Disoriented, she doesn't realize it's a railroad signal lamp located upstream. She begins walking toward it, away from Bobby and the rest of the campers.

Nancy Johnson has also been cast into the branches of a tree, for which she is supremely grateful. After she'd gone into the water, something had caught her by the neck and held her above the water. She had grabbed a board that was floating by, and it had lodged in the tree.

She pulls herself up to a higher limb, and tears a piece of her blouse to make a tourniquet for her left hand, which is bleeding profusely. She doesn't recall being cut. Very close by, she hears something. A voice.

Who's there? she asks, hopefully.

Aaaugh! Help me! Help!

I'm here! I'll help you! Who is it? Who are you?

Mama?

No, honey, I'm sorry. I'm not your mama. It's Nancy Johnson.

N-N-Nancy? It's me, Linda. Christensen.

Are you hurt?

I don't know. Not much. I'm scared.

I know. Where are you?

I'm in a tree…

Nancy hears panic creeping back into Linda's voice. *Me, too. Don't scream any more, Linda. We'll be all right now. Just hang on. I'm here. I'll be with you.*

They can still hear a cry now and then, but the sounds are growing fainter, and Nancy knows whoever is making them is being carried far downstream. When she senses Linda falling asleep or maybe going into shock, she talks to her, to bring her back and keep her from letting go and falling back into the moving water.

Nancy's mother is lying where she has been thrown a bit further downstream. She is crying. After a bit, Jennie tries pulling herself up, but is stopped by a piercing pain in her ribs. She lies still for quite a while, resting and wondering where her children are. The thought that they may still be alive and needing her motivates another attempt at movement. She realizes she's being held down by two logs she's wedged between.

Painfully, she extracts herself from their grip. As her eyes adjust to the darkness, she sees she has been tossed onto a debris pile. She crawls up higher and lies resting again. She can hear several people still crying for help, and the voices seem to be coming from above her. She realizes they must have gotten tangled in trees, but at least they're alive.

The water continues roaring. Jennie hears the snapping of large tree trunks under pressure from the water. As each tree is pushed down into the current, one of the nearby voices screams, then dies away. Whatever she's on is no longer moving. She realizes she will live.

Now she hears another voice, but it's quiet and soft, and close by. It's a child, crying.

"Is anybody there?" comes the small, frightened voice.

"Where are you?" Jennie asks, in the general direction of the sound.

She hears someone picking a way over to her. When the form draws closer, in the glow of a lightning flash she recognizes eleven-year-old Beth Deubel. The child's hair is matted and she has lost nearly all her clothing. Jennie's heart is torn.

Oh, Beth, she says, pulling the girl to her. *I'll keep you warm until we can get help.*

Beth asks if Jennie has seen her mother, Martha. Jennie admits she hasn't, and Beth begins crying again.

Honey, don't, Jennie says softly. *I haven't seen any of my children, either. We just have to believe that they're okay. God will watch over them, like he's watching over us.* She changes the subject, asking Beth how she got thrown on the same pile of debris with her.

Beth can't tell her. She doesn't remember. Jennie worries that perhaps Beth has been struck in the head and might have a concussion.

Let's go sit down, okay? We may be waiting a while. It's our job now to stay alive until someone comes to save us. She takes Beth's hand and leads her to a place that feels stable, as far from the sound of the rushing water as they can get. They huddle together, crying when they hear a child scream. They wait and wonder what has happened to their world.

On Lincoln Avenue in East Stroudsburg, Mr. and Mrs. George Van Gorder herd their kids and the family dog upstairs, then go back down to grab what little they can save from the water. As they make their way back upstairs, they hear the abrupt smashing of glass. The cellar windows are giving way to a powerful torrent of water, and it gushes in, filling the house.

A few minutes later, the lights go out. The wall of water that wiped out Camp Davis has reached the Interborough Bridge and rips it away, along with all the utility cables running beneath it.

The Van Gorders hear their furniture floating about downstairs and bumping into walls. Not taking any chances, they move up to the attic. There they huddle together in fear, wondering if the frame house will hold up against the raging water. They jump as a gigantic crash and a jerky vibration signal a car slamming into the porch and ripping it away from the house. More crashing and rumbling, as the house next door is sheared from its foundation and crumbles into the moving mass of debris.

George hears a strange whimpering and sticks his head out the tiny attic window to see what's making it. In the tall tree just outside, a small boy is perched. George can't know that the child has already been carried several miles by the water since being thrown into it at Camp Davis. He only sees the boy's body trembling with fear, and tries to calm the little fellow with soothing words. But the water is still rising, and the boy pleads with George to save him.

George knows the tree is out of reach, and begins tearing through the attic to find a rope, a pole, anything for the little boy to grab so George can pull him to safety. He can't locate anything long enough. All he can do is go back to the window and try to distract the child from the fear, and hope that the water stops coming up.

Mrs. Van Gorder can hear the boy's terrified pleas, and wraps her arms protectively around her own children. While thanking God for their safety, she prays desperately that the child outside will not be harmed.

Suddenly, a surge of the current tears the boy from his perch in the tree, and she hears George yell for him to grab something. But the boy submerges before George's eyes, and he does not come back up. There are no more cries now, and Mrs. Van Gorder rocks softly back and forth in the dark, tears streaming down her face.

The family sits in silence for a while, with George occasionally going to the window to monitor the water level and see if he can find anyone to summon for help. Then they hear voices and a thumping against the back of the house. George goes to the window and looks in that direction. There, on the hillside rising immediately behind it, several people are standing just above the waterline, wrestling with an extension ladder. They're attempting to poke the end of it into one of the Van Gorders' second story windows.

George hails them and tells them to wait a minute. He runs downstairs and raises the screen, reaching out to grab the ladder. He pulls it in and brings his family down to help them across to safety. The last one out, George realizes the dog won't be able to cross the ladder, and decides the best chance he has to make it is staying in the house.

Go back upstairs, now. Go on!

George hears the dog whimpering as he crosses the ladder, the water now touching its rungs. As the rescue crew pulls the ladder back across to the hillside, one of the Van Gorders' baby beds floats out the window. George wonders what other parts of their lives will follow it. He hopes the dog will be okay.

Rising

Friday, August 19
The wee hours to dawn

Just after midnight, Bill Coleman awakens to shaking by a counselor. The beam of a flashlight plays across his bunkmates' faces, rousing them as well.

"C'mon, guys, you gotta get up! The river's rising faster than we thought. Get your swim trunks on and bring a flashlight. Gather your stuff together and bring it up the hill to the main camp. We're gonna need your help moving boats and canoes out of the floodplain. Now move it!"

As the counselor moves on to the next tent, Bill and his bunkmates change hurriedly into their bathing trunks. They're excited, moved by the importance of their new job. This is the neatest thing that has ever happened at camp.

Those chosen to monitor the Culver Lake Dam in Branchville, New Jersey, are watching it bulge alarmingly now, as hours and hours of heavy rain have pushed it nearly to its limits. Reluctantly, they finally give permission for the firehouse to sound the alarm.

When the hideous blast lets loose around one a.m., few townspeople understand its meaning. Most are bewildered. Fire? In this weather?

Those in the most immediate danger are the first evacuated by the fire department. William Grippenburg, proprietor of the once stylish Park Place Hotel, now a down-at-the-heels tavern, realizes his fortunes have certainly spiraled. His establishment, directly in the path of any water that will surge from the dam, is doomed. Fatalistically, he begins handing out free bottles of liquor to his customers.

As they leave the place with their booty, they see water already covering Mill Street to a depth of two feet. Families on Broad Street, a block away, watch it creep over their floors, and the dam hasn't even given way.

After a while, the screaming and cries for help on the Brodhead Creek have mostly petered out, with one still reaching the ears of the LeCropane girls on the Pinebrook Inn porch now and then. The girls manage to sleep, but fitfully, because the loud roar of the water and other disconcerting sounds keep waking them. They're also still worried because they know they're not where they should be and that they're probably causing a great deal of concern to Aunt Lil and Uncle Henry.

Between about one o'clock and dawn, things quiet down at Pinebrook, and people are mostly in their cabins, sleeping. Staff members come around offering cans of fruit juice because there is no water to drink. The girls accept some, and try to go back to sleep.

Col. Heritage, calling from his Newtown command center, has arranged for a Bucks County Civil Defense communications network to be set up. By one-thirty on Friday morning, volunteer Bradley Algeo has opened the channels, with priority given to messages concerning the island campers.

As Helen Brown comes through the door at home in Stroudsburg, her niece greets her with relief and the news that Bill Wells, of the local Civil Defense, has left a message. Knowing her Army training and background, Bill thinks Helen's organizational skills and level head can be of great help. He wants her to report directly to the courthouse, get a typhus inoculation, and go to the Teacher's College in East Stroudsburg. She knows the school well, and he needs her help evacuating staff and students there, with the twin towns devastated and unable to support a busy campus right now.

Within moments, she's back out the door. Realizing the immensity of the event, historically minded Helen brings along her camera to record what she will experience.

It takes a good while to get herself processed in the chaotically busy Monroe County Courthouse. When she's finally finished, Helen is instructed to go to the Clearview School on Route 90 in East Stroudsburg. On the road north to Analomink from town, the school is functioning as the local CD headquarters in lieu of the completely destroyed Day Street Fire Hall, which had been the designated emergency operations center. When she reaches Clearview, officials tell her, she will be picked up by helicopter and taken to the college.

But there are no helicopters when she arrives at the school. They have all been commandeered to ferry search and rescue personnel, equipment and survival supplies. Search and rescue, thinks Helen…this really is serious. She spends more time trying to locate someone to take her to the college, and when she finally succeeds, the sun is reddening the horizon.

Ever resourceful, Helen hitches a ride in a sixteen-foot powerboat across the still-dangerous current of the Brodhead Creek at Stokes Mill. The ride is frightening, but they make it. She then hitches another ride up to the college with a passing driver.

She is met at the college by President Noonan, who shows her an official order, issued by Governor George Leader, to evacuate the school. He puts her in charge of the operation, handing her the Governor's Order so she can prove authority in requesting what she needs to get the job done.

Helen jumps right in, organizing six student cars into a convoy, and instructing students to leave their dorms and get in the cars. She leads the convoy over back roads, crossing the Brodhead to Analomink at a spot where the water has gone down somewhat and a temporary bridge has been thrown up. She gives the driver instructions where to take the students in Stroudsburg until they can safely return, then heads back to East Stroudsburg.

In the light of vehicle headlamps shining over flat land near the river, campers and counselors at Pahaquarra have been moving canoes, boats, and other equipment to high ground for two hours. Bill Coleman is wrestling yet another one up the hill. The grass has become matted from all the foot traffic, and the red clay begins oozing up between the blades, making it slick.

Bill loses his footing and slips, slamming face first onto the top of a guidepost. Stunned, he falls to the ground. He sees stars. When they clear, he watches raindrops sparkling down in the headlight beams. He wonders vaguely if his nose is broken.

Then someone is shining a flashlight in his face, and he hears a boy gasp.

"Wow . . . look at all the blood!"

Some of the other boys help him to the medical shack, where an older counselor cleans up his face and applies ice to his nose to stop the bleeding. Bill becomes aware that he's very cold, and begins to shiver rather violently. The medic, thinking this might be the first sign of shock, tells Bill to lie down on the cot and covers him with blankets. Once he's sure Bill isn't in danger of shock, he tells the boy just to sleep the rest of the night.

Bill, exhausted and in pain, is grateful. He drifts off immediately.

Residents of small river towns and vacation communities along both sides of the Delaware are extremely vulnerable to flooding. This is particularly true from Foul Rift to Sandts Eddy, where the channel drops twenty-two feet in half a mile. The river picks up speed over the drop, most of the banks are low, and quite a few of these towns are threatened by a secondary source: feeder creeks and streams. Hutchinson, New Jersey has Buckhorn Creek, Belvidere has Pophandusing Brook, and the Pennsylvania side has Martin's Creek. Most of these tributaries now back up furiously as the Delaware's volume increases to block their normal flow into it.

Beginning in the wee hours of Friday morning, some families accurately assess the flooding threat and begin moving furniture and valuables to safety in a desperate race against the river. Much of the work is done in waist-deep water.

June Schafer listens to her Newfoundland home creaking and groaning under the onslaught of water inside and around the building.

She has not been reassured by neighbor Bob Robacker's opinion of the soundness of its foundation, and considers waking the girls to dress them to go outside in case they are forced to leave. Finally, she decides she'll wait and take her chances. Waking them now could cause a lot of unnecessary fear.

Throughout the night the four adults sit tensely, listening to the water rush through the downstairs. They speak little, praying nothing large knocks the house off its moorings or crumbles the foundation itself. Toward dawn, they finally succumb to mental and physical exhaustion, and fall into fitful sleep.

All night long, seven-year-old John Birutta listens to fire sirens blowing as he lies in bed. He lives with his parents and two brothers on Market Street in Belvidere, New Jersey. The firehouse sits directly behind their home, so the incessant noise isn't something he can easily ignore. He wonders what could be going on to cause so much commotion, but eventually drifts off to sleep.

Meanwhile, across the river and to the south on River Road in Kintnersville, police are investigating what appears to be a traffic fatality. Around eleven p.m., Charles Sargant had heard a loud crashing in the brush behind his house near the Indian Rock Hotel. Running outside to see what caused it, he had found a delivery truck that had left the road and careened down the embankment above, hitting his raised concrete patio and the porch of the house. It had come to rest about twenty-five feet from the Delaware Canal, but hadn't overturned.

When he checked to see if the driver was okay, Sargant had found the body of nineteen-year-old Carl Schwarz not in the driver's seat, but pinned beneath an overturned refrigerator in the rear of the truck. He had phoned police, and everyone was finding the circumstances rather suspicious. The presence of a .22 caliber rifle in the cab caused the police to request an autopsy.

It didn't take long for word to spread about a possible murder in the small river community.

By three thirty a.m., the Port Jervis highway underpass on Route 6

between the railroad tracks and the Delaware River is completely underwater. Not only does this shut off a major traffic artery from Jervis, it also blocks one of the primary exit routes from Matamoras, its twin city in Pennsylvania. Already way above its normal height of three feet, the river continues to rise.

The Delaware now extends a full half-mile out of its banks. Main Street is beneath two feet of water, and other parts of Port Jervis are covered five to six feet deep. The entire First Ward beyond the railroad tracks, the tri-states area in the Fourth Ward, and all low areas of the city are ordered evacuated. Fire Department volunteers are assisting people in retreating from already flooded homes.

Residents with more foresight pack their things and leave before they become stranded. By the end of the operation, nearly two hundred people will be moved to a nearby Grange hall.

The city is now cut off from both auto and train travel, and the Tri-States Associated Telephone Company reports service out to the west and into Pike County. By six in the morning, the water level will crest just below twenty-four feet, and stay that high for an hour before finally beginning to recede.

In Washington, New Jersey, *Newark Evening News* reporter Dick Harpster is awakened at 4:00 a.m. by a telephone call. Earlier, his colleague, Vince Zarate, a reporter for the *Easton Express,* had called from his home in the Belvidere Hotel before he'd gone to bed, giving Dick the heads-up that the Delaware River was rising, and about to flood. The two often share leads and sources for stories of interest to both newspapers.

Vince's call had been a surprise, because Dick had seen the weather forecasts in all the papers, saying Diane was no longer a threat. He had noticed some rain locally, but nothing like that Connie had dropped; certainly not enough to cause any more flooding than that.

But this call is one he's been waiting for. Right after Vince's alert, Dick had called some of his State Patrol friends and asked to be notified if any flood-related activity was taking place. Now they're telling him the river is rising at three feet per hour, and they're on their way to Belvidere to rescue some islanders.

He thanks the dispatcher and hangs up. He then asks his wife to try to reach Vince and return the favor, but by now, the phone lines are dead in Belvidere. His wife sends him out the door with a thermos of hot coffee and an admonition to be careful, and he drives north to Belvidere.

The Belvidere Ambulance and Rescue Squad is already out on the river about four miles to the north. They have been summoned by shoreline residents who had heard the cries of frightened cottagers on Promises, Manunka Chunk, and Thomas Islands. They can't get to shore themselves, as their boats have already been washed away. Rescue crew members Nels Dalrymple and Lew Jones make several trips in the dangerous, debris-laden current to bring more than fifty of the vacationers to safety on shore.

The State Patrol is unaware that the island residents have been rescued already, and sets out in a motor launch over flooded cornfields where a current is barely discernible. Dick joins them, hoping to get some quotes and action shots. When they reach the river, the impressive whitewater and large pieces of wreckage shooting along in it are scary, even for a war veteran like Dick. He can't get any shots because the boat is bucking and heaving, and it's hard to maintain a steady stance. Still, the story is exciting, and it's one of the most compelling he's covered so far for the *Evening News.* He'll stay on the river most of the day.

Col. Heritage has been on the phone at his Newtown farm all night. His main concern is the welfare of campers and staff on the Delaware River islands above Erwinna. Reports relayed from bridge officers and the islands themselves indicate a continuous rise in the river's level. Soon the time element will become critical, but nothing can be done until daylight arrives.

The colonel has been in constant contact with Commander C. H. Franklin at Johnsville Naval Air Development Center at Mustin Field in Philadelphia. At this point, Johnsville becomes the control center for rescue operations in the Pennsylvania flood area. Calls have been coming in from other areas besides Bucks County. Port Jervis has called to request assistance in rescuing thirty children campers from Jubilee Ranch, a summer resort at Godeffroy, New

179

York. Two motorboats have already been swamped in the attempt, and the kids are beginning to suffer from exposure.

Cdr. Franklin sends the scramble order at five a.m. to the crews of four H-21C helicopters from the 509th Tactical Command at Fort Belvoir, Virginia. The squad has been on temporary duty at the West Point Military Academy, and will take off from there.

Franklin also dispatches an amphibious "duck" vehicle from West Point to Sparrowbush, New York, where 309 people are stranded at Eddy Farm resort. It's a large crowd to airlift, so two other ducks are sent there from Stewart Air Force Base and Monmouth Beach lifeboat station in New Jersey, while the Coast Guard sends a double-deck helicopter.

By six o'clock Friday morning, the colonel has also gotten HUP-type helicopters to the lower Neshaminy to provide airlift rescue to those stranded in trees and on rooftops by the upstart creek. The problem is more widespread than originally thought, and Squadron HU-2 from Lakehurst Naval Station in Atlantic City brings additional craft by eight a.m.

An hour later, Johnsville receives a similar request to help evacuate the Delaware camping islands. Water levels are beginning to threaten the ability of staff to keep the children safe, and estimates are that they will be completely overrun by one thirty in the afternoon.

As dawn breaks on Camp Pahaquarra, Bill Coleman wakes up with a headache and a very tender nose, but he's okay. Still in his swim trunks, he pushes open the door of the medical shack and scans the camp. It has stopped raining, but the river is higher than the night before. Incongruously, the sun is shining brightly, and he can tell the day will be hot and humid. Once his eyes adjust to the light, he goes off to seek his counselor and find out what's going on.

He's told not to blow regular Reveille this morning, but instead to sound the emergency assembly call. He does so several times before everyone makes it to the soggy parade ground. He and another scout are dispatched to run up the hills into the separate camping circles to spread the word about the rising water.

Everyone can see the river rising, and the boys are informed that they're needed to help secure the camp. With a sense of urgency, every-one sets to work lashing down buildings, moving equipment to higher ground, and tying up the new dock. At an expenditure of nearly eight thousand dollars, it's too precious an investment to allow it to take off downriver. When the most pressing tasks are completed, the boys are finally served breakfast.

Some boys are quite excited and have a hard time eating, but the older scouts and counselors dig in, knowing it might be a long day. There's no telling when another hot meal might be available. They are told that telephone service has gone out overnight and the Old Mine Road is flooded above and below them. They are isolated for a while, but not to worry: there is plenty of food and water in camp, and no one is in any danger. They can just keep moving up the mountain, if necessary. Most of the boys are high-spirited and see the flood as a unique adventure.

The sun is also beginning to lighten the sky behind the clouds in Branchville, when continuing rain and runoff from the mountainside finally forces Culver Dam to give way. Amid a tremendous cracking of tired, aged timbers and the sliding-in-a-tunnel sound of monstrous boulders grinding against each other, a massive column of water knocks a breach in the dam wall.

Logs split and explode outward as huge rocks spring out of the sockets they have occupied for so long. The pressure valve has finally let go, and the column of water shoots straight out. It plunges toward the ground and sprints toward Branchville below.

Sirens shriek, but it's too late. Whatever's in the way now has run out of luck. The eight-foot water wall smashes into buildings and rolls vehicles. Walls are splintered, foundations demolished. The water picks up the car being driven by general store owner Orrie Fields, surfing it toward a steep-sided basin near Garris' Garage. The car is flung into a tree, crushing the fingers of Charles Culver, who had climbed it in hopes of staying clear of the water. Orrie sees him wince and fall away as the car careens further.

The vehicle is now heading down the banks toward deep water collected at the bottom of the basin. In a last-ditch effort, Orrie reaches out the car window and grabs hold of a tractor as he's carried by. He holds fast, and the car's motion continues, allowing him to pull himself out, just before it hits the surface of the basin and sinks.

The main wall of water continues through town, sweeping Howe's Five and Ten Cent Store ahead of it and tossing it against the side of a storage barn. It tears loose a garage across from Dave's Bar and Grill, shattering it and tumbling its cars around among ton-weight slabs of its concrete floor. Mill Street buildings are gutted and left with roofs dangling.

Wielding the destructive power of the accumulated wreckage, the juggernaut easily flattens the puny obstruction of the lower dam, barely registering a brief check on its forward motion before charging full-speed into the Hoos and Fletcher lumberyard. It carries rafts of lumber along, pounding them into the railroad embankment and tearing the earth out from under the rails. They are left sagging in mid-air.

The torrent follows the course of Culver's Brook, scouring the sides wider until it reaches the underpass at Route 206. All the combined force of the rushing water and the scouring debris rips the concrete abutments out, leaving the roadway to collapse onto the rails below.

As the torrent loses momentum and spreads out in the area below town, rain continues to pour from the heavens, drenching those watching the destruction. Many swollen streams and spontaneous waterfalls are pouring into homes and weakening bridges.

Ironically, the home of Mrs. MacNellie, the current dam owner, is directly in the path of the crushing flow. Her son, Dean, and son-in-law, J.D. Reed, have evacuated the family from it, but have stayed behind to pump out the basement of water infiltrating from other sources. They're interrupted by the fire whistle. Knowing what it means, they scramble up a hill to avoid the deluge.

The water rushes in one end of the house and carries furniture and family keepsakes out the other. The men are caught by the edges of the rushing water, but are strong enough to swim out of its grip and climb to safety.

A pastor in town, seeing the water rush through the house and believing the men are still inside, is sadly on his way to inform Mrs. MacNellie of her loss when he runs into the pair, winded and drenched, but alive.

The MacNellie's century-old homestead survives, minus a porch, some outbuildings and a grove of ancient hardwoods. For decades to come, Mrs. MacNellie will have silt filtering out of her walls.

Customers of Portland, Pennsylvania's National Bank have been warned that the river might come up into the facility, and are provided access to their safe deposit boxes. Not everyone has made it in time, and when the water reaches fifteen feet deep in the streets and eleven feet inside the business district building, it floods the boxes and the vault.

Vault contents had been removed to the Pen Argyl Bank for secure storage the previous day, and it was a foresighted effort: The lack of electricity won't allow the bank to close its doors today.

At Marshall's Creek, just to the north, Randall Gabrielan is staying with his family at the Twin Falls housekeeping cottages on Route 209. The two waterfalls that usually flow peacefully over outcroppings in the creek now surge and tumble with a violence no one there remembers ever seeing before.

With the Minisink Hills in the background, the Coates Board and Box Company of East Stroudsburg languishes in inactivity with no electricity, no telephone service, and no delivery road. The macadam drive that had handled its traffic became part of a new channel for the Brodhead Creek, and all that remains is a rippling, buckled mess. Parts of its Empire Carton plant and other buildings were torn away, and access was cut off when two highway bridges and a railroad span were torn out nearby.
– Collection Monroe County Historical Association

Some bungalows near the river in Slateford are ruined, with three homes being carried off entirely. When the water recedes, one of them will be perched in a tree.

Along Route 402, twenty-four families are leaving their homes in Delaware Water Gap where the Brodhead Creek empties into the river. Here, too, the rapid rise surprises residents. Not everyone has time to move furniture to higher levels before they must abandon their homes.

Firemen are busy lashing ladders together so they can reach three men stranded on the roof of the Coates Board and Carton Company factory. The Brodhead is rushing so fast and at such high volume past the place that its water tower begins to tilt over like some drunken, stiff-legged spider next to a ten-foot gully where a macadam road had been just the day before.

Thirteen-year-old Charlie Rufe wakes up at five thirty on Friday morning at Camp Miller, the boys' camp run by the Lutheran Ministerium of Pennsylvania. Located just north of Shawnee-on-Delaware in the Water Gap, Camp Miller usually bustles with about 260 campers and staff, but this morning it's unusually quiet.

The previous evening's entertainment activities had been cancelled due to a campground that had turned into one large, soggy sponge. Charlie figures nobody's up yet, or at least not out on the grounds, which are probably still wet.

This is Charlie's sixth summer at Camp Miller, and he long ago relaxed into its easy rhythms of recreation, campfires, and enjoying the river. He's made lots of friends, and gets along especially well with another camper, Sumner Huber. Charlie will be sad when the summer's over and everyone must return to their hometowns to start school again.

He looks out the window and is flabbergasted by what he sees. The river, normally down two flights of steps on a steep embankment, is but thirty feet from his cabin door. It's spilling over the bank top in places.

He wakes his counselor to report the strange event. The counselor thinks he's dreaming and tells him to go back to sleep, but Charlie persists. Finally, the counselor gets up and has a look for himself. It's an abrupt end to the slow, easy summer. Within two hours, the camp will be an island.

The counselor immediately notifies the camp director about the danger from the encroaching river. While evacuation plans are being made, other campers are roused. Most of them, six to fifteen years of age, don't fully grasp the danger they're in, so no one feels frightened. On the contrary, the mood becomes festive.

Counselors bring a canoe to the Junior Area cabin circle and paddle it around. One cabin sits low enough that they can paddle in one door and out the other. Campers watch and laugh, enjoying their silly antics. One of them, fourteen-year-old Bob Bohm, is happy to see the sun for a change, after what seems like weeks of rain. He joins in the fun, playing in puddles deep enough to be called ponds.

Then the water floats one of the cabins off its cinderblocks. Someone reports that water is backing up from nearby cornfields over the camp access road. The mood of the camp changes from silly to serious as instruction comes over the loudspeaker to load knapsacks with sleeping bags or blankets and a change of clothing, as if packing for an overnight hike. Campers are told to stow their packs in the upper bunks of the cabins, then assemble in front of the camp office.

Charlie packs his sleeping bag, Bible, and a transistor radio. While waiting in the mess hall to be evacuated, he looks out the window again, and begins to get an idea how serious things might be: The trailer of an eighteen-wheel big rig floats by.

Twelve canoes and rowboats are hastily filled with clothes and camping supplies in an effort to save campers' belongings from the floodwater. These are chained to the basketball poles in hopes they'll rise with the water level but not float away.

The campers are instructed to form groups according to size. Joining hands, they create human chains to make sure everyone gets safely across the flooding access road and up steep Dutch Hill. One counselor leads each group, and others stand along the road to shore up the line if it breaks. From there, they will walk three miles along the upper road to the adult ministerial camp.

The current is fairly calm but getting stronger, so the smallest kids go first. By the time the taller boys like Charlie and Bob take their turn, the water is up to their waists and requires some strength to negotiate.

Bob feels Dick Geyer, the camper behind him, lose his grip on the camper behind him and get washed sideways. Bob's still hanging on to his hand, but Dick has difficulty getting to his feet. Counselors step in to pull him up and close the line. Everyone makes it up the hill, but none too soon. They watch, and within fifteen minutes, the water on the camp's middle ground is too deep to wade through.

Once at Ministerium, the boys see girls who have also been evacuated from their sister camp, Camp Hagan. Not all the girls have been moved, though, and Charlie's little sister is not at Ministerium. He wonders if she's okay, and whether their parents back in Easton know anything about what's going on.

Girls from Camp Hagan, the Lutheran girls' counterpart to Camp Miller, await transportation home as part of the massive Pocono summer camp evacuation that came to be known as "Operation Kid Lift." Media reports of death at "Camp Davis" led many parents to panic, wondering about the safety of their own children at various camps throughout the region. The evacuation was more about calming these fears than any real danger to the campers. Few camps were in any peril.   *– Collection Bob Stalgaitis*

With the rising of the sun, it's clear Paradise Falls has become less than idyllic. As soon as she can safely make it up the way to Harold Bates' cottage, Lydia Stielau asks him if he'd mind calling their home in Long Island. She wants to leave a message for Edward, letting him know they're okay, in case he's heard anything on the news about the flooding. Harold says he will, since the Stielaus' cottage doesn't have a phone. He makes the call when he gets back to his cottage, but Edward never gets the message. He and Carolyn are already on their way up.

Harry Leida knows that soon, his sister Jane will be hearing about the flooding in the Stroudsburgs and get worried about her son, Fred. Early in the morning, Harry walks the three miles into downtown East Stroudsburg to see what's going on, and whether the water has gone down enough for him to cross the bridge.

As he gets closer to the Flats, the streets begin to get muddy, and there is a foul, putrid stench in the air. He realizes it's coming from the mud that covers everything. In the already hot morning, the top layer is forming a dry crust, like the scab on a festering wound. Soon he sees huge piles of wreckage and debris—boards, garbage cans, boxes, tires, mangled lawn chairs—pushed up against fences and walls. When he reaches the Flats themselves, he barely recognizes the place. Cars are stacked up on each other, and entire blocks of houses are simply gone.

Harry is stunned and sickened by the devastation. He knows many of the people who live here. He even works with some of them at Line Material company. He remembers that he came to find a way to get Fred over to Stroudsburg and back down to Easton with his mother. Clearly, it won't be this way. The Interborough Bridge is gone, swept dozens of yards downstream, one of its steel spans pushed back along the far bank, the other in mid-channel where the roaring Brodhead had dropped it. Harry decides to try farther upstream.

Relieved to get out of the malodorous area, he strikes back north, walking as close as he dares venture along the still-high creek. He decides today isn't a good day to bring young Fred downtown. Too many chances he'll see something really disturbing, or maybe even get hurt.

When Harry gets back to his parents' house, he tells his mother to keep Fred occupied, that he's pretty sure he'll be able to get him out tomorrow. Meanwhile, he's going to head back downtown with his camera. The Flats are a mess and he doesn't think the plant will be open today. He asks to borrow their car to get down there, and lets her know it might be a long time before he gets back.

Incongruity

Friday, August 19
Dawn – 10:00 a.m.

As soon as it's light enough to see, the LeCropane girls and Marion Baker wake up and leave the Pinebrook Inn. Linda had lain awake most of the night, wondering what they would find when they went over to Davis Cabins in the morning. She runs ahead of her sister and their friend to a little knoll, where the flagpole is on the Inn's front lawn. What she sees makes her pull up short.

Yesterday, there had been trees obscuring the view across the Brodhead, but now all that has been washed away. Linda can see clear across the bank to the other side. No buildings obscure her view, either. The roads are gone; so are the cornfields and the cars. They've been replaced by a wash of round, light gray stones from the creek. The rubble stretches as far as she can see, interrupted only here and there by railroad cars strewn like children's blocks that have been carelessly tossed about.

Linda's breath catches in her throat. Davis'…is just…gone. "Sara! There's nothing there!"

Sara catches up to her little sister, out of breath. She stiffens as she beholds the vast, rubble-strewn wash that had been their summer home for more than half her life.

"Where did the people go?" Linda asks. She can't conceive that they have been washed away, too. Looking around wildly, she sees some small, white shapes on the side of a mountain, and points. "Maybe that's them." But they both know it isn't.

188

Marion has now come alongside the sisters, comprehending the very wrongness of the scene before them. The three just stand there, not knowing what to do.

After what seems an eternity, they walk toward the little bridge Linda had been the last to cross, less than twelve hours earlier. They peer over the guardrail to see only water and debris, and small islands breaking the surface. Then they notice Pinebrook's founder and director, Percy Crawford, standing there in his robe. The girls are stunned, since he has been on doctor-ordered bed rest since suffering a heart attack weeks earlier.

They study his face. His features are drawn from the strain and shock. Clearly, he's assessed the situation and has come to the inescapable conclusion that Davis Cabins—and everyone who had been in them—are gone. He notices the girls. A pained look crosses his face, then softens.

"How many of you are there?" he asks.

Sara replies, "Just the three of us."

Percy nods his head slowly, the full realization of the destruction hitting him. He continues to nod at the girls, and they know they'll be welcome to stay at Pinebrook. They also comprehend that Uncle Henry, Aunt Lil, and Honey, their old beagle, are probably dead.

The girls' thoughts drift as they stare over toward where their summer homes had been. Occasionally, they talk openly about the likelihood that everyone they knew at Davis' is dead.

They watch members of the Pinebrook staff, including the young men of the quartet, looking for bodies. When one is found, it is taken to the old Gish farm nearby, part of the Pinebrook property. The girls are told that someone has seen the recovery teams take Aunt Lil there, but they don't know if they mean their aunt or simply her body. Has she somehow survived?

The girls also see motorboats getting out on the water as it subsides, trying to rescue people standing out on islands of debris. Likely, some of these are survivors of Davis Cabins, but the girls can't know that.

The Pinebrook staff is solicitous of the girls' needs. Like the rest of the people at the Bible Retreat, the girls must drink water redolent of bleach, added to kill any bacteria in the compromised wells. There's plenty of food, but it's all sandwiches and things that don't require cooking, since there are no electrical or other services.

The scene of greatest destruction and loss of life in the Delaware Valley is this area just south of Analomink, where the Brodhead Creek widened from its usual 20 feet to 300 yards, and rose 20-30 feet inside of 15 minutes on the night of August 18, 1955. The main buildings and cabin circle of Pinebrook Bible Conference and Retreat are on the far left. Old highway 90 (now 191) is in the foreground. At center are the remains of the highway bridge that connected it to what is now Route 447.

The arrow at top left points to what is left of Davis Cabins—an expanse of bare ground with a single cement slab and a few well casings sticking up here and there where the earth around them has been washed away. The arrow at top right indicates the DL&W train, most of its cars still on the tracks, where the engine crew had taken refuge from the flood. They listened to the screams and cries of those perishing in the disintegrating buildings of Davis', while wondering if they'd be the next to go.

– Courtesy U.S. Army Depot at Tobyhanna

Bud Blandeau, a staffer, takes the girls under his wing, finding them comfortable bunks in one of the cabins. He also gives them some comic books to read so they can take their minds off the constant air of tragedy that surrounds them. Linda is grateful for the relief.

Later in the day, someone suggests to Linda, in passing, that she and Sara might be asked to identify some of the bodies. This frightens her terribly, so she hides for quite a while in the ladies' room.

Reporters have found their way onto the Pinebrook property and are asking to speak with the sisters and their friend. The girls remain blissfully unaware of this, as they are of Percy Crawford's orders for the reporters to vacate the property and leave the traumatized teens alone.

Bob Robacker hasn't slept well in his upstairs neighbors' apartment in Newfoundland. He has catnapped, awakened constantly by strange and unsettling noises, not just outside but also down in his own apartment. He has been keeping tabs on the water levels all night, and notices by one thirty a.m. that it has stopped rising. By three a.m., the beam of his flashlight reveals that it has begun to recede, to his great relief.

At dawn, his wife and their neighbors, Robert and June Schafer, awaken. Nobody has gotten much rest, and they all look haggard. Bob tells them the water has gone down, and now they're curious to see how the rest of their community has fared. June is also anxious to find some baby food, since she had been going to pick some up today. Otherwise, little Patricia won't have anything for lunch or supper.

As they all descend the stairs, they see a clear waterline at the third step, about two feet up. Things they hadn't been able to carry upstairs—larger furniture, books, and knick-knacks—are strewn about throughout the apartment. Bob's wife, Edith, is in no great hurry to experience the devastation of her home and neighborhood. She agrees to stay upstairs and watch the children, while her husband and the Schafers go downtown to survey the situation.

Everything in the Robackers' apartment is covered with a four-inch layer of dark, stinking silt. Their shoes squish into the muck as they venture out onto the porch for a first look.

The Pocono town of Newfoundland finds itself isolated by bridges and roads over and along the Wallenpaupack Creek torn out or missing entirely. A resident's connection to the Tobyhanna Signal Depot will prove fortuitous for the hamlet.
— *Courtesy U.S. Army Depot at Tobyhanna*

The neighbors step off into about ten inches of the same, dark mess, taking care not to lose their footing in the slippery stuff. A pile of dimensional lumber from the lumberyard has been deposited on the porch, and water is still knee-deep as far as they can see. The morning is bright and sunny, a strange and ironic counterpoint to the blatant destruction all around them.

Bob reminds his companions of the need to be careful where they walk. The still-muddy water may be obscuring sinkholes or other dangers beneath its surface, so they make their way slowly toward the downtown area. As they slog closer to their goal, they're joined by other members of their community. It seems everyone is out walking, wanting to know what has happened.

The three companions finally reach the downtown stretch of Newfoundland. The grocery store is tipped off its foundation, and the door hangs open. June enters and looks around. Of course, no one is there, so she finds a few jars of baby food and takes them. When she gets home, she'll make a list of what she's taken and pay the grocer later. The men have walked off to look around, so June proceeds to the office of their family physician, Dr. Frank Uridell, to see if he has any news.

While she waits to speak with the doctor, she watches a teenage boy being treated for exposure. It is young Ray Phillips of Greentown. She listens to his story of having held on all night to his grandmother's kitchen table before finally being washed away. He hasn't seen his grandmother, Kate Phillips, again, but had somehow managed to grab onto a tree limb and pull himself to safety in its higher branches until being rescued that morning by a canoeist. June is horrified by the tale, and wonders how many others have suffered a similar fate.

Finally, Dr. Uridell comes out to see her. He tells her that every area bridge has been washed out and the phone lines are all dead. In effect, Newfoundland is isolated from the outside world. He's not even sure that anyone knows they've been hit by the floods. He wishes he could give her better news, but he can't, and now he must return to helping those he can.

Shaken, June goes back outside to locate Robert. He and Bob have learned similar news about the bridges. She tells them the Phillips boy's story, and the men relate that they've heard nearly his entire family has been killed, along with several others. No one yet knows the total amount of fatalities, but it's clear the water has reached twelve feet deep in the lower part of town. June marvels at the destruction just half that depth has wrought at their place, and shudders.

The gravity of the situation begins to settle in. They wonder aloud about how they will keep enough food and find water that's not contaminated. The smell of the water and mud reminds them that sanitation will also soon become an issue. All around them, people exhibit a dazed look. The entire village is in shock, and nobody seems to know quite what to do.

By seven a.m., all volunteer firemen from Point Pleasant are working in teams to help relieve Carversville of its burden of mud. They'd had to take the back way in from Lumberville, since the center of town had been torn up and they'd been unable to get the trucks through.

They spend the morning pumping water from basements and hosing off filth-covered floors so the townspeople can begin to get back to normal. For most of the firefighters, it's already been a long night, and the days ahead loom with relentless need of their services.

Helen Brown's next assignment is to find housing for people from East Stroudsburg State Teacher's College infirmary and for town residents who had been evacuated from the Flats. After making the necessary arrangements, she uses a staff car from the college to begin the operation.

One of her first passengers is a woman in her twenties, who had been staying at the college infirmary. The woman is frantic because she had left her engagement and wedding rings in a drawer at her fiancé's trailer on the way to Bushkill Falls, where she lives. Helen assures her they'll be going right by that way and can stop to check about the rings.

When they get there, a neighbor who knows the woman comes to the road to greet her. The farmer tells her that the trailer has been washed away, but luckily, had come to rest against his barn. He volunteers to search it for her rings. When he opens the door, the small compartment is awash in several feet of dark, smelly mud. He scoops some out of the way to get to the drawer that the young woman has described. Pulling it open, he finds the box. Though soft with moisture, it is intact, and the rings are all there. He delivers it to the much-relieved and very grateful young woman, and Helen drives her on up Route 209 toward her family in Bushkill.

When they arrive, they see many people working to fill in the washed-out bridge over the Big Bushkill River. It's not yet sturdy enough to support vehicular traffic, so they leave the car and cross on foot. A man, one of the young woman's relatives, approaches them. He tells them he has hiked over the Old Hogback Road from the town of Delaware to seek out some food and supplies. He has only two dollars with him.

Helen informs him that the Red Cross and Civil Defense have organized shelters and dispensaries for those affected by the floods. She takes his address, and later gives it to her other niece, Jane, to deliver supplies to his family. Jane and her husband, Sonny, meet Helen and the young woman at their home in Bushkill. They agree to act as Helen's point people in the town, distributing supplies she will deliver several times over the coming weeks. The young woman leaves with her relative to go home to her parents.

Satisfied she has done all she can, Helen returns to the college, reporting on her delivery of the young woman and what she has seen in Bushkill. She arranges to have the promised supplies delivered there, then returns to her apartment to get some fresh clothes. Taking a circuitous route that avoids the worst of the washed-out roads and bridges, she drives over a temporary bridge that has been erected at Stokes Mill back into Stroudsburg. She finds that her apartment had been flooded while she was away, and all the clothes she'd put in the basement are ruined.

Her niece helps her find some things to wear, and Helen drives back up to the Lehighton Diner to retrieve her trailer, which contains some clothes and her other cameras. She realizes she'll need a place to live until things get cleaned up, so she tows it back to town. Its forty-gallon propane tank will allow her to cook and sleep there comfortably. She parks it by the college, where it will stay until permanent housing becomes available.

For the next few weeks, Helen will keep busy making food runs to Schuykill Haven, where she used to teach, bringing supplies back to Stroudsburg area churches for distribution to the stricken towns. She'll help in the cleanup effort and with Civil Defense in returning the Stroudsburgs to normal. And in the process, she'll document it all, creating one of the most thorough and extensive records of the worst disaster ever to hit Monroe County.

Col. Robert Angster, commanding officer of the Tobyhanna Army Signal Depot, had been aware of the devastation going on around the base since rescue calls had begun coming in late last night. At

Col. Robert Angster, commander of the Tobyhanna Signal Depot, points out an area of particular destruction to a government official on an aerial tour of the devastated Pocono region.

— Courtesy U.S. Army Depot at Tobyhanna

A military helicopter flies low over an unidentified area of the wooded Pocono Mountain region, looking for survivors and stranded residents and vacationers who may be injured or need rescuing from precarious situations. The flood established a link between the Tobyhanna Army Depot and its surrounding community that would remain even fifty years later. *— Courtesy U.S. Army Depot at Tobyhanna*

sunup, he had gone on an aerial survey of the surrounding Pocono region, and had been sickened by what he'd seen. He realized the potential for his command to function as a search-and-rescue base of operations, and how this function fit into the Army's mission to serve and protect its country.

This photo was taken by U.S. Army Lt. James Poole during a flyover of the ravaged Pocono region surrounding Tobyhanna Signal Depot. It shows the massive destruction and huge debris piles left in Henryville by the Brodhead Creek. In the upper left is the ruins of the Highway 90 bridge that has been torn out. That was just part of the destruction that included the washing away of several homes, a restaurant, service station and part of a resort.

— Courtesy U.S. Army Depot at Tobyhanna

Immediately upon returning to the base at eight thirty a.m., he had cancelled the schedule of regular activities and had implemented Operation Tempest Rapids, the base's most comprehensive disaster response ever. The large parking lot had been cleared of vehicles, light poles and wires to serve as an emergency heliport. Helicopters from the Army, Navy, Air Force and Marine Corps, along with light aircraft, had been moved into the lot and readied for dispatch.

Capt. Christopher Rossetti ran the emergency command post inside the guard control station at Tobyhanna Signal Depot, which included an amateur radio station to handle emergency communications on the FCC frequency established for such situations. It was staffed by ham radio operators from the post. — *Courtesy U.S. Army Depot at Tobyhanna*

Col. Angster and his deputy commander, Lt. Robert Glover, had established an emergency command post inside the base's guard control building. By nine thirty a.m., the depot's Military Affiliate Radio Station (MARS) K3WCQ had gone into operation under the command of Capt. Christopher Rossetti. It would handle emergency traffic on the Federal Communication Commission's decreed emergency frequency net, which consisted of amateur radio stations located throughout Pennsylvania and other affected states. Only traffic directly connected with the flood disaster and relief would be allowed over this net, assuring operators of utmost efficiency.

Capt. Rosetti had immediately set up a round-the-clock operation schedule, calling up "ham" operators on base who held FCC licenses to man the station. Nine such operators from Tobyhanna had responded right away, setting themselves up on a rotating basis to keep the center active twenty-four hours a day.

Now, Col. Angster is ready to begin what will become a twenty-six-day emergency operation in rescue, recovery and humanitarian aid. He and Col. Glover receive and screen all incoming requests for aid from the distressed area. They work to prioritize assignments in concert with Lt. Col. R.C. Spiedel, Deputy Commanding Officer of the Training Transportation Command, Aviation Group, at Fort Eustis, Virginia. Spiedel is in charge of air operations for the effort.

One of their first duties is establishing bases of operation in the field. Based on the calls that have come in and ongoing reports being monitored through various news and law enforcement agencies, the Tobyhanna command identifies the hardest-hit areas and sends key personnel to staff field operations.

An overturned car in a newly carved ditch at the Cresco train station attests to the ferocity of the flood torrents that ripped through the area and imperiled passengers stranded on the tracks by a series of washouts.   *– Courtesy U.S. Army Depot at Tobyhanna*

Stranded passengers, most headed to Scranton, mill about the platform at the Cresco train station, awaiting evacuation in Army buses, one of which sits in the foreground. Others, heading for more remote locations, were airlifted by helicopter. Below, one of the washouts that stranded them, at Devil's Hole.

— Courtesy U.S. Army Depot at Tobyhanna

Capt. Delbert Cole, Assistant Chief of the Stock Control Division, is assigned to coordinate operations at the Stroudsburgs. Lt. Col. John Woodburn, Transportation Officer, is put in charge of evacuating the passengers of the two DL&W trains marooned at Cresco and Tobyhanna. He dispatches helicopters to the tracks near Tobyhanna, while Army buses are sent to pick up those at the Cresco station and deliver them to safety. Lt. Col. Fred Sorady, Post Engineer, is sent to construct an emergency bridge to replace that washed out by the Wallenpaupack Creek at Rt. 490 in South Sterling. This effort will be crucial to enabling supplies to be brought into the stricken area.

Helicopter occupants got a bird's eye view of many post-flood activities, such as this one of the Rt. 611 bridge at Swiftwater, already being repaired by August 22, 1955.
– Courtesy U.S. Army Depot at Tobyhanna

Sorady's efforts, along with those of many others, rely heavily on the work of Major William Thorn, Provost Marshal, who is maintaining close coordination with the Pennsylvania State Police in furnishing updates on road conditions. Maj. Thorn sets out to survey the area for himself, and will eventually drive over five hundred miles of flood-damaged roads in the next week.

The Brodhead Creek undercut the banks and abutments of the highway bridge in Canadensis, finally toppling the critical traffic link into its raging waters. Like many other remote Pocono towns, Canadensis would remain isolated for quite some time before permanent repairs could be made.　　*– Courtesy U.S. Army Depot at Tobyhanna*

Barrett Township, including the ravaged Canadensis area, will receive food, potable water, medicine and other survival supplies due to the efforts of Capt. Donald Chirafisi, Chief Purchasing officer, Capt. John Cullen, Jr., of the Storage Division, and Lt. Robert Ironside, Jr., Assistant Adjutant. The Depot's Legal Advisor, Harold Shannon, coordinates the removal of the 48,000 quarts of milk aboard the train stranded at Tobyhanna. Through the permission of the railroad, the milk is airlifted by helicopter and distributed to flood survivors in the area before it can spoil in the heat.

Reconnaissance missions, in search of distressed survivors in need of rescue, are accompanied by Louis DePaul, Assistant to the Executive Officer, and Ken Banzhof from the personnel division. These two civilian employees of the Depot are Pocono natives and know the area well. They help helicopter pilots locate survivors stranded in trees, buildings and isolated areas.

Lt. Col. Vincent Fox, Chief of Maintenance, is tapped to coordinate the Newfoundland area effort. Knowing one of Tobyhanna's officers, Maj. Robert Schafer, lives in the area, Fox requests to be flown there. He wants to check on Schafer's condition, and if possible, to establish him as the area's base commander. Col. Angster gives the nod, and Fox readies himself to go into the field.

This Canadensis cottage may have been one of those from whose bedrooms sleeping Philadelphia vacationers dropped to their deaths into the raging Brodhead Creek, which had chewed away their foundations. — *Courtesy U.S. Army Depot at Tobyhanna*

Johnny Birutta and his brother Larry are riding with their mother and next-door neighbor Bob Michelson in Bob's station wagon. They're going across the Belvidere bridge to rescue some cats belonging to a friend of his mother's. The people are out of town and have called, frantic, hearing that their vacation trailer may be flooded and fearing for the lives of their pets. Bob is a barber, but no one's interested in having their hair cut today, so he's accompanying the Biruttas on their mission.

The water is rising, and Bob says they must hurry to get back before authorities close the bridge. Little John doesn't understand how the water can still be rising on such a beautiful, sunny day.

The four rescuers manage to find all the cats and bring them home safely to wait for their owners' return. Once back home, the Biruttas spend much of the morning watching the river engulf Market Street. It comes within about ten yards of their home.

John's dad takes the boys walking along the railroad tracks to the high ground north of the Belvidere Bridge. From there, they watch the brown, churning cauldron of river water flowing under and through the bridge. As Bob Michelson had anticipated, the span has now been closed to traffic, too vulnerable to floating debris to be safe. As they stand watching, a house rides the current to its demise, smashing into kindling against the bridge. It splinters into jagged boards, bubbling a last gasp before disappearing beneath the surface. Spellbound, the Birutta boys watch a show they'll never forget.

One of their neighbors, Ivan Sanderson, is having trouble with his own show. His roadside attraction, the Jungle Zoo, is in jeopardy. Nearly eighty wild animals are in danger of drowning as the Delaware River creeps ever nearer their cages. Most of them are being herded by keepers into a barn on a hill nearby, but several cannot practically be moved there.

Jocko the crocodile, a main attraction of the zoo, is seven feet long and weighs 240 pounds. He's simply too large to wrangle into the barn. A golden eagle and a Palestinian porcupine are also too unwieldy to relocate. Handler Edgar Schoenenberger is getting desperate, and begs Ivan to let the left-behind animals loose before they drown in their enclosures. Ivan reluctantly agrees.

Edgar opens the door and watches the eagle fly off toward Manunka Chunk Mountain. The porcupine swims away as its cage is opened. Now there's just Jocko to contend with. Edgar clenches a pair of wire cutters in his teeth and swims through neck-deep water to the alligator's cage. Just as he finishes cutting a large enough hole in its wire, Jocko slips through, crashes into the river, and disappears.

In Bushkill, Ellworth Peiffer is busy evacuating people from the cabin colony where he lives on the J. Russell Eshback farm. He had been watching the night before as boats from the colony near the water's edge, one by one, had broken free from their moorings and taken off downriver under the onslaught of the strengthening current.

Earlier this morning, as daylight had straggled across the fields between his home and the cabins, it revealed that the river was back-watering. The water has now completely surrounded the colony, and he's certain it will eventually overrun the cabins.

He motors out to what is now an island, waking anyone who has managed to sleep through the night, and telling them to gather their things and be ready to evacuate. Fortunately, most of the cottagers don't usually arrive until Friday, so there aren't as many to rescue as there might be.

It takes Ellworth three trips to remove thirteen adults, seven children and three dogs to safety. By mid-afternoon, all seventeen of the cottages will be washed away by the spreading Delaware.

Two miles south, eighty-two-year-old retired Judge E.E. Bonniwell and his semi-invalid wife are being evacuated from their cabin at Cakeout along the Big Bushkill Creek.

The settlement of thirty-five cabins is isolated, since the bridge over the creek had washed away early this morning on the only road leading to the enclave. The water has invaded the summer homes of three families here, and they've all escaped to their rooftops. The one consolation is that the rain has stopped and the day has dawned warm and sunny.

Mrs. Harold Griffin, her eleven-year-old son, and a Pen Argyl man make up the unlikely rescue team, typical of the spontaneous efforts of many ordinary individuals who find it in themselves to do extraordinary things this day.

Peter Barry is furious. He had spent the entire morning on Thursday painting the shutters on his family's new Buckmanville house. He stands before it now, and it looks as though it hasn't been touched. The drenching rains have washed away every vestige of his work. And of course today, it's clear, bright and sunny.

Heaving a sigh, he realizes there's nothing to do but start all over again. It's going to have to wait until he can get back into town for more paint. Besides, they're expecting guests for a housewarming dinner, and he won't have time to complete the project before they arrive this evening.

Peter's wife, Alice, has finished with her marketing in Lambertville and is driving back across the bridge to New Hope. She looks down and admires the swirling, rushing torrent. She has heard that the river is rising a foot an hour, but she can't concern herself with it. She must hurry home to make preparations for their visitors.

Across the river in Titusville, Dusty Scudder wakes to a warm, humid day. He stretches and rubs his eyes, and the glow of a rising sun illuminates his parents' porch, where he had fallen asleep. He grins. The sun means he and Mudguard will be able to get the boats out today, and he's ready to get moving. He goes into the house to get some breakfast and a shower. When he opens the door, he sees the family dog sitting on the hearth, a strange place and not very comfortable. Then he sees why. There are four inches of water everywhere else on the pine strip floor.

Dusty wakes his mom and makes sure everything else in the house is okay. There's no use trying to get rid of the water until it goes down, so he grabs a quick bite of breakfast and heads off to wake Mudguard. The two young men do what many other daredevils are doing today: they get in their motorboats and take advantage of the ability to zoom around everywhere they normally can't go in a boat. As a lark, Dusty has persuaded his mom and his cousin, Tommy, to go along.

They run the skiff up and down the river, in and around old abandoned houses and, foolishly, across the quickening current to the Pennsylvania side and up the canal. The current's not as strong as it will be later on this stretch of the river, as the crest hasn't yet reached down this far.

They make it halfway upriver to New Hope, then get bored. On the way back down, Dusty realizes the current has picked up, and now they're dodging trees, boards and huge rolls of paper from the mills upstream. He realizes they will be in serious trouble if they happen to shear a pin on the outboard motor. Just then, they run over the top of one of the camelback canal bridges and the propeller clips its railing. He hears the sickening, telltale *ring-ning-ning-ning-ning* of a sheared pin.

The boat continues its forward momentum into the main river channel, and Dusty looks up to see one of the Jersey side canal bridges just ahead. There's only about eighteen inches of space between the water's surface and the bridge deck. There's no time for a repair. Dusty looks at his mom and cousin in the bow of the boat, and knows he has to think fast.

The propeller still spins, allowing him to maintain some control and forward motion. He figures if he can angle the boat just right and hold steady, the current will push them across, just like the historical society people do when re-enacting Washington crossing the Delaware at Christmastime. He throttles way back, and the propeller catches just a bit.

In the nail-biting moments that follow, they edge slowly across the channel, drifting ever closer to the bridge looming just downstream. They notice Rev. Kilbury, the minister from the church, on the far bank. He doesn't realize they've sheared a pin. He thinks they're just drifting closer to the bridge to play chicken, and he's jumping up and down and waving them off. As the boat approaches the bank, he runs down to meet it.

Finally, Dusty tells Tommy to stand up in the bow and reach out for a tree that's hanging out from the bank. Tommy puts a "love-lock" hug on it, and Mudguard throws a rope to Rev. Kilbury, who pulls them to safety. The whole time, he's yelling at the boys about what a stupid trick it was to pull.

After they're back on shore, Dusty's mom, a bit shaken, heads for home. She tells the boys not to try anything else like that, just to stay off the water. They don't need to be told twice. They spend the rest of the day pulling in the neighborhood docks as the river rises. They listen to the mashing and grinding of rocks tumbling against the steel drums that keep them afloat, and have plenty of time to reflect on their good luck.

Cliff and Virginia Sutton have their hands full in Carpentersville. The river has been rising all night, and now Virginia's dad says he's sure it will come up and carry away the All Inn unless they do something to save it. It seems impossible, since it has stopped raining and the morning sky is blue and sunny, but Virginia admits the water is still coming up and agrees with her father.

Reluctantly, he saws a hole toward the corner of the roof and opens all the windows, even removing the screens. He explains to everyone that the less resistance the cottage offers to the water, the less likely it is to be ripped from its foundation. He's creating as much pass-through space for the water as possible.

Virginia, Cliff and the rest of the family pack up dishes and linens, stashing them in upper cupboards and cabinets. They may get wet there, but won't wash away, as long as the cottage stays intact. And if it washes away, they won't need the items anyway.

When they're done, they go over to LaFayette to help Virginia's aunts secure their cottage. Her father runs a huge, thick rope through the hole in the All Inn's roof and its windows, then around a massive oak tree just outside. They know they're right in taking such precautions when a work crew comes around to turn off electric service. It confirms their suspicions that the river will indeed invade their beloved cottage.

Down the road, thirteen-year-old Tom Zimmerman is enjoying the antics of his summer colony neighbors goofing around, paddling boats up and down the flooded roadway. It doesn't occur to him to be alarmed. Everyone is saying that the river will crest now that the rain has stopped, that it can't get much higher. But it does get higher, and soon Tom's mother calls him to come help move furniture and valuables to the second floor.

Meanwhile, neighbors Philip and Marie Baty and their five-year-old daughter Phyllis are making plans to leave for a beach day at Wildwood. The Batys live in a very old stone home, situated on two acres at the highest elevation between Carpentersville's two railroad crossings. People have come by to tell them the river is up, and Philip finds little Phyllis back in their horse pasture petting her pony, Betty. He asks her if she'd like to take a walk down to see the river. Phyllis scampers out to the road to meet him. It seems everyone is outside, and they talk with several neighbors along the way.

They reach the riverside and watch its latté-colored waters surging past, rising slowly the whole time. A neighbor talks with Phil about the probability of the water getting high enough to come in the cottages along the bank tops.

I just can't believe it, he says. *We didn't get that much rain, not even as much as from the last storm.*

No, agrees Phil, *but who knows how much they got up north of here?*

The men stand in silent consideration for a moment, then the neighbor asks Phil if he might store some of their valuable personal items up in his house until the flood's over.

I think it might be best, don't you? Phil replies.

His neighbor casts his eyes out over the water again, takes a deep breath, and nods.

Well then, Phil says, *I guess we'd better get at it.* He looks down at Phyllis, who's splashing about in a puddle with her little cowboy boots. *Wildwood will have to wait for another day, honey. Our neighbors need help.*

Phyllis looks up and nods, smiling.

That's my girl, Phil says, swinging her up over his shoulder. As he upends her, water cascades out of her boots over both of them, and they erupt in laughter.

They walk back to the house and Phil explains the change of plans to Marie. She climbs the stairs to clear some room in the attic while Phil goes to the barn to hitch his tractor to a hay wagon. He spends the remainder of the day driving it up and down the road, hauling his neighbors' belongings to safety.

Peggy Beling is waking up to the sun, pleased to see it after all the rain. She shuts off her alarm and begins getting ready for work. She's a door-to-door census taker for the Easton School District, working out of an elementary school office on downtown Second Street, between Northampton and Spring Garden Streets. It's a summer job, done to determine upcoming school populations for planning purposes. She works with three others and their boss on the second floor of the building.

As she dresses, she hears on WEST-AM that the Delaware River is rising. Only half-awake and busy getting ready, she's not paying much attention. After breakfast, she drives a car borrowed from her parents down Cottage Hill from their home in Forks Township. Turning right, she climbs Cottage Avenue, and looks down toward the river view she always enjoys.

The deck of the railroad bridge over the Lehigh River on Easton's Third Street is only about eight feet above the river's roiled surface as the flood continues to rise on August 19, 1955.
— Bradwin Roberts photo, collection Linda Roberts

She is shocked to see water almost to Front Street, and recalls the bulletin she'd heard earlier. She parks the car and greets her co-worker, Judy, who's already in the office. When their co-workers arrive, they all walk up into the clock tower attached to the building, to get a better view of the rising water.

They watch it creep over Front Street and begin swallowing the rise between Front and Second. They're discussing whether or not it will reach their office, and if it's smart for them to go out polling today. Then their supervisor, Attendance Officer Snyder, appears. He tells the young people that it would be a good idea if they all went home, because nobody is sure how high the water is going to get. He can't assure their safety.

It's the first inkling Peggy has that the situation could get serious. The fact becomes even clearer when she's unable to get back home the way she had come, because the backed-up waters of Bushkill Creek are already across Third Street at the foot of Cottage Hill. She drives to Thirteenth Street and across its higher-elevation bridge.

When she gets home, she asks her mother to drive her down Route 611 to the Fackenthal home. She's concerned about her fiancé's family and their property. Beautiful though it may be, it sits quite low along the river, and she knows it must be in jeopardy. Her mother is afraid they'll get stuck somewhere and refuses to drive her down. Their neighbor is already going that way later, and says she'll take Peggy down Frost Hollow Road and drop her off on Rt. 611, which is called Delaware Avenue there. It's all Peggy can do to keep herself occupied until after lunch.

Beneath the surface of the foreground water lies the Third Street Sunoco gas station. At the height of the crest, not a single part of the building was visible. Eventually, a fast-food restaurant will occupy the same site, and will be flooded in September, 2004 and April, 2005.   *— Bradwin Roberts photo, collection Linda Roberts*

Ed Stielau and his daughter, Carolyn, wonder what the holdup is ahead. They've reached Hackettstown on their way to join the rest of their family at their Paradise Falls cottage, but traffic is stopped. Ed thinks perhaps there may have been a washout from last night's heavy rain, but he doubts it. They didn't get that much, really.

He's startled when they finally pull into view of a National Guardsman, who's waving people off from proceeding further north. When it's his turn, Ed rolls down his window.

What's going on? he asks.

I'm sorry, sir, but I'm afraid I can't permit you to go any farther north, the guard replies. *Lots of roads and bridges are out up ahead.*

What? Ed says, incredulous. *We didn't have that much rain! How many are out?*

They got a lot more up north than we did, sir. Please turn around and go back home until the situation is resolved.

What 'situation?' It's just a few roads out. Can't you tell me another route I could take? My wife and kids are up in the Poconos, and they're expecting us to join them today.

The water in Easton's Northampton Street is even with that which covers the deck of the Free Bridge to Phillipsburg.

– *Bradwin Roberts photo, collection Linda Roberts*

Upon hearing this, the Guard's eyes soften a bit. He moves closer to the window and ducks his head level with Ed's. *Sir, I'm terribly sorry, but the whole Poconos region has been declared a disaster area. I'm not positive, but we've heard they got more than ten inches of rain yesterday. The mountains were all saturated. That water just ran off into all the rivers and…well, there has been serious flooding and a lot of damage. We're here to keep sightseers out of the area so rescue crews can do their jobs.*

Rescue crews! What…are people stranded? He thinks of Lydia and the girls, sitting at the foot of that slope. Or worse.

The soldier looks at Carolyn sitting next to her father. He doesn't want to alarm her, but he also needs to be honest with Ed.

Sir, yes, sir. There are some people stranded. And there is…news, from some of the camps. Not everyone…um, not everyone is accounted for.

Ed feels his blood run cold.

Where? Do you know where?

The guard is sympathetic.

No, sir, I'm sorry. I don't. All I know is that there are people reported missing and I'm not allowed to let any traffic through that might interfere with them being found. So please, go home and listen to the news. I'm sure your wife will call you as soon as she can. But that might be a while, just so you know. Most places don't have phone or electric service right now.

Blinking, Ed looks at the young man. He can see he's earnest and trying to be helpful. Ed leans closer.

Isn't there anywhere I can get through?

No sir, I'm truly sorry. You won't be getting anywhere near the Poconos today. Even if you could find a route that isn't roadblocked, it's probably only because you can't get through on it anyway. The soldier pauses, casting a glance at the long line of vehicles forming behind Ed's car. *Sir, I'm going to have to ask you to turn around now. The traffic's building up behind you.*

Yeah, sorry. Thanks for the information.

Ed puts the car in gear. As he looks out the passenger window to make sure the way is clear, he catches a glance at Carolyn. Her face is white, and her eyes are clouded with fear and concern.

It'll be okay, he tells her, with an assurance he doesn't feel. *Mr. Bates is up there. He wouldn't let anything happen to them. We'll just go home and wait for them to call.*

He turns the car around and begins one of the longest two-hour rides of his life.

The situation on the Delaware River islands is becoming critical, according to reports received by Col. Heritage at his command center in Newtown. Most of the Boy Scouts on Treasure Island have been able to get to shore in Pennsylvania using their regular ferry scows, but Pennington and Marshall are rapidly being overrun by the rising river. He puts in a desperate call to Johnsville Naval Base, requesting as many helicopters as they have to be dispatched immediately.

Cdr. Franklin has several H-21s and HUPs in the area already, but they're engaged in rescue operations of their own. The crafts' crews are plucking stranded people from rooftops, trees and telephone poles in lower Bucks County and elsewhere. Thinking quickly, he calls the Piasecki Helicopter Corporation in Moorestown to ask if they have any new craft available for use. Piasecki indicates that indeed, they have eight H-21s ready for delivery. Franklin tells them to mobilize. He dispatches Navy pilots and crew from Johnsville, and they ready the craft to fuel and fly to the islands near Erwinna, Pennsylvania.

Life rafts and jackets are loaded into a PBY plane, in case the children can't all be picked up before the landing area is totally flooded, which would prevent any further helicopter relief. All nine aircraft soon take off for the Delaware.

Jay Folkes and his wife, Sara Gardner, wake up to the sound of helicopters flying over their Tory Road home in Tinicum Township. They're immediately alarmed, because the *whop-whop-whop* of helicopter blades beating the air is not yet a familiar sound in 1955, and such a rarity can only mean trouble.

The night before, Jay and Sara had been listening to weather reports about the heavy rain when they discovered they had water coming in their basement. Worried about their children, six-year-old Lewis and eight-year-old Joan, who were attending the Presbyterian church camp on Pennington Island, they had driven down to the island's approach around midnight. They had been concerned for the island's safety, but the Point Pleasant fire department volunteer who had met them there had assured them everything was fine.

"Don't worry," he'd said. "This island's never been underwater." Indeed it had been underwater more than once in the past, but not in his lifetime. Like many others of his generation, he was unaware of this fact, and believed he was telling the truth to the worried parents.

Jay and Sara, having just moved that spring from Washington, D.C., know nothing of the area and had to trust the fireman. They had turned around and gone home to bed.

Now, hearing the helicopters, they telephone the camp's emergency number and are told that indeed, the river is flooding the island, but not to worry. Campers and staff are being airlifted to safety and can be picked up at the Frenchtown High School.

Army and Navy helicopters rendezvous in an Erwinna farm field before taking off to air-lift stranded campers and staff from three islands in the Delaware on August 19, 1955.
– Courtesy Tobyhanna Army Depot and the Boeing Corporation

Again, their lack of familiarity with the area gets in the way. They call the only person they can think of to ask directions. Local plumber "Malty" Schaible says he will meet them in Tinicum and lead the way.

They follow Malty several miles over muddy back roads to the Uhlerstown-Frenchtown Bridge, where he gives them instructions for finding the school once they get across. The river is already ominously high, and they're glad to get off the bridge.

On Pennington Island itself, the Gardner children are joining more than sixty fellow campers in gathering their belongings and piling them on the tables in the mess hall, the highest point in their camp. They have been told that the island is flooding and they need to sit in the mess hall until they can be evacuated.

One of the older campers is thirteen-year-old Elaine DeWinton. Having accompanied a friend to the camp, she has become a bit home-sick on her first lengthy stay away from her family. Now the disturbing

215

A group of counselors and other staff (right) await a signal from the pilot of a military helicopter, which has come to evacuate them from the Boy Scout camp on Treasure Island near Erwinna, that it's safe to get on board. The encroaching water is visible as the darker gray area at top of photo.

– Courtesy Tobyhanna Army Depot & the Boeing Corporation

news about the flooding has her terrified. She can't swim well, and begins wondering what will happen to them all. She even wonders if she'd be able to climb the flagpole if necessary to save herself. Finally, she just decides just to pray, asking God to save the camp.

It seems like a direct answer to her prayers when the counselors report that Navy helicopters are on the way to airlift them to the mainland. Because the camp is sponsored by Mt. Airy Presbyterian Church in Philadelphia, the campers will be taken to a firehouse on the Pennsylvania side, where their parents will pick them up.

Elaine is overjoyed, and awaits her turn to board the helicopter with a mixture of anticipation and anxiety. She has never been in any kind of aircraft before, and the choppers are large, very loud and intimidating.

The youngest campers are taken off the island first, and finally Elaine is strapped into a seat in the open passenger bay. Grateful for the seatbelt as the 'copter takes off, she watches out the side doorway as the trees fly by underneath. As the craft passes over the river and canal, she can see the coffee-colored water surging below and says another silent prayer of thanks.

On the other side of the island, Marie Petranto can see and hear the helicopters overhead as she and other counselors at the Campfire Girls camp try to keep their assembled charges calm. They've successfully gotten some of the younger campers across to the Pennsylvania mainland using their hand-pulled passenger barge, despite the strength of the current. However, as the last load had been starting across, the barge line had snapped, rendering that mode of transportation useless. It had just been lucky that no one had been hit by the flying line, or washed overboard into the roiling water.

Marie's friend and fellow counselor, Elsie Guidotti, is, at seventeen, older than most of the rest of the girls. She decides to take matters into her own hands.

"We've got to flag down one of the helicopters!" she tells Marie.

First, they must get the campers away from the water's edge and keep them together until they can be airlifted. They tie boats together in a circle and tie them to trees so they won't float away. They load the younger campers, who are shorter, into the boats to wait. Meanwhile, someone on staff has been able to get a message to Col. Heritage, and several choppers are now arriving to pick up the Campfire Girls.

One of the brand new Piasecki H-21s, already marked with Army insignia, lands first. The youngest campers are loaded on and it takes off, followed by a Navy ship. All the younger girls have been taken away by the time the water reaches chest-deep at the landing zone. The aircraft can no longer land without putting itself at risk. Instead, it hovers over the open area and drops a long rope with a knot at the end.

The older girls and counselors wait their turns in anchored rowboats, watching huge bubbles rise to the surface. From the smell that issues forth when they pop, the girls know they're indications of the camp's cesspools opening up beneath them. They're glad not to be standing in the water anymore.

In a photo taken by the crew of a helicopter waiting to airlift children and staff from Camp Wilson, a counselor wades in chest-deep water already covering Pennington Island. She is ferrying a canoe full of young campers from the bank barn used as the camp's crafts building, where they've been sheltering, toward the rescue craft.
– Courtesy Tobyhanna Army Depot and the Boeing Corporation

When it's her turn, Marie shinnies up the rope into the arms of flight-suited men waiting in the cargo bay. They pull her into the bay, which smells heavily of machine grease and aviation fuel. Marie can't wait to get out, but is thankful for the helicopter ride. The campers couldn't have waited but a few more minutes before they would have been in serious danger.

Donna Marcs wakes up in her cabin with other nine-year-olds at Camp Wilson on Marshall's Island, not far below Pennington in the river. Sunshine filters through the canvas top of the half log-walled structure, and she's happy the rain that had cancelled last night's sleep-out has finally ended. It was bad enough that she had arrived during the inundation from Connie last week, and she didn't want to spend her whole time at camp inside.

She throws back the tent flap, and her joy at seeing the sun is replaced by surprise at seeing the river topping its banks on the island. Usually, there is a fifteen-foot drop down to the water's edge. How can it be that the water's rising when the rain has stopped? It just doesn't make any sense...

218

Soon, counselors come around to the tents, telling the campers to put on their boots before walking to breakfast in the dining tent. They're also told to pack their things into their overnight bags.

What the campers don't know is that Wilson's director, Vernon Rossman, had been telephoned by the Bridge Commission guard at Frenchtown during the night, and warned that the river was rising dangerously fast. He had called the counselors together before first light and told them of the situation, stressing the need to stay calm so they could quickly evacuate the camp without causing panic.

The campers are delighted to be allowed to eat their morning cereal right out of the wax-lined boxes. They're told that the camp's dishwashers are malfunctioning, but the truth is that the staff knows there won't be time to wash dishes and get them put away before everyone must leave.

When they finish eating, the campers have a ball, playing in puddles all over the island and trying to catch the many frogs that have suddenly appeared on land.

After everyone has burned off some of the energy built up over days indoors, the counselors take everyone into the big bank barn used as a crafts building. The children are put to work making lanyards. Lots and lots of lanyards. Fortunately, none of the girls is overly curious about their confinement to the crafts barn. If anyone senses anything seriously wrong, they don't say anything. Most of them don't notice

Campers from the Delaware River islands are offloaded in a farm field in Erwinna, at the top of the bluffs. There, they'll be fed and kept safe until their parents arrive to pick them up. It's an experience they'll never forget.

– Courtesy Tobyhanna Army Depot and the Boeing Corporation

219

the counselors' frequent glances out at the river, which is beginning to overtake the island.

Every so often, the children are moved to a higher level of the barn to avoid the encroaching water.

Soon, the sound of helicopters is heard. It grows louder as several of the airships put down far enough from trees and buildings to be safe. Their rotors whip small ripples into the water, now covering the island several feet deep.

Donna and her fellow campers are herded down the banked ramp and into rowboats and canoes. Now they can't help but notice that much of the island has been overtaken by seriously deep water, but there's no time to panic.

The taller counselors pull them through the water to the waiting choppers. There, they are taken aboard by age, the youngest going first. As each chopper is filled, it lifts off in a whirl of air and noise, ferrying its passengers across the channel and the canal to a farmer's field in Erwinna.

For everyone along the river, it's going to be a long day.

A River Goes Mad

Friday, August 19
10:00 a.m. to Noon

Ned Harrington, who lives on a hill outside Carversville, has walked downtown to pick up his mail from the Post Office, which is housed in Bartleman's General Store. He sees one of the store's New Idea manure spreaders about 1500 yards down Fleecydale Road. There's a huge scar on the house where Jean Michener and Agnes Foster live, left by collisions with boulders and trees that had threatened to tear it down during the height of the Paunacussing Creek's rampage.

Ned is aghast at the damage. He hadn't even been aware of any flooding going on the night before. He becomes concerned, remembering that he'd left his Jeep at Harvey Frank's garage for repair. Harvey is standing in front of his shop, surveying the damage left by the water, which had gone in one door and out the other. There are several inches of mud covering everything. His gas pumps have been torn away and he tells Ned his apartment has also been damaged. He had only just returned from a Canadian fishing trip at five this morning; he certainly hadn't been expecting a welcome like this.

Ned finds his Jeep, now a sorry-looking, mud-spattered critter, and thinks it'll never run. But he gives it a try anyhow, and to his surprise, the engine turns over. Suddenly he's in great demand, with the only four-wheel drive vehicle that's still running. He's elected by several of his friends to make grocery and beer runs over roughened roads for everyone who has gathered in the square to begin the massive job of cleaning up.

Ned is only too happy to oblige, feeling that he owes this favor to his neighbors, since his home remains untouched by the misery. He stays around after each run to help people drag ruined items from their basements and shovel muck.

Elliott Highfield is dazed and slightly hypothermic when Scranton police sergeants Emil Zurcher and Thomas Tobin haul him off the garage roof and aboard their launch at 9:30 Friday morning. He tries to tell them what happened to Ella the night before as they take him to the hospital. The police take Elliott to State Hospital in a radio car, where his condition is reported as fair. He is sitting up and talking, trying to piece together the events that had led to his being there.

This striking AP Wirephoto captures the dramatic helicpter rescue of several people from a disintegrating house in Scranton's South Side early on Friday morning, August 19, 1955. By evening, it makes the front page of newspapers nationwide.
– Courtesy Scranton Times-Tribune

When interviewed later, his neighbors on nearby Union Avenue, Richter Avenue, and the rest of Ash Street say they could hear him calling for help all night, his voice growing weaker and weaker until they couldn't hear him at all. Five houses on Union Avenue have been knocked off their foundations, and the 1900 block of Richter Avenue has been completely covered in water.

At ten p.m., Mayor James Hanlon declares a state of emergency for the city. He closes down nearly every business not engaged in flood relief work. Restaurants that are still functional remain open to feed those without utilities. Mayor Hanlon imposes a nine p.m. curfew to discourage looting, and deploys National Guardsmen just to make sure no further harm will come to already devastated areas of his city.

Just an hour before, an Air Force helicopter had airlifted four occupants still stranded in their home on the Southside Flats near Washington and Birch. *Scranton Times* photographer John Greskovic Jr. had caught the dramatic rescue on film. Wire services pick it up, and newspaper readers across the country will get a glimpse of Scranton's plight on their front pages this evening. It is but one of too many tragic stories that will come out of the eastern seaboard in the next several weeks.

Around ten o'clock, one of the Carversville residents taps Will Dobron on the shoulder as he's pumping out yet another basement. He's told that his squad is being recalled immediately to Point Pleasant for more pressing work. It seems the Smithtown summer colony has phoned in an alarm, reporting that "a wall of water" is coming down the Delaware. Frightened riverside residents are calling for rapid evacuation help.

Will can't understand it. Just two hours earlier, they had made their way along the river toward Carversville. The river had looked high, but not threatening. Still, they take their directive seriously, and climb aboard their 1932 Hahn fire engine once more, to return home.

When they reach the stop sign on River Road, it's underwater. The guys look at each other in amazement. They lose no time in backtracking up the hill to Short Road and over high ground to reach those who need rescuing from the rising waters.

Immediately, they begin evacuating people and helping move what property they can. When everyone is safely on their way, Will and his brothers check out the situation at their own wire design and floral supply store, across from the Point Pleasant post office. Water is already invading the cellar, and the brothers and their firefighting comrades get to work moving their inventory out. Most of twenty-five tons of wire is hand-carried up over the bank behind the store to the Dobron's shop on Ferry Road. By the time they reach the end of the job, they're slogging through three feet of water, and realize this flood will be worse than the one in 1903.

All night, the Tinsman clan has been moving what they can out of harm's way. By dawn, they've even moved their vehicles up away from the river. As the sun comes up, Bill Tinsman phones his brother-in-law, who lives farther inland. He asks if he and his wife might consider taking care of a couple of their kids for a few days.

"Are you nuts?" comes the joking reply.

Silence.

"Why, what's the matter?"

Bill explains what's going on, and how they need to be able to work securing everything without worrying about the kids getting into danger. There is incredulity on the other end of the line.

"I'll be right over."

Bill and Sue place two of their other kids with Sue's mother, and another child with some friends for the duration of the emergency. Then, along with some family members and friends, they get down to the serious work of tying down everything in the lumber-yard that might float away.

Bill is busy securing piles of dimensional lumber in the yard, when he sees a pile across the road that's threatening to float off before he can get to it. He strips off his belt and pants with his wallet in the pocket, and lays them across a pile of lumber that he thinks can wait for him to secure the one in doubt. He swims across a mild current to get to it, realizing he must hurry if he is to save it. As he wrestles with the unruly pile near the river, he looks over the road just in time to see the other pile being lifted and carried away intact, pants and all.

Meanwhile, Sue continues to carry items upstairs in their house. She takes everything off the bookshelves below four feet. There are some large things simply impractical to move, a few antiques and a grandfather clock, so she just hopes for the best where they're concerned.

Lester Sciss has returned home to Upper Black Eddy from work across the river. He had left at seven, when the rising sun had made it plain the river was on a fast rise. He had driven across the Frenchtown-Uhlerstown Bridge, because the Milford-Upper Black Eddy span was already in danger of being breached. He'd puzzled at the situation. Sure, it had rained a good bit, but not as much as the last time. Yet here the river was, coming up serious. Well, who knew what had happened upriver?

He had been glad he was making the crossing early in the morning and didn't have to worry about what would be happening later on. He'd been even gladder of it when, as he neared home, he saw the river already seeping onto River Road in places. Now he tells his wife, Eleanor, that they'll probably stay dry because their house sits up so high. They agree they'd better start helping their neighbors who aren't so lucky to move their furniture and valuables out of reach of the water.

They keep an eye on the kids to make sure they don't get into trouble while they help neighbors bring things up out of their basements. Those whose houses are clearly going to be underwater even to the second floors bring their things to the Scisses' new shop building for safekeeping until the water goes down.

When they've moved all they can move, the Scisses decide to take a walk uptown to see how Upper Black Eddy is faring. They walk back along the canal towpath, because it sits higher than most of the surrounding fields. They watch as the fire company evacuates many of the residents. An elderly woman, Mrs. Dotter, refuses to get in the rowboat that the department has maneuvered to her window.

As they watch the ensuing argument, one of their neighbors calls their attention to a chicken coop floating down the river, complete with chickens on its roof. They move closer to see what else is coming down. For quite some time, they watch in awe as sheds, outbuildings and even houses bob in the current until they're pushed up against the bridge. Then, under the massive, brute force of the onrushing water, they explode in a salvo of snapping studs that sound like gunshots. The pop and tinkle of breaking glass provides a high counterpoint, and a low whoosh of air expelling from enclosed spaces beats a nearly subconscious bass line in the dreadful symphony of destruction.

Lester looks behind them and sees the water beginning to come up from the canal, as well. If it gets too deep, they won't be able to get back home, so he, Eleanor, and their neighbors start back down toward their houses. The water gets gradually deeper until they're wading waist-deep along the road back toward the river. They realize they've foolishly placed themselves in danger of being swept off their feet, and link hands to keep from losing anyone.

The group finally makes it back safely, and Lester checks on their two beagles in the kennel. The water's nowhere near it, but he'll continue checking it throughout the day. The water is coming up as much as two feet an hour for much of the time.

As the river continues to swallow much of Upper Black Eddy, the few homes around the Sciss property become a literal port in the storm for fire department rescue boats. They use the ersatz island as a stopover for a few moments' rest from their travails. Eleanor and the neighbor ladies make sandwiches and coffee for the rescue workers, who risk their lives to save their neighbors. They never do learn what happened to Mrs. Dotter.

There are a few less nobly motivated souls out on the water, as well. Lester, on the banks watching their swimming raft get torn away, now focuses with a mixture of amusement and concern on a man about twenty years old. The man wades out into the dangerous water to grab a rowboat that's shooting by, and somehow manages to snag it without being knocked off his feet. Flush with that victory, he next tries for a motorboat, but it's too much for him to handle. He gets swept out into the current.

Truly shaken now, he's clearly floundering. Lester shouts to him to get back to the bank before he drowns. Self-preservation triumphs over avarice, and the young man takes his advice and makes it to shore. The rowboat of his first conquest is taken by the current and wrapped around a tree, which the young man hangs onto until Lester and his son throw him a rope.

After pulling the man to safety, Les takes him back to the house and gives him a pair of dry trousers to wear. The man takes the next fire and rescue boat back to town. Lester never does see those pants again.

Robert Neyhart, a carrier pigeon hobbyist, wakes up at his home in East Stroudsburg worried about his teenage daughter, Mary Ann. She had left the night before to visit with friends in Stroudsburg over the weekend. Robert realizes he has no way of finding out if she's okay, with the bridges and phones out of commission. Then he gets an idea.

Robert straps message capsules to the legs of two of his pigeons and puts them in crates. Then he sets off to find someone who might be going over the Brodhead to the Stroudsburg side, but has no luck. He'll keep trying.

Meanwhile, the Civil Defense and related organizations have been busy since Thursday night in the twin boroughs of the Stroudsburgs. City and county officials have cooperated with local agencies to establish shelters, first aid stations and food canteens for those with nowhere to go. Local Boards of Health issue information regarding the safe use of water, including boiling before use.

The area hospital is cut off from both towns except by helicopter, so a medical dispensary has been set up by the Red Cross along with an emergency shelter at the Stroudsburg United Methodist Church. Eight doctors and forty-four nurses are rotating through a 24-hour schedule. All serve on a volunteer basis. Disaster victims, cardiac patients, diabetics, and others needing regular care are attended to. A dispensary is opened to administer typhus inoculations for those whose rescue and recovery work will take them into the contaminated waters.

Other shelters, at the VFW, YMCA, the Sherman Theater, and the State Teachers College, are staffed by graduate registered nurses, and will continue to be during the first critical week. Some nurses make their way on foot through the mud to staff outlying inoculation stations.

At the Monroe County Hospital in East Stroudsburg, the out-patient department is made available to walk-in disaster victims. Many staff employees are unable to make it to work, cut off by washed out roads and bridges. Helicopters are reserved for critical efforts, so at one point, 75 percent of staff duties such as laundry, dietetics, and general upkeep are performed by volunteers from the surrounding community who can get to the facility.

The effort is heartening, but the reality of the devastation is overwhelming. People are wandering through the streets of the twin boroughs. Some are looking for what's left of their homes and families. Others, who have perhaps already learned they haven't any homes to go back to, are in search of simpler things; something to eat and drink, a safe place to rest. Most are in a daze, disbelieving what they see with their own eyes. Familiar landmarks are strange-looking—disfigured or out of context—or gone entirely. People's usual thoroughfares are impassable beneath piles of debris, so movement is slow and uncertain.

Few ordinary citizens have information about the big picture yet. Rumors are rampant, and news comes in dribs and drabs, passed by word of mouth from those who have been out of the boroughs. What residents will eventually learn is that 776 houses have been destroyed or are temporarily uninhabitable, and all forty-two bridges in Monroe County are washed out.

Sixty-four people are reported dead and dozens missing in the county alone. Since they are cut off from the outside, the towns have only their own figures to go by, but to those who've heard it, such a figure seems plenty high without any additions from the outside.

Maj. Gen. Biddle has made good on his promise to interrupt the training of his five hundred National Guardsmen, moving them east from Fort Indiantown Gap to keep the peace and discourage looting. Seabees and the Army Corps of Engineers have moved into the towns and are already making headway in clearing debris from the streets and throwing up a temporary bridge over the Brodhead Creek.

A few miles upstream, Robert Lawyer, who had taken refuge in old Bertha Polly's cabin at Camp Davis, stands alone on the floodplain of the Brodhead Creek, which has receded considerably from its swollen vastness of the night before. He realizes he's the only survivor of the cabin. He can't remember much of what happened. Looking around, he sees water surrounding him in every direction, and sits down to wait for it to recede. At least the sun is out, and the chill of the night on his wet body is gone. He wonders how long it will be before he can hike out to find shelter and food.

Robert, a Marine, now hears the familiar sound of helicopter rotors thumping the air. He stands, waving his arms, attracting the attention of the crew of a helicopter on reconnaissance from Tobyhanna Signal Depot. The whirlybird sets down close by, on the wide stretch of grayish, rounded stones left by the raging creek water as it receded. Robert is helped aboard and wrapped in a blanket. Though the day is already heating up, he finds the warmth comforting, and finally relaxes back into his seat for the ride back to safety.

Seven-year-old Palmer Ward is antsy. He has been hearing about the river coming up from his father, *New Hope Gazette* publisher Allen Ward, since last night. Palmer wants to get out and see the rising tide for himself. He barely makes it through breakfast before finally being allowed to go outside, followed by a stern warning from his mother to be careful and stay out of danger's way. His father had come in late and was already gone, worried about the newspaper's press room and equipment on Main Street.

Palmer walks to the river from his home on Fisher's Alley. He's stunned at the height and swiftness of the water. Like many others, he passes the morning just watching all the improbable things being carried along in the current; outhouses, barrels, logs, and entire trees. A whole house floats by, a cat perched atop its roof.

Further north in Lumberville, Palmer's mother Alice is surveying the scene at the riverfront, where the Winans family had been the night before. Since then, the Cuttalossa Creek has washed out the road, taken off part of the Colligan's Cuttalossa Inn, and eroded its banks until neighbor George Ireland's car fell in.

Robbie Winans, also seven, stands in front of the inn, astonished to see water nearly up to its second floor. This time though, it's not the creek, but the Delaware River that invades the popular dining spot. He looks out over the river and watches in awe as an entire house floats by in the muddy water, wondering what will happen when it comes to the Point Pleasant Bridge.

Twelve families at the northern end of town near the Tinsman residence had evacuated overnight, when the Paunacussing Creek began tearing its way through their yards and homes. The Henry family lost half an acre of their property. Now the river has backed up into the creek channel and surrounded them on the porch roof of the Chutney House. They are in the process of being rescued by boat, and later on, the whole porch will wash away down the Delaware.

By midmorning, the river has breached its banks in Upper Black Eddy and is threatening to overrun the canal. Miriam "Mim" Stull is hanging out laundry in the backyard of their home on Bridge Street, between the river and the canal. Her husband, Sydney, is working on the railroad near Stockton, and she's not expecting him home until suppertime.

Suddenly, he appears around the corner of the house.

"You better jack that up," he says, loudly. "The water's coming up!"

Mim doesn't realize he's not kidding until she looks out toward the river and sees the water creeping up through the yards. Like many others that day, faced with an unprecedented situation, her immediate reaction to this realization will later seem ridiculous. She scurries around, collecting the laundry from where she's just hung it, and hurries back to the house.

Sydney tells her to gather the children and get out of there. Mim says she's got to stay and try to save some things first. The water is already invading the house. Syd isn't happy about leaving his family in this precarious situation, but knows his work has suddenly become critical. Without an intact roadbed, the trains won't be able to get people and goods out of harm's way. He has to return to work before the bridges go out and he can't get back across the river. He calls the fire department to come and get Mim and the kids with one of their rowboats, then takes off.

Mim is running about the house, frantically rushing precious items up the stairs. The children, Janet, Bob, and Ken, watch the water rise from the yard. Suddenly, the Post Office rises up from its moorings. It makes a left-hand turn and starts down River Road, almost as if someone is driving it. They giggle and point, calling Mim to come watch.

By the time the evacuation boat arrives, the water is up to Mim's waist, and she has called the children to stay close so they don't slip away beneath it. The Stulls pile into the long boat with a few of their belongings and some clothes, and are being rowed toward the canal bridge when someone notices the neighbor's dog, stranded and barking at the water all around him.

One of the firemen in the boat dives overboard and swims to the dog. He unhooks it from its leash and swims back to the boat with it. The dripping hound sits in the boat with the rest of the evacuees until they're all delivered to the foot of the Nockamixon Palisades. From there, the Stulls walk up Lodi Hill to bunk with Mim's brother for a few days. They'll stay there, Mim worrying about her husband's safety and the state of their home, until the water goes down and Syd returns from rebuilding washed-out railbeds near Stockton.

Next door, eight-year-old Marlyn Minder has been helping her mom, Ruth, put things upstairs since her dad, John, called earlier from his job at Riegel Paper across the river in Milford. He had warned them that the river was coming up, and that they should get ready to leave.

There isn't much in the way of big furniture they can fit up the curved staircase, even if they could lift it, so they concentrate on what they can carry. Ruth fills the bathtub with water so they'll have something to drink later if the well gets contaminated.

Marlyn and her sisters Sharon and Marion are still helping their mom move things when the firemen come through their front door in the rowboat to take them out. The girls just stare at the odd sight, and Ruth herds them into the boat. They, too, stay with relatives up on Bridgeton Hill until it's safe to return home. Their dad will forever rib Ruth about filling the bathtub with water, when it was flooded along with everything else in the house.

Just downriver, the helicopter rescues of the island campers are winding down. Marie Petranto's helicopter drops her and her fellow passengers in a field on the Pennsylvania side, where they will be safe until everyone has been evacuated from the flooding islands.

The one carrying Donna Marcs lands safely in Erwinna, where a bus takes her group to the firehouse. The campers are fed sandwiches for lunch, then wait until the rest of the campers and counselors are rescued. She hears that Director Rossman was the last one off the island, waiting in water up to his armpits, and that everyone was removed safely. Once everyone has been accounted for and fed, they are loaded onto buses and driven to Philadelphia, where bridges are still intact to allow New Jersey parents to come across and pick up their campers.

Elaine DeWinton lands in the same field, where she says a prayer of thanks. She also is taken for lunch at the firehouse, where her parents soon arrive and greet her with much joy and relief.

Jay Folkes and Sara Gardner reach Frenchtown High School, only to be told that the kids aren't there, but are being landed across the river in Erwinna. Growing frantic, they backtrack to the Frenchtown Bridge, now finding it blocked by a guard who tells them it's closed to further traffic.

Too much stuff coming down the river now, he explains. It's no longer safe to travel. There are houses and big tanks that could knock out a pier.

Jay explains their situation, and tells the guard he's determined to re-cross the river. Finally, the guard steps aside.

"You go at your own risk," he says.

And they do.

As they get farther from the banks, they can feel the bridge vibrate as it gets hit by debris coming downriver. The steel plates are rattling, and it feels to Jay and Sara as if the whole bridge wants to come off its pilings. Wanting more than anything to reach the far side, Jay nevertheless drives slowly, to avoid being tossed off the deck or causing further vibrations. He and Sara don't talk, just concentrate on getting across.

Once they gain the Pennsylvania side, Jay halts the car and lets out a huge sigh of relief. They look at each other with wide eyes.

"Now," says Jay, "how do we get to where the kids are?"

Look, says Sara, pointing to the sky downriver. *There are the helicopters!*

Jay turns the wheel and starts off to the south. He follows the airships cruising overhead, taking a right onto a road that takes them about a mile inland. As they drive up to the open field, they see large groups of children standing around, obviously waiting to be picked up.

Jay parks the car, and he and Sara start walking toward one of the groups. Suddenly, Lew and Joan are running toward them, elated after their harrowing ordeal to see their parents. Joan has just debarked her helicopter, and Lew is dirty from playing while his group waited. They're both very excited and talk all the way home about their adventure.

With everyone safely off the islands, Marie Petranto's group is finally ferried over to Frenchtown in their second helicopter ride of the day. They land in the baseball field and are led across the street to the high school, where they're given soup and sandwiches for lunch. After they eat, Marie goes around to all the campers she had been responsible for, to make sure they're okay. For the next two nights, her group will sleep on cots in the gym, worrying about whether their parents even know where they are.

Across the river in Kintnersville, Sally Packard is listening to her mother explain what all the sirens were about the night before. It seems a young deliveryman was found dead in a truck just down the road, and the radio is reporting that foul play is suspected. A murder, right here in Kintnersville! And on top of that, Old Fry is under-water, her mom says.

It can't be, Sally thinks. The rock formation they call Old Fry usually juts several feet out of the river between where Lehnenberg Road and Route 212 intersect Route 611. It's like some kind of regional icon to her, and she just can't imagine it being covered by the river. After breakfast, she goes down to see for herself. Sure enough, Old Fry is completely submerged beneath fast-running brown water.

Sally becomes concerned that her plans for the day will be ruined. She is supposed to go to Easton with her friend Nancy, who will drive. She'll drop Sally at the town circle to do some shopping while she puts in a few hours at her job at Metropolitan Edison, the electric power company on Second Street.

Sally is relieved when she gets back home to learn that their plans are still on. She calls Nancy, who says they'll just take the back roads through Durham and park her car at her sister's on the south side of Easton in case the water gets too high along the river. It's a beautiful day, and when Nancy picks her up, the young women are in high spirits after the lengthy spell of dreary weather.

They part company downtown, and Sally sits on the circle, waiting for the stores to open. She hears many people remarking that they'd never seen the river so high. After a pass through Orr's Department Store, she heads for Laubach's and is going up the escalator when all the power goes out. After the initial shock, people's eyes adjust, and they make their way down to the first floor, saying things like someone must have struck a power pole in their car. They make their way out into the street, where they're shocked by the sights.

Fire department volunteers and anyone with a rowboat are bringing MetEd employees out of the building. The river has risen at least ten feet since Sally last saw it, and Second Street is covered. The mood changes to one of serious concern. Nobody is panicking, but it's clear to Sally that most people are frightened by how fast and how far the water is coming up.

Nancy is in one of the boats coming out of MetEd, and she joins Sally. They see people climbing up and over the railroad trestle to the south side cliff, and decide they'd better get out while they can. They follow up the ladder and cross over the top of the railroad bridge. They stand watching and see the police begin to turn people away from the bridge they've just crossed as it becomes covered with water from the Lehigh River.

The young women make their way down off the cliff to Nancy's sister's house, where they listen to the news on the radio. Sally is worried about her family. She can't get through on the phone. Have they stayed in their house? Is it flooding? If so, have they made it safely out?

Nancy knows she won't be able to make it back home to Riegelsville, New Jersey, so she decides to stay overnight at her other sister's house in Springtown. Sally goes with her, and calls her boy-friend to come pick her up and take her back home to her parents' house. He says he won't be able to make it till later on, so she waits anxiously until he arrives.

Mildred Williams thinks things might get pretty bad with the flooding. She lives along Route 611 in Kintnersville, and the night before, she had been coming home from a PTA meeting in Upper Black Eddy when she blew out a tire because the rain had washed sharp stones onto River Road. She couldn't remember when it had rained so much as the past two weeks. The whole time she'd been changing the tire, she had been thinking about the truck driver they'd found dead just hours earlier, not even a mile up the road. All the women at the meeting had been talking about it. The police wouldn't say if it was an accident or not. She had been frightened by it, and that sense of dread had colored the evening.

Now her husband, Dick, is at work across the river at Riegel Paper, and she knows the river is coming up. Everyone's talking about it, but no one knows how high it will get.

She makes breakfast for her sons, Kenneth, Gary, and Leslie, and sits down to eat with them. Unexpectedly, Dick comes through the door and says he wants to go over to his parents' house. He says they've been sent home from work because the river is getting too high for them to wait any longer. He'd had to go down to the Frenchtown Bridge and come back up, because the Milford Bridge was already closed.

His parents live on the island where the Traugers sell produce from their farm, just north of the intersection of Routes 611 and 32. It's not far from hers and Dick's home, but because it's separated from the road by the canal, is quite vulnerable to rising river water. She sees he's concerned for their well-being, and agrees to go along.

The five of them pile in the car and drive to the island. Dick is relieved to see that all is well. No water is up over any part of the road.

Satisfied that everyone is safe, Mildred and Dick decide to drive around a while and see what's happening elsewhere in the area. They leave thirteen-year-old Kenny with his grandmother, just in case she needs something while her husband tends to his job as a caretaker on the canal, and drive off with the other two boys.

An hour later, they return to find the water has risen so high that they can't safely drive the car back over the canal bridge to the island. Kenny and his grandmother must have been watching for them, because as soon as they look up, the two are wading through water up to their knees to cross the bridge and get to the car. They also pick up Dick's dad, and bring them both back to their house to stay until it's safe to return to their place.

Kenny tells his parents that the water had come up so quickly that the only things they were able to move off the first floor were small, personal items. The furniture had to stay where it was. Mildred says she wonders what will happen to the woman who lives with her invalid mother, also out on the island. Everyone agrees they hope someone thinks to go out and get them with a boat, but Dick says it will be tricky, what with the current getting so strong.

They're all silent during the short ride back home.

Just before eight a.m., June Hissim had left her Kintnersville home for her job as a payroll clerk in the office at Whippany Paper. The company is located on the west side of Route 611, just north of its intersection with Route 212 coming from Durham. As she got north of Lehnenberg Road, she had seen that the river was in the road already. She believed her 1941 Studebaker could plow through it, so she continued on. The water had been higher than she thought, though, and the car had stalled.

She'd signaled a tractor-trailer driver to stop and he had pushed her car along the road and into the company garage. She had thanked him and gone into the building. When she'd opened the door, she could see that the water was already up to the first step going down to the basement. Still, her office mates Shirley Leh from across the river and her sister-in-law, Joyce Hissim, were already there working, so she had joined them and gotten to work.

Now it's about eleven o'clock, and their boss, Peter Ferrara, comes into the office.

I think you gals should probably get home, he says. *The water's getting pretty high, and we don't want you to get stuck here.* He watches the girls look at each other, as it dawns on them that the situation has become serious. *Be careful getting home now.*

June and Joyce leave together. June says she'll give Joyce a ride if she can get the car started again, and if not, at least they won't have to walk alone. She descends to where her car sits and turns the key. The engine turns over, shooting water out the exhaust pipe, and the car starts right up.

Relieved, the women take Sunday Road, the back way into Kintnersville, so they can avoid the flooded River Road. By the time June gets home, the river has expanded to within eight feet of her front door, and extends clear over to New Jersey.

236

By late morning, the Delaware is lapping the deck of the river's only remaining covered wooden bridge connecting Portland, Pennsylvania, with Columbia, New Jersey. Fifty-year veteran bridge tender Charles Newbaker had woken to find the river knocking on the back door of his family's house on a nearby stone levee. He had called for help evacuating his family and their possessions.

When the trucks arrived, everyone moved at a frantic pace to gather their things to be taken to safety. Still, it took longer than they'd anticipated, and by the time they finally drove away, water was coming in the first-floor windows. They'd had to wade to the trucks.

As his family drives away with their worldly possessions, Charles stays behind, in uniform and on duty, at the toll bridge.

The Delaware River has become the repository for runoff from every single over-taxed tributary in its vast watershed. Over the past several hours, its volume has increased exponentially, and it now begins to behave in an erratic, crazy manner never before seen by a living soul. It indiscriminately invades homes and businesses, churches and taverns, spaces sacred and profane. Anything in its reach is fair game to be swept into its overpowering current. Nothing is spared by this river gone mad.

On a farm along South Main Street in Phillipsburg, New Jersey, a blind draft horse named Bill stands in his stall, oblivious to the danger creeping up on him. His owner, Charles "Wingy" Snyder, has spared the creature from the heat of the day's sun by putting him in the barn. He's fond of the 25-year-old gray horse after all their years together. But now Wingy is unaware that his old friend is in peril.

Farther upstream, the creek that runs along the back of Wingy's property is backing up to form a lake, stopped up by a mass of debris collecting in a culvert that runs beneath the railroad tracks. Finally, the water pressure becomes too great, and the debris clog is pushed apart. The massive backlog of water bursts through the culvert and rushes over the creek banks into downstream properties, including Wingy's farm. The water is greedy, claiming yards and pastures for itself, and now it begins swallowing Wingy's barn, and the sightless horse along with it.

At first, Bill is aware only of a hissing sound as the water seeps among the long pieces of straw on the bottom of his stall. The snake-like sound stirs in the animal a primal urge to run, but there's no way out of the stall. Bill's heart begins to pound. Reflexively, his nostrils flare with faster respiration and the need to smell any danger. He hears the nervous snuffling of another horse in the next stall. His eyes widen as he senses stealthy, predatory movement all around. He snorts and paws at the ground in an instinctive threat posture, having no idea what threat is posed but certain that there is one.

The large, warm-blooded mammal becomes aware of a cool, wet sensation as the water creeps up over his hooves and fetlocks. He lets out a soft nicker, signaling the beginnings of fear. Now Bill begins pacing the confines of his stall.

The water continues to rise. Inside of an hour, it has gained enough speed and force to overcome the power of gravity and friction. Bill, in water most of the way up his neck, is unable to resist being lifted from where he stands. Then he hears yelling and splashing, and is aware that his barn mate is being removed by some men. He waits for them to come back for him, but the water is now pouring into the door left open by the rescuers.

Instinctively, Bill begins treading water, and concentrates on keeping his head above the surface. He's lifted clear of the stall door. Suddenly, he's bumped up against a wall and is spirited away from the wood and wire that has for so long defined his world. He's swirled about and carried along in the creek until it spits him out into the widening river.

Without any sense of direction, he soon works his way out into the current. There, he gets pelted with objects large and small, and the blind horse grows increasingly terrified. The whites of his eyes are now constantly exposed, though the functionality of this reflex was lost long ago. The larger impacts set the animal spinning in the current, and with no visual point of reference, Bill becomes disoriented. He thrashes his legs in the water, trying to gain a solid foothold, which serves only to tire him more quickly.

His long, tapered ears swivel about, just inches above the water's surface, searching desperately for something familiar to give him some bearings. Here and there, he does pick up the lowing of a frightened cow or the faint howling of a dog stranded atop a building and being carried along in the same current, but nothing that will return any sense of control.

As his strength wanes, Bill stops kicking any more than necessary to keep his head above water. His survival instinct takes over, and the fight-or-flight reflex relaxes, allowing his vulnerable body to absorb the harder impacts of floating debris without sustaining too much damage.

The men have been unable to get back to Bill, and know he's gone. He soon disappears from view altogether as he's carried around a bend in the river.

In New Hope, Sandy Smith is standing with her parents along the banks of the Delaware near her home on North Main Street, watching all sorts of things coming down the river. The morning heat and thick humidity already have black flies and other pests stirring annoyingly. Friends are standing with them, and everyone is talking about the probability that the river will leave its banks and flood their neighborhood.

Sandy sees her parents exchange meaningful glances. Just what they need before they leave on vacation…a flood. Her dad says they'd better get back to the house and start putting things up out of harm's way. They don't know how bad it'll get.

For the rest of the day, she helps them move furniture and valuables to the second floor of their house, and put other things up on cinder blocks. The canal begins to overflow and creep up their backyard. Fatalistically, her dad says they might as well eat steak for lunch, since they're going to lose the deep freeze in the cellar and everything in it. They've already lost electrical power. As her dad grills the steaks, Sandy sits with her mother watching the water cover the backyard.

While they eat their fancy lunches, local Civil Defense director Bob Icelow, being driven around in a truck, passes their house. He's issuing directives through a bullhorn, urging people in this section of town to evacuate, because they're expecting the canal and the river to merge.

Again, her parents exchange glances. Suddenly, nobody's hungry enough to finish their food. Her mother goes into the house to grab her pocketbook containing five hundred dollars they intended to use for their trip to Canada. She also removes their canary in its cage, and sets off to spend the night at her brother's house. Sandy and her father walk down the towpath toward Bridge Street, and join groups of other citizens heading for the Red Cross Shelter that's been set up at the New Hope/Solebury High School.

Joanne Shutt walks with her mom to the bank in Stroudsburg to withdraw some money so they all can get some breakfast. They're disappointed to learn that, with the electrical power out, the timed locks on the vault aren't working and no cash is available. They walk back to the hotel and tell her sister Barbara and their friend Mary Lou Lilius that they'll need to pool all their money together to be able to get something to eat. Between them, they have enough to make a trip to Driebe's Fruit Market, where they buy some oranges, peanut butter, crackers, and bread.

Mrs. Shutt is determined to make it back to their vacation home in Henryville. She navigates out of Stroudsburg and along back roads through Bartonsville to the west, then zig-zags back north. They encounter many closed roads from downed trees and washouts, and have to backtrack a lot. The trip seems endless to the girls, who are growing more frightened by the mile from the destruction they see and the news that's coming over the car radio.

Finally, they reach the haven of their mountaintop retreat, and everyone breathes a sigh of relief. Mrs. Shutt begins to worry anew. Her husband is supposed to be bringing Joanne's friend, Gwen Moore, with him from Chatham for the weekend, but there's no sign of them yet.

In fact, Mr. Shutt is indeed on his way up with Gwen, but they are turned back at Water Gap, where the Brodhead and Cherry Creeks have combined with the river to back up the whole town under twelve feet of water. None of the usual thoroughfares are even navigable. They have to drive down to Phillipsburg to find a bridge that's still open across the Delaware River.

They, too, are seeing the destruction left by the previous day's downpour and flooding. The going gets rougher as they venture farther north. Finally, concerned for Gwen's safety, Mr. Shutt stops at the Paradise Valley home of family friends, the Rosses. He asks if they will mind keeping her there until he finds a safe passage to their own cottage. They agree, and Mr. Shutt walks to the house of another friend, George.

Unaware that there is a back way open to their vacation home, Mr. Shutt asks George to help him construct an access across the

Swiftwater Creek. It's dangerous work, as the Swiftwater had been raging just as all the other waterways had, even taking out parts of resorts and golf courses farther downstream, and it's still not calmed down. However, George agrees, and the men take a couple axes and chop down a tree, allowing it to fall across the creek. Taking off his good clothes so he won't ruin them if he falls in or slips, Mr. Shutt crosses the tree trunk in his underwear. On the other side, he re-dresses and walks up Halbert Hill to his cottage.

When he arrives on foot and without Gwen, his wife and the girls are alarmed until he shares the story of their adventure.

Meanwhile, Barbara's boyfriend, Cam Mueller, has heard stories of the disaster coming out of the Poconos and worries for her safety. An adventurous young man, he leaves his home in Chatham to try to find her. He hitchhikes as far as he can in a vehicle, then manages to wangle a seat on one of the many helicopters flying into the Stroudsburgs. Knowing where the Shutts' vacation home is located, he hikes out of town toward Henryville.

He gets as far as the Lilius home before stopping to rest and get something to eat. The Liliuses are frantic, worried about their daughter, Mary Lou. She's been gone since Thursday, and they know she was going to the theater in Stroudsburg to see a movie with the Shutt girls. With no phone service, they haven't been able to call the Shutts, and they've been afraid to leave with as many washouts as are being reported.

The worried parents ask Cam to let them know if Mary Lou is all right, once he locates the Shutts. Mr. Lilius lends Cam a hunting rifle, and tells him to shoot it off three times once he finds Mary Lou. Fed and rested, Cam sets off toward the Shutts' property over the mountain.

Some time later, after Cam has found the Shutts and Mary Lou all safe and sound at their cottage, he walks down to the Henryville House Hotel, from which he knows the Liliuses will be able to hear him firing. Amid the wreckage of ripped-up homes, a ruined restaurant, service station and part of a resort left behind by the rampaging Brodhead Creek, he fires off three shots. Across the valley, the Liliuses, who have been waiting anxiously since he left, hear the signal and nearly cry with relief. As soon as it's safe to travel, the Shutts will return Mary Lou to her parents, and everyone will have a terrific tale of adventure to tell.

Kay Cody and her maid of honor, Joanne Martinelli, have weathered the night well at Joanne's home in Dunmore. They awaken to a bright, sunny morning, glad they had waited to try making it back to Mountainhome, where Kay is scheduled to marry Jake Sengel on Saturday at the Methodist church.

On their way out of town, they see some of the wreckage wrought by Roaring Brook near Scranton, but not the worst of it. They really don't have any idea how bad things had gotten overnight while they slept, and they're not expecting any trouble on the way back. But trouble has a way of showing up when least expected, and it finally makes an appearance as the young women pull into Daleville on Highway 435. There, they're stopped and told to turn around. No traffic is being allowed past the town, because so many roads ahead are dangerous or impassable.

Not to be put off, the girls turn around and head back north and then east to try to come in via Hawley, but they're stopped again. Becoming anxious that she won't be able to get back to prepare for her wedding, Kay tries to telephone Skytop Lodge, where her party is staying. The operator informs her that all lines into the Mountainhome-Cresco area are out because of the flood. So they head off even farther east, unaware that they're heading into another hard-hit area around Stroudsburg.

Another police officer stops the car and won't allow them to pass onto Route 611. He tells them the river is up over the road in many places, and it's too dangerous to travel. Kay, now desperate, is done being denied access.

"I have to get through!" she wails. "I'm getting married tomorrow!"

The officer sees her desperation and relents, stepping away from the car. He looks at her sternly.

"You go at your own risk," he warns.

Elated and relieved, the young women proceed toward Tobyhanna. When they get there, the water is still high from the night before, almost up to the car doors, but they press on.

Approaching Mt. Pocono, Kay tells Joanne to pull in to the lot at the High Point Inn. Ed Creen, a friend of Jake's, works there, and Kay wants to ask him a favor. Finding Ed inside, she explains their predicament and asks Ed if he would escort them the rest of the way to Skytop Lodge, to make sure they arrive safely.

Ed manages to get his supervisor to let him go, and he drives ahead of the girls to make sure they don't venture into any dangerous areas. He plows first through the flooded highway at Paradise, allowing Joanne to maneuver safely behind him.

It's almost noon before the mini-caravan reaches Cresco and Mountainhome. Everything is eerie and quiet, no people to be seen anywhere, no activity going on. Kate becomes frightened, and Joanne needs to get back to Skytop, where she's a half-day late for work.

As they reach the top of Canadensis Hill, they realize she won't be getting back this way. Water is roaring over the spot where the bridge had stood, very close to where Jake had abandoned his Ford the night before. Now both girls are scared. They drive anxiously back to Mountainhome, where Kate spots Jake. She wonders what he could be doing.

This view looks southwest along Route 90 (now 191) in Mountainhome, where yet another bridge has been torn out by the Brodhead Creek. In the lower right is Ravelli's restaurant, and the triangle at upper left is the front yard of the Mountainhome Methodist Church, where the Sengels will be married.

– Courtesy U.S. Army Depot at Tobyhanna

After they greet each other with much happiness and relief, she asks. He tells her he's on a body search-and-recovery detail, looking for the vacationers from Philadelphia who had been washed away from Price's Cottages up in Canadensis. She hesitates, not knowing what to do. It's a horrible, grim wake-up call for a young woman about to begin a new life.

Jake tells her more about what's happened while she was gone. He has found his car on its side, three hundred feet from where he'd left it, and his best man, Wolden Magann, hasn't shown up yet. He has no idea whether he'll show up at all, because no one knows what the roads are like elsewhere.

Fearful for his friend's safety and that of several other wedding party members and guests, they discuss whether they should go ahead with the wedding or not. It's scheduled for eleven o'clock the next morning. Both their parents and the maid of honor are present, so they finally agree to go ahead with the ceremony.

Down in Canadensis, Dale Price is driving his dad's new Ford F-600 dump truck toward town, hoping its higher road clearance will allow them to negotiate the leftover high water and debris in the road. When they reach Hwy. 290, they're glad for the truck. Leavitt Branch is over the road and spilling down toward the new Moravian Church into the Brodhead.

His dad tells Dale to drive strictly down the middle of the road, since they can't see the condition of the shoulders. Later, when the water recedes, they'll realize that this tactic probably saved the truck, if not their lives; the middle is all that's left of the road, with the gouged-out sides dropping off sharply into ravines on either side.

When they get into town, both men are awestruck by the extent of the damage. Grocery store owner Dan Russell is in his half-wrecked shop, eager to sell as much of his perishable goods as possible before they spoil in the heat with no refrigeration. No gas is available to fuel vehicles, since the electricity that powers the pumps is off. The only news coming into the area is coming over car radios unless someone has a battery-powered portable.

When they're done looking around, Dale decides to stay in town and join the search parties looking for bodies on the Brodhead, while his dad tries to round up men to help start the cleanup. He's glad he had always insisted on keeping his own fuel tank on premises at the house with a manual pump. It will come in handy over the next several days to fill the cleanup vehicles.

Walking alongside the Brodhead, Dale is impressed by the water, which still looks angry. The search for missing people will continue for days. On Monday, Dale finds the body of 42-year-old Helen White lodged in a tree, suggesting she may have survived the original plunge into the raging creek, but perhaps died later. Her death certificate lists drowning as the cause of death. The last of the bodies around Canadensis will be found on August 26th; that of little Jimmy Driscoll, eight years old.

His father, Joe, had waited until the water went down to come out of his tree perch. He had worked himself over to a pile of rocks that had boards from a wrecked outbuilding up against it, causing the water on its lee side to slow down. As the water slowly subsided back into the creek, he had realized the rocks were out of the main channel, facing a mountainside. Joe had kept his eyes on the mountain, and about nine thirty Friday morning sees what he thinks is a group of children walking along a road on it.

He shouts and gets their attention. They run toward him, and as they get closer, he can see they're not children but a rescue party. Three men wade out toward him, then toss a line. He ties the rope around his waist as they instruct him to, and they pull him in. The current is still fast, and the resistance pulls him underwater. He feels himself blacking out, his last thought the irony that he should live through the flood only to die in the rescue.

Moments later, he revives, spitting and gurgling, as six men are carrying him to higher ground. After they make sure he's okay, they take him to the home of Dr. Harold Tattersall on the mountainside. As they approach the porch, ten-year-old Barbara Harmer comes running outside, calling, "Oh, Uncle Joe!"

He's happy to see her, but still dazed from his experiences. He asks his rescuers, "Where are the rest of them? Is everybody all right?"

The men say nothing, looking away.

Barbara asks Joe if he had seen her mother and father, David and Violet Harmer. He admits that he hasn't.

Dr. Tattersall examines Joe, who is bruised from head to foot and cut in many places. The worst area is behind his knees, but the bruises are not large, just numerous. His hosts give him a cup of coffee and lay him on a cot with several blankets. Immediately, he falls into an exhausted sleep.

Some time later, Joe wakes up to the sound of a girl calling for her grandmother to heat a can of soup. Mrs. Tattersall gives Joe some of the doctor's clothing to wear. He asks if the rescue party has found anyone else alive, and is told that they had taken a woman to another house farther up the hill.

A Jeep arrives to take them all to a shelter in Mountainhome, and it's then that he learns the other survivor's identity. Violet Harmer, his sister, is put on a stretcher in the back of the vehicle. She sees her brother standing by.

"Wasn't God good to me?" she asks. "He left me Barbara."

Swallowing the lump in his throat, Joe gets into a seat and the Jeep heads down the mountain. From the back, they hear Violet's voice.

"Don't take me near the water!" she pleads, over and over.

Cruelly, one area newspaper, operating as so many had to on spotty information, reports a few days later that the White family, who had been thrown into the water along with the Driscolls and Harmers, has survived. In fact, Harry's body and that of his son, Joseph, have been found not far from where their wife and mother was recovered in the tree by Dale Price's search party.

Spirits are high among the Boy Scouts at Camp Pahaquarra. They are in no immediate danger from the flood, and the emergency is the kind of situation they have prepared for through their merit badge training.

The river has crept over the fields of the parade ground to reach Bill Coleman's Adirondack shack. The regular routine has been disrupted, and Bill doesn't open the camp store.

The boys watch the water rising quickly up the Old Mine Road, and several of them pass around a pair of binoculars. They watch one of the rustic vacation homes across the river. Someone is still inside it, irrationally bailing it out with a bucket and dumping the water out the window, back into the river. The boys discuss the futility of this behavior, and the danger that person has put himself in by remaining in the flooding house.

Soon, they grow tired of this activity and discuss the probability that their parents don't know whether they're safe or not. Someone gets the idea to paint a sign on the asphalt road, so one of the many aircraft flying over might see it and report back home to ease their parents' minds. The boys go to the supply hut for brushes and buckets of the ubiquitous white paint that's used on every wooden surface at the camp.

They locate a stretch of road unobscured by overhead foliage and not likely to flood, and begin their work. For the rest of the morning, they paint six-foot-high letters, spelling out "Tell Trenton Pahaquarra OK." Not long afterward, the pilot of a light plane radios in to a Jersey control tower that he has spotted the message, and it gets relayed to radio and television stations in time for the evening news. Many parents in the state capitol slept easier that night because of the boys' thoughtful work.

Some of that relief is undone when one of the campers, twelve-year-old Dennis Wene develops appendicitis later that afternoon and must be transported out of the camp to a hospital. All normal access routes are blocked and the telephone is out, so a group of six staffers volunteer to carry the ailing boy on a litter up over the back of Kittatinny Mountain and down the Appalachian Trail to a public road. They flag down a passing State Patrol squad that carries the boy until the trooper flags down a station wagon. The driver rushes the boy to Newton Memorial Hospital, where he is successfully operated on.

Dennis is a lucky boy: His appendix had ruptured, but infection had not yet set in by the time he was operated on. He owes his life to the accurate amateur diagnosis in camp and the quick efforts of his counselors to get him to a place where he could receive proper medical attention. The dramatic rescue garners much media interest from the time of the boy's arrival at the hospital. Not until the happy outcome identifying the boy can the other campers' parents relax again, knowing their own sons are safe.

The water continues to rise back at camp, now threatening the infirmary where Bill had spent the previous night. Some campers are detailed with an orderly removal of the medical equipment and supplies. The boat dock has now risen to the level of the road, and settles in the middle of it. The campers keep a close eye on it, making sure it doesn't float away.

Harry's Farm, a "rustic" resort for wealthy vacationers, sits below the camp. A boxer named Jersey Joe Woolsey has been running up and down its access road, training with one or two men on bicycles, and shadow boxing. It has been a treat for the boys to imagine him in the ring, surrounded by wealthy patrons waving hundred-dollar bills and glittering with diamonds.

Now they look down and see the farm almost completely underwater. As they watch, the maintenance building begins to creak and groan. Soon, it rises off its foundation and starts to float downriver. It runs into some trees and breaks up on impact, a magnificent booming and cracking signaling its disintegration. The staff and guests had already come up the hill to escape the rising water, and now one of the men stands with the boys to watch.

"There's five thousand dollars worth of tools in that building," he tells them, his expression unchanging. Bill is impressed. That's more than half his dad's annual income.

For the rest of the afternoon, the boys will watch homes across the river rise and take off downstream, hit trees and break apart. It's quite a show, and certainly not the entertainment they'd expected when they'd signed up for camp.

By evening, Bill Coleman's sleeping quarters will fall victim to the Delaware's hungry waters, and he'll have to finish the camping season in other digs. It's one he won't forget.

At her Bell Telephone operator's station, Greta Johnson has been fielding calls all morning asking if she knows anything about what's happening on the Delaware. Will it flood? What are the reports from upriver? Operators from other offices are also calling, wanting flood reports. Greta shares whatever information she knows for sure, careful not to spread misleading information or rumors, as her supervisor warns.

The next call Greta picks up is from her mother. She asks if Greta can come home. The water is going to come in their house, and her dad needs help moving the furniture. Greta asks her boss if she can go home for lunch. Her supervisor isn't happy about it with the heavy call volume they're getting, but she's understanding.

I can only spare you for an hour, Greta. Now go, and be careful.

When she gets home, she starts right in helping her dad. They put the cooking range up on sawhorses and move the clothes washer to a corner. When they finish with the big things, she helps him load other items into the back of his pickup truck. Her mom is standing on Main Street, monitoring the water level so they won't get stuck before they can move the stuff out.

As Greta reluctantly heads back up the street to work, she hears her mom urging her dad to hurry. He's still throwing things in the truck, and the water is now breaching the canal walls. They don't know that the river has overflowed farther north near Phillips Mill, adding pressure to the already overloaded canal and crumbling part of the earthen dike that separates the two.

Greta is frightened and sad, imagining what she might find when she gets off work. She takes one last look back, and is amazed to see three deer standing on their front porch, trying to escape the rising water. With a sick feeling in her stomach, she hurries back down to work.

Nancy Wolfe is a fourteen-year-old apprentice at the Bucks County Playhouse, one of New Hope's foremost attractions. During Thursday night's performance, the rain had fallen so quickly and heavily that the river had temporarily backed up to become level with the falls that usually tripped lightly where Ingham Creek emptied into the Delaware. The creek had also backed up, and with nowhere else to go, its waters spilled over onto the land surrounding the centuries-old former grist mill that housed the theater.

Suddenly, the Playhouse and the Playhouse Inn had become an island. Nancy had stood outside with the rest of the staff, watching in awe as nature's performance outstripped anything going on inside.

Then, as quickly as it had come up, the water had receded when the downpour had abated. By the time the play had ended, theater patrons filed out to see but wet asphalt and a few traces of grass bunches delineating where the water had been. It had been impressive enough that Nancy is wary as her mother drops her off at the Playhouse again this morning.

Her hometown of Carversville has been hit by creek floods overnight, and now there is talk of the river coming up. News-casters are mentioning all the rain that has fallen the whole length of the river, especially up north in the Poconos. Now it's all headed for New Hope, and they're warning of the possibility of dam breaks all over.

But the day is calm, the sky is clear, and the sun is shining brightly. The rain has left a fresh smell in the air, and it's a perfect summer day. Nancy walks behind the theater to take a look at the river. It's high, but not threatening. She has never seen it flood, and the concept is abstract to her, even after the previous evening's show from the creek.

Her assignment this week is to act as assistant in the theater office. At noon, she's sent to deliver a press release to the offices of the *Lambertville Beacon* newspaper. As she crosses the bridge over the Delaware, Nancy notices the water is nearly up to the road deck, and only then does she begin to understand the gravity of the situation. Afraid that she might become trapped in Lambertville if the water overflows the bridge, Nancy runs most of the way to the Beacon and all the way back to the playhouse.

By the time she returns, the water has reached the parking lot level, and the crew is moving everything out of the theater basement to the stage. Paint, props, costumes, equipment—everything is stacked up off the floor. Someone tells Nancy that a dam upriver has broken and the lower level of the theater will surely flood. She joins the stream of people moving whatever they can carry upstairs to the stage.

All the while, the river continues rising until, like the previous night, it completely surrounds the playhouse. By the time the base-ment is cleared, it has begun filling with water. The crew is receiving reports that the flood crest might actually reach higher than the stage level, so they go back into motion. Everything is carried up yet another level to the third-floor dressing rooms.

When they finish, the water has reached Main Street, and the crewmembers need to think about saving themselves from the encroaching flood. The stage door in the rear of the office is still above water, and someone has tied a rope to the railing there. Nancy follows it with her eyes and sees the other end tied to another railing at the end of the creek bridge on Main Street.

Each of the nearly twenty people in the crew must now pull themselves hand-over-hand along the rope, through the turbulent water and out to the street, which sits distinctly higher than the first floor of the playhouse. Nancy nervously eyes the debris shooting along in the current, wondering if she'll be able to hold on tight enough if something hits her.

Everyone manages to hang on and makes it safely to the street. Most of the crew live in rented rooms along Main Street, and they decide they'll all spend the night in the barn at the home of John and Jane Hess, on Aquetong Road in Solebury. Nancy, feeling very grown up, phones her mother to ask permission to go with them. Her mother is relieved to know she's safe, and since Nancy's father hasn't returned from work in New Jersey, is glad she can stay home in case he needs help getting home instead of having to come pick Nancy up.

One of the crewmembers has something in her room that she absolutely must retrieve, so they find someone with a boat willing to take them to fetch it, and Nancy is excited to be riding up Main Street in a boat.

As the water had been rising, the Red Cross had moved into town and set up a shelter in the high school gymnasium, complete with dry garments for those who couldn't get to their own. The crew makes a pit stop to take advantage of this much-needed replacement for their soaking clothes, then locates someone willing to drive them to the Hess's, where they set up camp for the night.

Swallowed Whole

Friday, August 19
Noon to 5:00 p.m.

At seven o'clock in the morning, employees of the DL&W Railroad had walked along the banks of the Brodhead Creek near their tracks in Analomink, looking for survivors from Camp Davis. The water had receded a great deal, though it was now in a new channel created by the flood. Bleached, rounded stones covered the area over which the water had expanded, and the sun was beginning to reflect brightly off of them, making it difficult to see.

Some movement caught their eyes along the tracks up ahead. It was Irene Weber, jumping up and down to stay warm. Her rescuers wrapped her in blankets to stop her shivering, and got her into a fire truck that took her down to Monroe County General Hospital in East Stroudsburg. The men then resumed their search.

Nobody had been left in the water, but they spotted two figures huddled atop a debris pile on the opposite bank. They hurried back and borrowed a motorboat. The two stranded survivors were Jennie Johnson and Beth Deubel, who cried with joy and relief as they were brought aboard the boat. Firemen were again called to transport the survivors to the hospital, to be treated for exposure, abrasions and bruises.

An hour later, Jennie Johnson's daughter, Nancy, and Linda Christensen were discovered, still clinging to trees in the middle of the creek. They were also transported to the hospital, but wouldn't learn about Mrs. Johnson's rescue until later.

Now the women and girls are resting in warm, clean hospital beds as doctors and nurses try to find out anything about their families. Not

Stroudsburg's Clearview School is taken over and used as an emergency operations center for search, rescue and recovery work following the ravaging of the area by the Brodhead Creek. Supplies, personnel and, eventually, bodies of victims are all brought here for appropriate disposition.

Tobyhanna Signal Depot's parking lot is quickly converted to a makeshift fueling and landing pad for the myriad helicopters used in the Pocono disaster area. Light standards, telephone poles and electrical wires are removed to make a safe space for air operations.
– Courtesy U.S. Army Depot at Tobyhanna

The famous Henryville House Hotel and a nearby restaurant feel the full impact of the Brodhead's wrath as it charges through the popular tourist area.
— Courtesy U.S. Army Depot at Tobyhanna

Guests at PennHills Lodge, another popular Pocono resort, have a few surprises waiting for them when the water recedes. Many emerge from their shelter in the lodge to find that their cars have been rearranged from where they'd been left in the parking lot.
— Collection Monroe County Public Library

until communication is established with the outside world and all urgent rescue traffic slows will the hospital be able to make information requests on behalf of their patients. It will be a long and excruciating wait.

Choppers launched from Tobyhanna Signal Depot make hundreds of search and rescue sorties before their task turns to the grim one of search and recovery. Bodies of unfortunate drowning victims are flown two at a time to the temporary morgue that has been established at Stroudsburg's Clearview School, south of the Analomink region on Route 90. There, they are quick-frozen and dispatched to any number of funeral homes and cold storage to await identification and burial.

— Courtesy U.S. Army Depot at Tobyhanna

Dorothy Shutt, Director of School and College Programs for the Southeastern Pennsylvania Chapter of the American Red Cross, is looking forward to taking a month off. She's just waiting out the last few days until her coworkers at the Philadelphia office return from their vacations. As usual, August is a slow time of year, so most of the staff plan their time off for this period. Her manager and assistant manager are both gone, as are both the Chapter and Disaster Chairmen and the Disaster Chief of Staff.

There has been a slight increase in activity lately, with the rains from Connie proving troublesome to a few spotty areas, but nothing that couldn't be handled with the dispatch of a few mobile canteens and aid stations. Dorothy is thankful, since anything major would devolve on her shoulders now, with all the "higher-ups" away.

Dorothy is beginning to think about lunch when the phone rings. It's a call from a Bucks County CD official. The Delaware River is flooding from this last bout of rain, and there have been reports that runoff in the mountains has caused significant flooding. Solid information is spotty, but there may even have been some deaths. There's the possibility that camps in the Poconos may need to be evacuated, since this heavy rain was unexpected, and no one knows if there will be more. Other reports will be issued as more information becomes available, but it would be a good idea to prepare for that evacuation.

Dorothy hangs up the phone, and suddenly she's not hungry anymore. Instead, she has a knot in her stomach. Something big is indeed happening, and it may get bigger. As ranking officer, the task of organizing and responding to the emergency has fallen on her.

In a few moments the initial shock wears off, and Dorothy falls back on her training. She kicks into active mode. She gathers her staff and they formulate "Plan A," the evacuation of Pocono camps and the establishment of emergency shelters. Dorothy details each member to different elements of the plan: activating communication networks, putting shelter staff on standby, stocking mobile canteens and aid stations, loading trucks with cots, blankets, and shelter supplies so they're ready to dispatch at a moment's notice.

A few hours later, just as these preparations are being completed, another call confirms that the flooding is serious and that evacuations should begin. Dorothy notifies her chapter branches in Monroe and Pike Counties, her call being patched through a network of emergency communication lines, since much of the telephone service is out in that area. Her contacts there confirm that, indeed, destruction in the Poconos is widespread.

She coordinates with Civil Defense officials to arrange helicopter removal of those whose camps are no longer accessible by road. They will be brought to bus stations that have access to roads outside the stricken mountain areas, and transported to Philadelphia's Reading Terminal. There, children will be distributed to their parents.

With the help of officials in Washington, social workers and trained volunteers are assembled to prepare handling the registration and distribution of all transportees. The largest scale operation of its kind in the area's history, which will quickly be dubbed "Operation Kidlift" by the news media, has begun.

Dorothy's own children are with their father at the Jersey shore, not due home until Labor Day. She knows they're safe and won't need her attention for a while. It's a good thing, because Dorothy won't get home tonight, and she won't get any sleep for the next thirty-six hours.

She receives instructions to travel to Bucks County and open an emergency shelter at the New Hope-Solebury high school. Dorothy assembles some trained staff and they make their way up to New Hope, where they will have eight hundred people to care for by nightfall.

Around midnight on Sunday, with the shelter operational, teams set up and running smoothly, and Dorothy confident that volunteers and evacuees can manage themselves, she finally succumbs to exhaustion. She finds a blanket and lies down in a quiet corner, where she is asleep as soon as her head hits the pillow. She'll sleep in catch-as-catch-can fashion for the next three weeks, while the shelter remains open.

Dorothy, as leader of the operation, must occasionally leave the shelter to meet people arriving with emergency supplies. She buys a pair of hip boots to save her clothes from all the mud.

When the shelter closes later, she'll be assigned to a "rumor squad," whose mission is to track down the source of rumors and either confirm or deny them. One rumor that she must confirm or disprove claims that a family isolated on an island in the Delaware had supposedly been sold bread and extra blankets by the Red Cross, whose services are always free. In fact, no families have been left on any islands, but she is never able to disprove that someone hasn't been taking advantage of the disaster by posing as a Red Cross worker and charging for relief supplies.

In her quest for information, she does learn that a Stroudsburg baker has managed to somehow keep his shop operational up and running. He is accepting contributions of flour and eggs to make bread, which he then donates to the Red Cross for distribution.

When it's all over, Dorothy never does get her vacation that year.

That Dorothy is able to get through to her Red Cross counterparts in Monroe and Pike Counties is due to the efforts of a bevy of dedicated volunteers who have turned their specialized skills from a hobby into a lifeline after the Poconos becomes a disaster area. A main communications artery for the region had been severed when the Interborough Bridge was torn out by the raging Brodhead Creek. Along with it went many utility cables that ran beneath its deck, including telephone lines.

Earlier Friday morning, Roy Keller, a Stroudsburg amateur radio operator, had already been in touch with Civil Defense officials in Harrisburg. His equipment was being powered by emergency current supplied by Monroe County's CD organization. He had worked with Charles Landis of Safe Harbor to contact Dr. Richard Gerstell, state CD director. Upon learning of the dire situation in Stroudsburg, Gerstell had immediately ordered two helicopters and other needed assistance rushed to the stricken towns.

By ten a.m., another "ham" operator, Charles Baker of Smith Street in East Stroudsburg, has rigged up a generator to run his rig. He establishes the first radio link with Stroudsburg's CD headquarters, employing runners between his home and the East Stroudsburg municipal building.

The Civil Air Patrol (CAP), also a volunteer organization, is able to establish a much-needed connection with the hospital, through the use of two AM frequency Gonset Communicator sets, affectionately known as "Gooney Boxes." These are some of the very first mobile amateur radio units, and get a serious workout during this emergency.

With Tobyhanna Signal Depot having set up its MARS station, K3WCQ, the hams now have a relay to handle emergency traffic between nearby and distant points. It relays messages ranging from urgent requests for evacuation, medical and food supplies to queries from anxious relatives about the welfare of their family members in the disaster area.

It's the kind of action amateur radio enthusiasts live for, and more distant hams aren't about to miss out. Richard Moll of Jenkintown piles all his equipment—which in 1955 means some serious bulk—into his vehicle and receives priority space on the irregular volunteer ferry boat service into East Stroudsburg. For several days, he operates from a cell-block at the police station. He receives permission to overstay his leave from the Army to continue rendering a more immediate kind of service to his country.

A five-car convoy of mobile equipment departs Bucks and Berks Counties on Sunday, with two of the sets ending up in East Stroudsburg, one in Analomink and a fourth in Stroudsburg. Later that day, radios and operators arrive from Allentown at Stokes Mill to assist in fire protection, since no water is in the mains in Stroudsburg. They also coordinate operations in a regular ferry service being set up across the Brodhead there. At least a dozen of Monroe County's own hams assist in maintaining communications until telephone service is restored to East Stroudsburg on Monday night.

The Signal Depot furnishes walkie-talkies and other equipment to aid in direct communication, and also makes it possible for the area's commercial radio station, WVPO, to resume broadcasting by providing a power generator. The AM station has been silent since quarter to eleven on Thursday night, when the power had gone out.

By two p.m. Friday, the generator is hooked up and "the little station that could" is back on the air. For the first hour, they adjust to the new system and wonder awkwardly what is appropriate to broadcast in such a situation. A few Civil Defense announcements come in and those are read.

At three o'clock, a woman stops by. She has been searching frantically for any information about the whereabouts of family members, whom she has been unable to contact. At her wit's end, she asks if WVPO will broadcast a message from her, in hopes that her relatives will hear it and know she's okay and where to find her. Station officials can think of no better way to be of service, and so they broadcast her message. It is the first in a constant flow of such messages that the station will broadcast throughout the weekend until midnight Sunday.

They never leave the air for more than three hours at a time, broadcasting a mix of personal messages, spot news, announcements, and recorded music. Amazingly, word gets out about the valiant effort and volunteers from all over the country begin pouring in to help the station staff itself to respond to the great need for its services. Soon they have three shifts of ten women working around the clock taking messages on four phones that they've managed to bring on line.

By the end of the emergency, the station will estimate that they've put more than fifteen thousand personal messages and more than ten thousand instructional or informational announcements over the air. Even station management and salespeople will do their part, acting as roving reporters to keep their communities informed of developments in place of regular newscasters, who can't yet get into the devastated area.

Later, WVPO will provide numerous tape-recorded coverage series of the event for other radio and TV stations outside of Monroe County. The effort will make the record books as the largest public service ever performed by a station of its power and size, and will earn the station's reputation as "the voice of the Poconos."

By noon, the Tinsmans have done everything they can to secure their home and lumberyard from the flood. The water is now up into the yard, too deep to safely navigate any longer. The current isn't as powerful as it is in the river channel itself, but the water is swirling around enough to begin picking up piles of lumber the Tinsmans weren't able to get to. It is also rising into the first floor of their home on Fleecydale Road. They resolve to stay with Bill's parents for the night.

They've moved their vehicles up on the hill, as have the neighbors they were able to warn the night before. Now there's nothing left to do but stand and watch all the strange cargo being carried along by the river. They watch piles of their lumber take off like rafts, and outbuildings smashed to kindling when they impact the Lumberville pedestrian bridge. Huge trees, oil tanks, 55-gallon drums, and massive rolls of paper from the mills in Riegelsville and Milford jockey for position in the current.

Clarence "Tom" Cochran is at work on his construction job, when he gets a call from his wife Anna at their home along the canal in Upper Black Eddy. Their house sits at the base of the palisades on Lodi Hill Road, and the water is getting high. It's been rising three or four inches an hour, and she's frightened and wants him to come home from work. By the time he gets there, the water has risen to the top of some small pine trees on their property.

The son of a canal locktender, Tom isn't easily put out. He's seen plenty in his years on the canal and on the river. He assures his wife that everything will be okay. The water's as high as it's ever been, and he can't imagine it'll get much worse. He opens the door to check the cellar, and finds it full of water. His two-year-old daughter Sandy's eyes grow large as she points to her little blue plastic tea set swirling on the surface. To keep her distracted so she doesn't become frightened, Tom rigs up a pole with line and hands it to her so she can "go fishing."

He switches on the radio and listens to the news and the forecast on WJZ-AM out of New York. They're not expecting any more rain, so that's good. But the water continues to rise. He turns the dial to a WEST out of Easton, and they report the river's level on the hour. Finally, the water begins coming in the house, and they decide the safest thing is for Anna and Sandy to go stay at the neighbor's house up the hill.

Tom stays in the house, wanting to be there if something happens. He watches as fish come in with the water now pouring through the windows. He can see it has reached almost over the tops of the cars parked outside. The water starts rising inside faster than outside, and Tom goes to check the drain in the corner of the house, thinking it must be clogged. It is…with a large carp trying to come in from below. It's a long, tense night of watching, listening and waiting, without knowing what it is, exactly, that he's waiting for.

The following day, as the water recedes, Tom is standing on his front porch. A neighbor walking by asks to bum a cigarette. Obliging, Tom walks across the yard to hand her one. Before he reaches her, he steps into a sinkhole and disappears beneath the water. When he resurfaces, he and his Pall Malls are completely soaked, so she doesn't get her smoke.

Just up River Road, May Snyder is beside herself. The bridge cops who came for lunch have just told her that the river will come into her luncheonette. She's still got a lunch crowd to feed, but she also has her own family's needs to think about. Her sons are helping in the shop, and she tells them to go up the hill to get their grandfather. He can help them move some of their things out of the house before the water comes up.

After they leave, she gets on the phone to her ice cream distributor to tell them to come pick up their product, because it's about to be ruined. There is no answer, so she decides she might as well give it away. She offers all her customers free cones.

Her father and mother show up with the boys, and they get to work loading May's washer and refrigerator and some of their more important personal items. They make a few more trips for clothes, and on the last one, snag the Snyders' three little Chihuahuas. Her mother, afraid of the water, eyes her nervously. May knows she doesn't want her to stay in the store any longer, but May feels compelled to save what she can of their home and business. Finally, her mom gets ready to leave.

"Just come up when you're ready," she says.

As the last of her lunch customers leave, May leaves the boys in charge and drives the family car across the canal bridge on Bridgeton Hill Road, far enough up the hill so it will stay out of the water. On her way back down, she walks to the front of the store and gazes across the wide expanse of the river at the Milford banks. A boy is clearly stranded in the water at the edge, and is waving his arms for help. May watches anxiously, knowing there's nothing she can do to help the child. Then she sees a fireman approach the boy and pull him to safety. It's a frightening experience, and she's a little shaken up.

Then she looks down her own side to the south. The river's already covering the road, and she sees something moving near the bridge. Shielding her eyes from the sun, she can make out a small building beginning to lift off its foundation. It's Ruth Gruver's Post Office!

The small wood building floats a short way into River Road, makes a turn south as though obeying a traffic sign, and wobbles away on the current. May doesn't know that Mrs. Gruver has just finished cleaning it out of all mail, cash, equipment and supplies, and removed the government property to her home for safekeeping.

The Post Office in Upper Black Eddy decides to take a trip down the Delaware.
— *Collection Miriam "Mim" Stull*

May just watches their little post office disappear into the river.

She's had enough. It's time to leave the store. She calls the boys and goes inside to take one more look around before abandoning it to the river. As she pulls the back door closed, oily brown water is coming through the front.

They walk up Bridgeton Hill Road until they get to the canal bridge, where the water is now so deep they can't walk anymore, but have to swim across to reach the car. No one speaks as May turns the key in the ignition and drives up the hill.

Up in Riegelsville, Barbara Slater's Post Office is also in jeopardy. She can see everyone around her leaving their homes and businesses and moving cars, but this is the Post Office. It's a government service, and nobody has told her she can leave, so she stays at her counter and watches the water rise.

Just around the corner on Delaware Road, her daughter, Dot Kale, is watching her neighbor, Alverna Apple, moving all her things to the second floor of her apartment. Mrs. Apple, who experienced the 1936 flood, advises Dot to do the same. Dot doesn't take her seriously. She hasn't heard anything about a flood coming, though she hasn't listened to the radio yet today. She knows the water is high, but at nineteen years old, has no concept of how high it can really get.

Dot's husband, Russ, is away in the mountains for a few days. When he gets back, they're scheduled to go down the shore, and he's due back any time now. It's a gorgeous, sunny day, and she's not about to get all excited about some water. Instead, she decides to join some of her friends down on the Riegelsville Bridge to watch the river rise.

The bridge is strong, built by the reputable Roebling company to replace the one that had been washed away in the 1903 flood. It's a beautifully designed iron structure, and no one's afraid it will go out, so the bridge guards allow people out on it to watch the water come up. And come up, it does. Soon, the phone and electrical utility cables strung just beneath the deck begin to flap in the strong current. It causes vibration on the bridge, and for the first time, Dot realizes that there might really be a serious flood. She decides she'd better take Mrs. Apple's advice and get busy.

Dot calls her brother James and he borrows her brother-in-law's farm tractor and hay trailer to move their furniture. But when he arrives with it, a local CD volunteer commandeers it to help move elderly residents from their apartments to the shelter up the hill at St. Peter's church. Some of the residents don't want to leave, and they are lifted bodily—chairs and all—out of their homes and onto the trailer.

Russ telephones Dot to let her know he's been dropped off at his mother's home near Deerhorn Creek in Durham. He needs Dot to go bring his car from where he'd parked it down by the river so they can hitch up a trailer to get his mom's things out of her basement. Dot asks him where it is, and he tells her he left it behind Ewald's Diner.

She begins to walk down to get it, when a policeman stops her. "Where you goin'?" he asks.

"I'm going to drive my car up here by Ewald's Diner," she replies.

"You better not," he warns, then adds more authoritatively, "You can't."

Dot thinks about paying two more years on a car they just bought, that won't even be there if she doesn't get it now. She won't be denied.

"You watch me," she says, then walks right on by. She walks a couple hundred yards toward the river across from Whippany Paper, the water up to her shorts. She finds the car, starts it up, and drives it back up the hill and to Russ' mother's place, where they will stay the night because Riegelsville is now underwater.

Four-year-old Chrissy Koehler is watching her mother running back and forth to talk with neighbors in their yard just around the corner from Dot Kale. She senses something is wrong, but can't quite figure it out. Too small to be allowed near the canal or river, she's unaware that they're rising. The canal is right across the street from her Victorian home on Durham Road, but Chrissy can't see it because it's not up over the road yet, so her mother's behavior is somewhat confusing.

Then she starts seeing other neighbors coming over to her yard, and everyone is talking excitedly. There's a sense of important activity, and she wants to know what's going on. She hears people talking about a flood, but she doesn't know what that is.

Chrissy's father is away on business in New York, so her mother asks some of the neighbors for help moving her many antiques to the second floor of their house. One of them agrees, and they begin moving furniture. Chrissy asks what's going on, and her mother, not wanting to frighten her or her one-year-old sister, Marlene, just tells them that Mommy is busy and they must stay inside the house until she's done. So the girls busy themselves with looking for Webbsy, their cat, who has gone somewhere to hide from all the commotion.

After what seems to Chrissy like a long time, the neighbor leaves, and her mother comes to talk with the girls. She tells them that the river is flooding and that the water is already into the canal and will soon be in the yard. They need to gather some clothes and get ready because a man is going to come pick them up to take them someplace where they'll be safe till the water goes back down. Chrissy asks if Webbsy can come, too, and her mother says yes.

Chrissy tells her where Webbsy is hiding and Mrs. Koehler goes to the attic for a box to put the cat in. To keep them busy while she packs a suitcase, she tells the girls to choose a few toys and books to bring with them.

By the time they're done packing, water has come into the front room of the house. It continues to rise, and is up to the second step on the stairs when a man rows a boat through the wide front door, right into their parlor. Mrs. Koehler and the girls are waiting for him on the third step. She hands the girls over the railing to him before stepping into the boat herself, carrying their suitcase.

St. Peter's Lutheran Church provides food and shelter for residents of Riegelsville, Pennsylvania, who are driven from their homes by the rising Delaware.
– Collection Bob Stalgaitis

Chrissy watches their house as he rows away. The man rows all the way up to Route 611, where he drops them off. She walks up the hill beside her mom, who carries Marlene in one arm and the suitcase in the other. Some nice people greet them at the church and show them some little beds they can sleep on. Her mother sits down on one and slides their suitcase under the one beside it, where she tells Chrissy she'll be sleeping with Marlene.

Chrissy looks around and sees many people she knows. She thinks this must be some kind of party. It's all very exciting.

Laura Slack is listening when Mrs. Fennimore, her host at their home on the Jersey Shore, calls back home to Hendricks Appliance store in Stockton. They've heard on the news about the flooding, and they want to know what they're missing. Amos Hendricks tells Mrs. Fennimore that they've taken the stock out of the store in a truck and hauled it across Centre Bridge to store it at a safe place on the Pennsylvania side. The driver has called to tell him that he won't be back over, because his was the last vehicle across before officials closed the bridge.

The women decide there's nothing much they can do now but wait to see what happens. Laura is still expecting her husband, Cliff, to come down on Saturday, so she agrees. They spend the rest of the day discussing what they might find when they get back home.

Mikey Edwards has worked all morning, checking people's groceries at the Acme Market in Lambertville. As the day wears on, more and more people are coming in to stock up on basics, talking about how they may not be able to go shopping for a while if the river really floods like the radio says it's going to.

On her lunch break, Mikey walks out to the parking lot and takes a look at Swan Creek, which runs right by the market on its way to the Delaware. It's very high, and she realizes that if the river really is flooding, it'll likely back up the creek. When she goes back in, she reports to her coworkers what she's seen. They begin discussing whether or not management will let them go home soon if it gets real bad, but no word comes from above.

Every fifteen minutes to half an hour, one of the employees goes outside to check on the creek level. After one of the longer intervals, someone says, *Look...there it is!*

Mikey looks toward the front and sees the brown water swirling in under the door and creeping across the shiny tile floor. She looks at the checker in the next lane and says, "It's time to get out of here."

Mikey and her workmates go to the office to ask the manager if he's going to close the store. He says he has no intention of doing such a thing, so they all look at each other. Finally, Mikey says, "Well, we're leaving. The water's already coming in. It's dangerous."

They start heading for the door, when the manager stops them. *At least help me get the stock up away from the water.*

So they quickly clear the bottom shelves of canned and box goods, produce and other merchandise. Then everyone heads for home to secure their own places or help friends and family with theirs.

Mikey walks around the corner to Choc's father, John's, house. She's amused to find him sitting on the stoop, dangling his feet in the water.

"Dad," she says, "We've got to get out of here."

He just looks at her and smiles. "Mikey, everything will be fine when the water recedes."

Inside, the water is up to her waist, and the kitchen table's floating in the living room with the sugar, creamer, and butter still on top. The refrigerator is also there, surprisingly still upright. She goes upstairs to fetch some clothes for John, and takes him back home with her.

Once inside, she calls Choc to see if he can come home. He tells her the Bridge Commission won't let him leave. He's needed to help keep traffic off the bridges. They're in danger of being swept downstream, and they can't allow people on them for liability reasons. They've been monitoring the river's rise, taking readings on the hour and reporting to radio and TV stations and Civil Defense officials.

Choc has been shuttling between the toll bridge and some of the free bridges up and down the river, doing whatever needs done. Traffic is backed up for miles around the river, with sightseers wanting to catch a glimpse of the high water. Choc says he doesn't know when he'll be able to get home.

It will be three days before Mikey sees her husband again. She hangs up and takes his father to his sister's house in Kingwood, where there's more room.

Harry Leida again walks down to Stokes Mill in East Stroudsburg, where a regular ferry has finally been established. He returns to Joyce's house, where she is overjoyed to see he is okay. He tells her what he's seen, and how much destruction there is on both sides of the Brodhead. She and her parents had been down Dreher Avenue as far as Main Street, but were afraid to venture farther. Harry tells her it's just as well, the place is a mess, and dangerous.

He tells Joyce that he's got to go back over and get Fred back to Easton, but she says they're saying all the roads are blocked, and there's no way to get in or out if it's not an emergency. He knows his sister will be frantic if she doesn't hear from them about her son. He says he's going out to his car to get his cameras, and take some photos of all the destruction. He's sure it's going to be a historic event, and someone should document it. By the time he's done, he thinks maybe someone will have cleared some of the roads. They kiss, and he's off again.

When he gets back across the creek, he heads back down to the Day Street Flats, where most of the worst destruction is. There, he runs into Gib Smrz, his boss at Line Material, who is there to survey the damage. Many of the Line Material employees live in the immediate vicinity, and the company is worried about them.

Since it's actually a workday, technically Harry should be on the job. Gib tells him to use his camera to capture images of all the L-M employees, their families and the damage to their homes. The company will be publishing a special issue of their employee newsletter about the flood. Happy to be able to do his work in good faith, Harry sets to work doing as his boss has asked. He spends the rest of the afternoon taking what will become some of the most graphic and poignant images of the flood's devastation. They'll soon be published in a special edition of the company's newsletter.

He captures images of Eugene Heller's car where it has come to rest after ramming the Firemen's Bingo Hall, and of the Van Gorders surveying the ruins of their house. George tells him that the one bright spot was that when they arrived in the morning, their dog was standing in the doorway, wagging its tail.

Eugene Heller's new Oldsmobile is finally located in the wreckage of the Firemen's Bingo Hall, where four women had drowned waiting for rides. Eugene's body will be found weeks later when a small girl slips on what she thinks is a rock in the park. It's Eugene's head, sticking out of the mud where he was buried, still clutching a metal folding chair that he'd managed to grab while being washed away by the Brodhead's swift current.
– Harry Leida photo, collection Ann Amato

Mr. and Mrs. Herb Fenner point out the utility pole that likely saved their lives. The pile of debris in the background had collected against it, shielding their small house from the worst force of the raging current. They escaped the flood by spending the night with their dogs on the roof.

Two of their dogs stayed inside, floating around on mattresses in the attic. When the water receded, their entire home was a sodden, stinking mess. The shot at right is what their bedroom looked like.

– Harry Leida photos, collection Ann Amato

From the looks of the rest of the place, Harry guesses it was the only bright spot. He takes a shot of Officer Lou Carmella and Harry Hinton going through the home of Harry's sister, Ethel Nevil. In the background is a clearly visible mudline up to the top of Lou's head, in the kitchen of the woman who just the night before had slipped from his grasp and disappeared beneath the dark water.

Harry documents what's left of the Fenners' bedroom and their dogs sniffing about among the furniture, which they dragged into the yard after coming down from their roof. And there's a photo of a bull-dozer hauling away what's left of the Burds' house trailer from the Flats.

Over the next few days, Harry will range over the entire area up to Analomink near Camp Davis, documenting the absolute carnage wrought by the Brodhead Creek. While he works, he asks around about open routes out of the towns.

One of the rescue workers tells him he's heard people are getting out by heading up toward Saylorsburg and coming around the back way.

When he's finished with his photography work, Harry heads back up to his parents' house and collects Fred and his suitcase. They again cross on a pontoon boat at Stokes Mill, and walk to Joyce's house. They say their goodbyes and Harry slowly picks his way back to his sister's house in Easton.

Bob Herman and his mother and sister walk back down to their home, afraid of what they might find. They haven't heard from Mr. Herman all night, and hope he's okay. They see the streets covered in what looks like sand dunes. A slight breeze blows off the street, and Bob realizes those dunes are ripples of foul-smelling mud.

When they come around front, Mr. Herman is already shoveling the disgusting layer of muck out of their house. They greet each other with much relief, and he tells them that the water did not reach the first floor. The bad news is that their basement is full of mud and water, and has ruined the furnace and Mrs. Herman's collection of sheet music for her piano and organ.

They look around at their neighbors' homes, some of which have clearly been infiltrated halfway up the second story, and say nothing. They know how lucky they are. They all get to work cleaning out their basement, and when that huge task is done, they head for their neighbors' homes to help them begin their recovery.

A couple days later, Bob's nineteen-year-old brother Don arrives from Allentown, where he has a summer job. He tells them of the destruction along the Lehigh River down that way, but says it's nothing compared to what's happened here at home. He and Bob go out on body recovery details. Bob doesn't find any, but Don does. He tells Bob the bodies they're finding are all green from being bruised by all the objects that must have struck them, and bloated from the heat.

Bob relates his experience on Lincoln Avenue, but leaves out the part about the man he couldn't reach. Despite his enjoyment of all the old men's fish stories he's grown up with, he'll never again be able to hear about "the one that got away" with a light heart. And it will be fifty haunted years before he shares his own.

Lydia Stielau is worried because she hasn't heard from her husband, Edward, and he and Carolyn haven't shown up. She has no idea that the relatively light damage they've had at their cottage in Paradise Falls has intensified to the south and east, and that Ed and Carolyn have been turned back at Hackettstown.

At breakfast, she and the girls had heard that another resort just down Route 90, Pocono Gardens, has been completely washed out, and that their guests escaped the rushing water by climbing up the hill to the highway. Now the girls are down at the tearoom, serving food to these refugees. She's glad they have something to keep them occupied after so many days cooped up in the cottage.

Ruth and Edna are glad, too. It's exciting, this break in the monotony of rain and gloom. Though it's beautiful and sunny outside, the girls are happy to be indoors today. One of the women they've served in the tearoom is telling her harrowing tale of escape from the marauding waters, and they hang on her every word.

> The woman and her young husband are honeymooning at the Gardens, when someone yells to get out, that a flash flood is coming. Her husband grabs her by the arm and she follows him, running to the hill behind their room. He begins clawing his way up the steep embankment, grasping on to tree roots that have been exposed by the eroding soil. She's hanging on for dear life around his waist.
>
> The water is rising so quickly, they're barely able to stay ahead of it. Now it's gaining on them, rising around her thighs. She's being battered by the trunks of downed trees and other debris, when suddenly, her husband reaches the top and pulls her to safety.

For emphasis, the woman swings her legs out from under the tablecloth and shows them the bruises. The girls stare in fascination, *ooh-ing* and *aah-ing*.

Later, when the girls' father is finally able to make it through to bring them home, they will pass people coming up from the ruined Stroudsburgs. At a rest stop, one person tells of a strange occurrence.

Mrs. Russell Lambert on Main Street there had lit a kerosene lamp when the power had gone out, then placed it on her dining room table. She then left the apartment to help her husband and son move their cars out of danger's path, and ended up going to her daughter's home to be safe overnight. The next day, when the water receded, they returned to find the lamp still burning on the table, though water marks on the wall indicated the table must have risen and fallen with the tide. It had happened so gently that it never disturbed the lamp, despite the violence the same water had caused outside.

As with every disaster, other such tales of the strange and ironic would become legend around the event.

Peggy Beling has finally arrived near the home of her fiancé, Mike Fackenthal. Her neighbor drops her off at the bottom of Frost Hollow Road, where it meets Rt. 611, known as Delaware Avenue at that part of Forks Township, just north of Easton. Peggy is stunned to see the river up over the road in some places. Her neighbor is worried about leaving her there, but Peggy assures her she'll stay in touch, and walks up 611 toward Mike's house.

When she arrives, she sees the house surrounded by about six inches of water, and knows it will get worse. She finds Mrs. Fackenthal and the rest of the family down below, helping neighbors in summer houses closer to the river move their furniture up to the road to keep it from the water. As Peggy pitches in to help, Mrs. Fackenthal tells her how their dog, Maggie, had woken them up, barking at three o'clock in the morning.

When they had gone to see what the commotion was about, they'd found her barking at the basement door. They shone a flashlight down the steps and it reflected back off water at the bottom. Maggie had heard it coming in and sounded the alarm.

The family had gone outside to secure Mr. Fackenthal's chicken coops, because they were already afloat. As they had sloshed through the water, they'd seen all kinds of animals fleeing the rising water, as well. Groundhogs and muskrats dodged snakes slithering up from the bottomlands. Then Mr. Fackenthal and his sons had gone to help their neighbors, the Laws, bring their rabbit hutches to high ground.

Once their animals were safe, they had helped another neighbor, Bill Johnson, tie his house to a tree so it wouldn't float away. They had run a rope through two corner windows in a bedroom and looped it around a huge tree. Then they had turned their attention to their own home.

Mr. Fackenthal, not believing the water would get immensely high, had capped a drainpipe running beneath the house and out both sides of the circular driveway, to keep it from coming up inside the house.

Now Peggy and the Fackenthals work through the afternoon to bring furniture and valuables to safety, until their yard along the road resembles a huge rummage sale. It's the same next door, at the YMCA's Waurenga Lodge.

The water continues to rise until it comes through the floorboards. Mrs. Fackenthal decides it's time she and Maggie go up the hill, and let the younger people finish securing the house.

The Fackenthal house on North Delaware Drive (Rt. 611) in Forks Township underwater nearly to its second floor as the river continues to rise. It will reach another foot over the level pictured here before it goes back down. The family is unable to move much of their furniture and valuables to safety. — Collection Margaret Fackenthal

Her son, John, rows a boat to the back door, and picks up his mom. She's standing there in her housedress with a folding chair, a portable radio, and a carton of Old Gold cigarettes. John helps her into the boat, and Maggie follows. John rows to the hill in the yard behind the house, where she gets out and sets up her chair. As the water continues creeping up the hill throughout the day, unflappable Janet Fackenthal simply moves her chair higher up the hill, and Maggie relocates herself right beside the chair.

Meanwhile, Mr. Fackenthal becomes chagrined at his earlier capping of the drain pipe. The water is now much higher than he'd expected it to go, having reached the windows and showing no sign of receding. He fears that it might build up too much resistance and push the house off its foundation, so he goes around opening all the windows to allow the water to just flow through. He sees the larger items they were unable to move—the refrigerator, freezer, upright piano—and knows they will be a total loss.

Peggy and Mike come by a little later and look in the side bay window at the family's dining room set floating. They think it would be neat to go swimming in the dining room, something they can tell their kids about when they're older. They begin climbing through the window, when they're stopped dead in their tracks by the booming voice of Mr. Fackenthal.

"Get the hell out of there!"

Unaware that their electrical service has been turned off by MetEd, he's fearful that the kids will be electrocuted if they go inside. They remain in the yard, shaken by this violent outburst by a man they usually know as quiet and reserved. It's the first real indication they have that things could get scary.

Still, young people will be young people, and Mike and Peggy decide to take a break from the work and enjoy the novelty of boating in people's yards. They tool around in Mike's fifteen-foot wooden boat with the 22-horsepower engine he's so proud of. As they go past the Wittens', three houses away, Mr. Witten calls to them from a second-story window.

Mr. Witten, the swimming coach at Easton's Lafayette College, had politely refused the Fackenthals' earlier offer to help them move their things out. He had insisted they were going to stay with the house. Now, with the relentless rising of the water, he changes his mind.

"I think we're going to have to evacuate," he admits. "Can you help me?"

The young people agree, and sidle the boat up to the window, removing their neighbors' family members and possessions. When they're done, Peggy and Mike take the boat back down along the bottoms of the yards. From there, they can see whole buildings coming down the river, complete with furniture inside. Some of them hit trees and break up. Lots of propane tanks are bobbing along dangerously on the surface.

Peggy thinks about the people who live in those cottages and wonders what they'll do. Then she realizes that soon, she and the Fackenthals are going to have to figure out what they're going to do for the night.

At the Portland, Pennsylvania, Civil Defense headquarters, messengers are pouring in with stacks of telegrams to let parents know their children in Pocono camps are all right. Pleas are issuing from the two-way radio for heavy burlap bags in which to wrap recovered bodies, and for volunteers to dig graves. CD officials radio back that cases of rubber gloves have been ordered for mortuary workers and rubber sheets to wrap the bodies in.

Just a bit past two in the afternoon, photographer Al Nittle of Bangor stands on the new Delaware River toll bridge between Portland and Columbia, New Jersey. They have been told by Charlie Newbaker, the bridge guard, that they do so at their own risk. Indeed, the new structure is trembling from the force of the water rushing below, and the impacts of all the flotsam being carried along in it.

Nevertheless, Al is intent on setting up his Speed Graphic to capture what he knows will be an historic event. About two hundred yards upstream, the last covered wooden bridge over the river is being battered by the river as well, and Al knows it will soon give up the ghost. His assistant, Joan Sandt, stands by with loaded film holders at the ready. Soon, their prescience pays off.

At two twenty p.m., the wooden structure begins cracking, and Al makes his first exposure. For the next forty seconds, amid a grinding and crashing that can be heard above the roar of the water, the two work as a well-oiled machine. Al shoots nine unforgettable images until the wooden wreckage strikes the toll bridge, causing a rumble and tremor. One section of the old bridge smashes to bits against the steel structure, and the rest flows intact beneath the toll bridge.

It has been a gamble whose costs would have been ultimate had it not paid off, but it has. Al's photos will run on the front pages of several area newspapers in the coming days, and contribute to a lasting historic record.

Seventy-five-year-old Charlie Newbaker watches what's left of the bridge—and his livelihood—float down the river toward Al and Joan. When it's out of sight, he turns to watch the river flowing through his home on the levee. Then he leaves to join his family.

The sorry remains of the Portland-Columbia span, last of the covered wooden bridges spanning the Delaware, stand as mute testament to the passing of another age.
– "River Jim" Abbott photo

The call from Portland comes in to the CD headquarters in Easton, warning them that the covered bridge has broken up and is on its way downriver toward them. The order is given to close the Northampton Street Free Bridge, and word is sent down the line to let other towns know what's coming.

At four p.m., Dr. Fred Phillips of Quakertown performs an autopsy on the body of nineteen-year-old Carl Schwarz of Souderton. Schwarz is the driver of the truck that had plunged over the embankment the night before, coming to rest on the patio of a residence.

When investigating officers had found a .22 caliber rifle under the seat, they'd notified Bucks County Coroner Russell Ferris. Ferris had in turn requested that Funeral Director Robert Snyder pay special attention to finding any suspicious marks while preparing the body. Snyder had indeed found two such marks, small puncture wounds behind the right ear and on the chest.

Now Dr. Phillips confirms that the punctures are entry wounds from two .22 caliber bullets. He tells the press that the death "seems to be a very cleverly planned murder," and the search is on for two other youths last seen with the dead farm products deliveryman.

Eighteen-year-old John Schnur and sixteen-year-old Virginia Tunstall are reported as having been seen hitch-hiking earlier in the morning near the Wa-Wa Diner south of Riegelsville. Two hundred dollars in cash had been found on the body during the original crime scene investigation, so police rule out robbery as a motive. Everyone is interested in why two young people could possibly want to kill another one in cold blood. As if the flood disaster isn't enough excitement, the press immediately wrings all the drama it can out of a small-town murder that might otherwise have made huge, black headlines.

This evening's *Philadelphia Inquirer* injects movie thriller status into the story, running it on the front page beneath the headline "Hunted Pair Vanish in Storm." Over the next several days, the couple is proven to be something less than "very clever," as the article describes the murder plot. It will be revealed as nothing more than a hot-blooded young man's jealous over-reaction to a rival's perceived threat. By Monday evening, the *Quakertown Free Press* will run the anti-climatic denouement under the disappointing deck "Youth Confesses Souderton Truck Driver's Murder," and the incident will fade into history as a sad sidelight to the enormous tragedy of the flood's destruction.

Twelve-year-old Barbara Fletcher is thinking about the man who had been sitting on a bench outside the bank in downtown Lambertville for the past several days, telling anyone who would listen that there was going to be a flood. Her younger sister Patty is on a camping trip with her 4-H Club up in Stokes State Forest near the Delaware Water Gap, and she's concerned about her. Everyone in town is either standing down near the river, watching it come up, or madly rushing around trying to move their possessions to higher ground.

Some of her own family members are in the latter group. Aunt Eleanor and Uncle "Hoot" (Charles) Dudbridge and their seven-year-old son Christopher live at the corner of North Union Street and Arnett Avenue, just two blocks from the canal. Barbara's family lives well away from the river, on the other side of Main Street, but she's concerned about her relatives. So is her dad, John.

Now she's following him downtown to beg Aunt Eleanor to leave her house just until the worst is over. Aunt Nel is a stubborn woman, though, and she's having none of it. Her husband and son leave with John to go to the firehouse, but Nel stays put.

John, who has gotten typhus shots so he can safely work in the dirty water, realizes his effort is wasted on his sister, and he takes Barbara with him to go join other volunteers who are helping evacuate those that want to leave. He rows up Union Street in his boat and lets Barbara out on the sidewalk on the east side of the street. Then he rows to the other side where they know an old lady lives alone.

He goes inside, and after a few moments, emerges with the woman. She's wearing a long skirt and apron, and a three-cornered scarf on her head. She's carrying a sack of her belongings in one hand and her cat in the other. Both she and the cat are shaking in terror.

Barbara looks closely at the old woman's wizened face, and sees that she is crying. A wave of compassion sweeps over the young girl, and she begins to cry, too. She watches as her father takes the sack from the old woman and puts it in the boat. Then he picks up the woman, who still holds tightly to her cat, and carries her to the boat, where he deposits her gingerly onto the front seat.

Barbara watches the rest of the evacuations. Then, when her dad rows the people to the shelter, she goes to the river to see what the problem-causer looks like.

All sorts of things are being carried along in the current: out-houses, bathtubs, lumber, hay bales and shingles. Huge trees are floating along upended, their gnarled roots exposed. A dead cow floats on its side. Between all these items, animals both wild and domestic all swim one way: downstream. It's an impressive education in the raw and indiscriminate power of nature for a young lady on the verge of adolescence.

Twenty-eight-year-old Jean DiRenzis is doing housework at her home on Easton's south side when she hears a radio announcer on WEST report that the river is rising and that a flood is quite possible. Their home isn't in the floodplain, so she's not worried.

She and her husband Rich love the neighborhood. The trains run daily from the Lehigh Valley, and the station is beautiful. It has a great little restaurant that serves really good lunches, and there's even a little bar where you can pass the time and see friends. There are lots of "mom and pop" stores—Champy's, Trump's, Fluck's, Schwar's—all within a five or six-block area. It's convenient for a growing family, and close to downtown. They enjoy walking there

There's no passing over the Glendon Bridge into Easton's south side when Rich DiRenzis tries to make it home after work on Friday afternoon.
— Bradwin Roberts photo, collection Linda Roberts

280

when the Ringling Brothers Circus comes to town, taking the kids to see the animals being unloaded. The schools are good and close by, and there's even a library extension within easy walking distance.

After an hour or so, Jean thinks it'll be about time for Rich to come home. He's working at his father's dry cleaning plant, Snow White Cleaners, on Freemansburg Avenue in Wilson Borough. For the first time, she becomes concerned, knowing he comes across the Glendon Bridge to get home, and that it's probably already underwater.

She picks up the phone to call him, but can't get through. Most of the phones in town are already out of service, including the one at the cleaners, so Rich can't call home, either. Of course, he doesn't think of doing so until his shift ends and he and his brother, Bill, are turned back at the Glendon Bridge.

At first, they decide to try walking home across the "two cent bridge" between the south side and Tenth Street, a rickety toll suspension span that sways even on a good day. But when they reach it, it has already been torn away by the current. They decide their only option is to return to work. Their father lives in an apartment above the shop, and they stay with him.

Jean has her two youngest daughters, Gail and Linda, with her. The eldest daughter, Kathy, and their son, Mike, are away at camp in the White Haven Area of the Poconos, near Hickory Run State Park. Jean has no idea that there has been any flooding up north, but still has a feeling of uneasiness as she gets the other kids ready for bed and Rich isn't home yet.

Crest

Friday, August 19
5:00 p.m. to Midnight

Jean Sinka, a seventeen-year-old student lab technician, is told to bring extra clothes to work with her when she comes in for her shift on Friday. Trenton's McKinley Memorial Hospital, where she works, has been notified that the Delaware River is flooding and that their facility on Brunswick Avenue may become isolated. They may need her help doing other duties if employees are unable to come in to work.

She's not surprised, then, when her shift is up and she's told to report to the hospital's School of Nursing dormitories. She gets time to eat and rest, then is put back to work serving food, busing trays, moving patients and doing whatever needs done. It's the only time she ever goes to work in dungarees, because the work requires more than her regular uniform will allow.

For three days and nights, she chooses to stay and help out. She and her coworkers are fed in the hospital cafeteria, and the dorms provide baths and showers. Everyone's abuzz over the flooding, and there's some fear over what they will find when they are finally able to go home. The days are long and she's exposed to much more of the hospital than she's ever seen, but it's gratifying to feel useful and needed. Everyone is working together as a team to get things done simply because they need done, and it's peculiarly satisfying.

Bill and Claire Talone are having an after-dinner drink in their backyard on Manor Lane in Yardley. They're relaxing and enjoying their rural yard, where they frequently see deer and raccoons. They're proud of their new home, which they'd built just a year earlier.

Bill had cut the lawn just before dinner so they could get a good look at the river, usually about a block away over the top of the canal bank. It has already crested, but the water is still high and makes a good conversation topic.

From somewhere upstream, the river gets a local boost in volume and overruns into the canal. It's simply more pressure than the old walls can take, and the bank suddenly explodes with the sound of a locomotive into the Talone's yard.

The explosion jars them out of their seats, and suddenly water is rushing up into the yard. Claire runs to the freezer to get all the meat that she'd just put away following a grocery trip the day before. Bill runs to the basement to shut off the circuit breaker box, then upstairs to corral their five cats on the third floor to keep them safe. Then he and Claire jump in their Buick and drive up Black Rock Road, where they're almost caught by the rising water.

They spend the night at Bill's sister's house, wondering what is becoming of their beloved new home.

Greta Johnson leaves her job at the phone company with a heavy heart, knowing she can't go home to Stockton. She wonders if there will even be a home to go to when the sun comes up. Her mother calls to tell her she'll be spending the night at her friend Mary Colligan's house.

Greta's dad and brother spend most of the night putting tar-paper over the roof on the cellar of the home they've been building, trying to make it livable on a permanent basis. Greta, having to work the next day, calls her fiancé, Nick Fresco, to come pick her up. She'll stay with his family until the end of her shift on Saturday, then join her dad and brother.

Dorothy Grider has had a strange feeling something's wrong during her entire train ride to Selinsgrove. After dinner, when her friend turns on the radio to hear the evening news, Dorothy learns the reason why.

The announcer reports the Delaware River has flooded, going on a rampage into most of the towns along its banks. Dorothy becomes heartsick, thinking of her beautiful bungalow in New Hope, and wondering if Lydia and Pops and Happy are okay. She tells her friend she must return home on tomorrow's first train.

The Tannersville Bridge, though only partially washed out, has the same effect as if it had been totally destroyed, as so many of the Monroe County spans have been—it's one more place where traffic can't traverse Route 611, a critical vehicular artery.
– Courtesy U.S. Army Depot at Tobyhanna

By the time the Schafers get back home from surveying the damage and talking to their neighbors in downtown Newfoundland, it's afternoon. While helping the Robackers shovel out the thick bed of stinking muck left in their apartment, they discuss what they have seen.

Cars, mashed and jumbled, some hanging partly from trees. Great, long gorges—some up to a hundred feet wide—gouged out of the earth by what had at one time been mere trickling streams. Boulders, weighing ten and fifteen tons, unearthed and pushed hundreds of yards, taking out everything in their paths.

Most ghastly of all, they report that most of the caskets in one of the community's cemeteries have been mostly disinterred. One concrete vault was carried away completely. It will later be found two miles away, its cover missing and its casket dumped alongside the vault, hanging open to reveal its long-decomposed occupant.

They take stock of their own damage. Both families' cars are total losses, but the Schafers are some of the very few people in town to have not-yet-common comprehensive auto insurance to cover their car's refurbishment. The Robackers, not as lucky, also suffer crippling damage to their lawnmower and garden tractor, but Bob is handy and will be able to revive them.

Around six p.m., a helicopter sets down in the field opposite their farmhouse, and Robert's colleague, Vince Fox, from Tobyhanna emerges from a circle of rotor wash. Robert runs out to meet the Lt. Colonel, who shares news of the surrounding area and of the Signal Depot's transformation into an emergency operations center.

Vince tells Robert that he'd like him to establish and assume command of a Newfoundland base of operations. This base will be responsible for evacuation of the sick and wounded, and to provide a supply line and communications link to the outside world. Robert readily accepts the assignment, and spends the next three weeks carrying out the mission to help get his hometown back into some semblance of order and normality.

In Erwinna, Dick DeGroot is standing with his father on the porch of a relative's farm, watching water engulf surrounding fields. He'll later learn that this water isn't from the river itself, but has backed up from the canal, whose locks have been opened to reduce pressure on its banks.

Dick, twenty, lives with his family above the Revere General Store in Nockamixon Township, up over Bridgeton Hill from the river. His father, Cornelius, is the local Justice of the Peace, and his mother, Helena, is the postmaster. They also own and operate the small country store. Dick and his dad have just come down the hill after closing for the day.

Dick is concerned because he is supposed to leave for New York City this evening, to start his senior year at Fordham University. But as far as they know, the bridges over the Delaware are all out or closed, and nobody flies such short distances in 1955. He's right to be concerned: it will be ten days before he's able to get over the river and into Manhattan, and he'll be late for orientation.

For now, he and his dad go back up the hill. Tomorrow, they'll report what they've seen to their many customers. As in many rural communities, this informational exchange is just another function served by the store. It's a natural crossroads of commerce and social interaction, and has one of the few telephones in the relatively poor area. Since the water began rising, the DeGroots have received many calls inquiring about conditions along the river. They'll continue to get them for the next few days, and will gladly pass along any news they learn.

A crowd gathers at the Kintnersville's intersection of Routes 611 and 32 to watch the Babbling Brook Restaurant and gas station get swallowed up by the confluence of the Delaware River and the Gallows Run. Not long after, the only remaining visible part of the building is its chimney.   *– Collection Mildred Williams*

Mildred Williams and her family join many from their Kintnersville neighborhood where Rt. 611 meets the river. Even the older folks who had been around in 1903 can't remember ever having seen the water so high. The Babbling Brook, a popular restaurant-ice cream stand-gas station, is completely underwater. All that's sticking up above the surface is its chimney and the top of the gas sign.

They learn that someone has tried to rescue the woman and her invalid mother who live near Dick's parents out on the island, but the water is just running too hard. Last anyone knows, the two women are stranded in their attic, and the water is up to its floor. All the men are saying that as soon as the water starts to go down and the current backs off, they'll go in with a boat to rescue them. Everyone wonders if the women can hold out that long.

The phones are still working away from the river, and Sally Packard has called her boyfriend to come pick her up from where she's staying in Springtown. He intends to drive her back to her parents, but they're not able to get that far down the hill. The water is too far up, and Sally just knows it has flooded her home.

She sees her parents standing in front of her aunts' home across Lehnenburg Road, up the hill a ways from their place. It's clear that everyone is safe, and Sally feels a wave of relief wash over her. They have a joyous reunion, crying and hugging, but the news isn't all good. Her parents tell her that the water has, indeed, invaded their home, and they won't know the extent of the damage until it recedes. For the time being, they'll all be staying with their aunts.

For now, they stand on the hill, looking out over the river that, only two nights ago, had brought Sally such peace. A bright green sedan floats by—driverless—followed by trees, telephone poles, and their wires. One of the poles separates from the rest, and floats over the top of Rt. 611. The current nudges it up against the huge plate glass window of Pagliaro's Chevrolet dealership. It squeaks along the surface of the glass, and the crowd waits for the glass to shatter. Miraculously, not a single pane breaks, and the pole just continues floating on downstream.

The expansive plate glass window of the Pagliaro Chevrolet dealership in Kintnersville miraculously survives an assault by a renegade telephone pole, nosing its way along as though on a leisurely shopping trip down the Delaware.

– Collection Ed Litschauer

Neighbors who have gathered to watch the river with them say the antique shop just down 611 has been completely washed away, taking all those beautiful old pieces of furniture with it.

Sally marvels at the silvery look of the water that reflects the evening sky as it runs over her home and through her neighbors' homes and businesses. That it can be so beautiful and at the same time so destructive is a wonder to her.

Trees act as battering rams to take out whole buildings along the Delaware just north of Kintnersville, near Sally Packard's home. Such scenes are abundant on both sides of the river, the entire length of the valley.

– Collection Bob Stalgaitis

The more recent addition to Harry Stryker's Raubsville home on Rt. 611 is separated from the original stone portion by the wrath of the Delaware, which deposits the frame section squarely across the critical traffic route.

— Collection Bob Stalgaitis

Just up River Road, Riegelsville and Raubsville are taking a beating. The home of one Raubsville resident, Harry Stryker, is torn in half by the force of the water. The half torn from its foundation is carried about fifty feet downstream, and will be left sitting astride Route 611.

As the sun sets, the last flights by an airplane shuttle service between Phillipsburg Airport and Easton wind down. All afternoon, people stranded on the opposite side of the river from where they want to be have rushed each plane as it rolls to a stop, hoping to secure a seat on the return flight.

Those watching the flooding Delaware from the Phillipsburg Hill section see the new addition to Jimmy's Hot Dog Stand swept away and piled up against the Free Bridge. Joining it are pieces of former homes, tires, freight car doors, trees, boxes, and barrels—all jammed up above the supports between the piers in the bridge's center section.

289

The murky, brown water sluices through the whole mess, creating a flapping of the loosely packed debris. It, in turn, causes the bridge to vibrate menacingly. It's a far cry from the clear, gentle current that had carried a tiny, white, flower-filled boat beneath the span on Memorial Day to honor the memory of lost war heroes.

The still-rising waters pour over the deck of the Free Bridge after covering the toll plaza before the Route 22 bridge, two to three feet deep. *Newark Evening News* reporter Dick Harpster, certain that the force of the water and all the debris being hurled at the Free Bridge will eventually knock it out, doesn't want to miss the chance for a historic shot. The problem is, he's on his way to Belvidere again, this time with a media contingent accompanying New Jersey State Senator Wayne Dumont. Dick prevails upon one of his photographer colleagues to sit along the river frontage to keep a vigil at the bridge.

Meanwhile, Dick travels once again to Manunka Chunk island, where he'd had the scare from the forceful current in the wee hours of the morning. The senator wants to see for himself what kind of devastation his constituents are enduring. He's about to get more than he's bargained for. Responding to shouts from some men at the water's edge, Dick accompanies the senator's cadre in joining them. They follow the downcast eyes of the men who had shouted, to behold a terrible sight.

Lying in the muck amid broken boards, pieces of foam rubber torn from mattresses and an oily residue on the water's surface is the pale, battered body of a large woman. She is completely nude, and her flesh is torn and discolored with bruises where she had been battered by pieces of wreckage. Everyone stands in stunned silence.

A raspy voice says, *Find something to cover her up, for God's sake.*

The men move slowly away from the woman's body, and Dick scribbles something in his notebook. They'll later learn that the woman is Faith Rowe Rickert, a farm wife who had been washed out of her home north of Camp Davis on the Brodhead Creek, Thursday night.

The front page of the *Easton Express'* evening edition is filled with boxes of last-minute bulletins, because the composing room hasn't finished setting its scheduled type before the power is shut down. As the rising Lehigh River threatens the Dock Street power station, the main switch is thrown. That the paper is published at all owes to the generous cooperation of another newspaper.

The *Bethlehem Globe-Times*, with an adjacent but noncompeting coverage area, takes delivery of the already-struck plates for most of the interior pages. They then accept late-developing story tidbits and fill the holes on those pages before printing the entire edition on its presses. A three-inch column at the bottom of the front page carries a notice of thanks from the *Express* to the *Globe*. Distribution of the papers takes place with assistance from the *Allentown Call-Chronicle*. Copies for New Jersey subscribers are flown across the river.

By this time, all bridges out of Easton are closed to auto traffic, with the river at 37.5 feet above normal low; just six inches below its all-time record high, set in 1903. It continues to rise, backing up the Lehigh River, which is also over flood stage and still rising. It has already backed up into the city's south side.

The view from the Glendon Heights bluffs is impressive, as the swollen Lehigh River, denied the ability to dump its burgeoning load into the already overburdened Delaware channel, backs up into Easton's industrial valley.

– Collection Rich and Jean DiRenzis

Where normally would be a view of the Lehigh River dam as it empties into the Delaware is now one continuous, churning channel. The railroad walkway in the foreground served as one of the last exit ways from the flooding city until it, too, was swallowed up by the encroaching water.
— Bradwin Roberts photo, collection Linda Roberts

A man who has suffered a heart attack is shuttled from South Easton across the Jersey Central Railroad trestle, along with an expectant mother about to deliver. Ambulances waiting at the Central's Fourth Street station take them to the hospital. The man is treated and reported in good condition in the evening paper, and the woman delivers a healthy baby girl less than three hours later.

Delivery trucks unable to reach their intended destinations or return to their bases leave shipments of food and other useful items at churches. The supplies will prove handy in coming days, as shelters are established to care for hundreds of displaced residents. The mayor calls out an extra shift of police officers to cover traffic control and all-night foot patrols to discourage looting.

Don Young, office manager of Easton's Employment Service, has been keeping a log all day, since he'd seen the first indications of flooding on his way in to work. From the first entry at seven forty-five a.m., recording a traffic jam on the bypass, he has made a steady stream of observations as the flood has progressed. He's spent the afternoon calling employers such as MetEd, Bean, Inc., and Collins & Maxwell to offer assistance in procuring emergency workers and cleanup laborers.

A dedicated state employee, Don now returns to the office after five thirty, because the river's still rising and he might be able to place more workers. He calls the mayor's office, the Civil Defense headquarters, and the Red Cross. Working by flashlight since the lunchtime power outage, Don won't leave until reports come in that the water has crested at nine p.m..

The water has completely submerged Riverside Park. On North Front Street, it stands ten feet deep, and it's creeping over Northampton. Herb and Sylvia Carle, along with many other merchants, haven't believed it will reach the downtown shopping district.

Their store, H. M. Carle Stationers, stands between First and Second Streets on Northampton Street. Nevertheless, they've kept their eye on the advancing river all afternoon. Now, when Sylvia calls Herb out back to see the edge of it just fifteen feet from their service entrance, they can't deny any longer that their enterprise is in danger.

Just upriver from Phillipsburg-Easton, the summer colony of Harmony suffers a particularly violent barrage from the Delaware. Its location on a knob of land that juts out into the river puts it in a vulnerable position to be pounded by the relentless current.
– Bradwin Roberts photo, collection Linda Roberts

Usually bustling Northampton Street is all but abandoned as merchants and businesses have long since lost their battle with the rising water of the Delaware.
— Bradwin Roberts photo, collection Linda Roberts

They spend an hour moving all their merchandise to the countertops. By the time they've finished, they're told that the Bridge Commission is expecting it to get still higher, so they move it up again. When the water reaches the foot of the store, they decide it's time to just move it all out. Passersby help them carry out reams of paper, typewriters, and desks. Sylvia's brother-in-law borrows a large bakery truck to help move the merchandise to garages offered on loan by others.

It's now late and dark outside. Dick Harpster loses his bid for a history-making photo. When large pieces of the Portland Covered Bridge from upstream finally tear out the center span of the Easton-Phillipsburg Free Bridge, it's too dark to see it coming without electric lights. Dick's photographer misses the shot.

The tired Carles lean against their doorway, wondering what else to take. Suddenly, someone approaches and tells them the river has just ripped out part of the Free Bridge at the foot of Northampton Street, and is now threatening the toll bridge. Sylvia becomes concerned, because their two sons are with their great uncle in Phillipsburg, across the river. He had been going to take them to the Poconos, but the flood had kept them home. She insists that he bring them home, and they make it across just moments before the last open local bridge is closed.

Most of Easton's heavy industry and retail stores have closed. Restaurants still managing to service clientele with a combination of cold food, candlelight, and rapidly melting ice stay open as long as they're able. Even these holdouts will soon be forced to close when the candles and ice run out. City water is turned off but not in any immediate danger of contamination, and gas service is off in some downtown sections. Firemen are engaged in rescue operations all over the city, and Easton's Disaster Committee members are evacuating its homeless people in boats.

Finally, as Mrs. Carle had feared, the Bushkill Street toll bridge to Phillipsburg is closed because the Bushkill Creek has backed up over its approaches.

Since six p.m., National Guardsmen have blocked entry to the railroad station from Fourth Street. Bus refugees, trying to get home

The Northampton Street Free Bridge, when it gave way to irresistible hydraulic force, severed not only a main commercial traffic artery, but also a critical communications junction for the entire northeast. Telephone and electrical service had been carried by cable bundles that ran beneath the bridge deck.

– Bradwin Roberts photo, collection Linda Roberts

to New York, or Phillipsburg residents wanting to cross the river to home after a long day at work are frustrated. The soldiers are also refusing entry to the CRR railroad bridge over the Lehigh River and the auto bridge over the Delaware.

Sightseers slip through when possible, placing themselves in danger to get a good look at the flood. They can see Eastoners on the Jersey side, wishing as fervently as their Phillipsburg counterparts to cross the river and get home for the weekend.

A commuter train shuffles irregularly back and forth across the railroad trestle, as officials feel more brave or cautious. Space on board comes at the cost of flashing the right kind of credentials, and many "regular joes" are seriously frustrated. No one really knows what the right credentials are, and people begin to perceive inequity in the way people are permitted to board. The atmosphere grows tense and the crowd becomes more restless as tempers fray in the relentless heat.

The Lehigh River is causing havoc elsewhere in its own valley, before it reaches the Delaware at Easton. Like the Delaware, the Lehigh is fed by tributaries that drain part of the Pocono Mountain

Would-be passengers at the Third Street railroad station pass the time river-watching, the latest in spectator sports. — *Collection Bob Stalgaitis*

region. One of those tributaries is the Tobyhanna Creek. Following the break of its quarry dam southwest of Warnertown, and the subsequent pressure collapse of the Pocono Lake dam, the Tobyhanna reaches a crest of 19.41 feet near the Rt. 940 bridge. Added to runoff from its other subwatersheds, this volume sends the Lehigh over its banks in many places.

One of those locations is Nazareth, where the planing mill at the Corner of Green and Prospect Streets is flooded.

The Lehigh also lashes Bethlehem, flooding out 14,500 workers from the Bethlehem Steel Company plant. More than 5,500 other workers are also displaced along the rest of its length, as well as along Monocacy Creek, backing up due to its inability to deposit its swelling contents into the Lehigh.

The worst destruction is prevented by floodwalls that have been built since the damaging 1942 flood, but the Lehigh will reach a crest of 25.9 feet before the day is out.

Similar cement retaining walls, installed by the WPA during the Great Depression, do a good job of containing the majority of extra volume in the Monocacy Creek. However, places such as underneath the Broad Street Bridge where these walls open up still experience overflow and flooding. Many homes and businesses beneath the Hill-to-Hill Bridge are underwater to their second stories. Rafts of lumber from the Brown-Bohrek yard float among houses as the sun goes down. A graphite mill and a large junkyard are also submerged.

Residents of Front Street in Allentown are being evacuated by boat, and the area bounded by Union and Chew Streets has become a huge lake. Jersey Central Railroad superintendent Charles Schlegel is on the phone, being interviewed by a newspaper editor about how the flood is affecting rail service. After answering questions about track washouts and line closures, Schlegel is questioned about the conditions there in Allentown.

"Why, I've got my feet in water in my office right now," he replies.

Against all odds, the under-staffed, under-trained, under-funded local Civil Defense organizations prove their mettle in meeting the needs of the widespread flood emergency. Volunteers rise to the occasion everywhere there is a need for rescue, recovery and provision for the basic human requirements of food, clothing and shelter. Even before the waters crest, these loose-knit agencies somehow manage to create working structures of organization that allow them to meet the most dire challenges of the disaster.

Their lack of training, equipment, and practice becomes evident in a few botched efforts, but overall, theirs is an amazing performance in the face of overwhelming stress on civil resources. Though more than one heated letter of complaint will show up in post-flood local newspapers, the CD organization as a whole will not again be underappreciated.

The summer colony at Carpentersville, New Jersey, takes the worst toll in overall destruction of property. Of 89 total homes and cottages, 83 are so badly damaged as to be rendered unlivable or are completely washed away.

— Collection Bob Stalgaitis

Gabe Kober of Huntingdon, New Jersey, is the coordinator of Civil Defense and Disaster Control for Pohatcong Township. He's working with his volunteer organization and the Alpha fire company to help the citizens of Carpentersville. Along with little Phyllis's father, Philip Baty, and some other neighbors, they're hauling furniture and clothing to safety on high ground by tractor and wagon.

Once a hoppin' nightspot, Hap's Pavilion in Carpentersville is left a scattered collection of tilted pilings, exposed plumbing and piles of debris. The community would never be the same after the loss of this gathering place.

What's left of the railroad tracks in the colony rivals the damage caused by General Sherman's Union forces on their march to the sea. — Collection Bob Stalgaitis

A few of the residents, having waited too long to safely walk out of their cottages, are evacuated by motorboats strong enough to negotiate the building current. Ironically, by the end of the flood emergency, Gabe will see his CD organization's ranks more than double in number, from 118 members to 280.

Where there is no formal CD organization, local fire and police departments, as well as emergency medical services and rescue squads keep flooding threats from turning into death notices. Mass evacuations, treetop helicopter rescues, swiftwater rescues and extractions from mudslides and road washouts are accomplished with amazing speed and effectiveness. Gratitude for their service will forge a lasting relationship of embrace and support between the departments and most of their communities.

Amateur radio operators up and down the Delaware Valley, as in Stroudsburg, apply skills acquired in their hobby to become the nerve centers of municipalities where all other communication has broken down.

In Easton, CD director Clarence Snyder establishes headquarters at the courthouse for a network that operates throughout eastern Pennsylvania and western New Jersey. Ten hams, most of them members of the Delaware-Lehigh Amateur Radio Club, rotate through a round-the-clock schedule. Many maintain contact with areas such as Phillipsburg and Stroudsburg, where no other means is available. The Easton base will process some five hundred messages before the weekend is out and telephone service is restored.

Two frequencies are used in the effort, a low band for contact with distant points, and a higher one to communicate with local mobile units. Messages are relayed for medical aid and blood donor requests, missing persons information, and transportation efforts. The Pike County Red Cross headquarters houses their ham base in Milford, Pennsylvania, which also suffers a lack of phone service.

Lewis Papp, a blind ham operator who has for years advised area residents of impending floods from his home station near Sandts Eddy, is unable to continue his service. All morning, he has manned his post, keeping in contact with New York State and answering hundreds of calls from anxious river residents. Suddenly, the river enters his home and swallows all his equipment, making it a total loss. Lewis will spend the remainder of the event at his sister's home in Martins Creek.

Gabe Kober's fourteen-year-old son, Bill, begins his transition to manhood as an emergency ham operator, manning a mobile unit for fifteen hours a day during cleanup operations. Pressed into service to replace the intended operator because his voice is clearer and more understandable over the airwaves, Bill notifies residents of when and where to get their typhoid shots, and check names against lists of people authorized to enter the area in a looting-prevention effort. He is responsible for ordering food and materials for cleanup crews, and working with other CD organizations to coordinate help from outside the area.

Social resources, too, prove invaluable as people are forced from their homes by the wild waters. Red Cross efforts in many communities are effective only because local churches, clubs, and civic organizations open their doors and coffers to make their facilities available as shelters. Where there are no shelters, neighbors take each other into their homes.

Farmers' neighbors help them round up scattered dairy herds from outside broken fences and lend a hand with manual milking, because Mother Nature doesn't wait when the electricity goes off. Everywhere, the only force greater than the flood's devastation is the groundswell of human kindness and decency, which overshadows relatively few instances of looting and price gouging.

Travelers approaching Phillipsburg, New Jersey, pass rest stops and restaurant parking lots with tractor-trailers lined up endlessly, some two abreast. On Highway 22 near the high school, auxiliary police and CD volunteers are screening traffic for local and through destinations, turning back anyone intending to cross the Delaware. They're told the closest passable span is in Camden.

Those who are allowed through find bumper-to-bumper traffic, with trucks lining the area around the high school, and the Phillipsburg Hill section an absolute jam. Cars inch along and pedestrians weave among them. Most vehicles carry sightseers trying to get a look at something most have never seen: river water reaching to second-story windows of buildings on the waterfront, and swirling through Center Square.

An aerial view reveals the absolute inundation of the Jersey Central Railroad station in Phillipsburg's Union Square. — *Collection Bob Stalgaitis*

Two small boys playing at a house on South Main and Pursell Streets are surprised to find fish jumping in the backyard. People stand on South Main, stunned to see hundreds of eels squirming about on the river bank. Apparently panicked from being tangled in weeds and trapped among floating debris, the long, slippery creatures are frantically leaping out of the river.

Hundreds of people gather in front of the Smart Set Furniture store along South Main Street as the river edges up to the window, waiting to see if it will overpower the glass and pour in. An almost carnival atmosphere prevails, as the humdrum of daily life is disrupted by an awesome display of nature's fury. At six thirty in the evening, the city's new emergency truck takes the first group of refugees from Union Square up to the shelter at the high school.

Several Boy Scouts decide to make their own contribution to community safety by helping evacuate hotels and apartments in Union Square. By seven thirty, the Emergency Squad is doing the same for residents along North Main Street. As elsewhere, some people refuse to leave their homes.

Summer colonies north of the sister cities are in trouble. Forks Township is about to issue a call for a hundred additional volunteers to help guard the river area from excessive looting overnight. Whole families, including small children, have been wading through waist-deep water all afternoon at Sandts Eddy. They're making a desperate attempt to remove furniture and other articles from their homes before the flood reaches full force. Businesses along Route 611—the Mineral Springs Hotel, Century Inn, Riverside Snack Bar, and Rothy's Appliance Store—are already inundated.

Martins Creek is in much the same straits. The Alpha Portland Cement Company has water in its packing house, which will eventually reach a depth of six feet. Their product, which is chemically activated when mixed with water, is turning to blocks before it even leaves the factory. Railroad delivery cars, sitting on the track spur outside, are halfway submerged. In nearby Riverwood Beach, nearly twenty cottages are submerged in water that will eventually lap at some of their ceilings.

The Alpha Portland Cement Company suffered not only damage to its physical plant, but also heavy losses to its inventory. Note branches and debris hanging from power lines.
– Collection Bob Stalgaitis

More than a dozen homes in DePue's Ferry are rapidly filling with water, and will wash down the river before the night is out. Water will reach six inches deep in the second-floor rooms of many others.

Residents at Conrad's Boarding House are helping each other remove their personal belongings. Mrs. Conrad had phoned all her neighbors earlier in the day, when she'd first heard the flood warnings on the radio. Now she's working with her family members to save their own belongings. Several of them vacate the porch just seconds before it collapses under a barrage of water and floating debris. It's time to leave.

Many area refugees will find a haven in the home of year-round resident Hart Chidsey, which overlooks the river from a high embankment. Standing there, they'll watch the river chewing away at their homes until darkness lowers the curtain on the sickening view.

Residents in Riverton are going through much the same experience, staying ahead of the water with help from the Civil Defense agency there. Camp Huribac, just outside of town, is evacuating its campers. Howard Bell is watching the river invade his Riverton Hotel, where it will reach a depth of four feet at crest. Two house trailers nearby have been washed away, and tractors have towed ten others to high ground. Under the bridge on the river, a large tree has become wedged, and part of a mangled rowboat is dangling from a guy wire. Engineers have closed the bridge to traffic, and are checking it for possible damage.

The Delaware Water Gap lives up to its name as the river swells to fill every available pocket of land between the slopes of the Kittatinny Range. It will be weeks before it is fully passable by traffic again.

– Collection
Bob Stalgaitis

304

This Foul Rift bungalow won't be providing any more lazy days by the river.

Another unfortunate summer cottage is ravaged and left to rot in the narrows north of Easton. It will be years before all of this kind of wreckage is either cleaned up or taken over by nature. — *Collection Bob Stalgaitis*

Across the bridge in the summer colonies of Belvidere, Brainards, Foul Rift, and Hutchinson, nearly every cottage or bungalow that hasn't washed away or been completely destroyed is being rendered uninhabitable. Small, foundationless homes are being picked up, flipped over, and dashed against trees and each other. Hutchinson's Oakhurst Café is being leveled, along with rows of homes and cottages. The residents are hauled away via horse and wagon, evacuated by the CD organizations and fire departments of Harmony Township and Delaware Park. When they return, they'll find just four out of their thirty-five homes still standing.

In Carpentersville, the Red Cross staff has already arrived to turn the Baty residence into an inoculation station as soon as the water goes down. Meanwhile, they help the Baty family and their neighbors carry their valuables upstairs, just in case the water does come up that far. The house is now disorganized, with little room to sit or sleep comfortably, so little Phyllis and her mom walk up the road to spend the night at her uncle's house. But Phyllis is too worried about her pony and the other animals in the barn to sleep.

After dark, when it's too dangerous to try moving anything else, Phyllis's dad brings Betty and the other horses up the road. Overjoyed, Phyllis runs outside and throws her arms around Betty's legs, feeling their wetness. The animals had been standing in about two feet of water in the pasture near the road. Minor has decided to bring them up the hill for the night, both as a safety precaution and to put his daughter's mind at ease.

Down the road, the Suttons sit outside most of the night to see if the All Inn will wash away. They can hear other cottages collapsing, being smashed in by other buildings now acting as battering rams, and the pieces hitting other things as they wash down the river. It's a long, tense night.

Riegelsville, New Jersey, takes water from the Delaware, though not to the extent that its twin across the river does. Downriver in Milford, however, things are a bit more serious.

The Riegel Ridge Paper Company, which employs so many on

both sides of the river, takes a serious hit. The river has invaded the plant, forcing the shutdown of the boilers and infiltrating into machinery and motors. The marauding water has defeated the best efforts of workmen who had previously plowed up earthen embankments, hoping to block the river's entry. In the yard, it's also carrying away finished stock and the lightweight coal that fires the boilers. The coal dust mixes with the water, silt, and raw sewage in the river to fill the cellar. It will leave a thick layer of disgusting black muck on the floor of farmer John Williamson's home, south of town. Company worker housing is also flooded the length of its presence on the Milford-Frenchtown Road.

The river is scooping loads of bulk and bagged feed out of the first floor of Cregar's Feed Mill, spinning the loose stuff out on top of the current in playful swirls that belie their danger. It picks Niece's Lumber Company virtually clean of its stock, a loss which will later prove an inadvertently fortuitous bit of chance for Howard Opdyke, another merchant destined to become a fixture in the valley. Moninghoff's Appliance Store loses a quantity of brand new stock housed in the home of the owner's father. They've been able only to

Employees of Cregar's Feed Mill in Frenchtown load a truck with stock in hopes of rescuing it from the rapidly encroaching floodwaters.

– Hunterdon County Democrat photo

save a few TV sets before they must abandon the residence to the rising water.

Mayor Charlie Sanderson is doing his best to keep from sleep-walking through his duties with Milford's Civil Defense agency, police and fire departments. They're helping with evacuations and trying to maintain some order.

Charlie had been summoned to his day job as a repairman at the Holland generating plant of the New Jersey Power & Light Company at five in the morning. He and his crew had put in a twelve-hour shift, removing vulnerable motors and gears from the machinery until ordered out for their own safety. Already exhausted, he'd then jumped right in to his public safety duties.

This view from Frenchtown across to Riverview Lunch and Dr. Uhler's house in Uhlertown/Upper Black Eddy reveals the extent to which the Delaware has infiltrated riverside homes and businesses. Note the house floating by in front.
– Hunterdon County Democrat photo

Looking across the bridge to Upper Black Eddy before the sun had gone down, he'd seen May Snyder's Riverview Lunch and Schuh's General Store submerged several feet up their second-story windows. If he'd had binoculars, he'd have seen the beautiful old windows on Dr. E. P. Uhler's graceful Victorian home pushed in, with water pouring through to sully the usually immaculate contents.

Now, with dark falling, the water has reached the bridge deck, and debris is giving the rail a pounding that will leave dents and scars when it goes back down. Volunteers with the Bucks County CD are in Upper Black Eddy, helping coordinate last-minute evacuations.

Most roads near the river have become impassable, and back roads made hazardous by the constant traffic on wet, muddy lanes through unbroken darkness. Topography, with the steep drop-off on the palisades side of Bridgeton and Narrows Hills, worsens the communications situation, but this is overcome by the use of two mobile radios. One is at the scene on the riverfront, with the other being used as a relay on the higher elevations.

Amphibious "ducks" from Forts Jay, Meade and Dix, are available on site. The small craft can't overcome the fifteen-knot current with their five-knot waterborne speed, and are rendered useless. They are dispatched to Yardley, where they're put to use in more negotiable situations, based at Leedom's dock. Working in concert with Naval powerboats, they perform splendidly in the less treacherous currents.

The Red Cross establishes itself at the Yardley Fire Station, and the Civil Air Patrol assumes air coverage responsibilities.

In Frenchtown, School superintendent Bert Light and CD Director Russ Gordon have spent the first part of the day around the high school, assisting with the helicopter evacuation of the island camps. Through that effort, they've established a good working relationship with the Hunterdon County Red Cross, the State Police, and other CD chapters of both states.

Telephone operators have fielded more calls than ever before. By four p.m., most of the rescued children had been on their way home, except for those whose homes were isolated and unreachable. That group includes Marie Petranto, who will have to wait a few more days to get home.

During and after the massive airlift, town officials also had to turn their attention to evacuation of some of their own riverfront residents. A bit farther back off the waterway, Bieber's Feed Mill has water already past the door sill, where it had crested in 1903. It will go two feet higher before it reaches its peak this time.

Along with its toll on human life and property, the flood is proving to be a decided enemy of poultry. Kerr Chickeries had lost

250,000 eggs in varied stages of incubation at the hatchery when the electricity had been turned off around three p.m.. Then, as the water rose, ten thousand live chicks had drowned in the nursery. Men who'd been in boats near the building say they could hear the chicks peeping pathetically inside, but it had been unsafe to enter the building to attempt any rescue.

Later, owner Sherwood Anderson would transfer the remainder of his stock to another hatchery in New Brunswick. Firemen in the area cleaning up mud and debris will discover a fire at the Kerr hatchery, and eleven companies will respond to the call to put out the blaze. Three firefighters will be injured in the effort. On Sunday night, a Stockton chicken coop will catch fire after being hit by lightning. It's one impromptu barbecue nobody's happy about.

The Turners' cottage in Byram was saved from washing away by the anchoring properties of its main water supply pipe, giving a whole new meaning to "plumber's helper."
— Collection Carol Turner Wolf

In Byram, the riverfront cottage fourteen-year-old Carol Turner shares with her parents has been pushed off its foundation, but the plumbing pipe running up to their kitchen sink pump has anchored it in place. The garages don't fare as well and disappear downriver. On Thursday when the rain had intensified, Carol had returned home to Philadelphia from the summer cottage with her family and their terrier, Shimpy. One of the last cars over the bridge to Point Pleasant before it washes away, they'll return in a few days to a changed world.

☼

On the other side of that bridge, seventeen-year-old Judy Castree has gathered with a small crowd of people at the Point Pleasant firehouse, which is built on a high knob. The back parking lot is underwater, but the structure itself is safe, and the crowd has joined Will Dobron and his firefighting comrades there.

Everyone's hoping to be given some assignment to help with the flood emergency. At this point, with night coming on and most places lacking electricity, there's not a lot anyone can do. Still, they all mill about, knowing if something does happen, the fire company will be notified and they'll hear about it, too.

After a few rather dull hours, they become aware of the sound of squealing pigs. They realize a sty must have been swept into the current from somewhere to the north, and is now floating down-river. Even in the dark, they can follow its progress by the changing sound of the squealing. Its volume grows louder, then remains unchanged for a few moments. They know its forward motion has been arrested by the accumulation of debris against the Point Pleasant-Byram Bridge.

The squeals continue to emanate from the sty's terrified passengers, then suddenly become drowned out by the sounds of old iron giving way in the current. The incredulous audience in the firehouse stands transfixed, listening to the creaking of several tons of fatigued metal twisting and popping its rivets, followed by a magnificent crashing and splashing.

"There goes our bridge!" someone shouts.

The toppled Byram-Point Pleasant Bridge lies in a heap of twisted metal. Though government officials promise to rebuild the span, budgetary calculations soon rule out the possibility. Its stone piers will stand for decades, reminding locals of the more convenient crossing they used to have.

– Tinsman family collection

The toppled span finally stops resisting the water's force and its mangled iron settles into piles in the still-raging current. As the tumult dies away, the firehouse crowd is amazed to once again hear the pigs. The squealing fades off into the distance as the sty, miraculously still afloat, makes its way downriver.

The Point Pleasant downtown area looks more like Atlantis as it is swallowed by the meeting of the river and the Delaware & Lehigh Canal.

– Collection Carol Turner Wolf

The following day, as the water recedes, Judy will survey the sodden remains of Gobblers restaurant and nightclub, and watch kids jumping off the roof of a submerged building into the muddy water near the town center. It's the last view she'll have of her hometown before leaving for college. The tumbling of the bridge is a story that will be told and retold in the area for years, as residents and visitors get used to the lack of a river crossing there.

Downriver in New Hope, a call is put in from the high school shelter for fifty cots to the county CD. It's one of several such requests that will be issued in the next twelve hours or so, as more people are displaced from their homes.

Larry Teel, an outboard marine dealer from Lambertville, is running one of his speedboats up and down the streets of New Hope, patrolling for any signs of people in distress. Around midnight, at the foot of Mechanicsville Road where it meets Main Street, he sees a candle burning in a second-story house window, which is now even with the surface of the water he's floating on.

He guides his boat through the window, and finds three people sitting there. Two of them are perched atop a piano, with the other occupying the bench. No one's playing; the water is covering the keys. Larry offers to evacuate them, to which they reply with a guffaw.

No thanks, their company and their gallon jug of gin will help them ride out the storm, they say. Not in a position to insist, Larry backs out the window and bids them good luck. As far as he knows, they are the only folks who will spend the night downtown.

The boys from Camp Miller and some of the girls from Camp Hagan are kept in close quarters at the adult Ministerium camp, with accommodations in short supply. One hundred forty of them are staying in one cabin, and that evening, the atmosphere grows tense as campers listen to Charlie's radio. With phone lines down, it's their only source of communication with the outside world for now. The announcer instructs in authoritative tones that anyone in their area who is on high ground should stay there. The campers wonder just how bad the situation is really getting.

Charlie spins the dial until he brings in a Philadelphia station. The campers are horrified to hear a news report say that Camp Miller has been wiped out with no survivors. What will their parents think? Now the kids are genuinely worried. Some of them stay up all night, listening to radio broadcasts that keep them up to date on what's happening elsewhere. They wonder how accurate any of them are, and the broadcasts produce little peace of mind.

Section III
Aftermath

The Morning After

Saturday, August 20, 1955

Just after midnight, the Hunterdon County CD-DC goes into action in New Jersey under the direction of county coordinator Albert Kahn. In the first real test of his organization's abilities, Al directs round-the-clock efforts from his Flemington headquarters. It's close enough to affected areas to be responsive, while not putting itself in danger from the Delaware, Raritan, or other flooding waterways.

By two fifteen Saturday morning, a state of emergency is declared in Lambertville, with the Delaware and Raritan Canal feeder breaking through its banks at Stockton. Just after three o'clock, roadblocks are set up to keep motorists from driving into dangerous, water-topped roadways, as well as to keep as much traffic as possible out of evacuation and repair zones.

Before the sister hurricanes had come through, the Delaware River at the Lambertville Bridge stood at a depth of 23 feet, 3 feet below normal, due to the extended drought. At six thirty Saturday morning, it crests there at 28.5 feet above normal.

By two p.m., Bucks County CD headquarters receives notification that everyone desiring evacuation has been safely removed from all riverfront communities from Riegelsville down to Bristol. The same is true for the camps on the river islands, including Mitters, Daddy Island, Owasia, and Hagan. Purchases are authorized for shelter food, and cots are dispatched to Riegelsville. Rescue craft—from

315

trucks and boats to air-sea rescue units—are dispatched from various locations including Reading, Pennsylvania and Massachusetts.

Flotsam from summer colonies upstream slams into the Washington Crossing bridge, which nonetheless manages to hold up under the strain.

– "River Jim" Abbott photo

Yardley is labeled by *The Trentonian* "a watery terror, abject and awesome." Civilians are barred entry, as the shattered city is placed under a state of emergency.

Many of its residents are engaged in the newly popular pastime of flood watching. With many businesses closed down, no electricity to keep buildings cool and nothing much better to do, thousands of people stay outside, entertaining themselves by watching the many and varied items floating rapidly downstream in the Delaware's muscular current.

Those upstream from the Yardley-Wilburtha Bridge can plainly see the mass of debris that has collected against it. The bank of wreckage has been building all night, with the majority of it being eddied over to the eastern bank. The pressure created by its water resistance threatens to collapse the bridge. The water now washes fully over its deck, and all parts of the bridge—railings, spans, and piers—are taking a tremendous beating.

At about eight a.m., a bungalow that has been swept downstream from one of the summer colonies slams into the bridge. It's the last straw for the beleaguered structure. It loses more than three spans, in excess of half its 902-foot length.

Jerry and Marian Detwiler return to their home in New Britain to find it has survived, but now holds a deep layer of mud in the basement and the entire first floor. Marian finds her stock pot, still full of the chicken she'd been cooking when the water had come up, sitting in the children's playroom, not a drop spilled. The kids' books and toys, however, are unsalvageable.

Jerry has to go back to his teaching job, so he stays at the house and begins the cleanup, aided by friends, neighbors and their entire Sunday School class. Marian and the kids stay at her parents' home in Hatfield until after her baby is born. A year later, they will relocate to higher ground.

The "Whip" ride at Chalfont's Forest Park amusement park is out of commission for awhile after being rearranged by the wild Neshaminy Creek.

– Collection John Malack

Just up the road, the owners of Forest Park amusement park are also digging out of the mud left by the raging Neshaminy Creek. It will be quite some time before the park can be reopened and popular rides like The Whip are again spinning riders into fits of laughter.

Three-week-old Alan Jackson is in the arms of his mother in the space they'll call home for the next several weeks. It's the kindergarten section of the Makefield School, and his older brothers, Robert and Don, are enjoying all the attention their family is getting. The media swarms about, taking pictures of "the youngest flood victim."

They'll make the papers as a human interest story, having been flooded out of their home just north of the Yardley boat ramp. Alan's parents have no insurance and won't be able to afford to bring the house back from its nearly destroyed state.

Alan will grow up in Levittown, far enough from the threatening waters of the Delaware to please his parents. It will also keep him from growing up as a "river kid," something he'll come to feel as a loss in his life. He'll grow up to develop his own relationship with the Delaware, working for the state of Pennsylvania as a bridge inspector. He'll see other floods on other rivers, some whose winter cargo of huge ice floes wrap deer around trees and strip the bark off for twenty feet above the ground. But it's the Delaware that will always hold his heart and capture his imagination.

As an adult, Alan will return to the Delaware again and again, rod and reel in hand, a boat sliding between him and the water. He'll contemplate his relationship to this living presence that has shaped his life directly and indirectly. He'll write a poem about the hold it still exerts on him. It will end not like a poem, but a love letter:

> Me and the Delaware River,
> Not always seeing eye to eye,
> But heritage runs deep and clear,
> So the river is where I'll die.

Others will grow to be not so fond of the river as respectful. When nine-year-old Randy Riggs had crossed the Yardley Bridge on Friday before it had been closed to traffic, he'd learned the power of the Delaware's waters. Rushing by just six feet beneath the tires of their '55 Chevy, it had been darned scary-looking. Then, hearing all the adults talk about nothing else but the impending flood, he had come to understand that serious changes may be afoot.

His parents express mostly a concern for Gus and Edna, family friends who live along the river in town. As the water rises, Randy stands on the East Afton Avenue canal bridge with his jaw agape, disbelieving how far into town the water has reached. The brown, cloudy stuff smells awful, and he's watching two people row a boat over the top of the pavement in front of Dilliplane's Studebaker dealership.

By Saturday, everyone's fears have become reality. Gus and Edna's home is flooded well into the second floor, and they lose everything, even the pet canaries they had moved upstairs for safety.

The Riggses, like many others, reach out to help their friends. Randy's parents give them clothing and furniture with which to start, and Randy uses money saved from his allowance to replace their canaries.

Everyone is inconvenienced by the new traffic patterns caused by all the bridges being out, but as he grows, Randy will come to see this change as a positive situation. It keeps his boyhood home a quaint, small town without much crime. Still, he'll never be able to come home again without picturing in his mind the river invading it without warning or mercy.

No one's going to be crossing the Yardley-Wilburtha bridge anytime soon. These cars wait on the Jersey side as the span loses its battle with the Delaware's powerful current in the morning on Saturday, August 20.   – *Trentonia Collection, Trenton Public Library*

Yardley doesn't remain alone for long in being forced to create new traffic patterns. Downstream, the Ewing Bridge becomes yet another casualty on the list of more than fifty bridges across the Delaware River that will be gone before the flood has ended.

At Trenton's Calhoun Street Bridge, the river crests at 20.53 feet, with water pouring into the streets at the rate of 329,000 cubic feet per second, or about 118 times the normal volume. The always-vulnerable Island section of town and parts of the south side are completely inundated, with furniture, debris, and even whole houses floating in the streets.

Mayor Donal Connolly is forced to abandon his basement apartment on River Street for the safety of the Stacy Trent Hotel. Residents fleeing their flooded neighborhoods combine with sightseers to form the city's worst traffic jam in history. Four thousand sandbags placed around the water plant save the city's drinking water supply from contamination, though Morrisville—across the river—isn't quite as lucky.

Nobody in Trenton becomes a casualty, but three Princeton residents drown in the swollen waters. Kenneth Workman and Patrick Maloney, two fifteen-year-old boys looking for some adventure, overturn in their canoe when they try to navigate the wild current of the Delaware. Township patrolman William Ellis, attempting to rescue the boys, also becomes victim to the river.

This aerial shot shows the tremendous power of the river current that battered, but didn't break the "Trenton Makes" Bridge. The homes and businesses around it took their share of punishment, as well.

– Collection New Jersey State Archives, Department of State

One tormented man, for reasons known only to him, finds the flood an opportune time to commit suicide. William Rinyu strips off his clothes and screams, "To hell with all of them!" before throwing himself into the surging water near the 1100 block of Lamberton Street.

Lorraine Fratto and Vince Arnone are a month away from being married. Right now, they are separated by ten blocks of Trenton's Vine Street. Lorraine lives with her mother at the corner of Vine and Princeton Avenue, while Vince lives with his parents and two brothers across the street and halfway down to Brunswick Avenue.

Theirs is a typical Italian neighborhood, lively and full of the sounds and smells of an open-air marketplace. The inviting aroma of baking bread drifts up from Rossi's on Paul Avenue, over by St. James Church. The pungent tang of freshly made sausage or beef roasting down at Marchine's Deli is enough to make your mouth water from blocks away.

On a walk down the street, you might encounter hucksters selling vegetables and fruits, calling out "Wahta-melone!" to draw your attention to the hefty, juicy melons. Or perhaps you'll see a milkman from Borden's or Castena's Dairy, descending his truck with a metal carrier full of chilled quart bottles clinking together. Kids play basketball in the street or on the playground down at Jefferson Chase Court.

The recent rainy weather has put a damper on the activity in the streets, and today, everyone is enjoying the abundant sunshine. Lorraine has been at her job at Westinghouse all day, and is looking forward to going home and getting out in the bright sun for a while. She thinks Vince might take advantage of the rare good weather to go fishing after getting off his job at Trenton Fabricated Metals.

The radio has been on at the metal shop, the music on WBUD-AM interspersed with news. Increasingly throughout the day, the main headlines have been stories coming out of the Pocono region about disastrous flooding, even deaths. Now it's talking about the Delaware absorbing all the runoff and coming up.

When Vince gets home, the phone rings. It's his brother, Tony.

"We need to go down to the store," he tells Vince, referring to Nadisco Electronics, where he works in summer between semesters at Lehigh University. "When I got off at five, the water was coming up Warren, past Front Street already. The store's going to be underwater!" Tony's manager lives in Newark and isn't aware of the impending flood.

"Okay, let's go then," says Vince.

"I'll be right there."

Tony stops by to get Vince, and they hustle down to Nadisco's. For the next hour or so, they move all the electronic equipment upstairs, while the water rises in the street. When they finish, a guy shows up out front with a pickup truck. He has a rowboat in the back, and tells the brothers he's going to row up Warren Street, right past the War Memorial building, just to see what's going on. He thinks it'll be a lark, and asks the guys if they want to join him.

The Delavue Grill, on River Road north of Trenton, is one of the "mom and pop" eateries that suffer greatly at the hands of the river. While these types of businesses were recovering, fast food chains were able to get a foothold in the valley.
– Trentonia Collection, Trenton Public Library

Tony declines, saying he still has things he needs to bring up from the store, but Vince is up for a little adventure. He helps the guy, who says his name is Gaza, pull the boat out of the truck and launch it. Vince and Gaza row down Warren and along a side street to the War Memorial. They're laughing at the novelty of it, when they cross Highway 29 and the current becomes very strong. It catches the boat and the two men just barely have enough strength to row out of it and back toward the steps.

As they reach the top step, they look at each other with amazement and not a little fear. They agree not to go back out in the dangerous current, since all they really wanted to do in the first place was see what's going on.

Rowing back up Warren Street, they're spotted by a lady who yells out her window. She says she's out of groceries and asks if they can help her. Vince thinks, Why not? He tells her to drop a list down. She wraps her grocery list in a twenty-dollar bill and wraps that around a quarter to give it some weight.

Vince tells her to have a rope ready to pull everything up, and he and Gaza make themselves useful. When they return, Vince yells up and the woman tosses down the end of a long line. Vince uses his fisherman's skills to tie a three-way knot around each of two bags and sends them up.

Then, either the woman has called friends or people have just watched the transaction, because about a dozen other people ask the same favor of the young men. Having nothing better to do, they oblige, and get a kick out of it. As they row past during their many trips, they notice that police have erected barricades across Warren and another cross street.

By the time they've finished their errands, it's beginning to get dark, and Vince decides it's time to get out of the current. He tells Gaza he'll help put the boat back in the truck, but Gaza wants to stay on, so Vince heads back to Nadisco's. He finds Tony resting on the steps. He has stacked everything on the second floor, and tells Vince he can't bring anything else up, so the brothers head home.

By Monday, most of the water will recede from the streets of Trenton, though residents of the Island won't return home until the end of August to begin the huge cleanup. New Jersey will order more than two thousand typhoid shots administered to residents within the week. Fifty years later, many of the city's homes will still have marks on their walls, bearing witness to just how high the Delaware crawled up the sides of the buildings.

Above Trenton, in Titusville, "River Jim" Abbott owns Abbott's Marine, a dealer in watercraft and outboard motors, and provider of dock space near his shop in Titusville. Jim is finally getting some rest. After three solid days of securing his docks from the flood, catnapping there while standing watch over customers' boats so they don't break away, and performing rescues and evacuations, Jim's in the hospital.

Nothing bad has happened to him; in fact, quite the opposite. Late Friday night, his wife had gone into labor with their first child. He'd come in from the river to keep his vigil, sitting in the lounge with several other daddies-to-be. While waiting, Jim had nodded off. When one of the other guys had woken him up, chiding him, Jim had simply pleaded exhaustion.

"Fellas, I've been up for three days straight, pulling boats and people out of the river!"

Jim and his wife commemorate the weather event by naming their daughter Lynne Diane. As soon as things have settled down around home, Jim is back out on the river, helping patrol the banks for stranded or distressed people and any looting or suspicious behavior.

On one such tour, performing rescues for the Lambertville Fire Department, he and his crewmates receive a report that someone has been swept into the river and is coming down on a log. They set off upriver in a motorboat to intercept the poor soul.

They scour the river up to the paper mill in Milford, but to no avail. Suddenly, a helicopter appears overhead. Out of its bay drops a board attached to a line. The paper tacked to it says, "Did you see a man on a log?" Apparently, their airborne counterparts have received the same report, and are having just as much luck. They never do find anyone on a log, and wonder if it's not a hoax. There will be a hoax the next night.

This helicopter is caught in mid-hover as it flies over the Delaware looking for a flood victim reported to be trapped in the channel on a mattress. The report turns out to be a hoax, when the "victim" turns out to be a dummy made of stuffed clothing that has been strapped to a mattress and launched downriver.

– *"River Jim" Abbott photo*

At six forty Sunday evening, the rescue squad receives a CD report that a body has been spotted floating downriver on a mattress. Anyone with a radio can hear the news, and the bridges that still stand are crowded with spectators looking for the stranded floater. At eight ten, the mattress floats by the squad boat, and the volunteers pull it in. Roped to the top is a crude dummy, fashioned from women's clothing. Two more reports come in about bodies in the water, and the squad members search the area until darkness forces them to call it off just after nine o'clock. No one ever knows whether the second call is a hoax.

Harvey Fisher, owner of Snuffy's General Store and Hot Dog Stand on River Road in Washington Crossing, New Jersey, calls in. The water's getting too high and he needs help evacuating. River Jim and his colleagues run their boats up to get Harvey out of his shop. The water's so high, they get their propellers caught in the electrical wires outside. Fortunately, the current has long since been turned off.

Snuffy's General Store in Washington Crossing, before the floodwaters had completed their work. The building remains on its foundation though surrounded by increasingly strong currents.

Snuffy's after the Delaware had its way with the popular neighborhood shop. The owners made a valiant effort to continue serving their customers, but were unable to keep the business going. The store was but one of dozens of casualties of the flood.

— "River Jim" Abbott photos

River Jim Abbott had marked a sturdy tree in New Jersey's Washington Crossing State Park at the highest point of the crest. Here, he returns later to post a sign marking it for posterity. The sign proves to be a popular souvenir for visitors, and after the second one is stolen, Jim replaces it with cheap, affordable placards.

— "River Jim" Abbott photo

As the river crests, Jim motors his boat through Washington Crossing State Park and nails a sign to a tree, right at the waterline, to commemorate the record-breaking flood. After the water goes down, he replaces it with a fancy, professionally lettered version. It and its immediate replacement disappear, taken by vandals or souvenir seekers. After that, Jim will continue to replace the sign when it goes missing over the years. He doesn't invest a lot of money in the replacements, knowing they, too, will eventually disappear.

Col. Fred Herr, Hunterdon County Red Cross Chairman, is hard at work establishing feeding centers, distributing food and cash for needs that won't wait. He had already established a center at Lambertville's First Baptist Church on Friday evening. Breakfast and supper are served at these centers, while lunch is provided by mobile canteen units. The canteen in Stockton serves meals to four hundred flood victims over the weekend.

Col. Lyman Burbank has been on the scene in Frenchtown since early Friday, assisting with evacuation, transportation, and temporary housing of the island campers. Disaster specialists from Red Cross national headquarters will arrive on Tuesday to interview and register distressed families for financial assistance in cleanup and recovery. This service is also performed at the Baptist church, as well as in a field office at the Frenchtown Borough Hall.

The same day, mobile canteen units will be sent from Morristown, and staffed by Lambertville volunteers. Local health authorities will also cooperate with the State Health Department to set up inoculation stations to administer typhus injections. These shots are mandatory for those living and working in the affected areas, especially if they come into contact with the contaminated water. More than four thousand people will be inoculated in Hunterdon County within the week.

John Ewing, of Lambertville's Rescue Squad, motors along over Ferry Street just before crossing South Main. Even three blocks in from the river, the water has filled basements and now it also threatens ground floors.

– Collection Heather Buchanan

With the Acme Market inundated beneath five or six feet of water, the only full service market in Lambertville is out of business for the time being. Some people don't drive, and the food canteens won't last forever. The Delaware Valley Council of Churches establishes a local food pantry to help people get back on their feet. It remains such a necessary community function that it will still be in operation on the flood's fiftieth anniversary.

The fire department is gratified that the new aerial ladder truck they've fought so hard to convince people was needed is getting a thorough breaking-in with second-floor rescues and evacuations. Immediately along the river, homes with indoor plumbing (still not a convenience taken for granted in 1955) will become popular, since many outhouses have been washed downriver. The disaster will be the impetus for the upgrade to such amenities when residents clean out and rebuild their damaged homes.

The city's new sewage disposal plant, which treats what's transported from that indoor plumbing, has sustained $25,000 in damage.

Floodwater has risen to the windows of the structure and filled the settling pits with mud. Many businesses have taken serious hits as well. Warehouse and shipping company Belmont Forwarders, filled to the ceiling, loses a $40,000 shipment received just Wednesday. Its total losses will be ten times that amount. Holcombe's Nursery will have $15,000 in damage, the Mercer Paper Tube Company, $45,000.

Precautions taken before the Acme Market had closed have been rendered irrelevant. Shifting the stock up one shelf was futile in the face of water that reached two-thirds of the way to the ceiling. Anything touched by the water will be destroyed by order of the Health Department. By the time workers can return to clean out the meat lockers, the heat will have begun to ferment the contents to the point where the doors practically explode open when pulled. The smell of rot that exudes from it will overwhelm some recovery workers.

Swank dining establishment "River's Edge" is now located decidedly inside the river, and won't be at the edge again for a week or so.

The Acme Market on South Union Street in Lambertville is completely wiped out by the backed-up waters of Swan Creek and the Delaware & Raritan Canal. Everything will have to be ripped out and replaced before it can open for business again.
– Collection Heather Buchanan

In Lambertville, it's common to see boats of all kinds tethered to parking meters (with some jokers even dropping in a coin or two) in front of various drinking establishments. With city water cut off, any place that has cool, drinkable refreshments is a popular stop. This is the view looking down Bridge Street toward the river.
— Collection Heather Buchanan

Though it suffers heavy losses in inventory, furnishings, and property damage, it will reopen within weeks.

In downtown Lambertville, most streets are covered with several feet of water. Rowboats can be seen tied to parking meters in front of Tommy Rousseau's Townhouse Bar, their owners having gone inside for something wet, if no longer cool.

The water will remain in some streets for a week. When it recedes, it'll leave a thick, mucky layer of putrid mud over everything it's touched. The hot sun intensifies the stink, and the top layer dries into a crackle pattern. A hard crust forms, breaking into patches along the cracks, and curling up at the edges like scabs on a festering wound.

All up and down the valley, the smell created by a mix of raw sewage, fuel oil, rotting food, and putrefying flesh is so appalling and intense that it can make a person feel faint in just a few seconds. Some people cut up onions and throw them on top of the mud until it can be cleared away, in a desperate attempt to mask some of the stench.

Sandy Smith Armitage will remember it as "a strange, dead smell." Sally Packard Ephross will describe it as "roadkill mixed with spoiled fruit, milk, and dead fish." Regardless of how they describe it, it's the single thing about the flood that will stick out most in the minds of the majority of survivors years later.

Some people who remain along the river, cleaning up their houses as best they can, will never be able to completely eradicate the smell. Over the years, during the particularly hot, humid periods that characterize Mid-Atlantic summers, they will catch a whiff of the mud, much toned-down in intensity. Those whose living spaces have been infiltrated by the floodwater will discover, during renovations years later, several feet of dried mud inside their walls. Others will experience the long-dried, ultra-fine stuff sifting up between floorboards or out of lighting switch plates and plug receptacles on their walls.

Many of these people will also notice a markedly less comfortable feeling in winter. Their walls retain far less heat, now that the insulation lies in a sodden heap between the bottom of the studs. Mold will cause problems for decades before it's identified as a serious health risk.

A new kind of decorative accent becomes de rigeur among riverfront properties: a high water mark on inside and outside walls, documenting the farthest reaches of the flood. Over the years, these marks become something of a badge of courage, bestowing bragging rights on those who survived the flood and returned to take up where their lives had been interrupted.

Not surprisingly, this practice is limited to the lower part of the flood area. In the northern reaches where the water has cost not just time and money but has taken a toll in lives, survivors are in a hurry to wash away the waterlines. They want nothing to remind them of the horror of the dark hours when the creeks tore apart their homes and carried off friends and relatives. They'll have enough of that to last them a lifetime, in the permanently changed landscape, diverted vehicle traffic, and missing persons.

Harry Leida learns that someone has begun ferry service between the Stroudsburgs across the Brodhead at Stokes Mill, and decides to get Fred across that way. He stops to ask how to get a ride, and a man tells him it's not an official service, just a couple guys with speedboats—private volunteers—providing a way for people to get back and forth. This pair will eventually grow to a contingent of ten boats that will work around the clock for four days, ferrying more than three thousand people across the creek.

The current is still raging when speedboat ferry crossings begin to be made at the ruined Stokes Mill bridge between the Stroudsburgs.
– Collection Monroe County Historical Association

Harry asks if he can bring his nephew across to get him back home to Easton. The guy says he can get him across the Brodhead, but that Harry might have a hard time getting the rest of the way to Easton, because Route 611 is underwater a good bit of the way south from there. Harry says he'll take his chances, and heads back to his parents' house to pick up Fred.

Friday evening, Sara and Linda LeCropane's parents had not heard about the Pocono flooding. When Mr. LeCropane had gotten off work at five o'clock, he went home to pick up his wife, and they had headed up to camp for the weekend. The entire ride normally took four hours, but they had only made it as far as Dingman's Ferry by eight o'clock, still several hours away. There, they'd encountered barricades and were told they could go no farther. Unable to figure out another way up, and unaware of the extent of the damage, they had turned around and gone home.

The girls' uncle, Frank "Bud" Martin, had been listening to his radio in his apartment next door to his sister and her husband late that night. He'd heard a report that Camp Davis had been wiped out, and had gone over to wake the girls' parents. They had switched on their own radio, and the broadcast soon repeated the awful news.

Soon, friends, relatives, and neighbors in the building had begun streaming in. They'd heard the news and assumed that the Hartigs and the girls had been lost. The phone had quickly gotten so busy that Buddy's girlfriend, Marge, began fielding calls for the distraught parents.

By Saturday morning, the sleepless night is catching up with the grief-stricken family as they wait for some word about their daughters and their friend.

In the afternoon, Bud Blandeau drives the three girls to Stroudsburg to try to contact their parents. They find a diner with a rare working pay phone and stand in one of the long lines. They're told the phones are only for emergency calls, so they aren't able to use them. Sara believes it's enough of an emergency that her parents don't know what has happened to them and stands in line anyway.

The man in front of her ends his call and hands her the receiver. When she puts it to her ear, Sara realizes the connection hasn't yet been broken. She gives the operator her parents' number.

Her mom, Edna, answers.

Sara, emotionally overwrought, says simply, "Mama!"

Edna is shocked. "Sara!"

Those in the LeCropanes' apartment, not knowing who is calling, believe this exclamation means Sara is being reported dead.

Sara regains her composure and adds, "And Linda is with me."

Mrs. LeCropane exclaims again, "And Linda!"

Hearing this, Mr. LeCropane believes both his daughters have been killed. "Sara's gone," he mutters, "and Linda, too." A deeply faithful man, he throws his hands into the air and quotes from the Biblical book of Job, "The Lord giveth and the Lord taketh away. Blessed be the name of the Lord."

His wife now realizes what he's thinking, and reaches up to get his attention. "No, Frank...they're alive!"

The rooms erupts in rejoicing.

The girls know their phone connection is tenuous and could go out at any time, and the line behind them is growing. Quickly, they both assure their parents that they're okay and are staying at Pinebrook. Before saying goodbye, they sadly report that the Hartigs are likely lost.

Edna, overwhelmed by the conversation, forgets to ask how they can get the girls home. One of the neighbors, Emma Mooney, asks her, "But what about the girls? You've got to go get them!" A moment of humor, if a bit dark, passes over the room and everyone can finally relax a bit.

The worried parents must wait until they can get through to the area to find out how they can pick up their daughters.

On Sunday afternoon, the girls are helping set the dining tables for dinner at Pinebrook, when someone tells Linda that more rain is predicted. She has had enough. She turns to Sara and says, "We've got to get out of here." She hasn't been truly afraid until this moment, but now she begins to panic, thinking they'll have to go through another flood. What if this time, Pinebrook is devastated?

Sara tries to calm her little sister, but everyone at Pinebrook seems to be harboring some level of similar anxiety.

Around three o'clock, the girls are standing on the road, not knowing what will become of them. Buses have finally been arriving to take Pinebrook campers home, but what are they to do? Suddenly, their parents' old "Woody" station wagon pulls up. A Red Cross flag hangs out the window, the passport, along with paperwork for Stroudsburg officials, that had allowed them to get through the road-blocks. Sara and Linda are so happy to be going home, and their parents and Uncle Buddy are relieved to see them, alive and well. Everyone hugs and cries, a mixture of joy and sadness.

Edna and her husband give Percy Crawford a donation in acknowledgment of the care that has been shown their daughters. They discuss the disappearance of Davis Cabins, and Percy expresses his deep sympathy for his longtime friends. Finally, the whole family stands by the tennis courts to say a group prayer of thanksgiving and to ask comfort for the families of the lost.

They get in the car and head for New York, Mr. LeCropane promising them the biggest steaks they can find for supper.

On the way back, they stop at Clearview School, now serving as a temporary morgue. Before they'd left Brooklyn, Mr. LeCropane had taped little photos of the Hartigs to the dashboard, to aid in identifying the bodies. He now goes inside to get through the gruesome task. When he comes back out, he reports that he's seen Aunt Lily.

"She looks just the way she always did," he says, "but she's bloated." He pauses, looking at his wife and children, then adds softly. "The only way I could identify Uncle Henry was by the ring on his finger. He was too disfigured." He spares his family the painful details, for which they're grateful.

The LeCropanes are a stoic bunch. They grieve quietly, tearlessly, on the way home. When they finally drop Marion Baker off at her apartment across the street, she is gratefully received by her family. The LeCropanes apologize profusely that the young woman has had to go through such an ordeal.

The next week goes by in a blur of visits from reporters and funerals for the Hartigs and for Mae and John Koch. The girls must buy dresses for the funerals, along with a few summer things, since all of their summer clothes have been washed away. Henry's brothers arrive to settle the Hartigs' estate. Edna retrieves a few things for the girls, as mementoes of their beloved aunt and uncle.

Just over a year later, Edna will die from the leukemia, and her funeral will be held in the same parlor as her late aunt's and uncle's had been. Sara and Linda will return once to Pinebrook, but find that to be so near to their familiar summer home and yet so far is more torturous than pleasant. It will be the last time.

The young women go on to attend Percy Crawford's The King's College, and life moves along. They get married and have children, but never forget their experience and how it has changed their lives. They know that the best plans based on the best information are not failsafe. Linda becomes determined to live intuitively, to enjoy life and to learn, but to be ready for the unexpected.

Nancy Johnson has been resting at the Monroe County Hospital since she and Linda Christensen had been picked up by rescue boats early Friday morning. Nancy has learned that her mother, Jennie, made it through their ordeal, but that her brothers are missing. She hasn't heard from her father, who has been unable to get through yet from New Jersey. Nancy has been treated for her hand injury, exposure, and multiple lacerations and bruises on her legs.

Linda has been staying at the Gish farm near demolished Camp Davis, where Irene Weber is also, waiting for her husband to arrive. Linda's father arrives to identify the bodies of his wife, sister, and sister-in-law. First, he accompanies Linda for her typhus injection at the Stroudsburg Methodist Church, where they're both interviewed by reporters. Clutching his daughter's hand, Mr. Christensen tells them, "I can't bear to think of those who are gone. I'm just thankful my little girl is safe and I have someone left."

Linda will appear with Nancy, standing on the cobblestones near where Camp Davis had stood, in a photo on the cover of "Diane Drowns Delaware Valley." The *Easton Express* will publish the photo essay a week after the flood. Nancy's bandaged hand will be plainly visible in the shot, as are both the girls' bruised legs.

Jennie Johnson is also interviewed by the press, and gives a detailed description of the house collapse and her time in the water. It does not jibe completely with her daughter's account, but highlights the confusion and mind-numbing fear the victims must have felt during their ordeal. She says she knows her sons are dead, and will soon find out she's right.

The body of her oldest, Roy, is being discovered as she speaks. Though his autopsy will list drowning as the cause of death, it carries the annotation "asphyxiation in flash flood, 15 min." His death had not been quick or merciful.

The corpse of Roy's brother David will be recovered the following day, amidst oppressive heat and a thunderstorm that gives everyone the jitters. Their mother's desperate state of mind will later become evident when it's discovered that she has misidentified the body of another camper, Jay Kehmna, and buried it as that of her son David. When the mix-up is discovered on September 8, Jay's body is disinterred and properly identified the next day.

Donnie Christensen's body won't be located until September 9. Mr. Christensen will identify his son by his plaid swim trunks and the Minerva wristwatch still strapped to his arm. Donnie's body will reveal the particular violence of the still-growing Brodhead Creek as it swept him and Bruce Thompson away. When Mr. Christensen moves closer to examine the boy's hair color, he will notice that his son's jaw is missing.

Irene Weber is shown in a large photo on the pages of the Stroudsburg *Daily Record*, slumped in despair against her husband as they await news of their children's fates. She also makes headlines as the bereaved mother who, despite losing two of her own children and four other family members, goes to the morgue to help identify the bodies of others lost in the disaster.

"I'm trying because I know it will help someone else," she says, "some of the families of our friends from the camp. We had been going there for seven years. Knowing them all so well makes it doubly hard."

Her pain will redouble, as she waits with her husband at the Gish farm for word of her children's recovery. Betty Jane won't be found until September third. Bobby's body will be found two days later, still strapped into the life vest his mother had put on in a vain attempt to save him. It had, in fact, done part of its job in helping him float. The water's recession had left him hanging where he'd stayed after Irene had lost him: at the top of the tree that had ripped him from his mother's arms.

Irene will wait nearly a year to gain some closure on the whole experience. Her sister-in-law will be the seventieth victim's body to be recovered. On July 11, 1956, Helen Lawyer's corpse will be found, the last adult still missing from the flood.

Her body will be discovered by an employee of the Department of Forests and Waters, working as part of a crew still cleaning up the remains of the Brodhead's destruction. Helen's corpse is found face down in the sand and mud. It's fairly well preserved from having been largely sealed off from the air by sand and mud until being disturbed by cleanup activities.

The gruesome discovery leaves only the body of Helen's nine-year-old daughter, Carol, still missing from the family. Carol's body won't turn up until August, 1969, when workers excavating the site of the new Stroudsburg Water Authority plant near Stokes Mill unearth her skeleton.

Many other bodies are located near where Helen Lawyer's body will eventually be found, on a narrow strip of sand that comes to be called "Death Island." Seventy-five rangers of the Civil Air Patrol, directed by state police, search the area near the Tru-Matic Machine Company on Route 190 in Stroudsburg. The remains of the Hartigs,

Edna Winfield, and Beth Deubel's mom, Martha, will be found in the vicinity on Sunday.

Helicopter pilots report spotting at least nine bodies floating in the "still wildly overflowing Delaware," according to the *New York Times*. Nobody knows yet if those bodies are from the Stroudsburg area.

To prevent another unfortunate confusion like that with the Johnson and Kehmna boys, CAP captain Dr. Floyd Shafer announces that the State Department of Health requires any remaining bodies not yet identified to be held for at least thirty days before they are buried.

Pennsylvania governor George Leader had flown to Mount Pocono Airport Friday evening, then was escorted by the State Police to CD headquarters in Stroudsburg. He will meet with Monroe County CD Director Judge Fred Davis and with General Biddle, who had hurried his National Guardsmen up from their emergency drill in Fort Indiantown Gap to the real thing in Stroudsburg. In the governor's entourage had been Dr. Maurice Goddard, Secretary of Forests and Waters in Harrisburg. Now the rest of the state is learning how serious things are in northeast Pennsylvania.

Monroe County, along with seven other counties, is declared a disaster area by the Small Business Administration. This clears the way to make federal aid available to those trying to recover. The *Daily Record* reports that it will soon be letting people know how to apply for such funding.

After a losing battle from eight o'clock Thursday evening until noon on Friday to get utilities back up and running, workmen have finally had some success. Bell Telephone is estimating it will be able to restore partial service to East Stroudsburg by the end of the weekend. Citizen volunteers are helping on the ground while a helicopter pulls a roll of cable across the settling Brodhead Creek to facilitate the repairs. Large areas of the county have had electrical power restored. An emergency substation is erected on Foxtown Hill to supply Stroudsburg, taking the place of the Power Dam substation that has been ripped away by McMichaels Creek.

Citizen's Gas Company reports that they can't accurately project a back-in-service date yet. State officials have rushed pumps and a chlorinator to Stroudsburg to help set up an emergency water supply system. In East Stroudsburg, water is being trucked in from local nursery reservoirs and treated before being dispensed to the public.

The paper also reports that less rain had fallen during Diane than Connie in the Stroudsburgs…not that it really matters. The eleven inches that had been dumped on Mount Pocono by eleven o'clock Thursday night and the additional two inches that had followed it were more than enough to seal the fate of any place along the Brodhead.

The federal Civil Defense agency shows up to survey the area and evaluate flood damage. Their report will reach President Eisenhower with recommendations for his declaration of disaster that would release federal aid to residents. Officials are estimating two million dollars' worth of damage to county highways alone.

More than five hundred homes are left uninhabitable in the twin boroughs. Red Cross shelters, food stations, and a clothing storehouse at the old Endicott Johnson Shoe Store are set up. When the majority of immediate basic needs have been met, officials will also set up stations to register applicants for flood relief funds. These will pay for immediate essentials, home repair or replacement, and occupational tools and equipment. Many area civic and religious organizations set up disaster relief drives and go all out in publicizing the great need of the stricken area. Donations will pour in from around the country and even from foreign lands, topping the $100,000 mark.

In 1948, when there had been a catastrophic flood in Holland as the sea breached the country's vital network of dikes, East Stroudsburg had declared itself a sister to one of the Dutch cities and sent funds to help its citizens recover. Now the European country, though itself still recovering from the ravages of the war, reciprocates with a shipment of hundreds of tulip bulbs so that the Pennsylvania town might have a bit of beauty in the spring. The flowers will be planted in the Lincoln Street park, and their riot of yellow color will seem even more lively against the backdrop of graying debris still left from the flood.

Without their usual recreational distractions, most of the kids from Camps Hagan and Miller are bored at the adult Lutheran

The remains of Camp Miller in the Delaware Water Gap are all that will greet visitors after the flood. The camp will be cleaned up and rebuilt in time to open for the next summer season.

— *Collection Bob Stalgaitis*

camp. A break in the monotony comes when a helicopter delivers giant boxes of Schaible's bread, hot dogs, and other food staples.

Charlie Rufe is asked to help unload the cargo, and he's glad for something to do. But as he goes to pick up a box of bread, he sees something that instantly sobers him: a pile of body bags. It's his first reality check, and he realizes how lucky he and his fellow campers have been. Two days later, he'll be picked up by his parents and driven to pick up his sister, still at Camp Hagan, and on his way home from a summer he'll never forget.

The following spring, the church will hold a clean-up day at Camp Miller. New cabins will have been built for a new junior area on higher ground, complete with concrete foundations and indoor plumbing. While raking the area, Bob Bohm will find his mess kit, but nothing else remains that he'd left behind.

Bob will return to the camp again, proud to be one of the campers who can claim "B.F." status: one who had been there Before the Flood, when camp life had been more rustic and challenging. He will also enjoy a double shot of prestige, as one of the campers who had actually been part of the now-famous human chain that had woven its way through the waters to safety.

Where the river has begun to go down, people emerge to assess their losses and the damage they will have to repair. Everywhere, they get to work with buckets of precious clean water, chlorine bleach and disinfectant to begin the arduous task of getting the mud off walls and floors. Some people, by the time they're finished with the seemingly endless task, will come to abhor the smell of these cleaning agents to the point where they can no longer stand to use them.

In Kintnersville, Sally Packard and her parents stay with her aunts while they scrub down their home. Following the time-honored Pennsylvania Dutch dictum that "many hands make light work," neighbors form cleaning brigades. They move from house to house, in much the fashion of the old-time harvest bee, until the work is done. Sally's father, using a snow shovel to scoop out the mud, notices a knot of well-dressed tourists gathered outside, gawking at the unfortunate flood victims. He figures he'll give them a show.

"Alene," he yells to his wife, flinging yet another scoop out into the yard, "when's the last time you cleaned this kitchen floor?" The group erupts in laughter, and everyone within earshot appreciates the injection of a little humor into the relentless tragedy of the situation.

When Sally needs a rest, she goes for a walk down Route 611. The asphalt has been rolled up like a carpet off the roadbed, and the Easton-Doylestown trolley tracks are twisted like pretzels. For years, Sally will think of the children who have drowned at Camp Davis, and hope that they died quickly and weren't afraid. She'll have night-mares about the river that before had been a source of such solace, but she'll never stop loving the Delaware.

Ed Litschauer goes down to the river to Riegelsville, where the Durham Paper Company has its warehouse next to Cooks Creek. The back of the warehouse has been ripped off, flooding the mill and machine room, and causing $1.5 million damage. The water has taken the huge, 37-inch rolls of paper and dumped them into the creek.

As soon as the water goes down, he and some buddies call Roy Fair, a contractor in Ferndale, to bring his truck to the river. They need help keeping the rolls from being carried off downriver. Roy runs his truck's towline around the rolls to keep them in place, while Ed and his friends tie planks together into a crude corral. Later, the company will be able to cut the rolls up and recycle the pulp into new paper.

The men manage to round up 106 of the rolls, paid by the plant manager with a case of beer to stay on the job till everything is secured. Several newspapers will mistakenly identify this operation as someone gathering oil drums.

Riegel Ridge Paper in Milford, New Jersey, is one of the hardest hit of all the businesses along the river. The area's largest employer estimates its losses in excess of $100,000 immediately after the flood. And so, the Delaware, which usually helps power the mill, brings it to a dead halt.

– Hunterdon County Democrat photo

Herman Hissim, an employee of Fair's, helps with much of the local cleanup efforts, including bulldozing the mass of debris left on the island in Kintnersville. His wife, June, goes back to work at Whippany Paper. Instead of their usual duties, the office gals set up tables and spread wet paperwork from the files out to dry in the sun. Some of the office furniture is beyond salvage. When it's time to move everything back in, they relocate the office to the floor above. For a long time, every time the river gets high, the employees will get nervous.

In Riegelsville, Dot Kale says goodbye to all their furniture and possessions. She and her husband will start over from scratch. As they rid their place of the mud and gunk, she's sick at all the preserved food they are forced to get rid of, for fear of contamination. For several days, they'll continue to take their meals at St Peter's Church, until they can secure cooking equipment of their own. Not knowing that the plaster walls will retain moisture for a while, Dot decides it's a good time to put up wallpaper after they scrub the mud off. That night, they awaken to a booming sound. The next morning, every single piece of paper has pulled off the wall and lies in a heap on the floor. The rapid fall of the long strips of glue-heavy paper striking the floor on its edges had caused the noise. She waits six months to attempt any further rehabilitation, and decides paint will do, this time.

North on Route 611, Don Young at the Easton Employment Service has dispatched two crews to help clean homes along North Delaware Drive, including the Fackenthal residence. He will continue to provide labor for the cleanup effort through the following Saturday. Then he'll make arrangements for blasters and dynamite to be sent to help workmen clear the remains of the cement bridge from the creek at Minisink Hills.

In a tragic coda to the flood, a teenage boy standing too close while watching the blasting will be killed by flying chunks of concrete.

The Fackenthals return to their flooded home in Forks Township. They never did get the basement drain unclogged, and Mr. Fackenthal is sickened at having to chop a hole in the beautiful wood dining room floor to let the water drain out. A huge gash has been scoured out of the lawn next to their house's foundation, and Mike helps fill it in. The family stays in the apartment at the Dennis' next door, while they rip out walls and floors and begin to rebuild.

Peggy Beling helps clean up the mess in what will one day become her own home, after she has married Mike and his parents

There's plenty of work to go around as the Fackenthals dig into their massive clean up job. Here, Mike fills in the deep ravine that has been gouged out around his home's foundation.

– Collection Margaret Fackenthal

pass on. At one point, they have an engineer come in to determine where the actual floodplain ends, which turns out to be the chair rail in their dining room.

Forty-nine years later, alone after Mike's passing, she'll have to leave again, when a hurricane called Ivan leaves another watery calling card. Again in April, 2005, she'll be driven from her house by the Delaware's floodwaters in a crest just beneath that of the 1903 Pumpkin Freshet. It will be the last time. Peggy decides she's had enough of fighting the river, and sells her home.

Rich DiRenzis is finally able to return home from his father's dry cleaning shop. He stays away from the river and takes the back way through Bethlehem and Hellertown, over Morgan's Hill. After a sleepless night of worrying about their kids at camp, Jean and Rich receive a call from friends in White Haven, who say the children are safe with them. The camp had called parents who lived nearby to come and get their children, so the friends had also picked up the DiRenzis kids. It's a tremendous relief, and all the DiRenzises can think about are those parents of the children from the camp in Analomink who are getting calls of a very different nature.

Nancy Wolfe returns with her stage crewmates to the Bucks County Playhouse in New Hope to find an unimaginable mess. The river has crested just at the bottom of the stage, soaking all the seats in the first dozen rows. Everything is covered in mud, and the box office and administrative office have waterlines halfway up their walls. The furniture is sitting wherever the water has set it down, and the playhouse porch is coated with several inches of slimy gunk that make it hazardous to walk.

The crew is overwhelmed, but feels compelled to do something to mitigate the damage. They attempt to sweep the mud from the premises, but it's a futile effort. As quickly as they sweep, more of the muck oozes over the area just cleared.

Late in the morning, the National Guard takes over the effort, astonishing Nancy with their speed and efficiency. They remove ruined desks to the parking lot and quickly sledgehammer them into piles of rubble. They blast away the seemingly endless mud in a few hours, with the help of high-pressure hoses. The popular entertainment

The river reaches the bottom of the show window of Benny Sidon's New Hope Pharmacy at the intersection of Main and Bridge Streets. The water is still rising in this shot, and will make such a mess of Benny's shop that it will drive him out of business. A small group of adventurous young men wait around all night in case there's an emergency.
– Hunterdon Democrat photo

venue will soon be back in action, drawing crowds to its beloved, if newly aromatic stage.

Just past Bridge Street to the north, Sandy Smith is helping distribute drinks and sandwiches from the mobile canteens to cleanup crews, having proven herself a danger to breakable items while her parents, aunt and uncle, and grandmother clean their homes. She watches fish jump up from deep puddles still in the road, and a boy riding his bicycle in water up to his waist. Her parents lose their boiler and the floors will have to be sanded, but the piano survives, needing only its legs replaced.

As the water recedes, it leaves huge nightcrawlers lying on the sidewalks, and her family responds to orders to report for typhoid shots at the high school. People's appliances stand in the gym, where they've been stored until the water goes down. After she's been home a while, Sandy becomes ill from the shots, developing bad chills and a sick stomach.

Her father hauls their ruined refrigerator into the yard where the water's still high, and opens the door. Packages of spoiled food float out of it and away with the current. When it's empty, he takes a look inside and realizes it's been ruined along with its content. He pushes the appliance itself off downriver.

Remembering the scare that had gone through her when the bull-horns had announced rescue crews looking for a body on a mattress, Sandy considers the implications of continuing to swim in the river, as she and her friends have always done. They decide not to swim under the docks anymore after a body is found there. Several more will be discovered lodged there in the months following the flood.

Just up Main Street, Dorothy Grider has returned from Selinsgrove to find her home a shambles. The carpeting is ruined, along with much of their furniture. Their kitchen appliances are all complete losses, and the basement needs pumping out. Dorothy's housemate, Lydia, and Lydia's father, "Pops," share their story of being evacuated in a motorboat as they all scrub the mud from their walls. As in many places, upholstered furniture lines their street, drying out or simply left for junk. A pile of ruined furniture in their yard looks as though it's ready for a bonfire. They stay with friends on Sugan Road until the place is livable again.

Dorothy Grider scrubs off her porch and the front of her house with bleach water to remove the smelly slime left by retreating flood waters. It's a disgusting job that for some area residents will last for months.

– Collection Dorothy Grider

Lydia Gudemann discusses how they'll handle the buckled floors in the living room with Dorothy Grider. Their home's cellar has fared even worse. Though they do their best to clean it thoroughly, a plumbing repairman will encounter a clod of mud falling off several pipes nearly fifty years later.

Lydia's father, "Pops," ponders how they'll replace all their ruined items, and what will become of all the debris on New Hope's now furniture-lined streets.

– Collection Dorothy Grider

The experience will force Dorothy to take a fresh look at her career. She understands now how quickly life can change, and decides it's too short to settle for less than what makes her happy. She calls her agent in New York, who rarely even sees the work she does, yet takes 10 percent of every project Dorothy illustrates. Dorothy hasn't required the agent's services to get new work in years, and she tells her it's time to terminate their contract. It's a good move. Dorothy's confidence as a businessperson gets a boost while her income increases. Considering all they'll need to replace in the house, the extra income will be welcome.

South of town, Peter and Alice Barry respond to calls for volunteers to help begin the cleanup in New Hope. They set out with shovels, mops, and buckets, and get a permit at the high school. Police lines are keeping anyone without authorization from entering the stricken town in an effort to prevent looting and the development of traffic problems tourists would surely create.

Not a car is in sight, just telephone linesmen and fire engines lining Main Street, along with rowboats tied to parking meters and trees. They arrive at the home of the Fausts, elderly family friends. There, the Barrys had enjoyed dinner just days before. The first floor is devoid of furniture, with four inches of thick, slippery glop coating the floors. The kitchen sinks overflows with brown, stagnant water, and the cabinets are littered with mud-covered pots and dishes.

Alice takes hold of the door and it falls off its hinges, then comes apart in her hands. Jars of freshly canned produce lie where they've been hurled into the mud, and tables are overturned in the summer kitchen. The electric clock on the stove has brown water trapped inside its face, and the walls show a waterline about five feet high. Mrs. Faust is sick about it, since they had just finished repainting and papering the walls in the spring. She moves about her house in a daze.

"I don't hardly know where to begin," she confides to Alice. Then, bending over, she reaches for something on the floor. "Well, we'll just save these here clothes pegs from the mud," she says, picking them out of the smelly ooze. "Some of them was my grandmother's."

Such pitiful scenes play themselves out over and over again, up and down the valley. Holding on to small memories seems to give stricken people some sense of control over what's happened to them.

In the days to come, Alice will accompany her friend Margaret Richie to Upper Black Eddy, in response to a call for volunteers from the Red Cross. They work a sixteen-hour day in the canteen and on telephone duty, fielding calls for information. She hears a rumor that an unknown man had spent the night on the canal towpath, clearing out the sluice gates to prevent it from flooding more than it already had.

Then the Mennonites begin to arrive in the flooded communities all along the river. Like many others, Peter Barry will work with them in helping to clean up New Hope. Their selfless service will impact the lives of thousands and its story will go on to become one of the least understood, yet most enduring legends of the flood.

Starting Over

Norm Good of the Blooming Glen Mennonite Church accepts an invitation to accompany his pilot neighbor, Andy Rosenberger, on a flyover of the flooded Delaware River region in Andy's light plane. They take off from Montgomery County Airport, flying over the Easton/Phillipsburg area first, then downriver to Philadelphia and back. The men are stunned and moved by the extent and severity of the devastation.

They return to a Sunday School annual picnic in full swing at Souder's Woods near Sellersville. They speak to Rev. Dave Derstine, saying perhaps there is some way their congregation can help. As the reverend walks in his front door in the evening, his phone is ringing.

It's Margaret Seylor, principal of a small school in Riegelsville. She asks him if there's any way he could send help for her stricken community. It's just the first of many incidents of the kind of timing the reverend can only perceive as God's will at work. After he hangs up, the pastor calls Norm Good and they decide to ask the congregation's help.

After church on Sunday, he gives the floor to Norm and Andy, who report what they'd seen the day before, and tell the congregation they believe they can be of help to the devastated communities. They ask for a hundred volunteers to go with them to Riegelsville the next day, telling them they'll need vehicles and equipment, too.

On Monday morning, nearly a hundred people show up at the church parking lot, and they caravan to Riegelsville. Rev. Derstine stays behind and calls Mrs. Seylor to let her know help is on the way.

He also makes arrangements for further cleanup efforts when this one is finished.

The Mennonite workers stay in Riegelsville all week, cleaning up the homes of mostly elderly or disabled residents, as well as Lundie's Hardware and Five & Dime, along the canal. One piece of equipment that makes a huge difference is the "Mud Hog" brought along by one of the men. It has the ability to vacuum and pump out even very thick mud, making short work of the massive job of cellar cleaning.

Mennonites from the Blooming Glen community begin their volunteer cleanup work in Riegelsville. The impromptu effort will soon evolve into an all-out attack on flood muck and debris, expanding to many riverside Pennsylvania towns.

– Collection Bob Stalgaitis

All during the week, after the tired workers arrive back home, they hear increasingly disturbing reports of even worse devastation in the Poconos region, including many deaths in the Stroudsburgs. Rev. Derstine believes they can help there, too, but has no idea who to contact. The following Saturday, Andy Rosenberger suggests they fly to the isolated cities and see for themselves what's going on, then determine if they can be of service. The pastor agrees, so they call Norm to join them, and the trio takes off.

Not having much experience with the area, they don't even know where the airport is. Using a road map, they find it on Route 209 and finally land there, taxiing to a small office building. They don't know if they'll find someone there, but a car parked in front of the building looks promising. They knock on the door, and Mary Hamlin, who co-owns the airport with her husband, greets them. They explain why they've come and ask her to call a taxi or bus to take them to East Stroudsburg.

Mary smiles, telling the men they probably won't be able to get into town. The National Guard is on duty, protecting the stricken towns from looters and annoying sightseers, so nobody's getting through without authorization. Still, she is sympathetic to their desire to be of service, and finally offers her own car.

You're welcome to use it if you think you can get into town, she says.

The three men thank her and drive to the checkpoint outside town. They explain to the Guard what their intentions are, and he allows them to pass. Now they have to locate the officials who can show them what needs done and authorize them to do it. Naturally, they head for the borough offices, not realizing that they're closed on Saturday. However, this Saturday, like everything else, is anything but normal. The councilmen are in a meeting with the mayor and other officials to decide where and how to begin cleaning up their city. The secretary answers the door and invites the men in to wait while she announces their presence.

Mayor Jesse Flory, upon hearing about the men and their mission, calls a halt to the meeting, inviting the three to speak. The reverend again feels God opening doors for them to be of service. He explains that they're from the Blooming Glen Mennonite Church Disaster Service, borrowing the name from a similar effort his brother had been part of in the Midwest. He offers their services to the cleanup effort.

The councilmen are receptive, asking how many people they can provide. The reverend does some quick calculating in his head, and boldly estimates that they could put together a crew of three hundred people by Monday. The room is completely silent, the group stunned by such an offer. Finally, Mayor Flory speaks up.

"Well, if that's the case, you should tour the area to see what needs done."

Norm rides up to the Canadensis area in a Jeep with the town's engineer to view the mangled downtown area. On the way back down, they stop at Analomink. There, Norm sees only a well casing sticking up from where he's told fourteen buildings, known collectively as Camp Davis, had stood less than two weeks earlier.

Andy and the reverend go with two separate groups of councilmen to tour East Stroudsburg itself. The pastor, something of a shutterbug, always brings his camera with him everywhere. In the Silk Mill Flats area on Lincoln Street, he sees an elderly woman in mud up to her shoulders, reaching into a pile of rubble.

When she comes back up with a Bible, he tries to capture the moment, but is unable to focus because his eyes are full of tears. This could be his mother, he thinks, or anyone else in his family. It will remain, in his mind, the most moving moment of the whole experience.

When Norm and the engineer return to town, they join the group at the Flats. He sees the waterline on a house near the Van Gorder residence, up above the attic window. If he hadn't seen it with his own eyes, he wouldn't have believed that the creek could have backed up like that.

Convinced of the need for their services, the Mennonite representatives leave for the airport, promising to stay in touch with the mayor over the weekend. They will be back on Monday. They plan their organizational strategy during the trip home.

When they get back, the reverend calls Rick Detweiler, overseer of the Blooming Glen Mennonite Conference, informing him of their activities. Rick is enthusiastically supportive. Then Rev. Derstine contacts several congregation members to recruit interested workers. He makes arrangements with the Shelly Lumber Company to provide equipment and safety gear, gloves, and tools. Owner Paul Shelly says he will give them everything they need, free of charge.

The Penn Ridge School District offers the use of their school buses to transport the workers back and forth, and the North Penn Goodwill Service pledges the use of their mobile canteen trucks to keep their workers fed and hydrated.

Finally, the minister calls a contact at the Quakertown Barracks of the Pennsylvania State Police, explaining that they will probably need an escort to maintain the safety of the workers in a large caravan of vehicles. He receives their immediate cooperation. He's told they'll work in concert with local police in the municipalities they'll pass through to make sure the convoy gets through with as few delays as possible.

Congregation member Bill Gross acts as volunteer coordinator at a meeting of potential workers that evening. The three organizers report specific details of their findings during the tour of the Poconos area, letting the workers know what they should expect. They hand out lists of clothing, tools, and equipment to bring, and ask those with pickup trucks to bring them along.

Doctor Norman Loxx is summoned to administer typhoid shots at his office the following day. When men and women begin showing up in the afternoon following Sunday services, the organizers are overwhelmed. It's clear they will have no trouble fulfilling their promise of three hundred volunteers.

Early Monday morning, twenty-seven buses and other vehicles are lined up, each bus carrying workers. Support vehicles carry the tools and equipment the crew will need. The State Patrol makes good on its promise of an escort as it accompanies the convoy to the outskirts of Allentown and Bethlehem, then picks up again on the outside of each town. The three organizers fly ahead to the Stroudsburgs, preparing for the arrival of the workers. They're met by City Engineer Leo Osterman, who drives them to Red Cross headquarters in downtown East Stroudsburg.

At eight o'clock, the buses and other vehicles arrive, making an impressive sight as they parade down streets that have been cleared to allow them through to the Red Cross offices. There, a councilman boards each bus, giving a brief overview of the site where they will be working. He goes over some safety rules, such as not to drink any tap water, and to expect that they may, in the course of their work, encounter dead bodies.

The buses then take off for their respective sites, and a group foreman for each crew is chosen on the way. The foreman will work with the councilmen to decide which buildings will be cleaned and in what order. The men will dig out basements, move heavy objects, and shovel mud from the floors, while women will scrub walls and floors, and wash dishes, linens, and other salvageable items that have been soiled by the floodwaters. Within half an hour, everyone is hard at work.

The Mud Hog is much appreciated, as shoveling mud up through tiny basement windows from inside a hot, filthy, stinking space is a challenge. But there is only one such piece of equipment, so most of

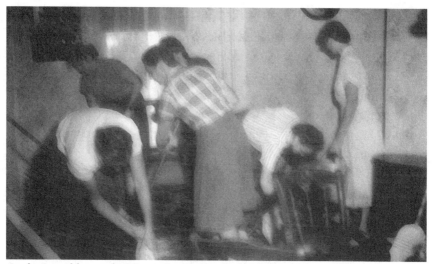

In the Stroudsburgs, the Mennonite workers develop a smooth process for methodically moving through affected areas. Men do the heavy lifting and shoveling and the outside work, while women take care of cleaning rooms, dishes, furniture and linens. By the time they're through, some people say the homes are cleaner than before the flood.
– Collection Bob Stalgaitis

the volunteers will endure the back-breaking, gag-inducing work. They wear high boots to protect themselves from the muck and anything hidden in it. Some men do, indeed, come across the bodies of flood victims, jammed beneath stairways or hanging in trees, as they clear away the thick deposits of mud.

The organizers are amazed at some of the tales they hear about some people's experiences during the flood, which are passed along from the flood victims by the workers. One story, in particular, seems to them to embody the kind of commitment they're showing in their own efforts:

> One man, whose wife is an invalid, realizes he has to get her to a higher level in the house when the water begins rising, sometimes by seven inches a minute. His wife, though, is a large woman, and he can't lift her by himself. He knows he won't be getting any help, because everyone else is trying to save their own lives and those of their families. Finally, as the water gathers around him and his wife, he sees that the water will float her body.

He waits until she's buoyed above the furniture, then grabs her under her arms and pulls her to the foot of the stairs. There, he waits until the water rises enough to lift her up the stairs. He does this for two flights of stairs, finally standing on a bed in the attic so he can hold his wife's head above the water. It continues to rise until it reaches to his own neck, and he begins to seriously fear that he won't be able to save either one of them.

Then he realizes that the water has stopped rising, and in fact is beginning to drop. He clings to his wife so she won't float away, helping her hold her head above water until finally, he collapses on the bed. He can't feel his arms, from holding them over his head for so long. What he does feel is gratitude that their lives have been spared.

The residents of the ravaged towns come by constantly, thanking the Mennonites profoundly for their kind and generous service. Everyone is impressed by the quality and speed of their work. The effort lasts through Labor Day, with the ranks changing as people return to their jobs or home duties, but the Mennonites are able to maintain the strength of their force.

Their work widens to include towns all along the river, and they are joined by members of other congregations from as far away as Lancaster, including those of other faiths. They're also joined by factory workers, union members, and others who just want to help. They welcome all sincere offers, and the work gets done.

As the volunteers finish up their work on Labor Day, grateful Stroudsburg residents wave and thank them as the buses roll away. Their police escorts have a special tribute in store for them: expeditious passage through the thick holiday traffic heading out of the Poconos. They have cleared alternating lanes through each city and town, running their squads ahead of and following the convoy, sirens blaring and lights flashing. The church workers will arrive home quickly, if a little frazzled from the fast driving.

When the Stroudsburg project is tallied for reporting to the Conference, the Blooming Glen Mennonite Church will have logged

135 houses cleaned in Stroudsburg and 230 in East Stroudsburg, 12,000 man hours, and all expenses covered by donation from the providers. The North Penn Goodwill Service, in providing support to the workers, will report having served 7,000 cups of coffee, 6,000 cups of lime juice and water, 3,100 sandwiches, 4,400 doughnuts and buns, and 22 quarts of soup.

While their work earns eternal gratitude from those communities able to get back on their feet more quickly than would otherwise have been possible, the Mennonites of Blooming Glen will be left with other lasting legacies as well. Their Mennonite Disaster Service will continue on as a vital arm of their living faith, providing meaningful expression of their devotion to God through service to His children.

Another, less direct result of their volunteerism will later prove that an act of service, while intrinsically worthwhile on its own, can have value far beyond its original intent.

Throughout the day, calls come in to Bucks County CD head-quarters for police, fire police and National Guard units to serve as deterrents to sightseers and looters in most of the river towns. As rescues are completed, helicopters begin to deliver food, supplies, and equipment to needy areas.

Nine-year-old Frank McCaffrey's body is found, pulled from a tree limb below the level of the creek at Garfield Street between First and Second Streets in Stroudsburg. Though the heat has already begun its gruesome work, the body is easy to identify. Examiners find a wallet in his pocket, containing a photo of Frank and his younger brother, Mike, with their collie dog.

The brothers will remain separated for almost a year, but not by great distance. On May 10, 1956, Mike's skeletal remains, still wearing his undershorts and dungarees, will be unearthed by farmer Arthur Wiest, as he does the spring plowing at his farm, "Shadowbrook," along the Brodhead's banks south of Analomink.

A concerted effort is made to find the body of Rev. Davis' grandson, Billy Liebfred, including organized searches manned by members of their church congregation. Though intensive, the searches fail. Billy's body is encased in a deep layer of mud on the bank of the Brodhead at the end of Lenox Avenue, near where the elderly Fenners had spent the terrifying night on their roof in the Day Street Flats of East Stroudsburg. Over the winter, the rising and falling of the stream water wears away the covering, exposing Billy's skull. Two teenage boys, looking for sites to place beaver traps, stumble across it sticking up from the mud on January 24, 1956.

At ten thirty Saturday night, a stranger runs into a restaurant in Sparrowbush, New York, just a few miles west of Port Jervis. He reports to the owner, a volunteer fireman, that the Wallenpaupack Dam has broken. It's the nightmare that every Tri-State resident fears. The stranger adds that firemen are evacuating everyone in a community up the river. Since the restaurant's phone is out of commission, he goes out to Highway 6 and begins to stop cars, warning them of the impending danger.

The second car he stops happens to be that of the Sparrowbush Fire Captain, who goes straight to the firehouse and radios the Fire Base in Port Jervis. He announces, "Emergency—Stand by," and waits until the frequency clears. All radios on the band wait at firehouses, headquarters and trucks for his next message. The captain then reports that he has been told by the fireman from Lumberland that the dam has gone out.

In Port Jervis, the Fire Chief is on a truck, pumping out a flooded cellar when he hears the horrifying news. He notifies the radio operator at fire headquarters to ask for a repeat and identification of the sender, to which the Sparrowbush captain obliges. The Port Jervis chief then tells his radio operator to check with the dam itself, going through the Middletown Fire Base radio station.

Meanwhile, the chief fire radio operator in Jervis takes it upon himself to assist in communication. He receives a telephone call from a resident, stating that fire trucks are driving through town, sounding their sirens and shouting for people to get out because the dam has broken. He decides, independently, to broadcast to the town's fire trucks that he believes the report is false and that headquarters is verifying as they speak. He tells them they are acting without orders, and to "cut it the hell out and get back to the fire house."

It's too late. The panic has begun. Cars are now in the streets, and people are clamoring for everyone to get out of town. Residents wake their neighbors, groups of terrified citizens descend on City Hall, CD headquarters, and other official centers. Railroad employees call the ticket office downtown to see if they know anything.

Just across the river in Matamoras, a car full of people is careening down the main street of town, and they're all yelling for everyone to leave. Someone hears the call and runs like a madman to the firehouse, blowing the siren before anyone there knows what he's doing or can stop him. Many people take this to mean the dam has broken, as rumors of such an impending disaster have been floating since the rain began. A mass exodus to the surrounding cliffs and mountains begins. When a real siren blows later to call firefighters to the scene of a fancy motel restaurant, people don't even know what to think anymore.

Those in Port Jervis can hear the continued siren blast issuing from Matamoras, causing alarm even to those who haven't heard their own city's warnings. Though police and fire officials are checking with their local CD headquarters for verification with the dam authorities via shortwave radio, the rush is on. People are leaving their homes in droves, some still in their pajamas.

Just after midnight, radio station WDLC goes back on the air after its usual eleven p.m. sign-off, to broadcast an emergency message. City officials announce that they have spoken with authorities at Wallenpaupack Dam, who have assured them that the structure is intact and still functioning properly. The dam break story is a rumor, and people should return to their homes.

Fifteen hundred people have already fled the community, and it will be days before they all return home. Once there, they will dig out of the mud and pump out basements, but most of the city's homes are still standing. Jerry Walter, a recent high school graduate, returns to his job at Romano's Drug Store on Pike Street. He'll tell his boss that everything looks normal, but that's before he opens the door to find seven feet of water in the store's basement.

Two hundred guests must be saved from the isolated Eddy Farm Hotel in Sparrowbush, and the Red Cross declares the entire region a disaster area. Around 5,500 tons of stinking, muddy debris will be cleared and removed to special dumps, which are covered with fifty tons of lime to suppress the odor and further contamination. The panicked evacuation will serve as the basis for a groundbreaking 1958 study by the National Research Council, titled "The Effects of a Threatening Rumor on a Disaster-Stricken Community." Officials will spend a significant amount of time and energy tracing down the source of the rumor, and putting in place reporting structures to assure that such a dangerous situation doesn't happen again.

The polluted, stagnant floodwater is a perfect breeding ground for mosquitoes, and authorities are concerned about the potential for a major outbreak of malaria or other blood-borne disease. The Bucks County Mosquito Control Commission rushes sprayers into New Hope and the surrounding area as soon as the water recedes. Director Art Walter appeals to residents and businesses to do their part in keeping the dangerous pests down by emptying all boats, bottles, cans and boxes of any remaining floodwater.

The *New Hope Gazette* runs other health news on the front page, including rules for steering clear of problems during the recovery period. Some recommendations are the thorough cleaning of homes intruded on by the water, getting injections for typhus and tetanus for skin lacerations of any kind.

Another strongly urged precaution is the boiling of tap water for twenty minutes before being used for drinking or cooking. Wells of public places known to be contaminated are listed and readers are warned against drinking from them. The Bucks County Health Department suggests putting a diluted mixture of chloride of lime into wells that have been covered by floodwater or that lie below the flood-water level, warning that filters will not properly decontaminate a well.

The paper quotes water analyst Ned Harrington of Carversville as pronouncing A. L. Lewis' sand pit well as uncontaminated, and offering potable water. The flood will put several area firms, such as Benny's Drug Store, out of business for good, but it proves a boon to Ned Harrington's water analysis service. Helping the area recover its private and municipal drinking water supplies will keep him busy enough to hire more employees. They remain busy, working seven days a week for months afterward.

It's such a boost for business that Ned sells his soil sampling division so he can keep up with the water work.

He'll go on to write a series of articles about the flood for the *New Hope Gazette*. In these, he argues—against his own self-interest—for a municipal water system for New Hope, and chastises rural residents for lazy land management practices that contribute to run-off problems. It's a message that will arise again for Ned and others along the river from time to time, and one that will remain largely unheeded even fifty years later. Nevertheless, Ned prospers with the overwhelming amount of orders for his water analysis and related services, and will ironically owe a great deal of his professional success to the flood that really got him started.

Lorraine Fratto is reading the Sunday *Trenton Times*. Under the mistaken headline, "Evacuating South Warren Street Residents By Boat," a big photo on the front page shows two guys rowing a boat in front of the shops. The caption reads, "Here Vince Arnone and Gaza Toth, who had been on the job since 9 p.m. Friday, assist another woman from her flooded home." She realizes Vince hadn't gone fishing.

Vince Arnone and Gaza Toth are captured on film as they survey the scene on Trenton's flooded South Warren Street. Vince's fiancée, Lorraine Fratto, only learns what her betrothed had been up to by seeing the photo on the newspaper's front page.
– Reprinted by permission of The Times, *Trenton, N.J., 1955. All rights reserved.*

360

The phone rings, and it's Vince. They laugh over the newspaper photo, and she teases him about being famous. He invites her to go with him to Mercer Airport. He hears there's an enterprising pilot at Ronson Aviation offering sightseeing flyovers of the flood area for fifteen bucks a seat. They take the trip with about twenty other people, and the pilot flies them down almost to Philadelphia, over the Fairless Steel Mill, along the Pennsylvania side of the river up past Riegelsville, then back down the Jersey side.

Seeing all the destruction to the north and hearing about the worst of it in the Poconos makes Vince and Lorraine realize how lucky Trenton is only to have experienced limited flood damage. It's an inconvenience not to have running water, especially for three weeks right before their wedding, but overall, they've been lucky.

In fact, about three hundred families had been evacuated under sometimes dangerous and trying conditions, directed by Freeholder William Falcey, Mercer County's CD coordinator. Ironically, the river had nearly invaded the State House in Trenton while it was in session with a hearing concerning drought control. Is boilers had been turned off to protect them from bursting, just in case the river did infiltrate, but it never did.

On his long way out of Stroudsburg on Friday, Harry Leida had passed by Miller's Butcher Shop on Rt. 611, just before he entered Bartonsville to turn down a back road toward Saylorsburg. Thomas Miller's establishment is popular for his excellent homemade sausage and bologna, and he moves quite a bit of inventory. To keep up with demand, he has installed a walk-in freezer to store the large sides of beef and pork he needs to make these specialties. Today, though, something different is being preserved in the deep cold of the freezer.

Thomas' son Wilmer, 28, like most able-bodied young men in the area, has been helping with the search and recovery effort for flood victims. This morning, he has gone with his friend, Dan Warner, to help bring bodies from where they have been recovered to a large, refrigerated trailer near the armory in East Stroudsburg. Dan is one of several funeral directors who have been brought to Clearview School by the authorities to process the great number of flood victims' bodies.

Once the bodies are trucked or airlifted to the school—depending on where they've been found—and legal paperwork begun on each, they are moved to the armory trailer. From there, they are prepared for identification and preservation until next of kin can be contacted and brought into the disaster area.

The problem is a lack of permanent morgue facilities. Those of the few funeral homes in the twin boroughs have a capacity for five bodies at most, planned for large auto or work accidents. All of them are filled by early morning on Sunday. By the end of the day, seventeen of the East Stroudsburg victims' bodies will be recovered, along with all four Stroudsburg victims (including the ladies from the bingo hall), and twenty of those from Camp Davis. And everyone knows there will be more on the way.

Dan Warner turns to Wilmer and asks if he thinks his father might allow them to use his walk-in freezer to store some of the bodies until they're claimed. Wilmer wonders about the sanitary issues, seeing as how food is stored there, too. Dan explains that by the time the bodies make it to the freezer, they will have been frozen and enclosed in locked steel containers. Personal effects will be attached to the outside of the containers for use in identification. Once someone makes a positive ID, the bodies will be taken back to the funeral home for burial. At no time will the food be exposed directly to the bodies.

Wilmer doesn't see how Thomas can refuse, and the two young men approach his father. As expected, Thomas understands the urgency of the need and gives his permission. Now the men must return to the refrigerated trailer to take the bodies to be frozen by high-powered motors procured by the Monroe County Coroner.

Wilmer moves among the bodies as he and Dan pick out those they've been assigned to. They're the Camp Davis victims. One large man is unable to remain well-covered by the sheet that has been laid over him. He had died clutching a tree limb, and the recovery crew had been unable to detach it from his rigor mortis grip. So he now lay on his back, arms sticking straight up in an unsettling pose, which appears to Wilmer a gesture of supplication. They have to put the man in a body bag, and eventually the steel container, with his arms still reaching out. It's a vision that will haunt Wilmer's memory for the rest of his life.

As the days wear on after the flood, and the area becomes more accessible to sightseers, Wilmer's wife, Susan, must chase away ghoulish thrill-seekers trying to get a glimpse of the bodies. She explains that the bodies are locked inside sealed containers, so there's nothing to see, anyway. Gee, some people! she thinks.

Monday, August 22, 1955

Cliff Slack drives back up through Trenton from the Jersey Shore to New Hope to take his wife, Laura, to work in the morning. She knows the bank will be a mess, and it's the first time she'll ever go to work in shorts, because the work will be hot and dirty.

The tellers, when they'd heard a flood was on the way, had called safe deposit box holders to come get their things, because the boxes were going to be inundated. Most people had made it in, but some who didn't lost their valuables.

The town's firemen come in to lift heavy accounting machines so the girls can clean underneath them. Bank directors armed with hair dryers are restoring soaked legal documents, and Laura and her fellow tellers today look more like laundresses. Lined up at ironing boards, they're drying and flattening stock certificates and bonds that had been underwater. Some certificates have more serious problems than rippled paper. The EE Series war bonds issued by the U.S. Postal Service had not been typed, but handwritten, and all the ink has washed off. To avert a crisis, they're all shipped back to the main Federal Bank building in Chicago to be replaced.

Laura looks around at everyone pitching in to make things right again, and thinks maybe not everything about the flood is bad. Unfortunately, not everyone can see through to the other side. At least two people who lose their homes commit suicide.

The *Easton Express* runs a small notice informing parents of campers from the Lutheran Ministerium complex, including Camps Miller and Hagan, that their children will be delivered at the clover-leaf intersection of Routes 611 and 402 near Stroudsburg, where they can be picked up during daylight hours.

Another story, headlined "Children Safe in 36 Camps In Pocono District," assures worried parents that the Red Cross is reporting all campers safe after a helicopter tour on Sunday. It lists the camps by name, also reporting the success of the emergency airlifts on the Delaware River islands.

Marie Petranto's group of campers finally learn that Campfire Girls administrators have called all their parents to tell them where to pick up their children. On Monday, with the river safely back within its banks and no longer threatening the bridges, they're bussed back across the Frenchtown Bridge and south to re-cross at Trenton's upper bridge, where they're finally dropped off at the Trenton YWCA.

Her mother is grateful she's safe and glad to see her, but when they hug, she pulls back.

You smell dreadful! she tells Marie.

In a statement that could come directly from a mother's handbook of nightmare scenarios, Marie explains that all the counselors had to stand in the water while the campers were in boats, and how they saw the cesspools opening up all around them.

Marie and the other girls haven't really noticed the smell themselves, since they all smell alike, but her clothes are ruined and she can't wait to take a bath and get cleaned up.

As they're driving home, Marie sees a pinball machine floating near Stacy Park and laughs. She and her friends Elsie and Marie become celebrities in the following weeks, sitting on interview panels fielding media questions at the Hotel Hildebrecht and Hotel Stacy Trent. It's a heady experience for the young ladies.

Within days, they all develop quarter-sized sores all over their bodies from exposure to the contaminated water. They have to go to Junior High Number Three for a three-week series of typhus shots. The sores leave long-lasting scars when they heal, but all three girls are able to return to school on time when it starts.

Two weeks after their rescue, the three become curious about what had happened to the camp. They borrow a rowboat and set out from the Pennsylvania side of the river to the island. They can't believe the utter devastation. Nothing is left of the camp. No buildings are standing, except a battered remnant of the mess hall. It's the last time they'll go to the island, and the end of Marie's tenure as a Campfire Girl.

She'll go on to marry and become a Campfire Boys and Girls den mother when her sons are little, but the flood has left more than physical scars as a mark on her life. After the trauma of the helicopter rides, she never likes to fly; an ironic twist for someone who makes her living as a travel agent.

At four thirty on the afternoon of Tuesday, August twenty-third, Col. Angster determines that his base's mission has been fulfilled, and terminates the Command Post of Operation Tempest Rapids. Although Tobyhanna Signal Depot will continue to render aid to the surrounding area as requested, the official mission is over. With assistance from Fort Eustis, Virginia, the officers, soldiers and civilian employees of Tobyhanna have wrought near-miracles for their civilian neighbors.

Over the past fifty-seven hours, the helicopter and amphibious aircraft pilots have flown 794 missions, during which they delivered 403,000 pounds of equipment, supplies, food, and medical serum. They have evacuated 795 civilians from dangerous situations to places of safety, performed 42 search and reconnaissance sorties, and evacuated 43 bodies from where they have been found to the temporary morgue at Clearview School.

The Army has issued for civilian use 22 generators, 1,422 batteries, a ton of lime to keep down the smell and infectiousness of exposed cesspools and open sewage, and 5,000 units of typhus vaccine. They have distributed 48,000 quarts of milk from the stranded train to those who had no food at all, along with 3,000 pounds of bread, 200 cases of C Rations, and 100,000 Halizone tablets to treat contaminated water before drinking.

Never again will the inhabitants of the rural Poconos look upon their military neighbor as a large, faceless entity with no connection to their lives. On August 31, the General Assembly in the Pennsylvania State House will issue a resolution on behalf of the commonwealth, expressing their gratitude to all the military, civil, and charitable agencies associated with the gargantuan relief effort.

The Tinsman family has their work cut out for them in recovering from the flood. After the water recedes, they will waste no time in cleaning up the old yard and building the new one. Still, the effects are long-lasting: they won't be fully restocked until the summer of 1957.   *– Collection Bill & Sue Tinsman*

Bill and Sue Tinsman had already been thinking about moving the lumberyard before the storm, but the flood now lends urgency to the situation. Bill calls J. C. Malloy Realty, with whom he and his dad have been chatting. They begin serious discussions about buying a lot with a summer cottage on it, farther downtown but higher up the hill.

They've never even been inside the house, but anything seems more attractive than having to stay in their house on Fleecydale Road, which has had water up to the ceiling on the first floor. By week's end, they'll own the house and move into it, using the previous owner's furniture and salvaging what they can from their flooded home. It will be a couple years before they can rehabilitate the old place enough to sell it.

The lumberyard is a complete wreck. They've lost much of their stock, and some of what's left is ruined. Friends and neighbors help them recover some lumber that has come to rest in an eddy below the pedestrian bridge. They have a flood sale, where they offer the damaged goods at serious price reductions to move it out and make room for cleanup.

The Tinsmans and their employees begin the long process of building proper facilities in the new upper yard, moving stock up there, and cleaning up the old yard. They'll build stock racks to accommodate forklift trucks, a huge improvement on the old manual method. It will take three or four years to completely clean up the mucky mess. They'll end up keeping both yards, but will drop their oil and coal supply sidelines to concentrate on building supplies. People's efforts at cleanup and rebuilding their own damaged places will keep Tinsman Lumber busy for years to come, and the surrounding communities will recover together.

Across the river to the north, young Howard Opdyke sees an opportunity that may not come again. He approaches Harry Niece, Sr. about the possibility of buying what's left of Niece's lumberyard in Frenchtown, on the river bank just to the north of the bridge. He hasn't a lot of capital, but then, there's not much left of the yard—it has sustained forty thousand dollars in damage. What's still valuable is mainly the location, a few buildings in need of repair, some spotty, damaged stock, and the customer list. Still, Howard sees it as a start on a future, and Harry appreciates an ambitious young entrepreneur.

The pitiful remnants of Niece's lumber yard in Frenchtown will become the basis for the very successful H.J. Opdyke Lumber, still a vital Delaware Valley merchant fifty years later.   *– Hunterdon County Democrat photo*

Frenchtown businesses will have a huge amount of work to do before they can open for business again, but they pull it off with aplomb.

– Hunterdon County Democrat photo

The transaction is made, and Harry generously holds the note so the young man can get a secure foothold with new inventory until he can pay it off. Howard appreciates the break, and works hard, slowly building inventory and a steady customer base. By 1958, he manages with help from family and a good staff to do well enough that the company can relocate to a less flood-vulnerable address. Thus begins the reign of H. J. Opdyke Lumber Company as one of the area's most solid and well-known businesses, still going strong fifty years later.

Other Frenchtown businesses won't be so lucky. The A&P Food Store takes some water, which endangers its grocery stock. It will have to endure a long, thorough cleanup before re-opening. Bieber's Feed Mill, taking water from Nishisakawick Creek as well as the river, has water to its windowsills. The road in front looks like a Venetian canal, with motorboats patrolling for looters and stranded people. The Pennsylvania Railroad station is also up to its windows in water, which crests at four o'clock on Saturday morning.

Large area employers such as Frenchtown Porcelain Company, Frederick A. Krause Associates plastic factory, and Gulf Oil bulk distribution facility all suffer considerable damage.

After being inundated by water, Kerr Chickeries then suffers an outbreak of fire. Aside from Kerr, other heavy poultry loss is incurred by farmer Abraham Mozes. Located west of the Atlantic bulk plant on the Milford Road, the farm's breeder house is completely submerged, drowning six thousand hens. In the sizzling days that follow, neighbors would call local officials to complain of the stench from their decomposing bodies. Alexandria Township's Board of Health will draw the unsavory task of collecting the carcasses for disposal in a mass trench.

Water has covered the Frenchtown-Uhlerstown Bridge by four inches, and about 450 feet of telephone cable has been ripped away from underneath. Unlike Upper Black Eddy, its cross-river neighbor, Frenchtown doesn't lose any houses. A total of seventy-five homes had been evacuated, with two hundred people taking refuge at the Fidelity Post of the American Legion. But most are already home, starting the cleanup.

After their rescue duties during the height of the flood emergency, firefighters are kept busy pumping out basements, shown here on Lambertville's North Union Street. Those who are helped by this public service won't soon forget.

– Collection Heather Buchanan

Lambertville has taken water as far east as south Main Street, where there's still a foot-and-a-half standing between Mount Hope and Bridge Streets. Again, no homes have washed away, though two are almost completely underwater. An evacuee shelter is operating at the Baptist Church, and the bridge to New Hope, though damaged on one span, has reopened to emergency traffic.

Choc Edwards finally makes it home after three days' straight duty with the Bridge Commission. After cleaning up his father's place with bleach and soapy water, he and Mikey pitch in to help their neighbors clean up their houses. When she's not cleaning, Mikey is down at the Acme, helping to put the shelves back upright and moving all the spoiled groceries to the dumpster. The Edwardses witness dozens of homes getting their basements pumped out, and like everyone else, begin to get used to the horrid smell issuing from the mud that covers everything.

Fifty years later, Mikey's still as feisty as ever. When asked if she concerns herself with the possibility of the river flooding again, she replies in typical fashion. "If you let that stuff worry you, you'd be in the nuthouse!"

Young Barbara Fletcher is relieved to know her uncle and cousin are returning to their home on Union Street, where her aunt had remained through the flood. She decides to visit them and notices that underground septic tanks are surfacing, springing up through the spongy ground from all the pressure put on them by the heavy floodwaters. Her aunt tells her that most of their furniture, including many antiques, will have to be discarded. The whole sad adventure will stick with her for the rest of her life, and she'll always wonder what happened to the old lady and her cat.

Barbara Fletcher Stires will move away from the river, consciously choosing not to live anywhere near the floodplain. But she still enjoys the river and the canal, walking the towpath and along the riverbank when she gets the chance. As she looks out over the lazy, swirling waters of the Delaware on a warm summer's day, she'll often recall when those clear waters turned muddy and angry, inspiring anything but serenity.

The immense hydraulic pressure put on saturated ground by the sheer weight of the water flowing over normally dry land has the effect of literally squeezing some septic and other tanks to the surface, as is visible at right in this photo from North Union Street in Lambertville. — Collection Heather Buchanan

By the time it's all over, Hunterdon County will declare over four million dollars in damage, and Bucks County will claim seventeen million, not including bridge damage. Hurricane Diane, having torn up the entire eastern seaboard with her damage, will make her way into the history books as the nation's first Billion Dollar Hurricane.

☼

In Raven Rock, New Jersey, the roadbed of a concrete-and-stone bridge is pulverized into little more than a pile of rubble. One home is left hanging halfway out in space, where its foundation has been washed away. Its owner will stabilize it with a quick carpentry brace until he can return solid earth beneath it. A new house on Raven Rock Road still stands upright, but is several yards away from the foundation it had been built upon.

The Belvidere Division of the Pennsylvania Railroad, running from Raven Rock to Stockton, has its tracks hanging in midair in some spots, the bank and ballast washed from beneath it. An emergency track laying project by work crews will have it restored within the week.

371

In Stockton, the Red Cross is serving about four hundred flood victims a day at their canteen. Without power or access to their homes, some people are having trouble taking care of even the most basic needs. Down the street, someone's chicken coop has come to rest on Bridge Street in front of one home, looking for all the world like it has pulled up to wait for some takeout food.

Greta Johnson is helping her parents sort through the wreckage of their home. The heavy wood door of the house is completely missing, so they take off their shoes and slide through the eighteen inches of mud to see if they can find anything worth salvaging.

Her mother's recipes are gone, as is her father's oak rolltop desk. Greta's clothes are missing from their storage place in the summer kitchen, but she does manage to locate all twelve pieces of her mother's set of carved bone-handled German silverware. The crocheted circles her mom has been making for her wedding gift, a bedspread, are all gone. The Johnsons shine flashlights into the remaining water but can see nothing but dark mud.

Mr. Johnson decides that now's the time to make their big move, instead of trying to recover in a rented house. He takes off work to finish the new house, using the money he has saved for supplies to turn it into a one-story Cape Cod model.

They'll start over with no furniture, but relatives come from New Hampshire to help her dad install the front picture window and other finishing touches. By Greta's wedding the following August, she's able to walk through the newly made plank door for her photos.

For years, she'll notice left-over debris still hanging in trees along the river. When her grown son moves into a home of his own along the Delaware, she'll feel compelled to constantly remind him to pay attention to the weather. And yet Greta Johnson Fresco stays in the area after all the destruction, putting down business roots as well, with a gift shop in Lahaska, across the river.

Just to the north in Byram, four of the summer colony's thirty-seven homes are gone, washed away by the flood. The rest bear scars from the beatings they've received from all manner of flotsam driven by the river. Backyards are littered with ruined furniture, television sets, wrecked lawn chairs, and bashed-up canoes jumbled together in standing water.

Carol Turner's family has returned to their cottage to find it lodged against a tree. Their garages are gone, and they find much of their furniture several houses away. Her terrier, Shimpy, is running about, sticking his nose into myriad corners and holes among the wreckage. To a dog, all the new and different scents are worthy of days' scampering about.

Carol's family is told they must report to the high school for typhoid shots. When they return, the fire company hoses away the worst of the mud, and the Turner family settles in to the seemingly endless task of wiping everything down with disinfectant. Her father contacts contractors to arrange the reseating of the cottage on its foundation. For the rest of the summer, they'll work at getting everything back to normal, even returning after school starts again to make sure it'll be decent to come back to next year.

The approach to the bridge that had carried traffic across the Delaware to Point Pleasant juts out into midair, looking somewhat lost. There are friends of Carol's in Point Pleasant that she'll never see again because the bridge never gets rebuilt. Besides the cost, one issue that keeps a replacement from being built is the lack of adequate space

The Point Pleasant-Byram Bridge is one of the conveniences of life that will never return to mid-river residents after the flood. Government budgetary studies will determine that it's not a financially viable project.

– Collection Carol Turner Wolf

to create a new access that will conform to building codes. From then on, the Turners will have to get to their cottage by crossing the river at Centre Bridge and driving up on the winding road through Stockton, since Hwy. 29 does not yet exist.

More friendships will go by the wayside when they learn that new zoning codes, enacted after the flood, disallow the rebuilding of cottages in the river's floodplain. There is one saving grace, though. With everyone pulling together to recover from the flood, neighbors who remain get to know each other better. The relationships are soon made official with the birth of the Byram Colony Association, which keeps the neighbors connected over the winter and provides social activities to entertain them in summer.

Reporter Dick Harpster will stay busy for weeks at the *Newark Evening News* with stories about the flood, its victims, and cleanup efforts. The event will help him solidify his reputation as a pro reporter. He later learns that a businessman from the Delaware Water Gap has salvaged much of the lumber from the old Portland-Columbia covered bridge, and has used it to build a summer home.

Up in Branchville, Mayor Willard Decker sits in a state of shock in front of the firehouse, which functions as the command center for salvage operations. The mayor has always been a booster for his city, and just three years earlier had sponsored the publication of a booklet on Branchville, titled "The Borough Beautiful." Many will come to believe that seeing his beloved hometown so ravaged contributed to his death, which occurs not long after the flood.

Forty-three-year-old Wilhelm Struss, a crane operator, is working on repairs to one of the town's damaged bridges. He gets down from his seat to help guide a ball hammer suspended from the crane, while the machine is being unloaded from its trailer. Suddenly, the machine goes off-balance and its arm swings into a power line carrying 4,300 volts of electricity. Wilhelm is instantly electrocuted. He is unable to be revived, though rescue crews will try for an hour.

As is so common in the wake of disaster, rumors run rampant everywhere, and few people know what's true and what isn't. New Jersey and Pennsylvania police are searching the river for four to six bodies that have been reported floating between Burlington and

Philadelphia. Nothing is found by boats or helicopters patrolling the waters.

Governor Robert Meyner's cabinet is meeting in an emergency session in Trenton to plan a strategy to cope with what is being called the worst disaster in the state's history. State CD officials are reporting that nearly four thousand people have been evacuated from home and work. Many others have reached a place of safety on their own. Civil Defense is working with the Pennsylvania governor's cabinet across the river to begin the process of restoring several broken bridge connections between the states.

In the midst of too much water, the state legislature continues its hearings on impounding river water for a New Jersey reservoir. Despite their immediate situation, nobody has forgotten the frighteningly dry summer that has just ended, and farmers aren't satisfied to depend solely on the whims of nature. Studies will be done, people will speak out on behalf of or against several different proposals. Eventually, the whole argument will be folded into the larger issue of damming the Delaware, both for flood control and water supply functions.

In Phillipsburg, the gas station across from what remains of Jim's Doggie Stand gleams wetly in the sunlight. The water is going down, revealing where the Delaware's waters have rushed through and the random nature of their destruction. Windows are broken, but their window boxes remain. Inside, battered red and white petunias still bloom, having clung to their soil as the deadly waters surged over them. It's a brave sight that gives hope to those who must begin rebuilding their lives and homes.

Traffic again flows over the Route 22 toll bridge into Easton, and work is already being done on the Free Bridge to get it back into commission. Stephen Mahl is a young laborer working for a subcontractor to Bell Telephone in the project to lay conduit that will carry cables beneath the repaired deck. These will replace those ripped away with the bridge's middle span. The conduits Stephen is replacing will carry the long distance line from New York and along the east coast. Others will replace torn-out electrical lines, local and long distance phone cables and water lines.

The Northampton Street Free Bridge, with its twisted and sagging deck, is a dangerous place to work for contractors replacing cabling for the all-important power and communications wires that have been torn out by the Delaware.

– River Jim Abbott photo

Unfortunately for Stephen and his boss, the job isn't a simple installation procedure. First the workers must jackhammer out the pavement on the approach to the bridge to access the lines they'll need to splice into. Those are located about five feet below the surface. Stephen is mainly a jackhammer operator, so he's immediately busy. Time is of the essence, since restoration of power and communication are of the utmost importance to everyone. This means exhausting work schedules for the work crews.

Stephen spends his first week on the job working around the clock, seven solid days. Temperatures are in the mid-to-high nineties, and it's backbreaking work. At first light, his duty is to start the compressors so there will be power built up for the air hammers by the time his crewmates arrive on the job. They can't just be left on, because they're too noisy and expensive to run around the clock. Then he jackhammers all day. When that shift ends, he becomes an auxiliary bridge guard, as much to protect equipment and the site from vandals and thieves as to make sure no one goes out on the ruptured bridge.

One of the official bridge guards, employed by the Bridge Commission, feels sorry for this young buck. He allows Stephen to sleep in the guard shack on the northeast corner of the crossing for a couple hours a night, while he keeps an eye on things. He wakes Stephen before going home each morning.

When the ditches are dug and the new cables spliced in, the crew must clear away all the debris that has collected on the underside of the bridge. They're required to wear safety ropes in case they fall, but most of the guys think of them more as a death sentence than a safety net. If they do fall into the water, the ropes will swing them up in the current and slam them against the underside of the bridge. It could be hard to get out of a wet rope and pull themselves to safety. Many of the guys simply slip out of the ropes as soon as they're out of the supervisor's sight. They'd rather take their chances against the river on their own.

On his first under-bridge foray, Stephen's never seen anything jammed so tightly with small twigs and various pieces of junk. They can't even work until they uncover the old conduits from all this buildup. It's hot, filthy, tedious and time-consuming work.

There's another crew on the Phillipsburg side doing the same thing, and working toward them. When they've finally got the conduit in place and the cables strung through it, the problem arises of how to get the lines across the gap in the span. The missing bridge deck hasn't even been bid out for replacement yet, but this work won't wait for that to happen, so they have to get creative. After numerous different approaches prove unsuccessful, the men get frustrated. Finally, Stephen suggests they get a bow and arrow, attach a line to it, then shoot it across. To that, they'll attach a heavier line, which in turn will pull the first cable end across. Everyone laughs, but then they realize that it just might work. It does.

While they're under the bridge deck, stringing the new cables, the men can look down and see all kinds of stuff still coming down the river. Refrigerators, oil tanks, picnic tables, and vehicle parts fly past, just inches below their feet. The water has turned from muddy brown to black, now draining off the dust of the coalfields and the topsoil of farm fields above Easton. Some of the debris that sticks up out of the water is still catching on the bridge, and the guys have to be careful not to get thumped and knocked off the girders by something passing below. It's a risky job.

It's also kind of frightening. Besides the danger of passing wreckage, there is the mystery factor. When the crew are pulling things out of the structure, they come across all kinds of mess. One day, a guy pulls out something that looks like a finger, and the rest of his crew gather around to check it out. Finally, they realize it's just a hot dog. That's when it occurs to them that none of them have had any kind of shots, and they're not wearing gloves. The problem is they couldn't reach into the small holes with gloves on, so they forego the safety accessory.

There's also the eeriness of the inky black water once the sun goes down, and…that other thing. The shooting thing.

When Stephen had first come out on the bridge in the evening, he'd talked for a while with a National Guardsman about enforcing the curfew. At one point, the Guard had looked right at him and said, "If you see any bastard looting, shoot 'em. Don't wait." It's rather a daunting responsibility for a young man with no law enforcement training. Fortunately, he never encounters such a situation.

Stephen's favorite time on the job is the morning. As he goes down to start up the compressors, the Red Cross comes around with their mobile canteen on Northampton Street. They park just above the waterline that shows where the flood has reached, and he walks up. Fortified by their good coffee and doughnuts, he's ready for another day. Two weeks later, his job is finished, and another crew comes in to complete the re-cabling operation.

Within days, an Easton man named George Stanko will decide he doesn't want to walk to the toll bridge or the temporary Bailey bridges the Army had erected upriver when he wants to get back across from a trip to a Phillipsburg tavern. He manages to get past the guard, and begins inching his way over the top of the bundled cables running between the permanent conduits that Stephen's crew and the others have installed across the gap in the bridge.

The guard suddenly notices him and starts yelling to get off of it and come back to the edge, but George isn't hearing it. He just wants to get home. He continues crawling on the cables, but then loses his balance and slips off. Down he falls, into the still swirling water. People on both sides can hear him splashing and crying for help, but it's no use. Nobody can reach him in time.

George will be the last official victim of the Hurricane Diane flood in Easton.

The bridge deck will be repaired by a $300,000 contract to Bethlehem Steel in 1956. While it's being fixed, engineers discover that the constant, prolonged force of the floodwater has stretched many of the original structural members, and they must be replaced. In the end, 220 tons of steel will be replaced. The job is finished ahead of schedule, and traffic is flowing again before Halloween of 1957. The "Gibraltar of the Delaware" has been saved.

Electric power is restored to most of Easton on August 26, 1955. Restaurants that had been submerged in the flood are returning to business as they show proof of sanitary conditions to the health department. The Red Cross opens a disaster office at the Moose Home, which also serves the Raubsville and Portland areas, and at least 130 people register for aid. Flooded-out residents are still quartered at their shelter at St. Mark's Evangelical and Reformed Church.

Ironically, the flood has caused a severe shortage of potable water, through damage and contamination. The city issues a proclamation prohibiting the use of city water except for domestic and public food preparation and minimum sanitary standards. This order effectively shuts down many businesses, adding to one of the hidden causes of suffering in the disaster. Many people lose workdays, and therefore paydays, making them victims of the flood even if they haven't been directly affected. The shortage will continue until the pumps at the Easton Water Company are repaired and back in operation, and the city's reservoir is refilled.

In a harbinger of cultural things to come, an early telethon is held by station WGLV on channels 3, 4, and 5 in the Lehigh Valley area. Performers and entertainers from New York appear and appeal for funds to help flood victims in Allentown, Bethlehem, and Easton. Civic service clubs in the area staff the phones, and contributors who bring their donations to the station are promised a chance to appear on camera. Even in the midst of carnage and destruction, the American fascination with celebrity is alive and kicking.

Like so much of the world, though, the Delaware Valley won't have much time to focus on frivolity before the second half of the century turns ugly. As it digs itself out of the muck, it will find itself embroiled in the Tocks Island Dam debate. One of the most vicious and divisive political battles ever fought, it's another of the flood's legacies.

By the time that contest reaches fever pitch, America will have stumbled its way through the civil unrest of the sixties and the assassinations of the Kennedys and Dr. Martin Luther King Jr. Hippies and flower children will be the social concern of the day, along with the war in Vietnam. That war will be gasping its last, but still exerting an influence on the nation strong enough to change the course of events in the Delaware Valley.

Regardless of what comes after, the flood of 1955 has left an indelible mark on the Valley. Even as those whose lives were directly touched by the surging waters pass from among us, they leave behind their stories and images to remind us that ours is a place in nature, not on top of it. Their experiences prove that we are—like all of creation—connected, and that what happens to one, happens to all. It's a lesson we'll do well to heed as developing technology tempts us ever closer to believing we can insulate ourselves from the vagaries of a living planet.

Epilogue

The River's Trembling Edge

The question of character and identity between the Delaware River and those with interests in the land on either side has been a constant back-and-forth throughout history. During times of upheaval, this motion has built to a tension that has resonated through life in the valley like music sings through a taut guitar string. During the natural upheaval of the 1955 flood, the tension is caused by immediate life-or-death struggles. During the inevitable man-made upheaval that will follow it, the banks of the Delaware will be pulled back and forth so often and so hard that it will tremble with rage and uncertainty.

When all is said and done, there will be a total of 184 (or 200, depending on your sources) deaths on America's Eastern Seaboard from the Hurricane Diane floods. 99 of those are in the Delaware Valley and watershed; 88 in Pennsylvania (along with 94 serious injuries) and 11 in New Jersey. It's a bitter pill for the stricken areas to swallow, on top of all the destruction and property loss. Despite the fact that natural disasters are usually out of anyone's control, many people in the affected areas succumb to the all-too-human tendency to seek a scapegoat onto which to pour their sense of loss and grief and anger.

The first and most obvious place to lay the blame is on the waterways themselves, particularly the Delaware River. Before the waters have even receded, calls for flood control scream off the editorial pages of newspapers and from the floors of statehouses. Everyone and their brothers have an opinion about "what should be done," though few truly understand the cause of the problem.

The reactive nature of politics touches off a flurry of demands for dams, levees and other structures to be built, with the intent of controlling nature's waterways. Rarely considered is something much more readily controlled: the behavior of those who put themselves in harm's way by choosing to build, live and work in the natural flood-plain of these waterways.

Little discussed among those clamoring for the government to "do something" is many people's unwillingness to acknowledge that the beauty and atmosphere of a life beside the river comes at a price. What really needs to be done is for everyone to acknowledge that trade-off, and make informed and honest choices about what they can and can't put up with.

Even along the river's tributaries, the choices are the same. Part of the massive destruction along the Brodhead Creek near the Stroudsburgs has been due to a Depression-era WPA project that had straightened the creek's natural curves. At the time it was done, the practice was not only condoned but recommended, based on the mistaken assumption that a straight waterway would be more easily maintained and controlled.

The last part is correct: It's far more convenient and less labor-intensive to mow grass, perform testing and equipment installations, and drive maintenance vehicles along a straight, smooth bank than a curved, bumpy one. But as experience and empirical research will prove, straightening (and sometimes even paving) any water channel has a frightfully effective and undesirable result: it actually speeds up the water's flow. This strengthens its destructive power during flooding. Effectively controlling such speed once it has been attained is nearly impossible, making any such waterway a coiled snake waiting to strike. It's never a matter of if, but when.

The corollary to this concept is that regardless of the care and engineering that may go into the re-routing of a streambed, nature usually wins in the long run. Engineered streams usually return—one way or another—to their original channels, or cut new ones that include a curving path of least resistance.

That the Brodhead had re-cut its channel in several places during the flood is irrefutable evidence of this. Many other streams, including ones in and around Scranton, had done the same, and those had been so violent that they literally changed the landscape forever.

The curves of a river or stream, along with the growth of plants and trees and the presence of rocks and other objects in and along its channel, slow the current through naturally occurring friction. Remove those obstacles, and you form a veritable chute that acts much like the ice tunnel in an Olympic luge competition. It provides a straight channel with smooth sides, creating the ideal environment for unimpeded speed — exactly the opposite of what you want in an urban or even semi-rural area near any sizable human population.

While the outcry for dams and other huge flood mitigation projects grabs the spotlight in the waning months of 1955, another school of thought is quietly taking hold in less visible parts of the Delaware Valley. In living rooms and around picnic tables, on lunch breaks and in the corners of classrooms, the flood has sparked another kind of conversation.

The jarring experience of the great flood induces introspection in some thoughtful people. It forces them to take a new approach to thinking about waterways. Instead of assigning fault and blame to insentient natural features, this discussion is more interested in applying common sense and claiming personal responsibility for human actions and decisions. Rather than being a divisive debate about who uses what and how they should be compensated, this conversation uses words such as "stewardship" and "conservation" and "interconnection."

It's a new conversation, at least among non-academic or -scientific types, that begins exploring ideas about the land, water and sky as parts of a larger, singular organism. It is the extension of a young environmental ethic based on the life work and writings of such pioneers as John Muir, Aldo Leopold, Sigurd Olsen and Pennsylvania's own Gifford Pinchot, and it will give birth in this region to the "watershed way of thinking."

This concept treats the land and its waterways as intimately interlocked with all other elements of nature, each as important as the other, and all invariably dependent on the health and viability of each other. It sees the natural influence exerted by and on waterways as occurring independently of human-imposed political boundaries.

A year after the flood, the popular *Bucks County Traveller* magazine runs a three-page article explaining the watershed idea to casual readers. It reports that several new watershed associations have formed, and that a few older ones are already implementing flood plans as part of their overall water management efforts. It holds up Solebury Township's Honey Hollow Creek organization and the Brandywine Valley Association as prime models, and reports recent efforts to form similar groups on the Perkiomen, Wissahickon and Neshaminy watersheds.

It's a still-small voice, but the ears into which it whispers belong to active, energetic and passionate believers. Some come to the idea through a natural extension of their personal beliefs. Others will be yanked in by a huge threat to their ways of life. In the years to come, these people will give the watershed movement a voice with which to be heard. As a kite that rises against the wind, this voice will begin to soar when it meets the resistance of overwhelming political force.

After the water recedes, Allentown will finally abandon attempts to develop the flood-prone land in its industrial valley along the Lehigh River. Funds are appropriated to clean it up and return it to mostly natural parklands, greenways and recreational areas. It will become the site of many of the city's local festivals in the latter part of the twentieth century, but will retain its problematic tendency to flood.

Robert Neyhart had been able to find a CD worker on his way to Analomink, to whom he gave his carrier pigeons. The CD worker had agreed to take the two birds to the place where Robert had said his daughter, Mary Ann, was supposed to be staying.

Later that day, the first bird had shown up back at Neyhart's home, carrying news of his daughter's safety. It was soon followed by the second bird, whose leg had another message strapped to its leg. Robert unwrapped it, reading, "There's a ferry taking people across at Stokes Mill. Meet me on the other side." Much relieved, he blessed his pigeons and headed for Stokes Mill.

In Stroudsburg, even after she rebuilds her wardrobe and her life, things won't be the same again for Helen Brown. In recognition of her service during the flood, she is tapped for a seat on the Monroe County Civil Defense council. She helps create a county-wide emergency management plan for mass care centers. This gets her noticed by the folks in Harrisburg, who ask her to come there to be a CD coordinator. She moves her travel trailer to the state capitol to work on the plan all the next summer.

When she returns, she notices the beginning of a great influx of people to her beloved Stroud Township, which had had a population around six thousand people when she was growing up. Fifty years later, that figure will grow to 150,000. Helen will mourn the loss of the small-town feeling of her home, and marvel at how many of the newcomers know nothing of the great cataclysm that has shaped their world.

The flood will, at best estimate, cost Monroe County $11,000,000 in damage to industry, $1,000,000 to commercial interests and shops, and $1,591,000 to residences, with 96 of them destroyed and 690 wrecked beyond habitability. 74 of its citizens and visitors will be dead, and some of their bodies will never be found. They will remain, fifty years later, beneath the dried mud of the Brodhead Creek or lodged somewhere under the waters of the Delaware River.

But even the worst of disasters have their hidden benefits. In Monroe County, those come in an amazing show of hometown pride and neighborly concern. One of the affected industries, the Ronson Corporation, shows its belief in the future of the area by breaking ground on its planned new manufacturing facility while that ground is still covered with mud and debris. The demonstration of optimism buoys spirits of local business boosters and common citizens alike.

"Just Between Us," the *Daily Record's* social column by Bobbie Westbrook, positively gushes over the dedication with which the social set, usually busy with dances and auxiliary meetings, weddings and civic events, is throwing itself into flood recovery efforts. It describes the "Clubwomen, who ordinarily at this time of year would be thinking of coming programs…working eight-hour days cooking at the feeding stations, washing the endless mountains of dishes with all the super-caution demanded by sanitarians, staffing the infirmaries, interviewing the stricken…and providing sympathetic ears."

It goes on to praise everyone from Girl Scouts to "those irresponsible (we thought) teen-agers…proving the most responsible of all in doing the tasks whether it's serving as auxiliary police or pushing the ferry boats away from landings or typing census lists from dawn till long after dark."

Society editors aren't known for their toughness, but Bobbie's a real pro. She can't get home from work, so she sets up a cot next to the press room, eats at food stations and doubles as a disaster reporter. When she finally does make it home four days after she becomes stranded, she finds eighteen other people there, taking refuge where it's available. The experience gives a whole new meaning to her duties as social editor.

Like the *Easton Express,* the *Daily Record* gets creative in finding ways to continue publishing its newspaper. Even after electricity is restored to its offices, typesetters lack their usual ability to melt down the lead that forms "slugs" of "hot type" for their composers to put together pages, because there is no gas service for the burners.

Resourceful employees find some bottled gas and a burner provided by a local farmer specializing in smoked meats. With such ingenuity and perseverance. the newspaper of the hardest-hit area in the Delaware Valley manages to miss just a single issue throughout the entire ordeal.

The generosity of fellow Americans swells the racks of the "department store" set up at the former Montgomery Wards location in Stroudsburg. A New York dress designer with a summer home there brings a carload of garments donated by manufacturers.

Monetary relief pours in via Red Cross donations. General Motors donates $100,000. Not to be outdone, the Ford Foundation gives $175,000. But most donations that make up the more than $10 million are small sums from ordinary citizens or office pools. Even foreign countries get into the act, with the Dominican Republic sending $200,000 worth of local products and Yugoslavia's President Tito sending condolences to flood victims.

A Stroudsburg taxi driver tells a newspaper reporter of a wonderful and unexpected result of the flood. "People on the hill who never spoke to the common folks are speaking to them now. What's more, they have them living in their homes. They invited them to move right in, folks who had lost their homes—gave them a room or two. In a way, the flood was good for this town."

Still, the air of tragedy hangs in the air as the unpleasant tasks of starting over are tackled. Eugene Heller, the man who'd left his wife at her parents' home to move his new car, is finally located on the last day of August. His body is found beneath several feet of mud in the bed of a small stream that runs through the Day Street playground. His car will be discovered in the remains of the fireman's bingo hall, where it had been driven by the current through one wall.

In the midst of the death and destruction, incredulous cleanup crews at the hall find unexpected new life. Just outside in the sweltering heat, cornstalks sprout from the still-moist mud. The plants have germinated from kernels that had been used as bingo card markers.

Bob and Edith Robacker live upstairs with the Schafers for a week while they get their apartment cleaned up. The hardwood floor of their Newfoundland home had swollen, but in the warm weather, it dries out quickly and settles back into place without cupping. June and Edith boil their families' drinking and cooking water on their grills until the electricity comes back on and June's doctor says their well has probably recharged itself with clean water.

The Red Cross stays at the school shelter until everyone returns home or finds somewhere else to go. Downtown, there is no traffic because all the connecting roads and bridges are closed. It's just as well, since no one can tell where the roads end and the yards begin, because everything looks the same; just a carpet of stones and mud.

About a month later, the Schafers must leave town for a funeral, and when they return, the cleanup is mostly finished. June notes that the landscape has been irrevocably changed, the roads and streambeds rearranged. For more than a year, June will lie in bed thinking she hears the water rushing through the downstairs again, and awaken later from flood-inspired nightmares. She's not sorry when Robert is transferred to Ohio.

Another lasting effect of the flood manifests itself in John Birutta of Belvidere. When he grows up, he becomes an advanced open water diver that can descend to 150 feet with no stress or problems. Yet he develops a strong, negative emotional reaction to riding or piloting a boat in rough waters. It harkens him back to the muddy water churning over and under the bridge that day in 1955.

For May Snyder in Upper Black Eddy, the flood means the end of an era. She will never go back to live in her house above the Riverview Lunch. After they scrub the walls of stuck-on macaroni and jelly from her larder, her family fixes it up and rents it out, later selling the whole building. They stay with her parents for two years, and May goes to work at the Frenchtown Porcelain Company, with many of the people who used to be her lunch customers. Finally, the Snyders move into their own home, another place in Upper Black Eddy, but one May makes sure has not ever been flooded by the river.

Near Carpentersville, New Jersey, an unlikely rescue is made two months after the flood. A railroad worker notices that for several days, he's seen an emaciated-looking horse munching on the leaves of trees between the right-of-way and the river. He knows Wingy Snyder, and has heard the story of his lost, blind horse. That evening, on his way home, he tells Wingy he thinks he knows where the horse might be.

Impossible! says Wingy. *That horse has been gone for months. Can't still be alive. That boy drowned, I tell ya.*

Don't you even want to check it out? asks his railroad friend.

Wingy squints an eye and scratches his stubbly chin. *What the hell,* he says. *I like that ol' nag. Show me.*

He grabs a halter and lead from the barn, and the two men head down to where the horse has been spotted. When they arrive, Wingy spies a very skinny horse, its ribs showing beneath a mud-matted coat. That can't be Bill, he thinks, but tries to get the horse's attention.

Hey, Bill! he says, his voice going soft.

Instantly, the horse's ears turn toward the sound of the beloved voice, then his face follows. The sightless eyes remain blank, but the horse whinnies softly and switches his tail. He begins walking toward Wingy.

Well, I'll be damned! is all Wingy can say. He walks over to his thin friend and slips the halter over his head. In the coming months, he'll fatten Bill up and put him back to work. The two friends will spend another decade together, and Bill will live to a ripe old age.

In October, resident Betty Conrad finds odd-looking tracks in the river sand at DePue's Ferry. She scans the water's edge for a sign of whatever might have made the strange impressions. Her eyes alight on the elongated head of Jocko the Croc, missing since the flood from Ivan Sanderson's Jungle Zoo in Manunka Chunk. The tropical croc had been lured to these waters by the warm discharge from the power plant. She calls the zoo and Edgar Schoenberger, who had saved the roadside celebrity by cutting him from his cage at the last minute, arrives with a lasso to bring him home. Jocko is later reported to be happily ensconced in his old digs.

Chris Koehler will grow up to marry Pat Wristen and eventually move back into the house she had shared with her sister and parents on the canal in Riegelsville. The Wristens, like the Fackenthals and many of their neighbors up and down the river, will be flooded again in the September, 2004 rains from Hurricane Ivan and then again in April, 2005 by heavy spring rains. The latter flood will crest at 33.32 feet, less than five feet below that of the record-breaking 1955 flood.

Mildred Williams will go with her husband to her parents-in-law's house on the island in Kintnersville to clean it up, while Dick's mom and dad stay at her home with the boys. When they get to the flooded place, she's amazed to find fish and eels flopping about in mud inside the house, along with the occasional water snake. Dick summons the fire company to come hose it all out, then he and Mildred get to work with soapy water and scrub brushes. She's nauseated by the horrible smell.

His parents will stay with them for a month while they build a new house to move into. The Red Cross will provide furniture for the new place, since theirs has all been ruined. To add insult to injury, someone breaks into the damaged house and steals some knives that hadn't been ruined. Dick's dad borrows a rowboat to take them over to clean the house while the water is still high, and when they come out to row back across, the boat is gone – someone else has taken it over to the other side of the canal! They think it might have been the knife thief, but they'll never know for sure.

It's early spring of 1956, and still no one has come to claim the last body in Thomas Miller's walk-in freezer. He knows it's a child, maybe six or seven, a little blond girl. Every time he goes into the freezer to get something, he sees her container, and it haunts him. How could someone just forget about this little girl?

What he doesn't know is that the little girl hasn't been forgotten, but that most of her family, the Lawyers, also died in the flood. Her brother, Robert, has been searching desperately for his little sister, Carol. In a few months, he will figure out the paperwork and will come to take her body home. But after the funeral director removes the freezer container, the whole situation is never explained to Thomas Miller. He will go to his own grave wondering what happened to the remains of the child he had come to think of as "the little angel."

In 1962, Blooming Glen Mennonite Church member Paul Longacre and his brother, Arlan, are in upstate New York, looking at some cattle to add to Paul's dairy herd. They're discussing the beauty of the area, and the talk turns to the ongoing effort to locate some affordable, appropriate property on which to build a children's church camp retreat. The newly formed Franconia Mennonite Camp Association, of which Arlan is a board member, has been charged with such a mission, but funds are limited and they haven't had much luck.

Driving back through the Canadensis area, the men see a sign reading "Property for Sale: Dalton, Canadensis." They stop at the Canadensis Post Office to inquire about where they might be able to find Mr. Dalton. The postmaster points to a gentlemen just getting into his Cadillac in the parking lot. It will be another of the oddly coincidental timings the church will consider providential. The Longacre brothers quickly catch Mr. Dalton before he drives off.

They tell him they're interested in the property he has posted for sale, and he inquires about the use they intend it for. They explain the children's camp concept, and he tells them the property isn't suitable for such a use, but that he has another parcel available that would be.

He takes the brothers out to Linn Lake Lodge, a former resort with buildings, a swimming pool, and other improvements.

It's a nice place, but the brothers think it's a bit too refined and perhaps not large enough at thirty-six acres. They're thinking of more rustic lodging that encourages healthy outdoor activity and communion with nature for growing children. Mr. Dalton says he's aware that the adjoining 240-acre lot is also available for sale, though it doesn't belong to him. Perhaps they can work something out for the sale of the entire acreage. The men are interested, but when they ask the selling price, Mr. Dalton tells them it's $350,000. Disappointed, the brothers admit it's way out of their range, and figure it's a deal that could never happen.

Mr. Dalton smiles, telling the men they don't know the best price he could get, and invites them back to his office to discuss it further. Once there, the Longacres explain the function of the camp as church-oriented, to give children and teenagers healthy activities to engage their bodies, minds and souls. They explain the mission of their church, the Blooming Glen Mennonites.

Mr. Dalton looks thoughtful for a moment, and walks over to a file cabinet, pulling out a drawer and thumbing through the folders. He finds what he's looking for and pulls it out. It's a sheaf of newspaper clippings from 1955, covering the flood in Canadensis and the Stroudsburgs. Several stories and pictures feature the Mennonites engaged in their volunteer cleanup duties. He points to one.

Is this your church? he asks.

The men nod. He looks at them for an extended moment.

That was an awful time for this area, he says. *Your people really helped us get back on our feet.* He pauses. *I think maybe we're in a position to reciprocate now. My price for the Lodge property is $175,000. I think I can help you get a good price on the other parcel, too.*

At this price, it'll be a stretch, but the Association can afford the land. The men schedule the first in a series of several meetings to set up the deal, and shake hands.

In early 1963, Mr. Dalton signs the sales agreement for his parcel. When the parties show up for the settlement meeting, he produces a check for $18,000, half the price of the second parcel of land. He gives it to the real estate agent, then tells the Mennonite Association representatives that he will hold the note on the property in lieu of the bank, allowing them to pay the $175,000 as they are comfortably able.

Now the Association will be able to use the extra money to immediately begin making improvements and building their new camp. Earlier than anyone has imagined, Spruce Lake Retreat is born, and continues the tradition of nurturing young people through the concept that service is one of the finest manifestations of faith.

Decades after the flood, R. Foster Winans is a reporter for *The Trentonian* newspaper, a ways downriver from his experience in front of Lumberville's Cuttalossa Inn that dark, rainy night in 1955. He talks his editor into allowing him to accompany a New Jersey Department of Environmental Protection (DEP) scientist on a canoe trip, collecting water samples to test for pollution on the Delaware.

The scientist tells him a story about a day in the '70s when a citizen had sent a rock in to the DEP. The man had found it in the river, but it was an exotic specimen that looked nothing like anything he'd ever seen come out of the Delaware. An investigation had uncovered the fact that a lapidary shop far to the north had been washed away during the flood of '55. The specimen had been part of its inventory, which had tumbled far downstream in the powerful current.

Across from Trenton in Morrisville, Bill Talone returns home, and notices all kinds of material from the Yardley Neckband Company hanging from trees along the canal. Their house no longer looks new, that's for sure. To his surprise, his television repairman, Bob Sanford, is waiting for him in a boat. He ferries Bill to the house over water standing on the low spots. They walk through several inches of water, which still flows through the garage.

Bill calls his friend Bill Crohl, a plumber from Langhorne, who brings a sump pump and runs it for most of the day to empty out the basement of the remaining water. When Claire arrives a few days later, she's just sick. Clinging to her kitchen walls are the dried contents of cereal boxes, and everything is black where fuel oil had risen into the first floor. She finds her favorite cookbook, and can't bring herself to throw it away, so she hangs it outside to dry in the hot sun.

A fireman is trolling the streets with a bullhorn to let everyone know that they can avail themselves of a hot meal at the town's community center. They won't have phone service for two weeks, and all the landscaping of which Bill had been so proud is gone. An FHA inspector shows up to help him salvage the house. He tells him to drill breather holes every four to five feet into their cedar siding to let it dry from the inside, and it works—no warping tears the boards away.

The government allows tax credits up to eight or ten thousand dollars, giving the Talones and many others a bit of relief for the next five years to help them catch up financially. Bill gets help from family members to re-do the landscaping before winter, and Claire proceeds to wash down the entire house with bleach water. They'll end up living there for the next fifteen years, and Claire will still be using the old, water-stained cookbook fifty years later.

Nearly twenty years after the flood, Joanne Shutt has married David Weiss, they are camping near a large reservoir in upstate New York. It's raining very hard, beating down on the metal roof of their camper van. Joanne becomes frightened, flashing back to her experience in the car while driving during that long-ago night in the Stroudsburgs. She begins to cry and tremble. Though she knows it's irrational, she is panicking, imagining they'll be swept away by the lake during the night. She insists David move the van farther from the water.

David flips on the headlights to show her that they're nowhere near the edge of the lake, but she's inconsolable until he finally agrees to relocate their campsite. She realizes the flood of 1955 will be with her forever.

Political response to the flood disaster is swift and broad-ranging. Local mayors and commissioners vote special funding to help their municipalities recover from the terrible blow. Pennsylvania Governor George Leader and New Jersey Governor Robert Meyner both visit ravaged regions of their respective states, setting up CD command posts and surveying the most damaged areas.

From Byers Peak Ranch in Fraser, Colorado, where he has been vacationing for several days, President Dwight Eisenhower sends a message that he is "highly gratified" with the work of the military in helping with the flood recovery and relief efforts in the eastern states and New England. He will fly to Philadelphia for a scheduled address to the city's Bar Association on August twenty-third, adding a helicopter flyover for an aerial inspection of the flooded regions nearby.

The president promises to call a special session of Congress, if necessary, to release emergency funding for disaster areas with all due haste. In mid-September, he will acknowledge activity by the U.S. Chamber of Commerce to help stricken businesses get back on their feet. On November 19, the U.S. Small Business Administration announces a grant of $23,700,000 in emergency, low-interest loans to northeastern state flood victims of Hurricane Diane in August and Hurricane Ione in October.

Under immense pressure from local and regional politicians, as well as the media, he also pledges that the federal government will get to work at once on a long-range flood prevention program. Included in this effort will be the genesis of the National Flood Insurance Program. He makes a passionate plea to the American people to donate "everything they can" to help their fellow citizens in need. Response continues to be generous, actually exceeding the million-dollar goal.

The second place where people rush to lay blame for the huge loss of life and property in the immediate wake of the flood is at the feet of the U.S. Weather Bureau. Not quite a week after the Brodhead Creek had careened madly through the Stroudsburgs, the *Daily Record* runs a story with the understated headline: "Forecasting Knowledge Held Insufficient Against Floods."

Anyone reading it must be snorting in derision, but the article, datelined "Washington" is full of earnestness on the part of Weather Bureau officials. Yet there is no sign of apology.

One could hardly have expected anything else. After all, meteorologists had been working under the severe handicap of a consistent lack of critical information. They had made every effort to express this in the most urgent terms to their professional associations, to the public, and—most importantly—to those whose responsibilities included funding the necessary research and development of modern forecasting equipment that would allow them to do a better job: Congress.

But elected officials are not about to allow this albatross to be hung around their necks, and the bureau knows it. Meteorologists, doing the best they can with the tools they have to work with, have no choice but to accept their post as whipping boy for this unfortunate turn of events.

Though they wouldn't dare discuss it openly, many weather professionals must be admitting in private moments that such a massive tragedy may indeed be the only thing that could possibly have made their point with such awful effectiveness. Nothing like some serious death and destruction to assure the attention of a distracted audience.

The fact is that what they've been afraid of all along—and have been warning about, if only someone would have listened—has come true. They had been left blind against a powerful force of nature, and even if they'd had the information they needed at the last minute, they'd have had no way to communicate it widely enough to make a difference in the outcome. Such a no-win scenario must be the ultimate in professional frustration, but now at least something is being done about it.

The article assures readers that "under enlarged appropriations for new facilities and research, officials reported steps had been underway even before the floods struck which will lead to 'great improvements' in the future."

The promised improvements will indeed come to pass. In the following decades, weather forecasting will take advantage of rapid developments in radar, satellite payloads, imaging technology, severe weather numerical models and measurement scales, and increased computing speed and power to overhaul both the substance and the appearance of weather forecasts. The twin hurricanes themselves have been a huge source of data that will eventually be analyzed and parsed for increased understanding of tropical storms and their effects. But immediately after the devastation, the words ring hollow for those whose lives have already been irrevocably changed.

One item toward the end of the article will prove prescient under later examination. It is pointed out that many of the streams that killed the most people and did the most property damage were ones without a history of severe flooding, and so were not equipped with water level gauges that might have helped the victims gain even a small head start on the flash floods. It will be a critical point in many political battles over major flood control project proposals to come.

In the end, nobody escapes the pointing finger of blame. Aside from the weather bureau, developers are blamed for "waterproofing" hilly regions with growing numbers of new homes, while city planners point to the over-industrialization of river valleys. Conservationists cite the danger of the increasing deforestation of the countryside and say the floods are clearly a result of poor land management practices.

Hydrologists are slapped for failure to bring the seriousness of a flood threat to public attention, and industry gets the blame for building plants smack-dab in the flood plains. Congress will ultimately also become a target of complaint by the Army Corps of Engineers for failing to appropriate more flood control money. But again, they put the ball back in the court of the states for not accepting monies already available.

What becomes clear in this endless public discussion is that, in some way, everyone has played a part in creating the circumstances in which an overland "perfect storm" could do as much damage as it did.

The crew of the freight locomotive at the DL&W Railroad yards in Analomink across from Camp Davis has been rescued after being stranded cab-deep in the muck left by the Brodhead Creek. Many of the railroad's tracks and other trains aren't as lucky. At Devil's Hole, the washout seen by the crew that had backed their train up to the Cresco station is now a gaping hole 250 feet wide. The track hangs suspended over it, eighty feet in mid-air. The Sussex branch of the line has been stripped down to the riverbed, and will be out of service until mid-October.

The Erie Railroad's turntable and maintenance yards at Port Jervis remain underwater for two days, necessitating replacement of most of the roadbed. Massive destruction has taken place on the fourteen-mile stretch of Erie track just west of Port Jervis, and there are several washouts at Shohola. Branches at Honesdale, Pennsylvania and Narrowsburg, New York are seriously damaged. Until they can be fixed, Erie trains are diverted onto parallel tracks of the Delaware & Hudson line, which had barely been touched. Later in the year, the Erie will sell this damaged stretch of track to the D&H to finance other flood repairs.

Other detours and re-routing take place nearly everywhere there is trackage alongside creeks and rivers. The Jersey Central has lost track between Jim Thorpe and White Haven, Pennsylvania, and the Lehigh Valley "Black Diamond" line loses two lines between Tannery and Penn Haven Junction.

What's left of the Lackawanna Railroad transports Bailey bridge sections into the Poconos for the Army Corps of Engineers before the water has even gone down. Before noon on August nineteenth, the DL&W has fifteen contractors working with the engineering department to restore the right-of-way. Passenger service is suspended for a week between Scranton and Hoboken, and continues westward on a limited basis.

Over the long haul, some of the railroads will not recover from the severe destruction to their lines. The New York, Ontario and Western is one of these. Though the Central New Jersey will survive, it will never again turn a profit after Diane's floods, and will leave Pennsylvania entirely in 1972. The Erie and the Lackawanna, both ailing and struggling under huge debt loads, will ultimately merge just to stay solvent.

The Erie shops in Scranton close up. After a five-day emergency declaration, the recovery begins. Severe water restrictions remain in place while the municipal system is brought back online.

This shot from 1961 shows the temporary Bailey Bridge trusses that supported the repaired Yardley Bridge. It would soon be replaced by the larger, higher and more modern designed Scudder Falls Bridge on Interstate 95 to the south.

— Collection D. Randy Riggs

The Army Corps of Engineers builds temporary bridges at Elm Street, Cedar Avenue and the nearly obliterated Ash Street, where the hapless Highfields had lived.

The city's Redevelopment Authority wastes no time in springing into action. They quickly produce two plans for rehabilitating the two hardest-hit areas. Five hundred dwellings in Scranton's South Side Flats are relocated, and the area will become a commercial center. The Little England section is simply gone. What little is left is bull-dozed and made into a greenway. Eventually, some businesses will move into the area. A serious flood control plan is begun. The entire effort will cost millions of dollars, but Scranton will not again be such a victim of its geography.

Having witnessed the amortization of federal government power in the formation of the Tennessee Valley Authority hydroelectric dam project, states on either side of the Delaware River had been determined not to lose control in a similar way when they got together in 1951 to assess their resources. Desiring to solve the area's water problems, New York, New Jersey, Pennsylvania and Delaware had formed a compact called the Interstate Commission on the Delaware River, or INCODEL, designed to operate without federal participation.

The organization had developed a comprehensive plan that includes managing the waterways—specifically the Delaware River—for the generation of hydroelectric power, navigation, water supply, flood control, pollution control and recreation. The plan is centralized around a series of proposed reservoirs meant primarily to increase New York City's water supply.

The dams that would create the reservoirs would also provide flood control and the recreational lakes. INCODEL had immediately run into problems, with New York and New Jersey approving the plan, but Pennsylvania not finding it satisfactory. Because the compact states could not agree on the plan itself, Congress failed to fund their approximately $16 million worth of projects. The project had been branded a failure, and the states had turned to a conservation approach—mostly reforestation—for flood control.

In 1954, the Watershed Protection and Flood Prevention Act had been passed by Congress in the wake of flooding destruction caused by Hurricane Hazel. The act sought federal-state-local cooperation to prevent such floods by setting stringent and specific percentages of water, forest and developed areas for any single project. The legislation had been so politically charged that it was amended no less than fourteen times in the next thirty years.

The fact is that nothing would have been enough to prevent the floods of August, 1955.

Under such rare and ideal storm conditions—fully saturated ground and streams swollen by a previous rain event, quickly followed by copious amounts of new precipitation—no one effort could have prevented some serious flooding. Again, the increasingly prevalent strategy of trying to identify a single "silver bullet" that would be the panacea to the flooding problem proves to be both naïve and ineffectual. The belief that there exists such a solution indicates a lack of understanding about the way nature works.

David Dempsey, a New York Times reporter, will write *FLOOD*, released the year after the 1955 event. The book will attempt to cover the storm, its floods, and the lasting effect over the Eastern Seaboard. Dempsey will correctly posit:

> The flood plain is just what its name implies—
> nature's safety valve—and one lives on it at his own
> risk. The risk, as we have seen, is considerable.

Still, the calls for flood control will not be ignored. The Monday after the flood, the *Easton Express'* editorial argues for engineering projects, saying "...natural forces can to some extent be tamed, some of their energy harnessed and turned to productive use. It is unlikely that the blow would have been so severe had the long-unheeded voice of the Lehigh Valley Flood Control Council been recognized in the government councils at Harrisburg and Washington."

Perhaps more effective in stirring public sentiment is the finger-pointing it does in the next paragraph:

> Citizens of this area can blame themselves for
> sending representatives to government who have
> failed to exert the force necessary to create public

works which would have alleviated or prevented the
1955 August flood.

Similar editorials appear in *The Phillipsburger,* the *Daily Record,*
the *Hunterdon Democrat-News* and other papers throughout the
affected regions. In a time when many are feeling impotent against
the ravages of nature, it's a comforting thought that engineered
structures will prevent such carnage in the future. The die is cast for
the Army Corps of Engineers to step, once again, into its traditional
roles of hero and rescuer.

The Corps does indeed prove its worth in helping carry off a
monumental cleanup job in nearly every stricken area. Even by 1955,
it has racked up an impressive track record of successful flood control
projects. These facts burnish the image of the can-do Corps as a knight
in shining armor fully capable of beating nature into submission
through huge engineering projects. What they don't take into account
are several other truisms, such as the fact that the majority of death
and destruction from Diane's rains took place on tributaries, not on
the main stem Delaware, and the inefficiency of the tendency to
reduce large, complex problems to a single-solution situation.

In an oft-repeated construction analogy, when a hammer is the
only tool in your belt, every challenge begins to look like a nail. The
tool available for offer by the harassed U.S. government is the Corps.

The Corps' official history says, "The floods of August 1955 did,
in fact, mark a major turning point in the scope and procedural emphasis
of the investigations under way in the Delaware Basin." Something
about these particular floods seems to breed understatement.

A public hearing had been held in July, 1950, in Philadelphia
under the auspices of INCODEL. Its purpose had been to review
the implications of a comprehensive study of the Delaware River
Basin, known informally as "The Valley Report." A field survey of
previous flood damage had been done by a consulting engineering firm.
Its findings had been included in the Valley Report, to support claims
of the need for flood control efforts. The report sparked, according
to Corps history, "a public mood of caution and defensiveness, due
partially to limited comprehension of the effects of the proposed

main stem dams." In short, the old suspicions of federally controlled hydroelectric power projects again surfaced.

The upshot was joint legislation between New Jersey and Pennsylvania to construct a dam at Wallpack Bend. Another result was the establishment by the state of Delaware of the Delaware River Basin Commission (DRBC), dependent for its long-term existence on similar action by the other three states. It took some time, but each of them did pass similar legislation, with Pennsylvania the last to do so in mid-July, 1955—a month before Diane's waters swelled the Delaware.

In January, 1956, four public hearings are held to feel out local views on flood control and other water issues in the seriously affected regions. In February, the Senate Public Works Committee adopts a resolution affecting the basin investigation, initiating feasibility studies for a main stem dam and reservoir.

The DRBC forms a Survey Commission, which first meets in March, 1956 to act on the recommendations of the study. According to the Corps history, "the site search was pursued by every available method of engineering, geologic and economic test for a dozen years." The result of this pursuit is the designation of Tocks Island, six miles above the Delaware Water Gap, as the best location for such a dam.

Private firms with interests in developing the power-generating capacity of the river lobby hard, using the '55 flood tragedy as a springboard to promote their business development agenda. By 1962, the DRBC has come around to be in favor of the federally controlled project.

The eventual full proposal for the Corps' anti-flood offensive includes plans for forty-seven dams throughout the Delaware watershed, including many on tributaries. The centerpiece, Tocks Island Dam, would flood 12,000 acres behind the dam at Tocks Island, all the way upstream to Port Jervis. It would be the largest dam east of the Mississippi River, costing $90 million. The anticipated completion date is 1975.

At first valley residents don't really believe the Corps is serious. Why would anyone want to make a huge lake out of one of the last major free-flowing rivers in the East? Not only would it destroy surrounding homes and farmlands, it would create ugly mudflats during times of drawdown during low flow periods. That would create eutrophication, or the buildup of algae from agricultural nutrients

running off into the stagnant water. Some people compare the anticipated result to a "gigantic cesspool."

Resistance to the plan begins quietly, then grows to open complaints and protests. Some residents sell their homes rather than wait
to be forced out, and legal battles sprout ahead of the encroaching
flooding anticipated in the dam's creation. The Corps listens to people's
complaints, then promptly ignores them.

Soon, everyone has an opinion about the project. Proponents of
the dam are backed by the government and media, so their positions
are given ample public exposure. Opponents are less well-organized
and funded, so theirs gets short shrift, at least in the beginning.

However, there are a few official voices taking a stand against
the dam. A passage from the July, 1957 Bucks County Council on
Civil Defense *Recap and Critique of the 1955 flood emergency* is
particularly eloquent in voicing the opposing argument:

> Who is there among us who would dare, through
> temerity, audacity, ignorance or political expediency, to
> put forth as true the concept that we can prevent floods?
>
> While there is no universal panacea of prevention,
> nonetheless control or minimizing of flooding is quite
> possible together with mitigating damage and disloca-
> tion. It cannot be done by a colossal project of large
> dams at a frightening cost of tax money to product
> that which would be a dire, ineluctable liability.
>
> ...But positive, constructive steps are possible; are
> worthwhile; and have been successfully applied since
> Roman times. The lessons so sorely learned during
> the hurricane and flood of 1936 were carefully put
> into practice in many localities in New England
> with the result that Diane did them relatively little
> harm. But those localities that had not taken precau-
> tions or practiced watershed improvement were
> indeed in dire circumstances.
>
> Perhaps the best example is verily almost in our
> own back yard, being the splendid local activities on
> the Brandywine, which result not only in the control
> of "run off," which causes floods, but also in conserving

topsoil and preserving that vitally important asset,
our ground water, which stupid prodigality has jeop-
ardized. The problem and its solution lies in each
locality's own door-yard! Also as they protect themselves, so they protect their neighbors, and are also in
their turn afforded protection.

The problem is that this report is authored by a non-authority
on water issues, and is seen by relatively few who can do anything
about the dam debate.

A few particularly active private citizens get involved and
organize the Delaware Valley Conservation Association to represent
the interests of valley residents opposed to the Tocks project. They
hold protests and erect road signs reading "A Pox on Tocks." Years of
political wrangling and positioning follow, with some residents actually
committing suicide rather than leave their lifelong homes.

A series of mismanagement steps and the exposure of a lack of
due diligence by both the federal government and the Corps produce
massive ill will and turn public sentiment against both them and the
dam. After all the heartache and tragedy on both sides and many
arguments for and against the dam, what finally kills the Tocks Island
project is a lack of funding. Much-needed federal money is siphoned
off to support the increasingly costly Vietnam War, leaving the Tocks
project seriously underfunded.

The compact states also begin to listen to studies indicating that
the dam will indeed cause eutrophication, and don't want the liability
of cleaning it up. New York and New Jersey pull their support from
the project. By 1975, only Pennsylvania still supports it.

After heavy lobbying from conservation interests, President Jimmy
Carter in 1978 officially designates part of the main stem Delaware as
a Wild and Scenic River, effectively squelching any further possibility
of the Tocks Island dam being completed. Though some of the tributary dams in the proposal, including flood control projects on the
Brodhead Creek and Lehigh River will be built, the main Tocks Island
dam project is dead.

Water engineer and environmental planner Richard Albert will
write the definitive treatment of the entire saga, publishing *Damming
the Delaware: The Rise and Fall of Tocks Island Dam* in 1988. Whether

swayed by Albert's authoritative and convincing treatise or simply wishing to cut its political losses and move on, Congress officially de-authorizes the dam-building project in 1992, to the chagrin of the Corps and the unmitigated glee of most valley residents.

The land that had been condemned and taken by the federal government through the doctrine of Eminent Domain is turned into the Delaware Water Gap National Recreation Area. It's a jewel of natural beauty that, fifty years after the flood, is enjoyed by five million people a year.

The struggle leaves a legacy of resentment, bitterness and government distrust among those whose lives are forever altered by the battle. However, even the most dug-in opponents of the dam admit that in the long run, their beloved, wild Delaware has been preserved by the park. Surrounding areas are testament to the rampant development that would otherwise likely have turned the acreage into a collection of condominium complexes, strip malls and vacation rental properties.

Still, struggles over flood control and responsible water management will continue to plague many of the areas affected by Diane's floods.

The very fine particulate character of Delaware River mud that makes it such a mess to clean up from a flooded home actually earns for it an improbable place in the annals of professional sports history.

Before use in professional league play, every baseball is "rubbed down" to take the hard-to-handle shine off its new leather. In the early years of the sport, the ball would be rubbed right before a game with a small bit of mud, mixed from playing field dirt and water. However, that tended to soften the leather too much, making the cover vulnerable to tampering and even to coming off when hit.

In 1938, Lena Blackburne, a coach for the old Philadelphia Athletics club, had a better idea. Familiar with the qualities of Delaware mud, he scoured tributaries near his home for some he could use. He eventually discovered a certain lode of muck, described as resembling a cross between chocolate pudding and whipped cold cream, that de-slicked the balls without discoloring or scratching them too much. Amazingly, it didn't smell bad, either. Other, similar concoctions were tried, but nothing else quite did the job. Soon, every major and most minor leagues in the sport were using Lena's "Magic Mud."

The business has been passed down among friends and families since then, and Major League Baseball alone buys 182 pounds of Lena Blackburne Rubbing Mud each year. The location of the exact spot where the mud is dug is officially a trade secret. Unofficially, those in the know say it's collected each year, at low tide, from a Delaware River tributary near the town of Palmyra, New Jersey.

The government's Civil Defense program will survive the Cold War years primarily as a response to the threat of nuclear warfare. It is responsible for designating and equipping public "fallout shelters," developing guidelines for attack drills and survival plans, and issuing warnings through the development of an Emergency Broadcast System. Its familiar yellow-and-black "pizza" symbol will at first alarm, then remind Americans of the constant threat of annihilation until the demise of the Soviet Union in 1989. In retrospect, many people will look back on the entire effort as a vestige of the quaint notion that widespread nuclear blasts are survivable in the long term.

With the reduced threat of nuclear war, Civil Defense will morph, through a tortuous and bewildering series of reorganizations and re-namings, into the Federal Emergency Management Agency (FEMA), with corresponding government bodies at the state and local levels. It will concentrate mainly on the threat of natural disasters until the terrorist attacks of September 11, 2001, when again a foreign enemy will emerge as a primary threat.

Ironically, many local Emergency Management Agencies, staffed primarily by volunteers, will be in much the same state of under-funded readiness and inadequate preparation before the attacks—though perhaps not considered such a joke—as local CD bodies had been before the floods of 1955. The amazing marshalling of these groups' resources into rapid, dedicated response during the terrorism again builds local prestige and appreciation of all public service groups, including police, fire and rescue units.

This esteem in which public servants are newly held once again proves well-earned during widespread, severe flooding along the Delaware and its tributaries during Hurricane Ivan in September, 2004 and again in April, 2005. Once again, selfless individuals working mostly as volunteers provide gallant rescues, this time making use of vastly improved technology for storm tracking, communication and reporting. As always, the Red Cross and private citizens provide extended comfort for evacuees and dedicated cleanup efforts.

And once again, despite all previous scientific and environmental studies showing the Delaware to be unsuitable for large dam projects, the clamor for flood control measures is renewed in public discourse and in the media.

The cycle will likely continue into the future, in time with the rhythms of nature, for as long as people live along the banks of the Delaware.

Notes

In the interest of making this a most readable book, the usual rigid format of footnoting was abandoned in favor of this less formal but equally functional Notes section. It is divided by chapter and page number for ease of use. To keep this ection concise, source entries are brief and may be referenced to fully expanded citations in the Bibliography. Those sources referenced with a single citation are fully noted here.

Common abbreviations:
NOAA - National Oceanic and Atmospheric Administration
NWS - National Weather Service, formerly U.S. Weather Bureau

Section I – The Calm

Chapter 1 – Between a War and a Hard Place

17 – Friday dawns red: Various weather records and newspaper accounts

21 – The newly robust automobile industry: "On This Day In History," History.com; dMarie Time Capsule website.

Chapter 2 – Connie

33 – His own recollections notwithstanding: The full story of Isaac Monroe Cline and the tragedy of the 1900 Galveston hurricane is masterfully told in Erik Larsen's *Isaac's Storm.*

37 – Surface waters were measuring: Weather and Circulation of August 1955.

37 – February and March 1955 had seen a surplus of precipitation: Philadelphia Area Historic Weather Data, Franklin Institute.

41 – The first intentional flight into a hurricane: The First Flight Into A Hurricane's Eye.

50-1 – Rainfall, wind and damage figures: from *The New Jersey Weather Book, The Philadelphia Area Weather Book, The World Almanac and Book of Facts 2001,* the Weather Bureau's *Technical Paper No. 26,* and various newspaper accounts.

51 – A High Point couple: Philadelphia Inquirer article, 8/14/1955, page 1.

51 – Unofficial estimates: Philadelphia Inquirer articles, 8/14/1955, pages 1+.

51 – With the storm past: Philadelphia Inquirer article, 8/14/1955.

53 – Connie threatens: Inside Line, Line Material Company newsletter, 10/1955.

53 – At her peak: "Hurricane Connie." *USA Today,* Chris Capella, 6/9/1999.

Chapter 3 – The Delaware: Cutting A Swath Through History

56 – The Delaware is one of the older rivers on our continent: The Geological Story of Pennsylvania

58 – Fast-forward to just over 20,000 years ago. Website of the Ontario Archaeological Society. The Archaeology of Ontario: Post-Ice Age Geography and the Environment. http://www.ontarioarchaeology.on.ca/oas/summary/post.htm

59 – By the time Europeans arrived: Delaware Diary.

62 – Six events with an average interval: Great Floods of Pennsylvania.

66 – In stark contrast: Tennessee Emergency Management Agency website http://www.tnema.org/Archives/EMHistory/TNCDHistory1.htm)

66 – The novel concept of the "planned community": Levittown, Pennsylvania: Building the Suburban Dream website

68 – A matter of insufficient technology: The Meteorologist In Your Life.

68 – The free bridges on the Delaware: Telephone interview with John Salaga, Delaware River Joint Toll Bridge Commission

Chapter 4 – Diane, The Jealous Sister

78 – While both hurricanes make landfall: Diane was at Category 3 intensity only as she crossed over Cape Fear, North Carolina. At final landfall, her winds had dropped into Category 2 range. NOAA *Technical Memorandum NWS TPC-1.*

81 – She has been absorbing it in abundance: An exhaustive recap of the meteorological factors contributing to the twin hurricanes' development is discussed in *The Weather and Circulation of August 1955.*

81 – Orographic enhancement: A full (though very technical) dissection of this and other related meteorological phenomena is contained in a NOAA research paper entitled "The Distribution of Precipitation over the Northeast Accompanying Landfalling and Transitioning Tropical Cyclones." Clarification of terms was provided in an email from on-air meteorologist Ben Gelber.

82 – The substantial rains from Connie: "Reservoirs Not Full In Spite of Rain," article from August 17, 1955 edition of *The Daily Record.* Stroudsburg, Pa.

88 – *An inch of rain:* "Figures Explain Reasons Behind Flood In Monroe." Article from *Easton Express.* August, 1955. Easton, Pa.

88 – *Hydrologists have proven:* "Upper Mississippi Flooding." American Weather Service Weatherbug.com website.
http://www.aws.com/aws_2001/greatesthits/default.asp?CID=61

Section II – The Storm

Chapter 5 – It Wasn't Supposed To Be This Way

93 – *This same issue of the newspaper:* "Area Awaits Heavy Rains," front page article from morning edition of *The Daily Record*, August 18, 1955. Stroudsburg, Pa.

94 – *But with other headlines:* "Tired Diane Puffs Way Into Virginia," front page article from morning edition of the *Philadelphia Inquirer.* Philadelphia, Pa, August 18, 1955.

99 – *In 1868 a small dam had been built:* "Flood: The Great Flood of 1955." Branchville website.

103 - *Uptown, farther from the brook:* "Neither Rain Nor Flood Nor… Stopped This Wedding!" Kathleen Cody Sengel. *Barrett Township Historical Society Newsletter.*

104 – *About 150 yards across the road:* "An Eyewitness Account of the Flood." Bob Robacker.

105 – *Just up the creek in Greentown:* "The Flood." *Carbondale Review.* Carbondale, Pa. 1955.

126 – *Dale Price was upset:* "Recollections of the Flood in 1955 in Canadensis." Dale Price. *Barrett Township Historical Society Newsletter.*

Chapter 6 – Hell In The Headwaters

101 – *The noisiest tributary of the Lackawanna:* "History of the Lackawanna Valley," Hollister.

101 – *Mechanics in the Erie yard are just finishing:* "Hurricane Diane," Gallagher.

102 – *Elliott and Ella Highfield: The Flood.* Carbondale Review.

106 – *Such distinguished personages: Remembrance of Rivers Past,* page 237. Ernest Schweibert. The Macmillan Company, New York. 1972.

107 – *Around five p.m.: FLOOD.* David Dempsey; various newspaper articles and weather reports.

Chapter 7 – Whole Worlds Wash Away

114 – *A heavy rain is falling:* Various newspaper articles and weather reports.

121 – His son works: "Flash Flood Rips Carversville." *New Hope Gazette.* Aug. 25, 1955.

121 – Little Robbie Winans: Email interview, R. Foster Winans.

122 – Sandy Smith has made it home: Personal interview, Sandy Smith Armitage.

125 – Lloyd Graff, committee member: "Camp Pahaquarra Survives Flood." *Hunterdon County Democrat.* Aug. 25, 1955.

130 – Only about a hundred yards upstream: Various newspaper articles (mostly from *The Daily Record)* and railroad reports.

130 – The nine cars of the DL&W's Train 5: "Hurricane Diane," Gallagher.

132 – All day, cottagers on the island's south side: Great Floods of Pennsylvania, Shank; various newspaper accounts.

Chapter 8 – Terror In The Night

133 – In Newtown, Col. Heritage is awakened: Incident report, Bucks County Council of Civil Defense, August 18-19, 1955.

135 – One of the town's merchants: The Flood. Carbondale Review.

139 – Meanwhile, down near Washington Avenue: ibid.

140 – East of town: "Hurricane Diane," Gallagher.

142 – In the Winter House at Camp Davis: Various newspaper accounts reporting interviews with Jennie and Nancy Johnson; interviews with Linda Lecropane Kelso.

148 – Earlier, Eugene Heller and his wife: Various newspaper accounts; personal statements at 50th Anniversary event, Monroe County Public Library, Aug. 14, 2005.

151 – Philadelphia vacationers at Price's Cottages: Various newspaper accounts, mostly Stroudsburg's *The Daily Record.*

156 – Back in Port Jervis: Various newspaper accounts; *The Effects of a Threatening Rumor on a Disaster-Stricken Community.* NRC report.

159 – For the first time in fifty-two years: Various newspaper accounts.

164 – The Van Gorder family is watching television: Inside Line.

165 – Back near the Day Street Flats: ibid., various newspaper accounts.

Chapter 9 – A River Goes Mad

176 – Residents of small river towns: Various newspaper accounts.

183 – Customers of Portland, Pennsylvania's National Bank: Various news accounts.

184 – Thirteen-year-old Charlie Rufe wakes up: "These campers escaped via motorboat." *Allentown Morning Call*, Aug. 13, 1995

195 – Col. Robert Angster, commanding officer: Operation Tempest Rapids report.

Chapter 10 – Swallowed Whole

204 – In Bushkill, Ellworth Peiffer: "20 Rescued By Boat From Cabin Colony." *Stroudsburg Daily Record*, August, 1955.

205 – Retired Judge E.E. Bonniwell: "Judge Bonniwell, Wife Saved in Flooded Cabin; Were Trapped 14 Hours." *Easton Express*, August, 1955.

208 – Thirteen-year-old Tom Zimmerman: "A Flood of Memories: Delaware River disaster remains vivid for survivors." *The Sunday Star Ledger*, August 20, 1995.

Chapter 11 – August 20th: The Morning After

222 – Elliott Highfield is dazed: "Wife, 60, Swept Away; Husband Clings to Roof." *Scranton Times*, August 19, 1955.

227 - Robert Neyhart, a carrier pigeon hobbyist: Article, *The Daily Record*. August, 1955.

237 - On a farm along South Main Street: Telephone interview, John Moyer. August 14, 2005.

245 - His father, Joe, had waited: Various newspaper accounts from *The Daily Record*. August, 1955

Chapter 12 – Starting Over

252 – At seven o'clock in the morning: Various newspaper accounts from *The Daily Record* and *Easton Express*. August, 1955.

258 – Earlier Friday morning, Roy Keller: Various newspaper accounts from *The Daily Record* and *Easton Express*. August, 1955.

277 – Seventy-five-year-old Charlie Newbaker: "Water Reached 15 Feet Outside Portland Bank." *Easton Express*, Aug. 22, 1955.

278 – At four p.m., Dr. Fred Phillips: Several newspaper accounts from *Easton Express, Doylestown Intelligencer, Philadelphia Inquirer*. August, 1955.

Chapter 13 – Crest

289 – The last flights by an airplane shuttle service: "Surging Lehigh, Delaware Rivers Isolate Easton, Strand Hundreds In Downtown Sections of City." *Easton Express*, August 20, 1955.

291 – By this time, all bridges out of Easton: "Late Developments." *Easton Express,* August 19, 1955.

293 – Herb and Sylvia Carle, along with many other merchants: "Hurricane of '55: Downtown Businesses Suffered." *Allentown Morning Call,* Easton Sunday Magazine. August 13, 1995.

292 – Don Young, office manager: Easton Employment Office report.

297 – Residents of Front Street: "Memories of Agnes flood back for locals," Devlin.

298 – Gabe Kober of Huntingdon, New Jersey: "Carpentersville: 31 of 89 Homes Destroyed." Page 6, *The Phillipsburger,* August 25, 1955

303 – Summer colonies north of the sister cities: "Loss Tremendous Along Delaware Up To Riverton." *Easton Express,* August 22, 1955.

Section III – The Aftermath

Chapter 14 – *The Morning After*

315 – Before the sister hurricanes had come through: Various news accounts in the *Hunterdon County Democrat* and the *New Hope Gazette.* August, 1955.

320 – At Trenton's Calhoun Street Bridge: Caption on back of New Jersey Dept. of Transportation official photo in the New Jersey State Archives collection.

320 – Mayor Donal Connolly is forced to abandon: "Receding River Leaves Many Millions in Losses." *Trenton Times,* August 21, 1955.

325 – At six forty Sunday evening: "Dummy placed On Mattress Is Cause of Search." *Easton Express,* August 22, 1955.

326 – Col. Fred Herr, Hunterdon County Red Cross Chairman: "The Great Flood Disaster of 1955." Photo essay. Democrat Press, Flemington, N.J. 1955.

327 – With the Acme Market inundated: Tape transcript from September 24, 2002 Reminiscence Meeting, Lambertville Historical Society.

329 – Rowboats can be seen tied to parking meters: ibid.

338 – In 1948, when there had been a catastrophic flood: Helen Brown interview.

Chapter 15 – *Starting Over*

349 – Norm Good of the Blooming Glen Mennonite Church: After the Rain: The Spruce Lake Story. Video.

356 - Nine-year-old Frank McCaffrey's body is found: This section is based on articles from several issues of *The Daily Record* in Stroudsburg, as well as on data contained in the coroner's reports of each victim.

357 – At ten thirty Saturday night: The Effects of a Threatening Rumor on a Disaster-Stricken Community. NRC report.

365 – Col. Angster determines: Operation Tempest Rapids report.

369 – Water has covered the Frenchtown-Uhlerstown Bridge: "Havoc of Storm Is Evident In Frenchtown Area." *Easton Express,* August 21, 1955.

373 – In Stockton, the Red Cross is serving: The Great Flood Disaster of 1955." Photo essay. Democrat Press, Flemington, N.J. 1955.

374 – Up in Branchville, Mayor Willard Decker: "Flood!" Official Branchville website.

375 – In the midst of too much water: "Receding River Leaves Many Millions in Losses." *Trenton Times,* August 21, 1955.

Epilogue – The River's Trembling Edge

382 – But as experience and empirical research will prove: "Disadvantages of River Channel Management." River Channel Management by Elizabeth Wall. http://users.aber.ac.uk/erw2/index4.htm; also "Flooding Hazards, Prediction & Human Intervention." by Prof. Stephen A. Nelson, Tulane University. April 2004. http://www.tulane.edu/~sanelson/geol204/floodhaz.htm

386 – A Stroudsburg taxi driver: FLOOD, David Dempsey

389 – In October, resident Betty Conrad finds odd-looking tracks: Delaware Diary, by Frank Dale.

393 – Political response to the flood disaster: "Meyner's Cabinet Meets To Discuss Flood Catastrophe." *Easton Express,* August 22, 1955; "Legislature To Act On Appropriation For Flood Relief." *Hunterdon County Democrat News,* August 25, 1955; several editorials from Delaware Valley newspapers.

393 – President Dwight Eisenhower sends a message: "Eisenhower Praises Army for Flood Relief." *The Philadelphia Inquirer,* August 22, 1955.

393 – He will fly to Philadelphia: "President Sees Flood, Pledges Fast Aid." *The Evening Bulletin,* Philadelphia. August 23, 1955, front page.

394 - In mid-September, he will acknowledge activity: National Archives and Records Administration. Archives item #214 - Dwight D. Eisenhower.

398 – The project had been branded a failure: Dick Albert interview.

405 – Soon, every major and most minor leagues: Lean Blackburne Baseball Rubbing Mud official website.

405 – Civil Defense will morph: The History of Civil Defense & Emergency Management in Tennessee website.

Appendix

1 - Meteorological and Hurricane Data

Tropical Storm Classification

Tropical systems go through several stages before developing into a full-fledged hurricane. The following defines the four stages of the development cycle, based on information from the Atlantic Oceanographic and Meteorological Laboratory (AOML). The AOML is the hurricane research division of the National Oceanic and Atmospheric Administration (NOAA). Windspeeds mentioned here are for those measured or estimated as the top speed sustained for one minute at 10 meters above the surface. Peak gusts would be on the order of 10-25 percent higher.

Tropical Disturbance

An individual tropical weather system of apparently organized convection (upward transfer of heat and moisture into the atmosphere from the surface). Generally 100 to 300 nautical miles in diameter, originating in the tropics or subtropics. Having a non-frontal migratory character, and maintaining its identity for 24 hours or more. It may or may not be associated with a detectable disturbance of the wind field. Surface upheavals associated with disturbances in the wind field and progressing through the tropics from east to west are also known as easterly waves.

Tropical Depression

A tropical cyclone (a gathering of thunderstorms that rotate around a central vortex) in which the maximum sustained windspeed (using the U.S. 1 minute average standard) is 38 m.p.h. (33 knots) or less. Depressions have a closed circulation.

Tropical Storm

A tropical cyclone in which the maximum sustained surface windspeed (using the U.S. 1 minute average standard) ranges from 39 to 73 m.p.h. (34 to 63 knots). The convection in tropical storms is usually more concentrated near the center, with outer rainfall organizing into distinct bands.

Hurricane

When winds in a tropical cyclone equal or exceed 74 m.p.h. (64 knots), it is called a hurricane (in the Atlantic and eastern and central Pacific Oceans). Hurricanes are further designated by categories on the Saffir-Simpson scale. Hurricanes in categories 3, 4 and 5 are known as Major or Intense Hurricanes.

The Saffir-Simpson Scale of Hurricane Intensity

In 1969, The World Meteorological Organization was preparing a report on structural damage to dwellings hit by windstorms. They recognized the need for a standardized scale to which all with weather-related interests could refer, concerning the strength of hurricanes. The task of formulating such a scale fell to Dr. Bob Simpson, director of the National Hurricane Center at the time, and his colleague Herbert Saffir, a consulting engineer.

The two men took into account that the destructive power of a hurricane depends on the way a number of factors combine: storm surge, wind, forward motion, the configuration of the land it strikes, and other aspects of the weather event. They came up with a five-category scale that assigns each hurricane (any tropical storm with sustained winds over 74 m.p.h.) a number, according to its intensity.

Mr. Saffir contributed applicable standards of potential for causing property damage, while Dr. Simpson added information regarding potential for storm surge heights that accompany hurricanes in each category. This information supplies a fairly reliable estimate of the potential property damage and flooding that may be expected along coastal areas faced with the imminent arrival of a hurricane.

The resulting Saffir-Simpson scale is now used by NOAA's hurricane forecasters to make storm comparisons easier, and to clarify to government emergency managers the predicted hazards of approaching hurricanes.

Examples

Category	Sustained Winds (MPH)	Description	Examples
1	74-95	Minimal	Florence 1988 LA; Charley 1988 NC
2	96-110	Moderate	Kate 1985 FL; Bob 1991 NY
3	111-130	Extensive	Alicia 1983 TX
4	131-155	Extreme	Andrew 1992 FL; Hugo 1989 NC
5	>155	Catastrophic	Camille 1969 MS; Labor Day Hurricane 1935 FL Keys

Category	Winds	Effects
One	74-95 mph	No real damage to building structures. Damage primarily to unanchored mobile homes, shrubbery, and trees. Also, some coastal road flooding and minor pier damage
Two	96-110 mph	Some roofing material, door, and window damage to buildings. Considerable damage to vegetation, mobile homes, and piers. Coastal and low-lying escape routes flood 2-4 hours before arrival of center. Small craft in unprotected anchorages break moorings.
Three	111-130 mph	Some structural damage to small residences and utility buildings with a minor amount of curtainwall failures. Mobile homes are destroyed. Flooding near the coast destroys smaller structures with larger structures damaged by floating debris. Terrain continuously lower than 5 feet ASL may be flooded inland 8 miles or more.
Four	131-155 mph	More extensive curtainwall failures with some complete roof structure failure on small residences. Major erosion of beach. Major damage to lower floors of structures near the shore. Terrain continuously lower than 10 feet ASL may be flooded requiring massive evacuation of residential areas inland as far as 6 miles.
Five	> 155 mph	Complete roof failure on many residences and industrial buildings. Some complete building failures with small utility buildings blown over or away. Major damage to lower floors of all structures located less than 15 feet ASL and within 500 yards of the shoreline. Massive evacuation of residential areas on low ground within 5 to 10 miles of the shoreline may be required.

Costliest U.S. Hurricanes 1900-2000 (unadjusted)

The 30 costliest tropical cyclones to strike the U.S. mainland. Damages are listed in US dollars and are not adjusted for inflation.

Rank	Hurricane	Year	Category	Damage
1	Andrew (SE FL, S.E. LA)	1992	5[a]	26,500,000,000
2	Hugo (SC)	1989	4	7,000,000,000
3	Floyd (Mid-Atlantic & N.E.)	1999	2	4,500,000,000
4	Fran (NC)	1996	3	3,200,000,000
5	Opal (N.W. FL, AL)	1995	3	3,000,000,000
6	Georges (FL Keys, MS, AL)	1998	2	2,310,000,000
7	Frederic (AL, MS)	1979	3	2,300,000,000
8	Agnes (FL, N.E.)	1972	1	2,100,000,000
9	Alicia (N. TX)	1983	3	2,000,000,000
10	Bob (NC, N.E.)	1991	2	1,500,000,000
11	Juan (LA)	1985	1	1,500,000,000
12	Camille (MS, S.E. LA, VA)	1969	5	1,420,700,000
13	Betsy (S.E. FL, S.E. LA)	1965	3	1,420,500,000
14	Elena (MS, AL, N.W. FL)	1985	3	1,250,000,000
15	Gloria (Eastern US)	1985	3[b]	900,000,000
16	Diane (N.E.US)	1955	1	831,700,000
17	Bonnie (NC, VA)	1998	2	720,000,000
18	Erin (N.W. FL)	1995	2	700,000,000
19	Allison (N. TX)	1989	TS[c]	500,000,000
19	Alberto (N.W. FL, GA, AL)	1994	TS[c]	500,000,000
19	Frances (TX)	1998	TS[c]	500,000,000
22	Eloise (N.W. FL)	1975	3	490,000,000
23	Carol (N.E. U.S.)	1954	3b	461,000,000
24	Celia (S. TX)	1970	3	453,000,000
25	Carla (N. & Central TX)	1961	4	408,000,000
26	Claudette (N. TX)	1979	TS[c]	400,000,000
26	Gordon (S. & Central FL, NC)	1994	TS[c]	400,000,000
28	Donna (FL, Eastern US)	1960	4	387,000,000
29	David (FL, Eastern US)	1979	2	320,000,000
30	Unnamed (New England)	1938	3[b]	306,000,000

Notes

a – Reclassified as Category 5 in 2002
b – Moving more than 30 miles per hour
c – Tropical Storm intensity
d – Tropical Depression

August, 1955 Southeastern Pennsylvania Weather Highlights

1955 Pre-Flood Precipitation
as measured at the Franklin Institute, Philadelphia

Month	Total Precipitation (Rain + snow)	Avg. Total	Deficit or Surplus Percentage from Avg.
January	3.17"	3.21"	-1%
February	9.22"	2.79"	+70%
March	7.5"	3.46"	+54%
April	1.9"	3.62"	-48%
May	1"	3.75"	-73%
June	4"	3.74"	+7%
July	1"	4.28"	-77%
August	9.7"	3.8"	+61%

Precipitation rounded to the nearest hundredth of an inch. Departure from averages rounded to nearest whole percent.

Source: Franklin Institute, Philadelphia

Hurricane Diane Flooding & Specific Precipitation Data

Aug. 18

Hurricane "Diane" moved into the NC coast then recurved to the NE, passing very near Philadelphia, then to the Southern coast of New England. Diane's heavy rains, up to 13" in the Poconos, added to those of Connie 5 days earlier, brought massive flooding to the Mid Atlantic and NE states during the next few days. The storm killed between 184 to 200 people, making it onto the Deadliest Atlantic Tropical Cyclones, 1492 to Present, list. (At least 25 deaths needed to make this list). Philadelphia received 0.16" on the 16th, 0.44" on the 17th, 2.32" on the 18th and 0.06" on the 19th, for a total of 2.98".

Aug. 19

Tropical Storm Diane brought torrential rain and flooding across the region.

The S. Branch of the Raritan River at Stanton, Hunterdon Co., NJ, rose to a record 15.2'. Flood stage is 8.0'.

The Bushkill River at Shoemakers, Monroe Co., PA, rose to a record 14.0'. Flood stage is 6.0'.

The Brodhead Creek at Minisink Hills, Monroe Co., PA, rose to a record 27.0', causing one of the worst disasters to hit the Poconos, killing more than 75 people. Some bodies remained missing for years. Flood stage is 10.0'.

The Delaware River rose to a record 37.4', with flood stage 21.0', at Tocks Island, Warren Co., NJ; a record 43.7', with flood stage 22.0', at Phillipsburg, Warren Co., NJ; a record 38.9', with flood stage 22.0', at Riegelsville, Warren Co., NJ; a record 27.8', with flood stage 16.0', at Frenchtown, Hunterdon Co., NJ; a record 28.4', with flood stage 18.0', at Stockton, Hunterdon Co.; and a record 26.0', with flood stage 13.0', at New Hope, Bucks Co., PA. The Neshaminy Creek at Langhorne, Bucks Co., PA, rose to a record 22.8'. Flood stage is 9.0'. (PHL)(USGS)

Aug. 20

The Delaware River at Washington Crossing, Mercer Co., NJ, rose to a record 27.8'. Flood stage is 20.0'. (USGS)

Source: Philadelphia/Mt. Holly National Weather Service

2 – Delaware River Crests

Peak Water Levels During Flood of Aug. 19-20, 1955

Bridge Location	Date	Time	Crest.Elev.	Ft. ANL
Lower Trenton-Morrisville	8/20/55	9:00 AM	21.99'	22.0'
Trenton Calhoun Street	8/20/55	9:00 AM	28.53'	18.53'
Yardley-Wilburtha	8/20/55	8:00 AM	41.49'	25.49'
Washington Crossing	8/20/55	7:00 AM	53.77'	27.77'
New Hope-Lambertville	8/20/55	6:00 AM	73.27'	24.27'
Centre Bridge-Stockton	8/20/55	5:00 AM	84.40'	30.40'
Lumberville-Raven Rock	8/20/55	4:00 AM	97.25'	31.25'
Pt. Pleasant-Byram	8/20/55	3:30 AM	105.32'	31.32'
Uhlertown-Frenchtown	8/20/55	2:00 AM	127.79'	27.0'
Upper Black Eddy-Milford	8/20/55	1:00 AM	140.25'	31.35'
Riegelsville	8/19/55	Midnight	164.02'	36.62'
Easton-Phillipsburg	8/19/55	10:30 PM	198.90'	43.7'
Riverton-Belvidere	8/19/55	9:00 PM	258.48'	28.38'
Portland-Columbia	8/19/55	7:00 PM	298.87'	29.27'

(ANL = Above Normal Low)

SOURCE: 1955 Annual Report - Delaware River Joint Toll Bridge Commission

3 – Delaware River Organizations

Advocacy & Environmental Groups

Delaware RiverKeeper Network
Main Office
P.O. Box 326
Washington Crossing, PA 18977-0326
Phone   215-369-1188
Fax   215-369-1181
Email   drkn@delawareriverkeeper.org
URL   http://www.delawareriverkeeper.org

A nonprofit, membership organization that has worked since 1988 to strengthen citizen protection of the Delaware River and its tributary watersheds. An affiliate of the American Littoral Society, a national conservation group, The Delaware Riverkeeper Network works throughout the Delaware's entire 13,539 square mile watershed, which includes portions of NY, NJ, PA and DE. Its programs include:

- a watershed-wide advocacy program
- River Resources Law Clinic, enforcing environmental laws in the watershed
- Tributary Task Force initiative, designed to organize and strengthen local communities working to protect local streams
- restoration projects organizing volunteers to restore eroded stream banks, using bio-engineering techniques
- a volunteer monitoring program with sites along the entire length of the River
- pollution hotlines
- student intern opportunities

The Delaware Riverkeeper is the voice of the Delaware River and its streams, and the Delaware Riverkeeper Network stands as a vigilant protector and defender of the river, its tributaries and its watershed. They are committed to restoring the natural balance where it has been lost and ensuring its preservation where it still exists.

Delaware River Foundation
PO Box 746
Hancock, NY 13783
Phone   607-637-3220
Email   info@delawareriverfoundation.org

The Delaware River Foundation is a not-for-profit organization dedicated to the Upper Delaware River system. Members include fishermen, local landowners and business people, organized in an effort to protect and improve the East Branch, West Branch and Main Stem Delaware River, as well as the Neversink River.

The organization's goals are to:

• Protect and improve the wild trout populations and the aquatic health in these rivers.
• Support cutting-edge, scientific modeling and cooperation with all parties to achieve a solution to better manage water releases and water temperatures on these rivers.
• Serve as a watchdog for the rivers and ensure that all parties follow through with any agreements and commitments.
• Work to improve fishing access, special regulations, and management decisions that will improve the fishery and the local economies.

Delaware Highlands Conservancy
P.O. Box 218
Hawley, PA 18428-0218
Phone   570-226-3164
Fax   570-226-3166
Email   info@delawarehighlands.org
URL   http://www.delawarehighlands.org

A non-profit land trust, founded in 1994, that works with landowners to conserve the natural and cultural heritage of the Upper Delaware River Region. The group's primary mission is to conserve the forests, farms and waters of the Upper Delaware River region by acquiring conservation easements, or land, from willing landowners.

The group's easements include farmlands, wetlands, working forest land, and other natural properties. They also maintain a small nature center, the Butterfly Barn, so children and adults can learn about the plants and wildlife native to this region, and how to care for their terrestrial and aquatic habitats.

The Conservancy is funded by contributions from hundreds of members and local business leaders who want to keep the Upper Delaware River region healthy, prosperous and alive.

Friends of the Upper Delaware River
P.O. Box 69
Minoa, NY 13116
Phone   866-230-3767 x74
Email   info@fudr.org
URL   http://www.fudr.org

An all-volunteer advocacy organization dedicated to protecting one of the last wild trout fisheries in the East.

Friends of the Delaware Canal
Susan Taylor, Director
145 South Main Street
New Hope, PA 18938
Phone 215-862-2021
Fax 215-862-2021
Email fodc@erols.com
URL http://www.fodc.org/

An independent, non-profit organization working to restore, preserve, and improve the Delaware Canal and its surroundings. The group's primary goals are to ensure that the Canal is fully-watered and the towpath trail is continuous. The Friends embrace this mission in order to
• sustain a unique link to the area's heritage
• care for and protect beautiful open space
• provide recreational opportunities for current and future generations.

The Friends' goals are accomplished through advocacy, community volunteerism, and educational and recreational programs. They sponsor walking tours, educational programs, informational meetings, clean-ups, fundraisers, and social events. Members receive a quarterly newsletter.

GreenTreks Network, Inc.
1420 Walnut Street, Suite 1304
Philadelphia, PA 19102
Phone 215-545-5880
Fax 215-545-5811
E-mail talktous@greentreks.org
URL http://www.greentreks.org

The mission of GreenTreks Network, Inc. is to make the health of the environment an intrinsic part of everyday life and to inspire individuals to make informed decisions that effect positive environmental change. They accomplish this through television and multimedia productions which tell entertaining and thought-provoking stories that present both the realities of the current environment and highlight possible solutions to environmental problems innovative outreach programs that are used to put educational tools directly into the hands of individuals, community groups and other organizations working for change.

Watershed Associations

Brodhead Watershed Association
Box 339
Henryville, PA 18332
Phone   570-839-1120
Email   questions@brodheadwatershed.org
URL   http://www.brodheadwatershed.org

The Brodhead Watershed Association (BWA) is a non-profit environmental organization dedicated to protecting and improving water quality and the environment in the Brodhead watershed. The BWA assists municipalities, residents, businesses and groups with protecting natural resources through education, workshops, seminars, public programs, stream monitoring and baseline data collection and stream cleanups.

The Brodhead watershed is located primarily in Monroe County and includes the Brodhead, Marshalls, McMichael, Paradise, and Pocono creeks and their tributaries. All the tributaries join the Brodhead Creek near Stroudsburg and flow to the Delaware River at a site just north of the Delaware Water Gap.

Gallows Run Watershed Association
PO Box 24
Kintnersville, PA 18930
Phone   610-346-8997
Email   info@grwabucks.org
URL   http://www.grwabucks.org

The Gallows Run Watershed Association (GRWA) is an independent non-profit organization dedicated to protecting the quality of the natural resources of the Gallows Run Watershed. The group advocates on behalf of sound environmental stewardship, sustainable land management, and the preservation of the rural character of Durham and Nockamixon townships in Pennsylvania.

Their tools include educational outreach, active participation in the legal processes that affect local land use, and a strategic partnership with other organizations that share their objectives.

Musconetcong Watershed Association
Beth Styler Barry, Executive Director
PO Box 113
Asbury, NJ 08802
Phone   908-537-7060
Email   beth@musconetcong.org
URL   http://www.musconetcong.org

Appendix

The Musconetcong Watershed Association (MWA) is a non-profit organization incorporated in 1992 to protect and enhance the Musconetcong River and its related resources. MWA members are kept informed about issues concerning the watershed by receiving quarterly issues of the *Musconetcong River News*.

MWA's primary mission is education and awareness. They carry out grassroots activities including educational programs, municipal government outreach, workshops and seminars for the public, stream cleanups and outdoor educational programs.

Government Bodies

The Delaware River Basin Commission
P.O. Box 7360
West Trenton, NJ 08628-0360
Phone   609-883-9500
FAX   609-883-9522
Email   clarke.rupert@drbc.state.nj.us
URL   http://www.state.nj.us/drbc/drbc.htm

An interstate compact between Delaware, New Jersey, Pennsylvania and New York and the United States federal government, created in 1961 to provide an agency through which the signatories could join together as equal partners in river basin planning, development and regulation.

Commission programs include water quality protection, water supply allocation, regulatory review (permitting), water conservation initiatives, watershed planning, drought management, flood control, and recreation. The DRBC is funded by the signatory parties, project review fees, water use charges, and fines, as well as federal, state, and private grants.

Pennsylvania Organization for Watersheds and Rivers, Inc.
610 North Third St.
Harrisburg, PA 17101
Phone   717-234-7910
Fax   717-234-7929
Email   info@pawatersheds.org
URL   http://www.pawatersheds.org

POWR advocates for the protection, restoration and enjoyment of the commonwealth's water resources, and conducts programs that foster stewardship, communication, leadership and action.

Delaware & Raritan Canal Commission
PO Box 539
Stockton, NJ 08559
Phone   609-397-2000
Fax   609-397-2001
Email   drcc@blast.net
URL   http://www.dandrcanal.com/drcc/index.html

An administrative body established in October, 1974 to accomplish three main tasks:

• Review and approve, reject or modify any action by the State in the Canal Park, or any permit for action in the park

• undertake planning for the development of the Canal Park

• Prepare and administer a land use regulatory program that will protect the Canal Park from the harmful impacts of new development in central New Jersey.

History & Heritage
Delaware & Lehigh Heritage Corridor
National Park Service, U.S. Dept. of the Interior
URL   http://www.nps.gov/dele/

A collection of people, places and events that helped shape the American nation. The Corridor passes through five Pennsylvania counties bursting with heritage and brimming with outdoor adventure. Canals and railroads-remnants of Northeastern Pennsylvania's prosperous coal age-form the spine of this more than 150-mile Corridor. Contains a history trail marked with stories about hearty lumberjacks, coal miners, lock tenders, canalers and railroaders. Outdoor recreation enthusiasts can explore quiet canal paths, challenging bike trails and the rippling waters of the Delaware and Lehigh Rivers.

Delaware & Raritan Canal State Park
625 Canal Road
Somerset, NJ 08873
Phone   732-873-3050
Email   inquiries@dandrcanal.com
URL   http://www.dandrcanal.com/park_index.html

The 70-mile Delaware and Raritan Canal State Park is one of central New Jersey's most popular recreational corridors for canoeing, jogging, hiking, bicycling, fishing and horseback riding. The canal and the park are part of the National Recreation Trail System, as well as a valuable wildlife corridor connecting fields and forests.

With its wooden bridges and 19th century bridge tender houses, remnants of locks, cobblestone spillways and handbuilt stone-arched culverts, the canal is also a tremendous attraction for history lovers. The upper portion of the feeder canal follows the Delaware River through historic New Jersey towns such as Frenchtown, Stockton and Lambertville. The main canal passes the Port Mercer bridge tender's house, through the charming villages of Kingston and Griggstown to Blackwells Mills, ending up in New Brunswick.

Delaware River Mill Society
PO Box 298
Stockton, NJ 08559
Phone   609-397-3586
Fax   609-397-3913
Email   drms@netcarrier.com
URL   http://home2.netcarrier.com/~drms/

A group of local citizens and interested members who, in 1976, obtained a long-term lease giving their group the responsibility to "restore, preserve, operate, maintain and interpret" the Prallsville Mills site. The Mills were included on the National Register of Historic Places in 1973. The entire property became part of the Delaware & Raritan Canal State Park in 1974.

The Mill has become a place of cultural and environmental events attracting wide spread participation. Concerts, art exhibitions, antique shows, holiday parties, school fund-raiser auctions, meetings, as well as private parties, are a source of income for restoration and maintenance of the site.

Bibliography

Books

Barnes, John H. and W.D. Sevon, *The Geological Story of Pennsylvania*. Fourth Series. Harrisburg, PA. Commonwealth of Pennsylvania Department of Conservation and Natural Resources, Bureau of Topographic and Geologic Survey, 2002.

Dale, Frank. *Bridges over the Delaware River: A History of Crossings*. New Brunswick, N.J. Rutgers University Press, 2003.

Dale, Frank. *Delaware Diary: Episodes in the Life of a River*. New Brunswick, N.J. Rutgers University Press, 1996.

Dempsey, David. *FLOOD*. Original edition. New York, N.Y. Ballantine Books, 1956.

Gelber, Ben. *Pocono Weather: A History of Eastern Pennsylvania, the Poconos, and Northwestern New Jersey*. Revised edition. Stroudsburg, Pa. Uriel Publishing, 1998.

Gelber, Ben. *The Pennsylvania Weather Book*. Princeton, N.J. Rutgers University Press, 2002.

Larsen, Erik. *Isaac's Storm: A Man, A Time, and the Deadliest Hurricane in History*. New York, N.Y. Crown Publishers, 1999.

Ludlum, David M. *The New Jersey Weather Book*. New Brunswick, N.J. Rutgers University Press, 1983.

Nese, Dr. Jon M. and Schwartz, Glenn. *The Philadelphia Area Weather Book*. Philadelphia, Pa. Temple University Press, 2002.

Shank, William, P.E. *Great Floods of Pennsylvania: A Two-Century History*. Second Edition. Annapolis, MD. American Canal and Transportation Center, 2001.

Stutz, Bruce. *Natural Lives, Modern Times: People and Places of the Delaware River*. New York, NY. Crown Publishers, Inc. 1992.

Toomey, David. Stormchaser: *The Hurricane Hunters and Their Fateful Flight into Hurricane Janet*. New York, NY. W.W. Norton & Company, 2002.

Magazine, Newspaper and Newsletter Articles

[Note: So many contemporary news articles from affected flood areas were used that listing them all would be impractical. Those listed here are special for one reason or another, either for their uniquely qualified authorship, historical reportage or because they come from publications that lay readers might not otherwise hear of.]

And the Floods Came. J. Silas Graybill, ed. *Mission News* newsletter. Franconia Mennonite Board of Missions and Charities. September, 1955.

Special Flood Anniversary Edition Newsletter. Barrett Township Historical Society. Mountainhome, PA. January, 2005.

The First Weather Officer to Fly Into A Hurricane. Al Moyers, Air Force Weather Historian, and Jerry White, Deputy Air Force Weather Historian. Air Force Weather Historian, Volume 1, Issue 3, quarterly newsletter of the Air Force Weather History Office. Summer, 2003. https://afweather.afwa.af.mil/ docs/AFW_Historian_Newsletter_1-3.pdf

Inside Line. Employee newsletter of the Line Material Company. East Stroudsburg, PA. Special Pennsylvania Flood Edition. October, 1955.

The Legacy of Tocks Island Dam: A Three-Part Perspective. David Pierce, *Pocono Record.* August 12-14, 2001.

Memories of Agnes flood back for locals. Ron Devlin, *Allentown Morning Call.* June 23, 2002.

The Meteorologist In Your Life. Patrick Hughes. *Weatherwise* magazine, June 1, 1995.

What Diane Taught Us: Bucks Moves to Save Its Land. Edward A. Miller. *Bucks County Traveller* magazine. August, 1956.

Essays, Correspondence and Personal Accounts

1955-56, Moving to New Hope, Hurricane & Flood. Diary entry by Alice Barry. Stockton, N.J. Covers period of August 18-28, 1955.

An Eyewitness Account of the Flood. Robert Robacker. Monroe County Historical Association files. 1955.

The First Flight Into A Hurricane's Eye. Personal recollection by Lt. Col. Ralph O'Hair, U.S. Army Air Force (Ret.). As reported in The 1943 Surprise Hurricane. NOAA History: Stories and Tales of the Weather Service. Lew Fincher, Hurricane Consultant and Bill Read, Houston/Galveston Area National Weather Service. http://www.history.noaa.gov/stories_tales/surprise.html

Floods On the Delaware River. Personal handwritten essay by George Wyker. Spruance Library Collection, Bucks County Historical Society. Doylestown, Pa.

N.A.R.A. Eisenhower Administration (1953-1961) Archives item #214 - Dwight D.

Eisenhower. Telegram to the President of the United States Chamber of Commerce on Assistance Given Flood Disaster Area. Released at Lowry AFB, Denver, Co. September 12, 1955.

Neither Rain Nor Flood Nor...Stopped This Wedding! Kathleen Cody Sengel. *Barrett Township Historical Society Newsletter.* Vol. 13, No. 1. January, 2005.

Recollections of the Flood in 1955 in Canadensis. Dale Price as told to Lew Parks. *Barrett Township Historical Society Newsletter.* Vol. 13, No. 1. January, 2005.

Letter and poem. Alan Jackson. October 10, 2004.

Written personal account. Dorothy Schloss Shutt. October 5, 2004.

Written personal account. Joanne Shutt Weiss. October 5, 2004.

Technical Data, Reports and Monographs
August 18, 1955 – A Demon Named Diane. Report, on file at Monroe County Historical Association. Gracann Bush. May 25, 1971.

Bulletins and Advisories on Hurricane "Connie." Issued by Weather Bureau Office, Miami, Florida and Weather Bureau Airport Station, Washington, D.C. Covering 0100 EST August 4, 1955 through 1400 EST August 13, 1955. United States Department of Commerce, Weather Bureau. Washington, D.C., 1955.

Bulletins and Advisories on Hurricane "Diane." Issued by Weather Bureau Office, Miami, Florida and Weather Bureau Airport Station, Washington, D.C. Covering 0700 EST August 11, 1955 through 2300 EST August 17, 1955. United States Department of Commerce, Weather Bureau. Washington, D.C., 1955.

Coroner's Reports, August 18-19, 1955 Flood Victims. Office of the Coroner. Monroe County Courthouse, East Stroudsburg, Pa.

Delaware River and Neshaminy Creek, Bucks County Flood, 18 and 19 August, 1955. Incident report. A. M. Heritage, Col. U.S. Army (Ret.), Director Bucks County Council of Civil Defense; Col. John Cummings, Curator Bucks County Historical Society, Historian for Bucks County Council of Civil Defense. Doylestown, Pa.

Deadliest, Costliest, and Most Intense United States Hurricanes From 1900 to 2000 (and Other Frequently Requested Hurricane Facts). NOAA Technical Memorandum NWS TPC-1. J. Jarrell, et al. Miami, FL, 2001.

Distribution of Precipitation over the Northeast Accompanying Landfalling and Transitioning Tropical Cyclones. David DeLuca, et al. Originally presented at the 20th Conference on Weather Analysis and Forecasting. Seattle, WA, January 11-15, 2004.

The Effects of a Threatening Rumor on a Disaster-Stricken Community. National Research Council report, 1958. Pub. National Academies Press, Washington, D.C. Available online at http://books.nap.edu/books/ARC000010/html/5.html

Extent and Frequency of Floods in the Vicinity of Easton, Pa. – Phillipsburg, N.J.
Open-file report prepared by George Farlekas. United States Department of the
Interior Geological Survey, prepared in cooperation with the Delaware River Basin
Commission. Trenton, N.J. October, 1965.

Floods: The Awesome Power. Informational pamphlet. U.S. Department of Commerce,
National Oceanic and Atmospheric Administration, and the National Weather
Service. Washington, D.C. August, 2002.

Highways: a review of the New Jersey State Highway Department, 1954-1962. New
Jersey State Highway Department. Trenton, N.J. 1962.

Historical Weather Data, Philadelphia, Pa. Washington, DC. The *Washington Post* online.
http://www.washingtonpost.com/wp-srv/weather/longterm/historical/data/
Philadelphia_pa.htm

Hurricanes Connie, Diane and Ione. Online archives, National Oceanic and
Atmospheric Administration. http://www.csc.noaa.gov/products/nchaz/htm/1955.htm.

Memorable Hurricanes of the United States Since 1873. NOAA Technical
Memorandum NWS SR-56. Arnold Sugg, et al. U.S. Department of Commerce,
Southern Region. Fort Worth, Tex., 1971.

North Atlantic Hurricanes and Tropical Disturbances, Year 1955. U.S. Weather
Bureau. Miami, Fla., 1955.

Northampton Street Bridge. History and description. Lehigh Valley Section of the
American Society of Civil Engineers. http://sections.asce.org/Lehigh/site

Operation Tempest Rapids: Report of search, rescue and recovery operations by U.S.
Army at Tobyhanna Signal Depot from August 19-23, 1955. Col. Robert Angster,
Commander. 1955.

Philadelphia Area Historic Weather Data. Philadelphia, Pa. Franklin Institute, online.
http://www.fi.edu/weather/data2/index.html.

*Report of the Delaware River Port Authority to the governors and legislatures of the
Commonwealth of Pennsylvania and the state of New Jersey.* The Authority, 1955.
Delaware River Port Authority, Camden, N.J.

Structure No. 260 – Riegelsville Toll-Supported Bridge. Internal history and technical
specifications. Delaware River Joint Toll Bridge Commission. Morrisville, Pa.

*Technical Paper No. 26: Hurricane Rains and Floods of August 1955, Carolinas to
New England.* Paul H. Kutschenreuter. U.S. Department of Commerce, Weather
Bureau. Washington, D.C. 1956.

Topographical Maps of New Jersey, New York and Pennsylvania. TerraServer and
TopoZone online. http://www.terraserver.com. http://www.topozone.com.

Watershed Protection and Flood Prevention Act. (16 U.S.C. 1001-1009, Chapter 18; P.L. 566, August 4, 1954; 68 Stat. 666)

Weather and Circulation of August 1955: Including the Climatological Background for Hurricanes Connie and Diane. Jerome Namias and Carlos R. Dunn, Extended Forecast Section, U.S. Weather Bureau, Washington, D.C. Excerpt from *Monthly Weather Review.* August, 1955.

Working in Pennsylvania: A History of the Department of Labor & Industry. Chapter 3, 1940-1970. "Hurricane Diane Report Log, Easton Employment Office." Donald A. Young, Office Manager. August 19-27, 1955.

Wyoming-Jefferson Divisions Maintenance-of-Way Personnel File Index. Erie Railroad. Post-flood records, in custody of Steamtown National Historic Site. Scranton, Pa.

Specialized Photo Essays of the 1955 Flood
Booklets published by regional newspapers immediately following the flood.

Diane Drowns Delaware Valley. Easton, Pa. *The Easton Express,* 1955.

The Great Flood Disaster of 1955. Flemington, N.J. The Democrat Press, 1955.

The Flood: Photo Highlights of Northeastern Pennsylvania's Worst Disaster. Carbondale, Pa. *Carbondale Review.* 1955.

The Flood of 1955. Blairstown, N.J. *Blairstown Press,* 1955.

Primary Source Interviews
Abbott, James. In-person interview. 6/17/2003.

Ace, Libby. Indirect personal interview from author's questions through caretaker Joanne Cesarini. 3/3/2005. Also personal interview by Barbara Beckwith. 10/2004

Amato, Ann. Several email and telephone conversations, plus an in-person interview with Harry Leida's niece, at her home in State College, PA. 6/26/2003.

Armitage, Sandy Smith. In-person interview. 7/11/2003.

Arnone, Vince and Lorraine. In-person interview. 7/14/2003.

Balliet, Jean Sinka. Email interview. 9/16/2004.

Barry, Peter and Alice. In-person interview. 6/29/2004.

Beecken, Elaine DeWinton. Several written narratives and follow-up telephone conversation between 8/25-9/15/2004.

Birutta, John. Email interviews. 9/23/2004 and 10/21/2004.

Bohm, Robert K. Email and mail interview and personal narrative. 10/6/2004.

Bowman, Craig. In-person conversation. 4/10/2003.

Brown, Helen G. In-person interview at her home in Stroudsburg, PA. 8/30/2004.

Cochran, Clarence. In-person interview. 6/21/2004.

Coleman, William H. In-person interview. 3/17/2003.

DeGroot, Richard J. In-person interview. 6/9/2003.

Detwiler, Marian. Mail survey. 10/20/2004.

DiRenzis, Richard and Jean. In-person interview. 6/30/2004.

Dobron, William Sr. From narrative compiled by his daughter, Tammy. 7/10/2004.

Duvall, Richard. Mail survey. 6/24/2004.

Edwards, Donald F. and Marion J. Telephone interview. 10/24/2004.

Edwards, Leroy. Telephone interview. 1/7/2005.

Ephross, Sally Packard. In-person interview. 3/24/2003.

Fackenthal, Margaret Beling. In-person interview. 6/27/2004.

Farrell, Gertrude Miller. Letters and telephone conversations, 4/14-10/13/2004.

Folkes, Jay. Telephone interview. 1/23/2005.

Fresco, Greta Johnson. In-person interview. 3/27/2003.

Gabrielan, Randall. Email interview. 9/14/2004.

Gelber, Ben. In-person interview, East Stroudsburg Lincoln Street Park, Day Street Flats. 8/6/2004.

Gordon, Phyllis Baty. Email interviews. 3/2-4/2004.

Grider, Dorothy. In-person interview. 4/24/2003.

Harpster, Richard. In-person interview. 6/8/2003.

Harrington, Edwin. In-person interview. 4/18/2003.

Herman, Robert. Series of mail and email interviews, 10/5-28/2004

Herr, William. Telephone interview.10/14/2004.

Hissim, Herman and June. Telephone interview. 4/1/2003.

Jesiolowski, Edmund. In-person interview. 5/14/2003.

Kale, Dorothy. In-person interview. 6/1/2003.

Kennedy, Nancy Wolfe. Personal narrative and email followup. Summer 2004.

Larison, Ruth Stielau. Telephone interview, 1/6/2005.

Leida, Joyce Hewitt. Telephone interview with Harry Leida's widow. 2/24/2005.

Line, Donna Marcs. Telephone interview. 1/12/2005.

Litschauer, Edmund. In-person interview. 5/14/2003.

Mahl, Stephen. In-person interview. 10/10/2004.

Maxwell, Robert. In-person interview. 1/16/2005.

Opdyke, Jack. In-person interview. Summer, 2004.

Palmer, Carol Peri. Mail survey. 6/22/2004.

Riggs, D. Randy. Telephone interview. 1/12/2005.

Salaga, John. Superintendent, District I, Delaware River Joint Toll Bridge Commission. Telephone interview, 10/15/2004.

Santin, Marie Petranto. Telephone interview. 10/13/2004.

Scarborough, Kenneth. Telephone interview. 10/13/2004.

Schafer, June. Telephone interviews, 10/13-14/2004.

Sciss, Lester and Eleanor. In-person interview. 5/14/2003.

Scudder, Charles M. In-person interview. 6/17/2003.

Singer, Herbert. Email interview through his granddaughter, Sandra Singer Rauschenberger. 5/8/2003.

Slack, Laura B. In-person interview. 8/25/2004.

Snyder, May. In-person interview. 6/21/2004.

Stires, Barbara Fletcher. Email interview. 10/27/2004.

Stull, Miriam. In-person interview. 6/21/2004.

Sutton, Clifford and Virginia. In-person interview. 5/27/2003.

Talone, William and Claire. In-person interview. 8/18/2003.

Thran, Charles. Telephone message. 11/20/2004.

Tinsman, William Sr. In-person interview. 4/10/2003.

Ward, Palmer. Email interview. 8/20/2004.

Weber, Sandra Cochran. Email interview. 1/21/2004.

Williams, Marlyn Minder. In-person interview. 6/21/2004

Williams, Mildred. In-person interview. 6/21/2004

Wilson, Judy Castree. Telephone interview. 1/12/2005.

Winans, R. Foster. Email interview. 1/21/2003.

Wolf, Carol Turner. In-person interview. 8/20/2003.

Wristen, Christine Koehler. In-person interview. 6/10/2003.

Zorbas, Jane Leida. In-person interview with Harry Leida's sister, at her daughter's home in State College, PA. 6/26/2003

Secondary Source Interviews
Gross, Daryl. Series of email and telephone interviews on the topic of the Blooming Glen Mennonite Church participation in cleanup from the flood. Westover, MD. Fall 2004.

Knecht, Donna. Tobyhanna Township administrative office. Telephone interview, 1/27/05. Concerning the dam break on Pocono Lake, Donna consulted a crewmember of the Tobyhanna Township Public Works Department, who had lived there during the 1955 flood. He provided details of the dam break and its results.

van Rossum, Maya. Delaware RiverKeeper Network. Email interview. September, 2004.

Tapes, Videos and DVDs
After the Rain: The Spruce Lake Story. The birth of the Bucks County Mennonite Disaster Service. Franconia Mennonite Camp Association. Canadensis, PA. © 2003, Legacy Video

The Flood of 1955. Helen Brown. Produced by East Stroudsburg University, 1998.

Reminiscence Meeting, September 24, 2002. Lambertville Historical Society, audio cassette tape transcript.

Websites
1955: Underwater. Chris Baud of *The Trentonian.* 1955: Trenton's Worst Flood. http://www.capitalcentury.com/1955.html

Bethlehem Flood of 1955. Joe Gerencher. Moravian College. http://home.moravian.edu/users/phys/mejjg01/geology/images/Flood_1955/bethlehem_flood_of_1955.htm

Brodhead Watershed Conservation Plan. Pennsylvania Department of Conservation and Natural Resources. Pennsylvania state website. http://www.dcnr.state.pa.us/brc/rivers/riversconservation/registry/brdhistoric.pdf

Calculation of Flood Forces. Hydrostatic pressure data. http://64.233.161.104/

The History of Civil Defense & Emergency Management in Tennessee. Includes full history of FEMA development. http://www.tnema.org/Archives/EMHistory/TNCDHistory.htm

Flood: The Great Flood of 1955. Village of Branchville, New Jersey website. http://www.Branchville-nj.com/flood.html

Floodwater force. AWS Convergence Technologies, Inc. Weatherbug site. http://www.aws.com/aws_2001/greatesthits/default.asp?CID=61

History of Levittown, The. City of Levittown, PA official website. http://www.levittownpa.org/Levittown.html

History of the Lackawanna Valley. H. Hollister, M.D. Excerpt from the Sixth edition, 1903. http://www.freehaunt.org/slocumhollow.htm

Hurricane Diane. William C. Gallagher, 1998. http://www.rr-fallenflags.org/el/before/diane.html

Lena Blackburne Baseball Rubbing Mud. http://baseballrubbingmud.com

Levittown, Pennsylvania: Building the Suburban Dream. State Museum of Pennsylvania. http://server1.fandm.edu/levittown/default.html

Pennsylvania Highways. Webring member, the Pennsylvania Highways Network, which consists of websites devoted to all aspects of the highway system of the Commonwealth of Pennsylvania.   http://www.pahighways.com

The Power of a Doubled River. "Ask A Scientist" Environmental Earth Science Archive. http://www.Newton.dep.anl.gov/askasci/env99/env251.htm

Red, White and Blue Highways: The story of the U.S. Interstate. http://www.factmonster.com/spot/interstate1.html

Upper Brodhead Creek Subwatershed. Brodhead Watershed Association official website. http://www.brodheadwatershed.org/1.htm

Wanderings: Inside the Francis E. Walter Dam. A journal by Al Zagofsky. http://home.ptd.net/~azagofsk/wanderings/wanderpg1.html

Water Safety Course Instruction. Information on the force of moving water. http://www.shawnalladio.com/k38/k38_tayenaka.htm

Watershed Protection and Flood Prevention Act, 1954. Digest of Federal Resource Laws of Interest to the U.S. Fish and Wildlife Service. US Fish & Wildlife Service website. http://laws.fws.gov/lawsdigest/watrshd.html

Acknowledgments

This project began innocently enough. I found a copy of "Diane Drowns Delaware Valley," a photo essay booklet published a week after the flood by the *Easton Express*. After reading it, I promptly forgot about it until a few years ago, when I remembered that the fiftieth anniversary of the event would soon be upon us. As a columnist for the *Bucks County Herald,* I wanted to write a series of columns about it for that anniversary. Realizing I had to do all the research anyway, I figured I may as well write an entire book. It seemed fitting, since no one—surprisingly—had so recognized this major natural disaster.

I soon realized why. It turned out to be a monumental undertaking, and basically laid claim to my life for three years. As with most worthwhile efforts, it soon became a labor of love that sometimes bordered on obsession. Most of the time, I wasn't even sure it would ever get published. The only way it finally did see print was through an almost unbelievable set of circumstances, including the support of an amazingly diverse yet dedicated collection of individuals and organizations.

Many people contribute to an undertaking such as this book, in many different capacities. No author of any historical documentary can be successful without the support of understanding families, interested friends and coworkers, helpful research librarians, museum curators and media archivists, and of course, professional colleagues.

I am no exception, and the following few pages are devoted with much humility and gratitude to all those whose interest and support gave me the strength to plow ahead. Even when daunting work loomed ahead of me, testing my courage and resolve to complete it, the kind words and encouragement of my friends and family were enough to get me back in that chair in front of the computer.

I have attempted to include everyone who deserves recognition for their parts in making this book a reality. If I have inadvertently left anyone out, please don't take it as ingratitude. Simply understand that five boxes of paperwork make an easy place to lose things. I have genuinely appreciated every single supportive comment and action from every person who offered them.

A few people deserve special recognition for having gone above and beyond in their efforts to help me, and I want to mention them first:

Bridget Wingert, Editor of the *Bucks County Herald* newspaper, gave me the initial push to start the project. Her positive response to my inquiries about doing an article series about the flood allowed that idea to morph into this book. Without her encouragement in the very early stages, I would never have even started it.

The book would likely not have seen the light of day without the absolute dedication of my friend and colleague, R. Foster Winans. His belief in the importance of the work and his incredible enthusiasm helped sustain me through an often difficult process.

Some of that difficulty arose when my mother, Nina W. Shafer, passed away very suddenly and unexpectedly during what should have been the last phase of writing the manuscript. She had been unwaveringly supportive of my writing career. She even helped me with the research for this book by accompanying me on interviews with flood survivors. I will always cherish that memory. Thanks, Mom. I wish you could have been here to see the end result. I choose to believe you're enjoying it anyway.

Special thanks to my nephew, Tucker, whose visit just before I went into the last leg of revisions and production helped me move past losing Mom so I could finish the work. What a blessing his serene presence was. His mother—my sister and respected colleague—Rebecca Valentine, performed miracles of time management to edit and index this huge manuscript while working on a book of her own. Any remaining errors are solely my own. Thanks, Beck.

Three people in particular are to be commended for performing some of the most unglamorous "grunt work" necessary to create this work. Noreen Wickert, a most kind and generous soul and a valued friend, and Caryn and Casey Newton, two delightful and talented young ladies, spent an entire summer helping me with research and data entry. They all spent numerous hours at the challenging task of taking interview notes, both in single-subject sessions and in groups. They then hunched over ancient, slow computers and put up with temperamental tape recorders to transcribe those notes. This book owes everything to their steadfast work, and I will be ever grateful for that and for their company, which made the workdays pass more quickly.

The interest and generosity of Buz and Linda Teacher helped make this book possible. They lent their considerable publishing experience and social connections to planning the book and helping raise funds for its production, and asked nothing in return. Their involvement and kindness have been a gift.

Tim White and Maya van Rossum of the Delaware RiverKeeper Network lent their expertise to my inquiries about certain aspects of the river, and were enthusiastic about working with us to promote the book. I am proud that a portion of the proceeds from the sale of each copy will go to support their amazing organization. Its efforts to protect the Delaware from harm help ensure there will always be a river worth writing about.

As a member of the Bucks County Historical Society, I frequent their Spruance Library to perform a good deal of research for this and other projects. I thank librarian Fran Waite for her aid in locating the many sources I required, and for helping keep this archive one of Bucks County's many treasures.

Sandy Weber graciously allowed me to use her Bucks County Hair Company and Day Spa as a space in which to perform group interviews. Not only that, she was kind enough to videotape the proceedings, thereby creating a valuable oral history artifact in itself. Sandy shared with me her own memories of the flood, and also helped locate other interview subjects, including her dad, Clarence "Tom" Cochran.

Karen Ackerman, one of Sandy's stylists, also helped a great deal in identifying and assembling the interviewees. Two of those subjects were her mother, Marlyn Williams, and her grandmother, Mildred Williams. Karen's enthusiasm and invaluable ambassadorship on behalf of this project have been evident from Day One, and it's this kind of support that keeps an author going over the long haul.

Suzanne Forbes, a delightful and generous spirit whose personal and professional dedication to the welfare of the river is both inspiration and aspiration for me, was also a bulwark of enthusiasm. She put me in touch with many people who helped it along, and gave freely of her valuable advice and network connections. Like many others, she was also there with tremendous moral support and positive energy when I really needed it.

Chris Handschin of the Haycock Township Historical Society was a source of early and ongoing support.

Lance Metz of the National Canal Museum Archives and Bill Minneo of the Delaware & Lehigh Canal National Heritage Corridor helped me decide where to begin related parts of my research.

Renee Bristow lent me a scrapbook about the flood kept by her friend, Violet Apple, who generously allowed me to use it.

Subjects

Not everyone I interviewed for this book appears in the text, for any number of reasons. However, they all gave of their time and interest to participate in the process. Their names are listed in the "Subjects" section of the Bibliography. A few of them deserve special recognition.

Helen Brown was a most engaging and informative interview subject, as well as an avid supporter of the project. Helen is a respected local historian in her own right, and should be considered a national treasure.

A few interview subjects found me through various channels, and went out of their way to share their stories through letters, emails, and phone calls. I appreciate the interest and effort put forth in this way by: Gertrude Miller Farrell; Debra Girard; Lynn Greening; Torie Makarewicz; Bob Maxwell; Carol Peri Palmer; Herbert Singer and Sandra Singer Rauschenberger.

Peggy Beling Fackenthal not only submitted to one of the more lengthy interviews, she also lent me her family photos of the flood, and welcomed me into her home to see how it had been restored after the flood. We became friends, and she once again gave me a tour through her home after it had been seriously flooded—for the third time—in April, 2005. That was enough for Peggy, and I wish her a less eventful life in her new place.

Meteorologist and East Stroudsburg native Ben Gelber and his mom, Judy, helped me obtain a copy of Ben's work, *The Pocono Weather Book*, which served as a major source of research for this work. Ben also made the trip from his home in Cincinnati to give me a personal, on-site interview at the Day Street Flats in his hometown, helping very much to bring the horrible reality of the night of August 18, 1955, to life in my mind. His consistent support has been a true gift.

Daryl Gross was incredibly patient and generous with his time in helping me tell the flood story. He was responsive through several emails and phone interviews to my questions about the involvement of the Blooming Glen Mennonite Church in the recovery effort. He shared a copy of the video produced by the Church about this fascinating story, and I highly recommend its viewing to anyone who is interested in the positive, lasting effects of the flood (and yes, there are some. See *Appendix – Resources*).

I interviewed local historian Edwin "Ned" Harrington of Carversville for this story. He also shared his photo collection. Ned has for years written columns for the *New Hope Gazette* and the *Bucks County Herald*, and is a well known and respected person in the river valley. I so appreciate his kindness and encouragement.

Karen Johnson generously gave permission to use material from her website in reconstructing the Branchville dam break incident.

Fellow writer Brenda Lange put me in touch with more than a few interview subjects, including her mother, Ruth Stielau Larison. I am eternally grateful for her early championing of the idea of this book. Such peer support is so important.

Don Lynch provided hydrology information about why the Tocks Island Dam couldn't have been a viable project.

Linda LeCropane Kelso and Sara LeCropane Kershaw found me and became the saviors of the story, helping me correct quite a few inaccuracies I had obtained from other sources about what really happened at Davis Cabins in Analomink. Their contributions of (often painful) memories and family photos make this book a hundred times better than it would otherwise have been. Their friendly support of the project has been such a gift.

Donna Knecht of Tobyhanna Township took time out of her busy day not only to answer questions about the Pocono Lake dam break, but also did an impromptu secondhand interview of one of the township's Public Works employees who was there during the flood.

John Malack was dogged in his determination to have me return phone calls so he could lend me his photos of the Forest Park damage in Chalfont, and also generously offered use of his videotape of the floodwaters.

Weather Channel™ Storm Analyst Dr. Jon Nese was incredibly kind, patient, and generous with both his time and his knowledge in agreeing to proof the manuscript for weather accuracy, and to write the Foreword. For a true weather weenie like me, it has been a real thrill to work with such distinguished professionals.

David Pierce, *Pocono Record* reporter, kindly responded to email requests for clarification about some of his reportage about the Tocks Island Dam.

Lester and Eleanor Sciss were most generous with a lengthy interview and allowing me access to their family flood photos. Their patience in letting me hang on to them while I found time for scanning is much appreciated, and their personal take on the story was enlightening.

Brian St. Pierre gave me a digitized copy of his father's 16mm film of the flood, and went far out of his way to get it into my hands.

Bill Tinsman, Sr., granted me a most entertaining and informative personal interview, as well as having patience with me while I scanned his photo collection. I feel fortunate to have been able to interview a member of a family that is such an integral part of the history of Bucks County along the river.

Louise Wile helped me locate a booklet that turned out to be invaluable to my research, and was very kind in her support of my work.

Nancy Wolfe-Kennedy has been a huge cheerleader throughout this project, and her wonderful flood memories enrich this story.

Some people went above and beyond, either by contributing more than an interview, putting me in touch with other subjects, introducing me to new research sources, or trusting me with their personal photo collections. This kind of generosity also represents a leap of faith. I'd like to give special recognition to the following individuals:

Hilary Bentman and Kelly Madsen of the *Doylestown Intelligencer*; the late Doris Brandes; Heather Buchanan; Vicky and David Child; Lisa Collins; Pam Eelman; Carolyn Evans; Martin and Paula Focazio; John D. Harrison, Jr.; Curt Herr; George Houseworth; Anne Lyons; Laura and Harvey Mirsky; Denise Morano; April Tierney; Gloria Kosco; Marc Mappen, Karl Niederer and Joseph Klett of the State of New Jersey; Dorothy Moon; David Pierce; Linda Roberts for the generous use of her father's color photo collection of the Easton area; Diana Rollar; Denny and Pidge Smith; Inge Snipes; and Bridget Wingert.

In this vein, I would especially like to thank Barbara Shutt Beckwith, who allowed me to use her interview with Libby Ace, as well as putting me in touch with Libby through her caretaker. Barbara also helped me get copies of the narratives of her mom and her sister, for the stories about the Stroudsburgs, Henryville and the Philadelphia Red Cross efforts.

Jeff Apgar and Melanie Graham sought me out and gave me a bundle of 1955 newspapers containing contemporary flood coverage. These proved invaluable in my research, and in helping me discover other information sources. Many, many thanks.

Marlene Arnholt and Rick Kintzel of the *Doylestown Intelligencer* were very generous in securing for me reprint rights to their photo of me doing research.

Sara Burns of the Riegelsville (Pennsylvania) Public Library has been a bulwark of enthusiastic support for this project, and generously provided access to and permissions for the library's Marge Sneckenburg and Violet Apple photo collections. Nancy McEvoy also helped with the technical part of getting these photos. The visual content hereof is far richer for this generosity.

Along with some engaging cyber-conversation, journalist Neil deMause generously gave me permission to use part of his article "High Water Mark" from his online (and entertaining) magazine *Here*. Frank Dale allowed me to cite his wonderful *Delaware Diary*.

Research Sources

Several individuals went out of their way to help me navigate public and private historical collections, and it is to these folks I owe a great deal of whatever success this book has.

Sincere thanks from the bottom of this researcher's heart goes to: Jim Cantore, Weather Channel™ Storm Tracker, for the formula to determine the force of moving water; Susan Gesford, Assistant Editor at the *Pocono Shopper,* for her assistance in identifying an article; Wendy Hughes and Jane Moyer for their assistance in my research of their collections at the Northampton County Historical Association and Museum; Amy Leiser, Curator at the Monroe County Historical Association, for her help with archival research and assistance with permissions and digitizing of photos from their collection; Stephanie Cooper for helping me locate resources and gain permission to scan photos in the collection of the Eastern Monroe Public Library; the archivists at the *Hunterdon County Democrat;* and Jerry Moon of the *Scranton Times-Tribune.*

Michael Lombardi, Boeing Company Historian, gave permission to use the helicopter photos that originally appeared in the *Vertrol* publication of the Piasecki Helicopter Company. Wendy Nardi, curator of the Trentonia Collection, helped me navigate her holdings at the Trenton Public Library. Joanne Nestor, Principal Photographer at the New Jersey State Archives, gave friendly assistance with archival photo research and digitizing, and had patience with the production end of the process. Kevin Toolan and Terry Williams of the Tobyhanna Army Depot provided personal research assistance, access to the Signal Depot archives, scanning of and permission to use their photos.

B. J. Bachman, Monroe County archivist, deserves a medal for her dogged determination to locate the long-lost coroner's records from 1955. I know others in the future will appreciate her dedicated efforts as much as I. Alvin Hall helped me locate a photo from the Barrett Township Historical Society newsletter, and Larry Gering allowed me to use his old photos of Camp Pahaquarra.

Hard-to-find weather information from 1955 was made available to me through the interest and efforts of several government offices. Thanks to: Ethan Gibney, NOAA Coastal Services, and Robert Britter, head librarian at the National Hurricane Center, for locating old National Weather Service documents.

The unearthing of some long-buried reports was graciously performed by several librarians, archivists and veteran meteorologists at the National Oceanic and Atmospheric Association (NOAA) and the National Weather Service (NWS).

Other various research assistance, greatly appreciated, was provided by: Kim Bloxdorf of Joel Whitburn's Record Research for contemporary music facts; Frank Curcio; Robert D. Griffin of Bergen Historic Books, Inc.; Donna Jenssen, Secretary of the Hunterdon County Cultural & Heritage Commission; Linda Spalinski, Delaware River Joint Toll Bridge Commission; and Gary Saretzky.

Contributors
More than a few people responded generously and immediately to a request for donations that would allow me to self-publish this book. Whether due to their sincere interest in seeing the book in print, a desire to help someone who really needed it, or simply to shut me up after listening to me go on about this project for three years, these people saved it from becoming a sad idea that would have been nice, had it actually happened. You are reading this because of their generosity and belief in my ability to make it happen. I will be forever grateful for both of these gifts, and for the monetary or in-kind donations they contributed to allow me to continue with publication. They are:
Clarence Berger, Susan Bertrand, Janet Brueggeman, Norine Kevolic, Tom and Anne Lyons, Jerrianne Mecham, Laura Pritchard, Patty Rutledge, Todd and Lori Stone, Rebecca Valentine, Sandy Weber, Noreen Wickert, Linda Wisniewski, and Chris Wristen.
Particularly generous donations were made by: H.J. Opdyke Lumber of Frenchtown, who sponsored the first printing; and Vicky and David Child, whose contribution allowed me to retain legal rights to my work. The Childs have also been enthusiastic supporters of this project from its inception, as well as invaluable promotional partners.
I also must thank my friends and family for their unwavering support. My cousin, Chris Snyder, is a quiet rock of support, and her mom, my aunt Helen Benner, is always ready with an encouraging word.
I am especially grateful and indebted to my partner, Shelly Sickbert, for putting up with three years of my not being available or only half-present for nearly everything. Many, many house projects went undone or half-finished for too long, and countless other sacrifices were made by her in service to the completion of this project.
A writer must be dedicated to her work, but that's her own choice. Those she drags along into it have little choice, and the patience and indulgence of those closest to us are gifts we dare not think we can live or be productive without. Such support is quiet but long-suffering, and is most important of all in allowing us to create. Thanks, Shel. You're the best.

About the Author

Mary A. Shafer is a native Pennsylvanian. She spent her childhood summers in the south-central part of the state, and grew to know and love Pennsylvania and its history. She lived in Wisconsin for thirty years before returning in 1997, and now resides in Bucks County.

An honor student at the University of Wisconsin campuses at Stout and Milwaukee, she earned her Associate of Applied Science degree in commercial art and communications at Milwaukee Area Technical College and went on to teach there. She now teaches in several community school programs in Bucks County, and as a private tutor.

Mary makes her living at The Word Forge, a full-service freelance writing firm. She is also a columnist for the *Bucks County Herald.*

Her first book, *Wisconsin, The Way We Were: 1845-1945*, was published by Heartland Press in 1993. 1995 saw the release of Ms. Shafer's second book, *Rural America: A Pictorial Folk Memory,* by Willow Creek Press. It won a Best Book award from the Mid-America Publishers Association.

Her work has appeared in numerous trade and consumer magazines and newspapers. She has also contributed to literary anthologies and garnered an Honorable Mention from Montgomery College, Maryland for an essay in their *Potomac Review.* She is currently working on *Lonely Cottage Road,* a Civil War-era novel set in her home township of Nockamixon. She receives help typing, filing and with general clerical duties from Idgie, the inbox kitty.

She is a member of the National Writers Union and the Writers Room of Bucks County, as well as several local and national historical societies and historic preservation groups.

Mary is a National Weather Service certified SkyWarn weather spotter and a self-described "weather weenie." She serves as volunteer communications coordinator and heads the NWS StormReady Community initiative for the Nockamixon Township Emergency Management Agency.

Mary welcomes visitors to this book's website at http://www.55flood.com, and response to the book at floodbook@thewordforge.com.

Index